Business Structure, Business Culture and the Industrial District

Modern Economic and Social History

General Editor: Derek H. Aldcroft

Titles in this series include:

Raleigh and the British Bicycle Industry
Roger Lloyd-Jones and M. J. Lewis

Battles for the Standard:
Bimetallism and the Spread of the Gold Standard
in the Nineteenth Century
Ted Wilson

Railways in Britain and the United States, 1830–1940:
Studies in Economic and Business History
Geoffrey Channon

Trade Unions and the Economy: 1870–2000
Derek H. Aldcroft and Michael J. Oliver

Gales:
A Study in Brewing, Business and Family History
Barry Stapleton and James H. Thomas

The Skilled Compositor, 1850–1914:
An Aristocrat among Working Men
Patrick Duffy

Technology, Industrial Conflict and the Development of
Technical Education in 19th-Century England
Bernard Cronin

Wheels and Deals:
The Automotive Industry in Twentieth-Century Australia
Robert Conlon and John Perkins

Merchants and Migrations:
Germans and Americans in Connection, 1776–1835
Sam A. Mustafa

Demons and Domesticity:
A History of Women and the English Gas Industry, 1889–1939
Anne Clendinning

Business Structure, Business Culture and the Industrial District

The Potteries, *c*.1850–1914

Andrew Popp

Ashgate

Aldershot • Burlington USA • Singapore • Sydney

Published by
Ashgate Publishing Limited
Gower House
Croft Road
Aldershot
Hants GU11 3HR
England

Ashgate Publishing Company
131 Main Street
Burlington
Vermont, 05401–5600
USA

Ashgate website: http://www.ashgate.com

British Library Cataloguing in Publication Data
Popp, Andrew
Business Structure, Business Culture and the Industrial District: The Potteries, c. 1850–1914. – (Modern Economic and Social History)
1. Pottery industry—England—Staffordshire—History. 2. Pottery industry—Location—England—Staffordshire—History. 3. Industrial districts—Great Britain—History. I. Title.
338.4'76666'0942464'0903

US Library of Congress Cataloging in Publication Data
Popp, Andrew
Business Structure, Business Culture and the Industrial District: The Potteries, c. 1850–1914 / Andrew Popp
p. cm. – (Modern Economic and Social History)
Includes bibliographical references.
1. Pottery industry—England—Staffordshire—History. 2. Industrial districts—England—Staffordshire—History. 3. Staffordshire (England)—Economic conditions. 4. Pottery, English—History. I. Title. II. Modern Economic and Social History.
HD9612.7.E54P67 2001
338.4'7666394246–dc21 2001022832

ISBN 0 7546 0176 5

This book is printed on acid free paper.

Printed and bound in Great Britain by MPG Books Ltd, Bodmin, Cornwall

Contents

List of tables

Preface

British business history has in recent years increasingly recognized the extent to which industrialization has been characterized by a marked process of localization or clustering, the formation of what Alfred Marshall famously termed 'industrial districts'. Amongst the most renowned and interesting of such industrial districts is that dedicated to the manufacture of pottery in North Staffordshire. This study aims to explore the business history of the North Staffordshire Potteries during a critical but hitherto neglected period in its history, from the mid-nineteenth century to the eve of World War One.

However, before preceding any further, I must acknowledge several very important debts. My own interest in the region and its industry has deep roots in a long period of residence in the city of Stoke-on-Trent in the 1980s. However, I owe the awakening of an interest in business history, and in industrial districts in particular, very largely to Professor Roger Lloyd-Jones and Dr. Myrddin Lewis. Together they have done much to equip me with the tools I deploy here and to spur me on in my work. Their support and advice over a number of years has been absolutely invaluable. A similarly important role has also been played by Dr. John F. Wilson in providing both encouragement and always positive and insightful critiques. At the same time the company of fellow doctoral students Mark Eason and Tim Willis lightened many a difficult day. A host of colleagues from across the business history community have made further useful contributions. And without the belief of Professor Derek Aldcroft, as series editor, this study may well have never seen the light of day.

Equally vital has been the advice and help offered by a host of librarians, archivists and companies. I wish to thank especially the staff of the Stoke-on-Trent City Archive service based in Hanley Library, Joan Jones, archivist at Mintons, all staff at Jesse Shirley and Co. and the Pinfold and Bennett families.

Finally, but very far from least, I cannot do enough to thank my family; my parents, my parents-in-law and, most of all, my wife and children. I could not have managed without their support through some difficult times. This book is, then, for Diane, Theo and Clara.

Modern Economic and Social History

General Editor's Preface

Economic and social history has been a flourishing subject of scholarly study during recent decades. Not only has the volume of literature increased enormously but the range of interest in time, space and subject matter has broadened considerably so that today there are many sub-branches of the subject which have developed considerable status in their own right.

One of the aims of this series is to encourage the publication of scholarly monographs on any aspect of modern economic and social history. The geographical coverage is worldwide and contributions on non-British themes will be especially welcome. While emphasis will be placed on works embodying original research, it is also intended that the series should provide the opportunity to publish studies of a more general and thematic nature which offer a reappraisal or critical analysis of major issues of debate.

Derek H. Aldcroft

Manchester Metropolitan University

CHAPTER ONE

Business structure, business culture and the industrial district

Introduction

This study is concerned with the regional clustering of industries. The manufacturing economy of Britain in the nineteenth century was to a very great extent an economy of such clusters, amongst the most intense of which was that dedicated to the manufacture of pottery located in North Staffordshire. The growth and development of that regional industrial cluster will be explored from the mid-nineteenth century to the outbreak of World War One. In the one hundred and fifty years preceding 1850 the North Staffordshire Potteries experienced a process of prodigious growth and change.[1] Growing together, industry and region established their identities and characteristics as significant elements within the landscape of British industrialization. Clustered tightly together, the region's many firms were competitive and vibrant, both masters and men confident in their varied skills and proud of the wares they sold across the globe. Growth had been extensive rather than intensive, predicated on product rather than process innovation, and expressed through a multiplication of firms and through the prevalence of personal or proprietary capitalism. Specialization by firm, again by product rather than by process, had been a natural corollary of this pattern. Pottery manufacture had originally flourished in the region on the basis of natural resource endowments, largely in the form of plentiful and accessible coals and clays, but those advantages had for some time been supplemented or even supplanted by a matrix of factors that reinforced localization: the progressive elaboration and application of human resources, the growth of auxiliary trades, links to important sources of raw materials and mercantile networks, the emergence of locally generated circuits of credit and finance, the institutionalization of associationist impulses both within and across labour and capital, the emergence of a powerful collective reputation.

National localization of pottery manufacture in North Staffordshire was in turn matched by micro-localization within the districts and the six contiguous townships of which it was composed. Running from north to south, Tunstall was

[1] L. Weatherill, *The Pottery Trade and North Staffordshire, 1660–1760* (Manchester, Manchester University Press, 1971).

viewed as centre of medium to large firms concentrating on staple tablewares for the North American market, Burslem, the 'mother town' of the Potteries, was by the later nineteenth century losing ground to neighbouring and rapidly expanding Hanley, but still contained many firms, some of them of considerable size and longevity. Hanley's emergence as the de facto centre of the district was multidimensional. Its population of manufacturing firms grew apace, both in number and in the scale of some individual enterprises. These firms also varied widely in the product and market orientations, stretching from tiny shops making Parian statuary to large concerns making fine china and earthenware for export markets. The town also began to develop concentrations of auxiliary firms supplying intermediate products and other services. Furthermore, the retailing sector also expanded dramatically, leading to its condemnation by novelist Arnold Bennett for draining the commercial life out of the centre of ancient Burslem.[2] Stoke-on-Trent contained fewer firms than perhaps any town except Tunstall. A number of those firms were, however, amongst the largest and most prestigious in the entire district. Fenton and Longton, the two most southern townships, were commonly viewed as home to a teeming mass of small and often transient shops concentrating on the production of cheap china destined largely for the domestic market. This study will broadly confirm this traditional view of patterns of sectoral localization within the district, but we will also uncover the subtleties, complexities and dynamics of those patterns.

Around this core of industrial life had grown both a distinctive social world and a unique urban environment, one mapped upon the other.[3] Relatively isolated from great centres of industrialization to the north and the south, customs of work and leisure, dialect and even diet were all highly specific to the locale. However, as in manufacturing, so in life and place diversity ruled. Appearing homogenous to the outsider, the Potteries were internally differentiated along a host of dimensions, represented most obviously in a highly fragmented civic structure, politically but perhaps not culturally resolved through the struggle for Federation in the first years of the twentieth century.[4]

The growth of the industry during the period associated with the classic Industrial Revolution has been relatively well served by economic historians and the impact of that process on patterns of social change by social and labour

---

[2] A. Bennett, *The Old Wives' Tale* (London, Dent, 1954); but see also J. Stobart, 'Patterns of Urban Retailing: Suburbanisation, Centralisation, and Hierarchies in the Potteries Conurbation, 1872–1932', *Journal of Regional and Local Studies*, Vol. 18, No. 1 (1998).

[3] R. Whipp, *Patterns of Labour: Work and Social Change in the Pottery Industry*, (London, 1990); M. Dupree, *Family Structure in the North Staffordshire Potteries, 1840–1880* (Oxford, Clarendon Press, 1995).

[4] J. Stobart and C. Thomas, 'Cultural Capital and Competition in the Five Towns', (forthcoming).

historians.[5] However, the period that followed the mid century has been largely neglected by business and economic historians.

Yet, in the six or seven decades that followed the mid century, the North Staffordshire pottery industry was to face unprecedented challenges. In particular, the rise of protectionism and of foreign industries, principally in continental Europe and the United States, threatened both export and domestic markets. On a more distant horizon, Japan appeared ready to emerge as a yet more potent rival. The response of the pottery industry to those challenges may be crudely characterized as a deepening commitment to established patterns of development, but under rapidly altering conditions. A proliferation of products remained the key motif, though often on the basis of insignificant stylistic variations. Mechanization was, in comparison, hesitant. A few large firms struggled to reorient their growth along more intensive lines but were repeatedly swamped in waves of small start-ups. Growth in demand did not stagnate so much as become unstable, in terms of both level and composition, increasing uncertainty and channelling the terms of competition away from quality and differentiation and towards price, a harsher arena. At the same time, such systemic disincentives to opportunism as existed within the district showed a marked tendency to weaken, undermining notions of 'the trade'. In this climate it was not so much growth as profitability that suffered. Equally importantly, confidence dissipated or turned to bluster and collective understandings, actions and bodies, temporary and situational at the best of times, repeatedly fractured.

The two decades from the mid-1870s, in particular, appeared to represent a prolonged period of crisis. This crisis was understood at the time to have both short and long-term dimensions. Intense competition threatened the immediate survival of individual firms and many, old and new, large and small alike, succumbed. More fundamentally, developments posed serious questions about the long-term viability of existing structures and strategies, at the level of both the firm and the industry. In essence, the industry appeared to be faced with a choice between alternative developmental paths. This choice presented itself along a range of dimensions, in terms of batch versus mass production, craft and skill versus repetition and mechanization, personal versus corporate capitalism. Thus, though closely identified with the First Industrial Revolution, pottery, as a styled consumer durable amenable to the rapidly advancing arts of branding, advertising and induced stylistic obsolescence, also potentially represented one aspect of the nascent Second Industrial Revolution, the creation of new patterns of mass consumption.[6] The explicit contemporary framing of the choices facing

---

5 Weatherill, *North Staffordshire*; J. Thomas, *The Rise of the Staffordshire Potteries* (Bath, Adams & Dart, 1971); N. McKendrick, 'Josiah Wedgwood: An Eighteenth Century Entrepreneur in Salesmanship and Marketing Techniques', *The Economic History Review*, Vol. 12, No. 3 (1960); Whipp, *Patterns of Labour*; Dupree, *Family Structure*.

6 P. Scranton, *Endless Novelty: Specialty Production and American Industrialization, 1865–1925* (Princeton, N.J., Princeton University Press, 1997).

the industry in these terms, reflecting the discursive, self-reflective potential of the actors concerned, is as of much interest to the historian as the patterning of the choices actually made.

Intense debate ensued within the industry and district. These debates echoed those in popular and academic economics and a reading of writers such as Marshall, Hobson, Chapman and Shadwell serves to introduce and delimit our concerns and to sketch the contours of our analytical framework.[7] In essence, Marshall and others sought to outline the scope of those alternative possibilities already identified by potters and to identify the forces structuring the range of likely but far from inevitable outcomes.

This study aims to make a contribution not only to our knowledge of the North Staffordshire pottery industry, but also, given the regional structuring of the economy, to British business history more generally. In British business and economic history a powerful but essentially teleological concern with decline has long oriented questions and analytical approaches around two basic poles. On the one hand, assuming wide-ranging scope for effective intervention in the process of economic development, the actor is either accused of failure or exonerated, according to the precepts of a narrowly defined economic rationality. On the other, the impact individuals are able to make on historically unfolding patterns is severely constrained by institutional and other external rigidities.[8] Crucially, in both the Chandlerian paradigm and the institutional rigidity thesis there is traced a direct relationship between issues of agency, whether of its failure or its constrained position, and the prolonged commitment of British manufacturing industry to an increasingly inappropriate structure of many small, non-integrated and personally managed firms. This developmental path, alternatively condemned by Chandler and celebrated by Scranton, has formed the locus of recent debates on the long-run development of the British industrial economy.[9]

Increasingly, however, effort is being focused more on reconstructing and analysing the contexts and frameworks within which actors individually and collectively identified themselves, took decisions and participated in business as

7 A. Marshall, *Principles of Economics* (Basingstoke, Macmillan, 1952); J.A. Hobson, *The Evolution of Modern Capitalism: A Study of Machine Production* (2nd. Edition, London, Walter Scott, 1906); S.J. Chapman, *The Lancashire Cotton Industry: A Study in Economic Development* (Clifton, N.J., Augustus M. Kelley, 1973); A. Shadwell, *Industrial Efficiency: A Comparative Study of Industrial Life in England, Germany and America* (London, Longmans, Green & Co., 1906).

8 A.J. Chandler, *Scale and Scope: The Dynamics of Industrial Capitalism* (Cambridge, Mass., Harvard University Press, 1990); D. McCloskey, *Economic Maturity and Entrepreneurial Decline: British Iron and Steel, 1870–1913* (Cambridge, Mass., Harvard University Press, 1973); B. Elbaum and W. Lazonick, *The Decline of the British Economy* (Oxford, Oxford University Press, 1987).

9 Chandler, *Scale and Scope*; Scranton, *Endless Novelty*; R. Lloyd-Jones and M.J. Lewis, 'Personal Capitalism and British Industrial Decline: The Personally Managed Firm and Business Strategy in Sheffield, 1880–1920', *Business History Review*, 68 (1994), pp. 364–411.

a socially and spatially embedded activity. The regionally clustered industry appears the most promising unit of analysis through which this project can be furthered. This work aims to contribute to that effort by adopting a focus that will fall equally on the *firm* and on the *industry as a whole*.[10] The study has three basic themes; industry structure, business strategy and business culture, unifying these through sustained exploration of their interaction in the context of intense spatial clustering. Thus, the perspective adopted is informed by the concept of the Industrial District. This introductory chapter will explore the scope, utility and implications of that perspective.

The Industrial District model

The Industrial District model posits a form of socio-spatial organization supportive of particular patterns of industrial development. However, as William Lazonick has noted, this organizational form varies across regional and national boundaries and over time; the challenge facing historians is to begin to account for that variation and its impact.[11] The study of industrial districts requires judgements regarding two fundamental and interdependent balances. That is between, first, individual agency and systemic or collective effects, and, second, what we may term industry-specific effects and idiosyncratic, region-specific effects.

Recent formulations of the industrial district model are largely clear in how they view these balances; for empirical and analytical purposes systemic and regional effects are privileged over individual agency and industry effects. Such judgements limit the industrial district model in three ways. They provide weak perspectives on, first, the long-run competitive advantage of clustered industries and, second, on the adaptive capabilities or dynamics of such complex systems. Finally, they do not allow for an explanation of the diversity of social organization displayed by industrial districts over space and time. The model is also often based on stylized distinctions between mass production and flexible specialization, and between markets and networks. In sum, the model is held to capture conditions positive to the promotion of regional industrial development. However, these biases have emerged from and reflect flaws in the way in which industrial districts have come to be defined, both conceptually and empirically.

As Mark Casson has argued, many studies have used 'predicted characteristics to identify industrial districts through casual empiricism', rather than any objective measurement of clustering. This methodology runs the risk that it will

[10] J.F. Wilson, 'Industrial History: Towards a Definition', *Journal of Industrial History*, Vol. 1, No. 1 (1998), pp. 1–8.

[11] W. Lazonick, 'Review of C. Sabel and J. Zeitlin, Worlds of Possibilities', *Business History Review*, Vol. 73, No. 2 (1999), p. 313.

'merely assume what it is supposed to prove' and has had a highly reductive effect on the industrial district debate.[12] Thus, Staber, for example, claims that 'district relations are expected to be more stable, *because they are embedded in a social milieu that rewards cooperation*', or that trust is particularly important in 'networks that reward innovation and change, *as those in industrial districts*'.[13]

In objective terms the historical clustering of the British pottery industry in North Staffordshire is not to be doubted. The identification of that region as an industrial district on the basis of the commonly used predicted characteristics is, however, less certain. As this study will repeatedly reveal, the Potteries could be a very fractious and divided place. And yet the industry persisted and survived, and whilst cotton has all but disappeared from Lancashire, Stoke-on-Trent remains a globally important centre of pottery manufacture. How can this survival be explained and to what extent does it suggest that the industrial district model requires re-evaluation?

Writers in the modern tradition of the industrial district would claim that successful Industrial Districts possess resources and dimensions absent from the Marshallian framework. Thus, before turning to the insights to be derived from Marshall, it seems necessary to first examine the later evolution of the model. Drawing principally on the example of northern Italy in the second half of the twentieth century, authors such as Sabel, Zeitlin, Piore and others in the 1970s and 1980s developed a form of counterfactual or phantom teleology in which small-scale and flexible production remained viable and unvanquished by throughput mass production, giantism and corporatism.[14] The novel ingredient in this project was an emphasis on the particular way in which industrial districts are constituted as social organizations as the key determinant of their resilience and strength. In Staber's words: 'The embeddedness of firms in a distinctive local social fabric is a key feature of the industrial district model'.[15] In this vision the co-ordinating corporate body became not the integrated Chandlerian firm but the community.

We need at this point to examine prevailing judgements with regard to those central balances identified above, and to unravel their implications. Staber neatly encapsulates these judgements or preferences in a table laying out the assumed characteristics of district networks, but they were also prominent in the work of

---

[12] M. Casson, 'Analysing Regional Business Networks: An Economic Perspective,' Discussion paper, Department of Economics, University of Reading (1999), p. 6.

[13] U. Staber, 'The Social Embeddedness of Industrial District Networks', in U. Staber, N. Schaefer and B. Sharma (eds.), *Business Networks: Prospects for Regional Development* (Berlin, de Gruyter, 1996), p. 154 & p. 154–5, (emphases added).

[14] M. Piore and C. Sabel, *The Second Industrial Divide: Prospects for Prosperity* (New York, Basic Books, 1984); C. Sabel and J. Zeitlin, 'Historical Alternatives to Mass Production: Politics, Markets and Technology in Nineteenth Century Industrialization', *Past and Present*, No. 108 (1985); E. Goodman, J. Bamford and P. Saynor (eds.), *Small Firms and Industrial Districts in Italy* (London, Routledge, 1989).

[15] Staber, 'Social Embeddedness', p. 148.

Sabel, Zeitlin and Piore in the mid-1980s. Staber's table, for example, explicitly identifies 'communities, clans, families, professions', as opposed to 'firms, entrepreneurs', as the 'key actors' in the 'ideal-typical industrial district', This series of bipolar contrasts is continued, see Table 1.

Yet viewing social and market mechanisms in this way, as dichotomous rather than interwoven, seems unsustainable. Similarly unproven is the assumption that any socialization process arising from industrial clustering will necessarily result in a unitary culture. Even the simple observation, made in the Potteries at the opening of the twentieth century, that 'there is probably no industry in the world so concentrated [as pottery], and yet so chaotic in respect to ... customs' throws doubts upon this possibility.[16]

Table 1.1
Stylized comparison of perspectives on business networks

Key Features	Market View	Institutionalist View
Key actors	Firms, entrepreneurs	Communities, clans, families, professions
Principal motives	Material benefits, private gain	Collective identity, collective gain
Normative foundation	Property rights, constitutional rights	Customary practices, cultural correctness
Basis of compliance	Expedience, efficiency	Social obligation
Guiding principle of coordination	Dispersed competition	Solidarity, local cooperation
Ideational resources	Calculative rationality	Trust

Source: Staber, 'Social Embeddedness,' p. 158.

In order to sustain this version of industrial districts, and in particular the distinctive emphasis on co-operation, focus has been concentrated firmly on vertical exchange linkages within the local division of labour, at the expense of attention to the competitive rules operating across horizontal divisions. Economic

16 *The Pottery and Glass Trades Gazette* (hereafter *Pottery Gazette*), May 1900, p. 557.

analysis, so far as it is present, effectively identifies reduced transaction costs between non-competing elements as the principal source of district competitiveness, downgrading the importance of potential and realized economies of scale and scope inherent in the vertical and horizontal structuring of a clustered industry and sidelining the stimulus of competitive impulses.

This focus naturally favours evidence of characteristics such as locally defined reserves of identity, trust and social cohesion, together constituting a moral economy that fostered a balance between co-operation and competition and supported innovation and flexibility. Thus, according to Sabel and Zeitlin, industrial districts developed beyond the realisation of simple agglomeration economies to the point where:

> sentiments fused into an ethos that reconciled and gave immediate human content to the claims of ambition and competition on the one hand and community and co-operation on the other ... The central and defining experience of each new generation was automatic and collective induction into the local industry.[17]

But identities, trust and cohesion are properties that require stability, problematizing analysis of the impact of destabilizing influences, not least of which is the inexorable passage of time. Such influences are potentially many, flowing not only in the long run from technological change and from secular change in the structure of product markets and in the short-run from trade cycles, but also from the dynamics of clustering itself. Thus, paradoxically, prolonged technological stability may have a similarly destabilizing effect as technological revolution by progressively lowering barriers to entry, perhaps to a point accessible to individuals relatively resistant to inculcation in district codes of 'customary practices, cultural correctness,' and 'social obligations'.[18] While exchange linkages in the Potteries did at times thicken sufficiently to constitute networks as defined in the industrial district literature, such networks, as Chapter 8 of this study will demonstrate, could be highly situational, breaking down both during trade depression and under pressures exerted by structural change within the district.

Similarly, Marshall's often abused notion of 'industrial atmosphere' referred not to any such process of socialization but to the progressive development of local resource endowments, especially human resources, which would also necessarily disrupt the local division of labour in the long run, and with it the patterning of exchange relationships. How sociability is maintained in the face of the need constantly to remake exchange relationships, not only with new actors but against a constantly shifting context, is not adequately addressed. Indeed, the literature on business culture points to the tendency for 'adaptive difficulties as

---

[17] Sabel and Zeitlin, 'Historical Alternatives', p. 152.

[18] Staber, 'Social Embeddedness', p. 158.

[the] environment changes to the point where some of [a group's] assumptions are no longer valid'.[19] The heavily socialized business networks of the 'ideal-typical' industrial district seem to contain a similar potential for adaptive inertia. Nor do these criticisms begin to question the strength of the empirical evidence for effectiveness of socialization in overcoming bounded rationality and countering the threat of opportunism.[20]

However, perhaps the most serious implications flowing from the privileging of systemic or collective effects, linked to region-specific factors or conditions, are those concerned with questions of agency, co-ordination and governance. Systemic or collective co-ordination of the order proposed by the industrial district model clearly requires a form of implicit or explicit governance if it is to be meaningfully distinguished from the co-ordination achieved by markets.[21] Here again the typologies of governance structures found in industrial districts, such as that proposed by Sabel and Zeitlin in their seminal paper of 1985, are disappointingly limited and static, breaking down when their application to the historical record is attempted. Their typology of institutional mechanisms of governance, running from the municipal, through the paternal to the federated family firm, has little relevance in the context of, say, Sheffield or Lancashire. Nor, as will be shown in Chapter 9 of this study, does it illuminate the history of associational activity, formal and informal, in the Potteries in the nineteenth century.

Similarly, and in turn, the range of wider socio-cultural environments, especially in terms of political economy, in which industrial districts are likely to flourish has been restricted by the emphasis on collective over individual agency. The development of a stable and unitary sense of the collective necessarily presupposes that participants share a common background in a political culture that is, at the very least, not inimical to such a project. This is most obvious in the frequent dominance of local government in Italian industrial districts by the Communist Party or by Catholic Christian Democracy.[22] But this would also seem to render the emergence of industrial districts unlikely in environments characterized by, for example, a laissez-faire political economy, such as Britain was in the nineteenth century.

---

19 E.H. Schein, *Organizational Culture and Leadership* (London, Josey-Bass, 1992), p. 2.

20 See Casson, 'Analysing Regional Business Networks'.

21 There is often a strong tendency in district studies to view markets and competition as essentially and inherently asocial. Staber, for example, claims that 'the presence of strong social bonds distinguishes industrial districts from other, more instrumentally oriented production agglomerations, where co-location is valued mostly for the realization of external economies of scale and where producers see themselves as independent competitors'. 'Social Embeddedness', p. 152. However, such views amongst actors are, of course, as much a property of the social system they inhabit as those favoured by the district model.

22 C. Trigilia, 'Small-Firm Development and Political Subcultures in Italy', in Goodman et al., *Small Firms*, pp. 174–197.

The cumulative outcome of these interlinked implications to privileging the regionally and socially embedded collective is the almost total absence of a role for the entrepreneur and, with him, for business strategy also.[23] The actor/entrepreneur does play a far more prominent role in a recent reformulation of the industrial district/flexible specialization paradigm by Sabel and Zeitlin.[24] However, this work still fails firmly to anchor the actor in the context of industry structure and its determinants and neglects the range of external economies available to specific clusters.

Central to the theoretical structure of the recent work is a stated aim 'to clear the way for a recharacterization of the actors that takes account both of their capacity for self-reflection and the resulting interplay between the constitution of their interests and identities on the one hand and the context in which they operate on the other'.[25] However, this aim, whilst admirable in itself and addressing some limitations in their earlier work, introduces fresh difficulties.

As has been argued here, in the works of the mid-1980s the actor, though ultimately the arbiter of business decisions, was a largely abstract figure, closely identified with and submerged in the greater social body, typically the community. His identity, values, preferences and frameworks for decision taking appeared to coincide to a very high degree with some larger, though imperfectly defined, grouping. Consensual, though implicit, rules were the mechanism by which aggregation from the individual to the collective was achieved within this theoretical framework. However, just as the institutional rigidity thesis never adequately resolved the issue of the relationship between individual agents and the institutions of which they were a part, so the industrial district model devalued the possibility of fragmented, fragile and situational coalitions of interests, identities and values existing within the socio-economic and cultural systems of industrial districts. By recasting the actor as a more mutable, self-reflective, and 'deliberate' figure, Sabel and Zeitlin's recent work recognises this issue.[26] This vision is grounded by the wider claim that for historians 'the study of the economy has become the study of the adjustment to ever changing contexts'.[27]

Thus they progress to claims with which we have little serious dispute here, for example that actors have in the past 'rarely interpreted economic and technological progress as continual and ineluctable progression towards a single set of practices ... a sphere of transhistorical permanency'.[28] Thus, actors in the

---

[23] Casson, 'Analysing Regional Business Networks'.

[24] C.F. Sabel and J. Zeitlin, 'Stories, Strategies, Structures: Rethinking Historical Alternatives to Mass Produciton', in C.F. Sabel and J. Zeitlin (eds.), *Worlds of Possibilties: Flexibility and Mass Production* (Cambridge, Cambridge University Press, 1997), pp. 1–33.

[25] Ibid., p. 6.

[26] Ibid., p. 1.

[27] Ibid., p. 1.

[28] Ibid., p. 3.

Potteries were, as Sabel and Zeitlin claim, aware not only of 'changing standards of efficiency' but also of their 'institutional concomitants'. They could 'typically see ... connections between the use of machines and the organization of the firm on the one hand and the structure of the latter's markets and institutional context on the other'.[29] The principal trade journal of the pottery industry, the *Pottery and Glass Trades Gazette*, argued in November 1900, for example, that

> looking backward and forward, it can scarcely be doubted that the next decade will see the practical extinction of the small factory-at least as regards crockery. Competition, ever growing keener will cut profits down to the last farthing ... This, of course, means capital, means large turnovers, and large factories. Whether the smaller businesses are eaten up by the large, or the trust system introduced, remains to be seen, but ... the small manufactory is doomed.[30]

Less satisfactory however are the mechanisms through which it is proposed actors moved from this clear vision of their interdependence with the context in which they were operating to the formulation of 'strategizing' decisions and actions able to alter that context. In essence, from being too circumscribed by immersion in the collective moral economy and collective identity the actor has become liberated to a degree that seems implausible. As Joseph Melling has argued, the Sabel/Zeitlin thesis increasingly 'turns on our accepting that the various actors and business strategists whom they depict were indeed extremely well informed about the environment in which they functioned and the various options which were available' and the evidence for this is 'at least open to serious debate'.[31]

However, this is not simply an issue of evidence. Analytical clarity does not extend, for example, to a discussion of the importance of and difference, if any, between 'the intended and unintended consequences' of actors' actions. More fundamentally, those carriers of adjustment to external stimuli identified as the most important by Sabel and Zeitlin seem in fact to be exactly those beyond the control of the actor. Thus, though professing a desire to construct less a 'epochal' narrative of industrialization, the 'real work' of adjustment is attributed to 'individuals' acting to 'reconstruct ... formative institutions upon which economic activity depends ... from time to desperate time'.[32]

Do not the most fundamental reconstructions seem more likely though to stem from a process of accretion. A process in which each individual decision, though in itself self-reflective and 'strategizing', cannot, in combination with other like

---

[29] Ibid., p.12.

[30] *Pottery Gazette*, November 1900, p. 1248.

[31] J. Melling, 'Review of C. Sabel and J. Zeitlin, *World of Possibilities*', *Business History*, Vol. 4o, No. 3 (1998), p. 175.

[32] Sabel & Zeitlin, 'Stories, Strategies, Structures,' p. 10.

decisions, constitute a broader but similarly reflective and strategic process. Thus, as Hannan and Carroll argue:

> Organizational worlds transform over time in two sharply different ways. Some individual organizations adjust their routines and behavior in response to changed environmental conditions, as the conventional theories emphasize. But another key mechanism operates as well - populations of organizations evolve because some existing organizations perish and other (sometimes novel) organizations emerge. In other words, economic, political and social transformation entails both *adaption* by individual organizations and *selection* at the level of populations of organizations.

Crucially, Hannan and Carroll observe that, 'few organizations succeed in solving their adaptive problems for very long in a turbulent world. Hence few of them acheive either great longevity or social power. There is an indisputable, though often overlooked, danger in generalizing from a few well-known success stories to broad classes of organizations'.[33] It was with the contradictions of the apparent need for systemic change, and their individual and even collective powerlessness to achieve it, that some potters grappled in the late nineteenth century.

Thus, the firm plays a very marginal role in Sabel and Zeitlin's account of reflection and action, as indeed it did in the earlier work. Reference to the firm is restricted largely to the claim that: 'Adjustment through natality and mortality ... carries the burden of change when the changes are small'.[34] Despite the use of the language of natality and mortality, firm entry and exit are not naturally occurring phenomena, instead each reflects a clear and purposeful decision taken often in the past by the individual actor. Marshall's intense interest in the birth and death of firms was far from peripheral. Marginalizing the decision to enter an industry in particular seems unnecessarily to downgrade the importance of the entrepreneurial, that is 'strategizing', actor.

Thus, in reality, might the firm not be one of the most powerful vehicles through which individual reflective and strategizing decisions in the economic sphere are expressed, particularly in economies characterized by personal capitalism? Moreover, might not such decisions, through their sheer weight of numbers, be also the pre-eminent mechanism of adjustment to a constantly altering context? This was certainly the view of some commentators in the pottery industry, who understood also that, in their cumulative effect, such decisions contained the counter potential to block fundamental institutional adjustment. It was a myriad of individual entry decisions that dictated that the pottery industry remain highly fragmented and competitive in structure. These

---

[33] M.T. Hannan and G.R. Carroll, *Dynamics of Organizational Populations: Density, Legitimation and Competition* (Oxford, Oxford University Press, 1992), p. 4.

[34] Ibid., p. 10.

arguments suggest the need to progress beyond the typical claim that 'the ideal-typical industrial district describes agglomerations of mostly small and medium-sized firms', to a more precise desciption of industry structure over time.[35]

It is not even clear that Sabel and Zeitlin consider industry structure as an element of the context within which actors strategize. It is our contention that industry structure not only determined the range of external economies available within a district but also formed a central plank in the decision-making framework of actors, especially in clustered industries where structure was both observable and relatively intelligible and could be mapped onto the social structure of the district. Position within the structure of an industry, whilst never stable, was a constant source of self-identity, of identification with others, of interests, preferences and values. Industry structure, it is fair to say, was the principal subject of a highly self-reflective discourse within the trade press of the pottery industry, a discourse that could, for example, simultaneously recognise the legitimacy of individual entry decisions and lament their systemic impact on the industry as a whole. Discussion of industry structure prompts a return to the concept of the industrial district as originally articulated in the late nineteenth century by Alfred Marshall.

Marshall, Hobson and the Industrial District

Working from a basis in inductive empiricism, Marshall and others attempted to adumbrate laws of economic development from observation of contemporary Britain. In their studies of industrial organization, explored largely in relation to manufacturing industry, Marshall and Hobson had three principal concerns. The first was with the structure of industries and the range of factors shaping those structures. Second, they focused on the business strategies concomitant with various industrial structures, business strategy being viewed as the orientation of firms and industries to the pursuit of particular classes of economy. Third, both authors displayed an intense interest in the 'localization' of industries, its causes and likely future patterns. In turn, industry structure, business strategy and patterns of localization were seen as subject to the influence of two broad forces derived from classical Smithian economics. These were mechanization (and an associated evolution in the division of labour) and change in markets, both in their size and in their composition. Finally, in Marshall in particular, analysis of the interaction of structure, strategy, localization and dynamic forces takes place

[35] Staber, 'Social Embeddedness', p. 148. As Staber himself notes; 'While the theoretical logic of the distric model stresses the dynamic and innovative aspects of foundings, researchers have generally performed empirical analyses with static data sets that assume stability and equilibrium'. U. Staber, 'An Ecological Perspective on Entrepreneurship in Industrial Districts', *Entrepreneurship and Regional Development*, Vol. 9 (1997), p. 45.

within a far from peripheral perspective on the wider organization and value systems of society, particularly in terms of political economy, and an intense regard for the impact of historical patterns of development.

For both Marshall and Hobson, industry structure was widely conceived and included not only the number and size of firms, but also the complexity of their organization, both within and between firms, patterns and degrees of integration, horizontal and vertical, and the factors affecting rates of births and deaths of firms. And again for both Marshall and Hobson, industry structure, technology (or 'mechanization' more normally), markets and business strategy were linked by the overriding central question of 'what are the conditions under which the economies of production arising from division of labour can be best secured'.[36] Pursuing this question Marshall notes:

> We may divide the economies arising from an increase in the scale of production of any kinds of goods, into two classes-firstly, those dependent on the general development of the industry; and secondly those dependent on the resources of the individual houses of business engaged in it, on their organization and the efficiency of their management. We may call the former *external economies*, and the latter *internal economies*.[37]

Having introduced this most important distinction, Marshall immediately proceeds to lay the foundation stone of the industrial district concept by proposing to examine 'those very important external economies which can often be secured by the concentration of many small businesses of a similar character in particular industries: or, as is commonly said by the localization of industry'.[38]

A fundamental point needs to be drawn out from this foundation. For Marshall the chief engines of growth were 'economies of production' and such economies were driven by increasing mechanization and division of labour deployed in the pursuit of ever-larger volumes of production. Economies of scale, not of scope or of any other type, are the underpinning of modern economic development. The centrality of scale and volume heavily informs Marshall's consideration of the differing advantages of single large businesses on the one hand and of clusters of smaller businesses on the other. Here, he is asking not whether large and small firms in fact pursue quite different classes of economies but to what extent each is fitted to pursue the same central, technologically driven 'economies of production' arising from scale and standardization. As Paul Krugman has argued, Marshall's analysis of localization 'depends crucially on at least some degree of economies of scale ... It is only the presence of increasing returns that makes a large center of production able to have more efficient and more diverse suppliers

---

36 Marshall, p. 219.

37 Ibid., p. 221.

38 Ibid., p. 221.

than a small one'.[39] Here we go to the heart of the falsity of sharp distinctions between flexible specialization and mass production, which are relative rather than absolute terms. Thus, relative to contemporary developments in bulk steel or soap, the Potteries in the later nineteenth century was not a site of mass production, but relative to the Potteries of one hundred years earlier it was in the sense that, in aggregate, the scale of production had increased many times over, bringing in train increasing returns.

The same point is reinforced by the illustration Marshall drew from the Lancashire cotton industry. Thus, Marshall argues that the 'chief' economy in production available to disintegrated industries is that arising, however achieved, from the:

> parcelling out of demand for various sorts of the same class of product (so) that each business can specialise its plant on a narrow range of goods, and yet keep it running with but little interruption. This specialization is ... thoroughly effected without conscious effort in the Lancashire cotton industry and especially in the branches of it that are in the hands of a multitude of independent businesses of moderate size.[40]

We see here that the success of Lancashire in the nineteenth century was dependent on the presence of several factors. As Bellandi has argued, 'a system of small firms can achieve the full utilization of specialized instruments of production (and of specialized labour)' when 'the production process is decomposable and its components are conveniently divided among the firms of the system'.[41] It was perhaps a considerable constraint on the pottery industry that its production process was not readily decomposable, yet was also unsophisticated enough as to impose no serious barriers to entry. The result was a structure of intense horizontal segmentation combined with insignificant vertical segmentation, restricting the access of individual firms to a market where consumer preferences were ill-defined yet undergoing a shift that increasingly privileged the mass-consumption of standardized products. These preliminary observations, based in Marshallian analysis, are an indication of the necessity and utility of considering together industry structure, technologies and markets.

But it should further be noted that in the above passage, Marshall, bringing into play industry structure, business strategy (in terms of an orientation towards standardization) and socio-political factors (in terms of the 'independence' of the business units), observes, as very few have done since, that the great Lancashire industrial district was, despite its vertically disintegrated structure, dedicated to the production of large volumes of standardized goods, albeit in batches rather

39 P. Krugman, *Geography and Trade* (Cambridge, Mass., MIT Press, 1993), p. 49.

40 Marshall, *Industry and Trade* p. 601.

41 M. Bellandi, 'The Industrial District in Marshall', in Goodman et al., *Small Firms*, p. 138.

than through mass production. Indeed, the exploration of all classes of economies, and especially of economies of production related to scale, have been largely neglected in the more recent industrial district literature.[42] They should be a central concern given that mass production and flexible specialization are explicitly construed by many of the latter's proponents as competing rather than as parallel paradigms of industrial organization. Where the broad issue of economies is addressed in the recent literature it is largely in terms of economies of scope, typically approached obliquely through references to flexibility. However, this approach begs the assumption that the principal advantage of districts lay in the pursuit of such economies, or that such economies find a natural corollary in particular, prescribed forms of firm and industry structures. For some industries, given their technologies and markets, and largely independent of their localization in *specific* districts, this was clearly not so. In other words, available economies were very often industry rather than region-specific.

Marshall was far from uninterested in economies other than those of large-scale production. He addressed the importance of remaining 'supple' where customers are 'under the influence of western fluctuations of fashion',[43] and noted the importance of clustering to the realization of economies of marketing, in labour markets, in transactions and in markets for inputs.[44] We shall have cause throughout this study to return to a more detailed consideration of Marshall's observations on these further economies. Moreover, as the reference to clustering suggests, some of *these* economies, unlike those of scale, may be classified as regional rather than industry specific effects. Indeed, their operation largely depended on clustering and were derived from the historical localization of the industry, in effect leading to what is now characterized as embeddedness. But in each case these further economies serve largely to aid smaller manufacturers in swimming with, rather than against, a drift towards large-scale production and standardization.

Markets, as well as structure and strategy, were also important to Marshall and Hobson. Unlike in more recent formulations, where change in the market is held in a constant but superficial state of ferment that advantages producers capable of short-term flexibility, for Marshall and Hobson change in markets, though hard to predict, was also progressive and directional. Markets were then an important force stimulating the dynamic interaction of structure and strategy. Technology, and more especially mechanization, acted in this process as a further enabling instrument. Thus, Marshall insisted:

---

42 S. Broadberry and A. Marrison, 'External Economies of Scale in the Lancashire Cotton Industry, 1900–1930', (Unpublished paper, 2000); M. Russo, 'Technical Change and the Industrial District: The Role of Inter-firm Relations in the Growth and Transformation of Ceramic Tile Production in Italy', in Goodman et al., *Small Firms*, pp. 198–222.

43 Marshall, *Trade and Industry*, p. 230–231.

44 Marshall, *Principles*, p. 225.

> It is the largeness of markets, the increased demand for great numbers of things of the same kind, and in some cases of things made with great accuracy, that leads to the subdivision of labour; the chief effect of the improvement of machinery is to cheapen and make more accurate the work which would anyhow have been subdivided.[45]

The growth of markets is not entirely monolithic, however. As Hobson argued, 'as human life continues, the art of living must continually change, and each change alters the value attached to the several forms of consumption, and so to the industrial processes engaged in the supply of different utilities'.[46]

The 'value' attached by consumers to products could in many instances constrain the realization of conventional economies of scale, substituting 'an "art" economy ... for a "routine" or "machine" economy'.[47] However, Hobson goes on to counsel that 'This does not necessarily imply the execution of such orders by small businesses. A large pottery company often employs a number of designers and skilled crafstmen in order to stimulate and supply the more refined demands of high grade customers'.[48] This last observation is apposite and accurate; individually many of the largest firms in the Potteries were predicated on economies of scope as much as of scale. As noted above, it cannot be assumed that there is a necessary correlation between firm-scale and mode of production.[49]

However, the impact of this evolution in the 'art of living' interacts with constant expansion in the geographical scope of competition, through improvements in transport and communication technologies, to ensure that 'this world competition, however free it may become, can lead to no finality, no settled appointment of industrial activity to the several parts of the world'.[50] Thus, the dynamic interaction of industries, technology and markets is expressed also in dynamic patterns of localization.

Marshall's exploration of the multitude of factors affecting the balance between competing forms of industrial organization extended beyond the structure of industries to a consideration of the internal organization of the firms comprising those industries. Here, Marshall identified powerful forces tending to promote an increasing division of labour in the work of management, inevitably leading to a decline in what is now recognised as personal capitalism, occurring in tandem with an increasing orientation towards large-scale production. Indeed,

---

45 Ibid., p. 212.

46 Hobson, *Evolution*, p. 159.

47 Ibid., p. 131.

48 Ibid., p. 131–2.

49 See, Scranton, *Endless Novelty*; R.L. Blaszczyk, '"Reign of the Robots": The Homer Laughlin China Company and Flexible Mass Production', *Technology and Culture*, Vol. 36, No. 4 (1995). Blaszczyk claims that the 'story of technological innovation at Homer Laughlin ... suggests that the models of batch and mass production are not exclusive categories', p. 910–11.

50 Hobson, *Evolution*, p. 159.

for Marshall, the 'advantages and disadvantages of the subdivision of the work of business management' was the 'central problem of the modern organization of industry'. It was in this area also that Hobson identified the most powerful forces promoting the survival of small firms, arguing that such survivals were due either to the absence of forces promoting scale or the presence of countervailing forces. Thus, some:

> small businesses ... survive because of certain features in the materials or processes which are involved which give importance to those personal qualities of skill, care, judgement, and character incapable of being evoked, controlled and applied effectively under the routine economy of the large business ... the only substantial limit to the growth of a business, from the standpoint of economy of supply, has reference to the application of administrative power ... The chief cause of the survival of small forms of business in many highly-skilled trades was found to be the necessity of direct detailed attention on the part of a responsible interested workman or employer.[51]

It will be noted that these forces promoting the survival of small businesses are, in the first instance, industry rather than region specific and also essentially negative. Clustering may lead to processes of socialization that reinforce such forces, but is not their fundamental cause. Marshall was also well aware that such a process of socialization offered no guaranteed bulwark against changing conditions, and may even impede effective reaction, famously arguing that 'even a little obstiancy or inertia may ruin an old home of industry whose conditions are changing; and ... the opening out of new sources of supply or new markets for sale may quickly overbear the strength which old districts have inherited from past conditions'.[52]

Of central importance here, as we have already noted, is the fact that for both Marshall and Hobson, despite their insistence on the market and technological imperatives driving the evolution of industrial economies, the forces tending to promote large scale firms, internal economies and geographical dispersal were frequently met by countervailing forces. Their work is marked by a distinct and significant indeterminacy, stemming no doubt from their empirical methodologies. What is most important, though, is that they predicted no necessary demise of small scale business or of clusters of such firms able to realize external economies of scale, and in so refusing they echoed the beliefs of potters convinced of the continued viability of the established developmental patterns of the industry in the face of external change.

Moreover, it is instructive to stress that Marshall's analysis of the linkages between structure, strategy and localization, was located within a broad and

---

[51] Ibid., p. 133 and p. 139.

[52] Marshall, *Trade and Industry*, p. 287.

profound vision of the processes underlying the very long-run development of human societies and economies. Whilst many of the features of this philosophical framework now appear outmoded, others, emphasising the interplay of choice, chance, history and environment in structuring outcomes, are most salient to developing an historical perspective on the evolution of industrial districts. In particular, we wish to emphasise here Marshall's insistence on the dual importance of the 'heredity' element in history and on the growing 'deliberation' displayed by modern individuals, particularly in their economic lives.[53] Furthermore, Marshall recognised that this 'deliberation', this 'self reliance ... [and] promptness of choice and judgement', was practised by an economic man as capable of 'ethical' action and motives as he was of being economically rational.[54] In other words, whilst actors were increasingly self-conscious and thoughtful when considering options and making choices a far wider range of motives than the purely utilitarian could and often did come into play, not least in the sphere of business activity. Taken together with the detailed empirical work on industry structure, this framework forms a sophisticated exegesis that firmly eschews either a rigid economic or social determinism and paints man as a self-aware and self-interested, yet strongly social animal, operating within but subservient to neither historical nor systemic forces on the one hand or abstract and ahistorical economic laws on the other.

None of this is to deny the reality or the importance of collective value systems, but is instead to question both their form, their cohesiveness and their impacts. The relationship between localization and social embeddedness will be viewed, as it was by Marshall, not only as an outcome of various historical processes, but also as a dynamic influencing further developments. The business culture of the Potteries will be posited as the leaven that stimulated the interaction of industrial and social organization. In order to focus on its dynamic properties, business culture is conceptualized here not as a set of values or agreed upon rules but as a discourse, having (multiple) contributors, form (modes of expression) and content. It will be argued that notions of places, present in the Marshallian model in the form of *genius loci*, formed a central core of this discourse and that such notions can usefully be explored through the understandings of place developed by geographer Doreen Massey.[55] By focusing on historically unfolding conceptions of place we may begin to answer Lazonick's call for exploration of variety in socio-economic organizations over space and time and Staber's for investigation into the '*content* of social relations ... [and] the *mechanisms* by which social structures constrain or facilitate economic action'.[56]

---

[53] Marshall, *Principles*, p. 203 and p. 4.

[54] Ibid., p. 4 and p. vi.

[55] D. Massey, 'Places and Their Pasts,' *History Workshop Journal*, 39 (1995), pp. 182–92.

[56] Staber, 'Social Embeddeness', p. 157.

Conclusion

We may now make a preliminary summation of how the work of Marshall, Hobson and others can inform our approach as historians to understanding clustered industries. At the most general level they provide us with an empirical reminder of the wide and heterogeneous array of clustered industries found in Britain, Europe and North America in the late nineteenth and early twentieth centuries, warning us away from constructing a canonical form of the industrial district model.

At the level of specific district studies they point first to the reconstruction of industry structure over time, and its relationship to evolving divisions of labour and technological imperatives. This should not, however, be mistaken for a simple technological determinism. The development and utilization of technologies should be seen as a historically and socially situated process, affected in clustered industries by the accretion of human resource endowments in particular; that is, by the 'industrial atmosphere' identified by Marshall as the principal mechanism through which skill is transmitted and transformed.

But industry structure evolves in response not only to technology and the evolving division of manual labour but also of the labour of management. As Hobson argued, this division in part reflects requirements imposed by technologies, materials and markets, but is also again an historically and culturally situated process in which certain forms of management receive cultural validation. Before proceeding to some of the implications of this statement, it is vital to reiterate that industry structure, the organization of the labour of management, technological development and the size and composition of markets intersect to influence business strategy, that is the orientation of firms and industries to the market and to the pursuit of a range of economies, internal and external.

In turning to the socio-cultural validation of forms of business activity, a Marshallian framework suggests several important qualifications to more recent models of the industrial district. First, just as strong assumptions of rationality and profit maximization derived from neo-classical economics have been progressively abandoned as extraneous to historical analyses, so strong assumptions of 'automatic induction' into a cohesive district-wide moral economy should be replaced by the weaker assumption that self-interested reciprocity is the only *necessary* product of spatial proximity. This assumption does not negate the bulk of the advantages associated with the strong assumptions of social cohesion found in later models of the industrial district, but allows greater freedom for the play of competition and entrepreneurship, and thus has profound implication for the analysis of industrial districts as social organizations. At the same time, this weaker assumption does not preclude the emergence of networks based in higher levels of trust, but views them as likely to have a basis in sectional coalitions of interest rather than in any more pervasive system of values. Such systems are at any rate unlikely to escape instability and, to adopt the language of Hannan and Carroll, are prey to the potential for legitimation crises.[57]

Moreover, it is clear from Marshall's work that the socio-cultural validation of forms of business activity and roles occurred within a national as well as a regional context, directing attention to questions of political economy. Of particular interest will be conceptions of the relationship between the self and business activity within and between competing models of political economy.

Where prolonged clustering undoubtedly did have an important impact was in the generation of notions of place, represented in both Marshall and Hobson as *genius loci*. However, as Massey's work suggests, it is rarely plausible for understandings of place to be unitary, even within a geographical unit displaying homogeneity along many other dimensions. Instead, place is more often a contested concept which is, moreover, used to validate particular forms of action and visions of the future. This last argument is of especial pertinence given the view advanced here that in the late nineteenth century the North Staffordshire pottery industry faced a series of choices concerning future developmental patterns.

A Marshallian framework suggests, then, the investigation of a matrix of factors displaying complex lines of causality. Most importantly, causality is no longer seen as flowing primarily from the fact of clustering to a range of other outcomes. Thus the balance between agency and industry specific effects on the one hand and collective and region specific effects on the other becomes much more evenly and finally judged. At the same time, the systems described and analysed by Marshall were highly dynamic, with both industry structures and the social institutions that supported them open to destabilization and reconfiguration by a range of both endogenous and exogenous forces.

These forces, as we have already noted, fall into two basic categories, those stemming from technological changes and those from changes in markets, both cyclical and secular. Developments in technologies and markets could compound or counteract one another. Thus, in the Potteries in the last quarter of the nineteenth century a period of relative technological stability progressively lowered the cost of entry. At the same time, changes in market structures and preferences, induced by changes in the 'art of living', by changes in channels of distribution and by the different market orientations of emergent foreign competitors, collided with the increasingly competitive structure of the industry. The result, in short order, was waves of price wars, business failures and depressed profitability. What balance there had been between co-operation and competition, claimed as a distinctive characteristic of industrial districts, dissipated rapidly. Moreover, a collapse in retained profits available for investment coincided with highly equivocal attitudes towards mechanization *per*

57 Hannan and Carroll, *Dynamics of Organizational Populations*.

se, heightening technological stasis. In turn, analysis of this double bind increasingly focused on issues of industry structure and the proliferation of small firms in particular, fuelling intra-district tensions and undermining forms of business organization and activity previously validated by the business culture of the region.

In the twentieth century, however, a largely exogenous technological innovation, the tunnel kiln, a capital intensive and essentially flow process technology, eventually began to reconfigure the structure of the North Staffordshire pottery industry, leading to the emergence of a much stronger core of large integrated firms. In both cases, these complex causalities and dynamics shifted either structural and/or behavioural patterns away from those predicted for the 'ideal-typical industrial district' without significantly altering statistical measures of clustering, such as the proportion of national employment or output in the ceramic sector generated in the region. Clearly, any industrial district model needs to be flexible enough to take account of the impact of such outcomes, rather than simply ruling that the cluster no longer constitutes an industrial district.

Given the intensely regional patterning of the British manufacturing economy in the nineteenth century, it is hoped that this perspective will prove fruitful for other studies in British business history. First, there is a need to justify through detailed empirical research Zeitlin's assertion that: 'It would ... be the height of perversity to argue that while Alfred Marshall invented the (industrial district) concept in turn-of-the-century Britain, its true empirical referent would only appear in Italy half a century later', furthering a 'necessary move ... away from a "thick," "closed" model of the industrial district based on a stylised account of the Italian experience towards a "thin," "open" model capable of accommodating a variety of empirically observable forms'. Most importantly, and fully in the Marshallian tradition, such a model would 'not assume that industrial districts are necessarily flexible, consensual or otherwise successful'.[58]

More specifically, intensely spatially clustered, wedded to a structure of many small and medium-sized personally managed firms and reliant on market mechanisms to reach heterogeneous markets with a wide range of differentiated products, the pottery industry exemplified many of the characteristics at the heart of the Chandlerian critique of British business during the Second Industrial Revolution. Reflecting on the complex roots of this industry's vicissitudes, and survival, will serve to further a necessary re-evaluation of the Chandlerian paradigm. That re-evaluation is, of course, already underway and has been characterized by a rejuvenated interest in both regional economies and business networks. Given this recent turn in British business history, this study aims to offer fresh and robust insights into the relationship between clustering and the

[58] J. Zeitlin, 'Why are There No Industrial Districts in the UK?,' in A. Bagnasco and C. Sabel (eds.), *Small and Medium Enterprises* (London, Pinter, 1995), p. 102.

growth, development and resilience of industries under conditions of environmental changes. That task is begun in the next chapter by reconstructing the structure of the North Staffordshire pottery industry from 1860 to 1913–15, laying a solid empirical foundation for the remainder of the study.

CHAPTER TWO

The business structure of the North Staffordshire pottery industry, 1860–1914

Introduction

The status of Stoke-on-Trent as the primary site of ceramic manufacture in Britain and, indeed, much of the world, was firmly established by the mid-nineteenth century. The district entered the second half of the century as the seat of a confident and commanding industry. Commentators noted a 'maturity', which American Consul Edward Lane ascribed to 'concentration of effort combined with an industrial existence of two hundred years'.[1] However, the business structure of this vigorous and expanding manufacturing industry has received little empirical investigation. It has long been assumed that the industry was largely comprised of many small and medium sized firms, above which towered a handful of firms both much larger and more famous.[2] However, this picture has not been verified or the mechanisms that lay behind its growth and development uncovered.

Business structure, 1850–1914

Detailed reconstruction of business structure is vital therefore. Without it we cannot adequately assess the interrelationships between the units comprising the total 'business system' of the industrial district.[3] Nor is it possible to address the Chandlerian critique that an atomistic and small-scale structure inhibited the dynamic qualities of the British economy during the second industrial revolution, a critique increasingly prefigured in the trade press of the pottery industry in this period. This chapter will reconstruct the business structure of the industry over time, examining the number and size of firms, their sectoral and spatial dispersal,

---

[1] *The Pottery Gazette*, November 1879, p. 428 and May 1883, p. 451.

[2] Whipp, *Patterns of Labour*.

[3] R. Lloyd-Jones and M.J. Lewis, *Manchester and the Age of the Factory* (London, Croom Helm, 1988), p. 2.

concentration ratios and the mechanisms whereby both firms and industry grew. The chapter will first concentrate on manufacturing firms, those actually making ceramic wares. Subsequently, the auxiliary sector, which supplied a range of inputs and services to manufacturing firms, will also be considered.

Given the paucity of suitable data for the nineteenth century, the reconstruction of the structure of the industry has been carried out using data extracted from Borough rate books. In particular the rateable values (RV) of premises are used as a proxy for the fixed capital assets of the firm, allowing for the categorization of firms by size.[4] Careful cross-referencing with numerous trade directories and other sources has enabled more detailed histories of some firms to be constructed, giving life to the aggregate figures. Whilst numerous rate books survive their coverage is not complete. In particular rate books from the second half of the nineteenth century are extant for only two of the district's six Boroughs, Stoke-upon-Trent and Hanley. However, for both of these Boroughs there exist runs of rate books that allow industry structure to be traced over time (the series are, for Stoke-upon-Trent, 1878, 1886 and 1898 and, for Hanley, 1872, 1882 and 1892). For the period 1900–14 such useful runs do not exist. However, rate books for all six Boroughs do exist for at least one of the years 1913–15; these have been aggregated to form a very detailed portrait of industry structure on the eve of World War One.

In their reconstruction of the business structure of Manchester in the first decades of the nineteenth century Lloyd-Jones and Lewis focused on the 'struggle' between two 'quite different modes of production', the factory and the warehouse.[5] In the Potteries there were no such competing modes of production but instead a struggle shaped by the very different scales on which the same mode of production could be and was organized. The predominant structural characteristic of the North Staffordshire pottery industry was a combination of intense horizontal fragmentation and considerable vertical integration. Vertical specialization by firm was only significant in the supply and initial preparation of some raw materials. Within this structure were firms of very different sizes, from those employing less than ten hands to those with more than 1500. These firms nonetheless performed very nearly the same set of operations, comprising all of the major steps in the production of ceramic goods. Small manufacturing firms were very rarely partial process firms. In larger units individual departments would be larger and the division of labour, highly advanced throughout the

---

4 For detailed discussion of the methodological issues associated with this technique see Lloyd-Jones and Lewis, *Manchester*, Chapter 3. For other applications see R. Lloyd-Jones and A.A. Le Roux, 'The Size of Firms in the Cotton Industry: Manchester, 1815–1841', *Economic History Review*, Vol. 33, No. 1 (1980); G. Timmins, 'Concentration and Integration in the Sheffield Crucible Steel Industry', *Business History*, Vol. 24 (1982); M.J. Lewis, *The Growth and Development of Sheffield's Industrial Structure, 1880–1930*, (Unpublished Ph.D. thesis, Sheffield City Polytechnic, 1989).

5 Lloyd-Jones and Lewis, *Manchester*, p. 2–3.

industry, certainly more elaborate. Generally, however, large and small firms were different in quantitative rather than qualitative terms. Nor were larger firms necessarily more mechanized or more capital intensive. A progressive extension of the division of labour since the eighteenth century had not resulted in the emergence of vertical specialization by firm because the semi-finished product, as it moved through many stages of processing, remained fragile. This fact alone dictated that firms be vertically integrated. A lack of mechanization ensured however that it did not dictate that they be also large.

Not all of these firms were direct competitors with one another. A more elaborate division of labour often allowed larger firms to compete on the basis of the greater quality and wider scope of their product ranges. But towards the close the century, partly it would seem as a result of changes in consumer preferences, substitutability across these differentiating boundaries grew, bringing the large and prestigious and the small and new into ever closer competition. These shifts both originated and were reflected in the business structure of the district.

Certainly firms were numerous, the Borough Rate Books covering the years 1913–15 detail a total of 220 firms, the vast majority of them occupying whole, single premises. This figure in fact represented a decline from the number of firms seen even just one or two decades earlier. With nineteenth-century rate books extant for only two of the district's six Boroughs we are reliant on trade directories for a gauge of the total size of the industry in earlier periods. The picture they paint is one of uninterrupted growth in the number of firms from the mid-1860s until the early 1880s, whereafter the number of firms stagnated before falling. Thus the total population of firms contracted between 1853 and 1866 before surging by thirty-nine per cent between 1866 and 1882. Between 1882 and 1892 the firm population fell by just one per cent but then between 1892 and 1914 slumped by some nearly sixteen per cent.[6]

However, this period witnessed other structural shifts as important as those in the number of firms active in the industry. The total and average rateable value of the 220 firms of 1913–15 are presented in Table 2.1. An average RV of £286 per firm would locate the typical firm as a medium size unit, within the range RV £151–500. This figure echoes those for the firm populations of two individual boroughs in the late nineteenth century, where, in Hanley in 1882–3 and in Stoke-on-Trent in 1898, the average RV was respectively £238 and £370. It seems that the broad outlines of the size structure of the industry were relatively stable over a period of more than three decades

[6] *Slater's Classified Directory: The Potteries* (Manchester, I. Slater, 1853); *Keates & Ford's Directory of the Potteries and Newcastle-under-Lyme* (Hanley, Keates & Ford, 1865–6); *Keates' Directory of the Staffordshire Potteries and Newcastle-under-Lyme* (Hanley, Keates & Ford, 1882); *Keates' Gazetteer and Directory of the Staffordshire Potteries* (Hanley, Keates & Ford, 1892).

Table 2.1
The population of manufacturing firms in Stoke-on-Trent, 1913–15

No. Of Firms	Total RV (£)	Average RV (£)
220	62,890	286

Source: Tunstall Borough Rate Book, 1913; Burslem Borough Rate Book, 1914; Hanley Borough Rate Book, 1914, Stoke-on-Trent Borough Rate Book, 1914, Fenton Borough Rate Book, 1915; Longton Borough Rate Book, 1913 (Hereafter Rate Books, 1913–15).

Was the industry in fact characterized by a 'typical' firm of medium size? Lewis has shown that possible answers to this question may be reached through constructing industry type and size categories. Attempts at classification by industry type do not prove fruitful for the pottery industry. In part this reflects weaknesses in the sources, where, in rate books and trade directories, fullness and precision are lacking. For instance in the Hanley Borough Rate Book of 1862 the premises of all pottery firms are recorded simply as manufactories. In all later rate books both this generic term and a more precise specification of the type of product made are used in an apparently arbitrary way for different firms. Similarly, all trade directories vary in the detailed categorization of firms. However, difficulties in constructing sectoral categorizations also reflect a flexibility characteristic throughout the industry. However, simple size categories still have much to tell us about the growth and development of the industry, of the balances between firms of different sizes and, in turn, of the implications of those balances for the business strategies of firms. Mapping the total population of firms in Hanley in 1882 results in the size categories presented in Table 2.2.

Table 2.2
Firm size categories by RV, 1882

Size Category (RV) (£)	Description
1–150	Small
151–500	Medium
501–1000	Large
1000+	Giant

Source: Hanley Borough Rate Book, 1882.

Sorting the 220 firms of 1913–15 according to this categorization results in the distribution of firms presented in Table 2.3. Clearly, small and medium sized firms did dominate the industry, at least numerically, at the close of the period under study, a period which had been perceived by many as one of great turmoil and change in the industry and which some had predicted would witness the demise of small firms 'except for artistic and special purposes'.[7]

Table 2.3
The size structure of manufacturing firm population, 1913–15

Size	No	%
Small	90	41
Medium	99	45
Large	17	8
Giant	14	6
Total	220	100

Source: Rate Books, 1913–15.

The size structure of the population of firms in Hanley between 1862 and 1882, presented in Table 2.4, suggests a gradual shift away from the dominance of small firms, but this trend was not decisive.

Table 2.4
The size of firms in Hanley, 1862–82

	1862		1872		1882	
Size	No.	%	No.	%	No.	%
Small	30	75	28	64	41	62
Medium	8	20	10	23	17	26
Large	2	5	5	11	3	4
Giant	–	–	1	2	5	8
Total	40	100	44	100	66	100

Source: Hanley Borough Rate Books, 1862, 1872 & 1882.

At a simple quantitative level then, the charge levelled by both Chandler and Elbaum and Lazonick is valid for the pottery industry, which was characterized by a highly atomized and overwhelmingly small-scale structure. As might be

[7] *The Pottery Gazette*, November 1900, p.1248.

expected this form of business structure was reflected in very low industrial concentration ratios, as demonstrated in Table 2.5.

Table 2.5
Estimates of industrial concentration, 1913–15

% of 3 largest firms to total RV	% of 4 largest firms to total RV
9.16	11.28

Source: Rate Books, 1913–15.

Table 2.4 touches upon important issues relating to the growth of the industry. However, it is first necessary to indicate how the firm population of 1913–15 was unevenly distributed across the six Boroughs of the Potteries in terms of both number and size. There were for example eighty-nine firms in Longton in 1913 but only fifteen in Tunstall. At the same time however the average RV of firms in Tunstall was somewhat more than double that of firms in Longton, where the average RV was the lowest in the district. Indeed, only in Fenton and Longton was the average RV lower than the aggregate district average RV, broadly confirming the traditional picture of firm size distribution across the district. The total RV and average RV of individual Boroughs are presented in Table 2.6 and the size structures of their firm populations in Table 2.7.

Table 2.6
Total and average RV by borough, 1913–15

Borough	No. of Firms	Total RV (£)	Average RV (£)
Tunstall	15	7782	518
Burslem	26	8895	329
Hanley	46	13,393	291
S-o-T	21	9911	471
Fenton	23	6212	270
Longton	89	16,697	188

Source: Rate Books, 1913–15.

These tables cast a subtly different light on the traditional picture of firm distribution across the district. Fenton in particular, whilst it had no giant-sized firms, had an above average number of large firms and a very high proportion of medium-sized firms. In Hanley, on the other hand, small firms were relatively more numerous than in any other Borough, including Longton. These figures are important for they contextualize the debates that took place within the region over trends in industry structure.

Table 2.7.1
Size structure of firm population by borough, 1913–15

	Tunstall		Burslem		Hanley	
Size	No.	%	No.	%	No.	%
Small	3	20	9	35	26	57
Medium	5	33	11	42	13	29
Large	4	27	5	19	2	4
Giant	3	20	1	4	5	11
Total	15	100	26	100	46	100

Source: Rate Books, 1913–15.

Table 2.7.2
Size structure of firm population by borough, 1913–15

	S-o-T		Fenton		Longton	
Size	No.	%	No.	%	No.	%
Small	5	24	5	22	42	47
Medium	11	52	16	70	43	48
Large	1	5	2	9	3	3
Giant	4	19	–	–	1	1
Total	21	100	23	100	89	100

Source: Rate Books, 1913–15.

Analysis of the data for 1913–15 allows only for the creation of a static picture however. Comparable data from the nineteenth century are more limited but are nonetheless sufficient to provide a number of insights into the patterns of growth displayed by both individual firms and the industry as a whole. Uncovering these patterns provides one step towards understanding the relationship between individual agents and their actions, on the one hand, and the systemic effects of those actions on the other.

Discussion of the growth of industries in British business history has to a large extent been conditioned by the work of Marshall and in particular by his so-called 'trees of the forest' analogy. This analogy proposed that a circular mobility, from the bottom upwards and from the top downwards, is largely responsible for the growth and regeneration of industries and of the firms of which they are composed. Empirical explorations of this thesis have produced conflicting results. Lloyd-Jones and La Roux, building on a critique developed by Steindl, subjected the 'Marshallian growth path' to a test in the context of the cotton industry in the first half of the nineteenth century. Their calculations provided 'strong support for Steindl's claim that small firms wither away in large numbers before they had any opportunity to grow'.[8] Examining rates of entry, exit and mobility between 1815 and 1833 they found that a decisive shift away from small to medium and large-scale firms was the result almost entirely of firm entry, not firm mobility. They concluded:

> The evidence for the cotton industry therefore does not appear to support Marshall, since it was the entry firm rather than the upward mobile firm that acted as a catalyst for change in firm population structure ... Firms did not grow by the laborious Marshallian route, starting small and gradually growing to maturity.[9]

Lewis too orientates his examination of the growth and development of the Sheffield iron and steel industries around Marshall's analogy but his findings suggest a different conclusion. According to Lewis Steindl's proposition of a negative correlation between mortality rates and firm size 'is not supported by the Sheffield evidence'.[10] Lewis demonstrates an impressive survival rate amongst small firms of fifty nine per cent between 1880 and 1901 and an upward size mobility rate of seventeen per cent amongst the small firms present in 1880.[11] In general his data provide support for Marshall. The contribution that evidence from the pottery industry has to make to this debate is unequivocal. Thus, in the population of firms in Hanley between 1872 and 1882 we find a survival rate amongst small firms of fifty-seven per cent and an upward mobility rate of thirty-two per cent. A biographical history of the population of firms of 1882 provides further detail and is presented in Table 2.8.

Most striking is the importance of the contribution made by upwardly mobile firms to the growth and composition of the medium, large and giant size categories. Indeed, entry firms had no role to play at all in the growth of the two

---

[8] R. Lloyd-Jones and A.A. La Roux, 'Marshall and the Birth and Death of Firms: The Growth and Size Distribution of Firms in the Early Nineteenth Century Cotton Industry', *Business History*, Vol. 24, No. 1 (1982), p. 143.

[9] Ibid., p. 146.

[10] Lewis, 'Growth and Development', p. 39.

[11] Ibid., p. 37.

largest size categories and were significant only amongst small firms. Evidence of the importance of mobility over entry for the growth and structure of the industry is decisively reinforced by a similar biographical history of the population of firms in Hanley in 1872. Again entry firms had made no contribution to the large and giant size categories. Of the five large firms of 1872, the pool from which four of the five giant firms of 1882 grew, four had displayed upward mobility from the medium size category between 1862 and 1872. Similarly, the one giant firm of 1872, Brown, Westhead, Moore and Co., RV £1524, had been a large firm in 1862, RV £528. The smaller population of firms in Stoke-upon-Trent showed even greater longevity and growth potential. Between 1879 and 1886 the total population of firms in the Borough displayed a survival rate of sixty-seven per cent, whilst the mobility rate amongst small firms was thirty-three per cent.

Table 2.8
Biographical history of firm population in Hanley, 1882

	Size category									
	Small		Medium		Large		Giant		Total	
Firm type	No.	%	No.	%	No.	%	No.	%	No.	%
Survival:										
Static	8	20	6	35	2	67	1	20	17	26
Mobile:										
Up	–	–	9	53	1	33	4	80	14	21
Down	–	–	–	–	–	–	–	–	–	–
All	8	20	15	88	3	100	5	100	31	47
Entry:	33	80	2	12	–	–	–	–	35	53
Total	41	100	17	100	3	100	5	100	66	100

Source: Hanley Borough Rate Books, 1872 & 1882.

Clearly, entry into the small and medium size categories and then growth from that point had a substantial impact on the structure of the North Staffordshire pottery industry in the late nineteenth century. As was true also of the metal trades in Sheffield, Marshall's 'trees of the forest' analogy does provide a useful encapsulation of the growth mechanism operating in the pottery industry. The mass of small firms evident in the categorization of the industry by firm size was a fertile source of further growth, a proportion of such firms 'though of less material strength, [having] on their side the vigour of youth'.[12]

Thus, whilst Farnie argues that in this period the cotton industry 'ceased to fulfil its historic function as a vehicle of social mobility', the widespread belief that in potting 'the people who ... succeed in our business are men who have risen from the bench' was not simply a romantic fiction.[13] In the context of a national climate of laissez-faire political economy, the survival and growth of a proportion of small firms, to a considerable size in some cases, served to legitimize and encourage the position and activities of smaller manufacturers, so widely viewed as a destabilizing influence by large established firms and the trade press. Though the trade press might plead that 'it is only in exceptional circumstances that the small capitalist or affluent artisan can by an investment of his savings in manufacture rise to a position of easy competence', independent proprietary capitalism appeared to remain a viable aspiration for many skilled workers, the group from which most industry entrants were drawn.[14] Recognizing the validity of that view, and its cultural context, including not only the national framework but also a very strong local identification with potting as a way of life, serves to contextualize later explorations of the contours of, and potential points of weakness in, the political economy of the Potteries industrial district.

Details help to flesh out and give human content to these mechanisms and to also illustrate how spatial mobility and an evolution of governance structures often accompanied the size mobility of a firm. The trajectories of individual firms could be spectacular, probably none more so than that of the firm of Thomas Twyford, one of the first dedicated manufacturers of sanitary wares. In 1862 Thomas Twyford occupied two rented properties on Bath Street, Hanley, a manufactory (RV £37) and, very unusually, part of an adjacent factory (RV £9). In 1872 the firm was working in the same properties, their rateable values having grown by a modest amount. By 1882 the firm, now in the hands of Thomas's son, also Thomas, occupied and owned a single factory in Bath Street with an RV of £161, placing the firm at the lower end of the medium-size category. In 1887, however, the firm moved into purpose built premises on Cliffe Bank which, by 1914, commanded an RV of £2200, making the firm second to none in the industry in size.[15]

---

12 Marshall, *Principles*, p. 263.

13 D.A. Farnie, *The English Cotton Industry and the World Market, 1815-1896*, (Oxford, Oxford University Press, 1979), p. 120; Godfrey Wedgwood, quoted in 'The Technicality of Potting', *The Pottery Gazette*, May 1885, p. 560.

14 Anon, 'Some Commercial Aspects of Potting', *The Pottery Gazette*, May 1884, p. 536. The link between small aspirant capitalists and laissez-faire ideology seemed clear to the *Pottery Gazette*, which complained of the 'teaching of moralists who are forever holding up the mirror of success and pointing out the achievements of the few.' Ibid., p. 536.

15 Hanley Borough Rate Books, 1862, 1872, 1882 and 1914.

A perhaps more typical example though is that of the partnership Wardle and Ash, who in 1862 were manufacturing parian statuary at a rented property on centrally located Broad Street, Hanley. This, like many parian shops, was a tiny concern, with an RV of just £12. The firm was not listed in *Slater's Commercial Directory* of the town published that year. By 1872 Wardle and Ash had separated, but both remained in business. George Ash occupied a rented factory on St James Street, Hanley, RV £33. *Kelly's* directory recorded this business as Ash & Co., indicating the formation of a new partnership. Wardle too had acquired a new partnership, based at a works in Slippery Lane, RV £28. Both men had survived the 1860s as manufacturers, but had achieved little growth. Their paths were to diverge in the following decade. Ash remained in the rented property on St James Street, its RV increasing to £44 by 1882, perhaps through modest capital investment. Wardle, in comparison, prospered. Now in partnership with D. Jones he still occupied the small site on Slippery Lane, its RV too having grown, to £40. But he also now owned a far more substantial factory on Victoria Road with an RV of £170. With a combined RV of £210 for the two works, Wardle and Co., manufacturers of parian and majolica, were a medium-sized firm of at least twenty years standing.[16]

The change in Wardle's station in life should not be underestimated. In twenty years he had progressed from marginal artisanal manufacture, his origins almost certainly being at the workbench, where he would probably have continued to labour as a fledgling boss, to the status and security of property ownership. At the same time, however, it should be stressed that success was the exception and that the small firm population in particular could still display considerable instability, impacting heavily on the tenor of the trade. Despite respectable rates of survival and growth, surviving small firms were repeatedly swamped by waves of new entrants. This process seemed to build over time and showed a cyclical relationship with the waves of failures that also swept the trade. Thus entry firms represented sixty-four per cent of the small firm population in 1872 but eighty per cent in 1882. Similarly, in the Borough of Stoke-upon-Trent, the period 1878–1886 witnessed an extremely high birth rate amongst small firms, ninety-two per cent of small firms in 1886 were new entrants, and, relative to Hanley, a low death rate, thirty-three per cent of small firms present in 1878 exited before 1886. However, in the ensuing period, that is 1886–1898, the death rate amongst small firms accelerated dramatically and seventy-five per cent of small firms present in 1886 had failed by 1889. Attempts to correlate data from Rate Books and trade directories serve only to emphasise this instability, considerable numbers of firms appearing in one source but not the other and vice versa. The

---

[16] Hanley Borough Rate Books, 1862, 1872 and 1882; *Slater's Commercial Directory* (Manchester, I. Slater, 1862); *Post Office Directory of Staffordshire* (London, 1872); *Keates and Ford's Directoryof the Staffordshire Potteries and Newcastle* (Hanley, Keates and Ford, 1882). Jewitt records a Wardle & Co. as still active in Hanley in 1900. G.A. Godden, *Jewitt's Ceramic Art of Great Britain, 1800–1900*, (London, Barrie and Jenkins, 1972), p. 81.

majority were tiny, transient or both. In other words, neither Rate Books nor directories, compiled in the same year, were able to keep up with or agree on the composition of the district's shifting population of firms. Contemporaries were forced to acknowledge that 'We do not even know the number of manufactories or firms in the potteries of Staffordshire'.[17] Turnover in the firm population, particularly at the bottom end of the size range, was to have a significant impact on the general tenor of the trade. Trust was just one casualty of this process, a theme to which we shall have cause to return.

Again it is instructive to trace these structural patterns at the micro-level. Sabel and Zeitlin, building on the work of Philip Scranton, claim that firms in industrial districts in the nineteenth century were 'not enduring units of production but rather temporary combinations of machines and skills directed at the achievement of particular tasks: the "constant" in the Philadelphia textile industry was the "mill building rather than the firm"'.[18] If this is so then attention to property rather than firms also allows access to the constant tramp of start-ups and failures. A typical example is the manufactory on Broad Street, Hanley, owned by E. Bostock. In 1862 these works were occupied by the partnership of Rickhuss and Wilkinson, RV £77, manufacturing china, in 1872 by Taylor and Tunnicliffe, RV £101, and in 1882 by Mary Massey, earthenware and figurine manufacturer, RV £142. A very similar example is that of a works on Liverpool Road, Stoke-upon-Trent. This 'potbank' was being worked by Stanway and Co., makers of china, earthenware and parian, in 1878, RV £53, by earthenware manufacturers Shingler, Travers and Co. In 1886, RV £57 and by J. Bevington in 1989, RV £45. Of these, only Taylor and Tunnicliffe enjoyed any genuine longevity. Whilst Sabel and Zeitlin trace some of the vitality of industrial districts to this kind of pattern, it seems equally likely that such firms had not enjoyed sufficient time to develop significant reputations, either for their probity of for their wares.

Having considered the structure of the manufacuring sector of the pottery industry we turn now to that of the auxiliary trades.

The auxiliary sector

Despite the considerable vertical integration of manufacturing firms, the Potteries still generated and relied on an important auxiliary sector that provided a range of goods and services. Pottery firms were then, in Scranton's typology of specialty manufacturing, a blend of 'integrated anchors', however weakly anchored many were in this sea of competing firms, and 'networked specialists' reliant on

---

[17] *The Pottery Gazette*, September 1890, p. 818.

[18] Sabel and Zeitlin, 'Historical Alternatives', p. 149.

'specialist auxiliaries'.[19] As Scranton is at pains to stress though, 'there was no single model for specialty manufacturing, no core around which deviations or innovations can confidently be arranged'.[20]

Scranton notes that such formations 'in turn had spatial consequences', and we will have cause to explore the spatial patterning of the auxiliary sector within the Potteries industrial district, and in particular the extent to which the location of auxiliary firms lead to the formation of contacts that reached across the internal boundaries of the district.[21] However, shifts in the size of the auxiliary sector, both in absolute terms and relative to the manufacturing sector, and in the array of functions performed by auxiliary firms will first be assessed. Again the lack of nineteenth-century rate books for all Boroughs makes definitive statements difficult, nonetheless it is possible to clearly identify a number of important trends.

First a profile of the total population of auxiliary firms in 1913–15 is presented in Table 2.9 and the size structure of that population in Table 2.10.

Table 2.9
The population of auxiliary firms in Stoke-on-Trent, 1913–15

No. of Firms	Total RV (£)	Average RV (£)
87	8039	92

Source: Rate Books, 1913–15.

As might be expected, the small-scale structure of the auxiliary sector was even more pronounced than that of the manufacturing sector. Moreover, decline in the number of auxiliary firms seems to have been more rapid than that of manufacturing firms. Extrapolating from the evidence available for the Boroughs of Stoke-upon-Trent and Hanley suggests a total population of auxiliary firms in the late nineteenth century in the region of 190, double that for 1913–15. At the same time, as was true also of manufacturing firms generally, the average RV of auxiliary firms had shown some modest growth in the two Boroughs for which direct comparisons are possible; from RV £69 in Stoke-upon-Trent in 1898 to RV £133 in 1914 and from RV £125 in Hanley in 1882 to RV £135 in 1914. However, the auxiliary sector also shrank relative to the manufacturing sector. Between 1862 and 1882 the total RV of auxiliary firms in Hanley as a proportion of the total RV of manufacturing firms in that Borough averaged twenty-nine per

[19] Scranton, *Endless Novelty*, p. 21.
[20] Ibid., p.21.
[21] Ibid., p.18.

cent. In 1914 the total RV of the auxiliary sector in Hanley represented just nineteen per cent of the total RV of the town's manufacturing sector.

Table 2.10
The size structure of auxiliary firm population, 1913–15

Size	No.	%
Small	65	70
Medium	20	23
Large	2	2
Giant	–	–
Total	87	100

Source: Rate Books, 1913–15.

Table 2.11
The size of auxiliary firms in Hanley, 1862–82

	1862		1872		1882	
Size	No.	%	No.	%	No.	%
Small	19	86	20	74	27	69
Medium	3	14	7	26	9	23
Large	–	–	–	–	3	8
Giant	–	–	–	–	–	–
Total	22	100	27	100	39	100

Source: Hanley Borough Rate Books, 1862, 1872 & 1882.

These data suggest that the two or three decades spanning the turn of the century witnessed the reversal of two earlier trends. First, comparison of Tables 2.10 and 2.11 indicates how, having steadily declined in importance from 1862 to 1882, the small firm category had by 1914 once again grown relative to other size categories in the auxiliary sector. Second, as we have seen, in the years immediately preceding 1914 the auxiliary sector had contracted more rapidly than the manufacturing sector, in terms of both the number of firms and the relative total RV of the two sectors. In contrast, in earlier decades the population of auxiliary firms had actually been growing more rapidly than that of manufacturing firms, suggesting a process of increased disintegration. Detailed evidence from rate books indicates that this trend was most pronounced in Stoke-upon-Trent, where between 1886 and 1898 the population of manufacturing firms grew by twenty three per cent but that of auxiliary firms by some ninety-three per cent. Trade directories give a broader picture. These suggest the population of auxiliary firms grew by eleven per cent between 1853 and 1866 and then by nearly fifty per cent between 1866 and 1882. The next decade though witnessed a collapse in firm numbers of some thirteen per cent. The population of manufacturing firms, whilst also growing by eleven per cent between 1853 and 1866, expanded less dramatically between 1866 and 1882, adding thirty-nine per cent to firm numbers. However, in the decade 1882 to 1892, in which the auxiliary sector was heavily hit, the number of manufacturing firms was essentially static.[22]

Contracting more rapidly than the manufacturing sector, both in absolute and relative terms, and once again moving towards, rather than away from a small-scale structure, the auxiliary sector seems at the close of this period to have been withering, occuping an increasingly marginal position within the overall business structure of the Potteries industrial district. One possible inference is that as the average size of manufacturing firms grew integration was increasing, the division of labour by firm fading and the capabilities and resources of the total business system of the district becoming less important to individual firms.

However, alterations in the structure of the auxiliary sector had qualitative as well as quantitative dimensions. In the nineteenth century the majority of auxiliary firms, and certainly the largest and most important, supplied and prepared a range of inputs for pottery manufacture. Thus a number of mills ground and otherwise processed a range of materials, including clay, bone and flint. These mills, requiring a range of heavy machinery and a power source, were relatively capital intensive and often larger than many manufacturing firms. Chapter 7 will explore in detail one such firm, Jesse Shirley and Sons. Some such firms were independent specialists but others, especially from the 1880s, were combined manufacturers and millers, these firms will also be examined in Chapter 7. Other firms made colours and glazes, assembled crates for packing wares, or manufactured stilts and spurs, small ceramic pieces used to separate wares during firing. Most of these firms were very small, often with RVs of less than £10. A very small group of so-called 'potter's engineers' made machinery for the industry.

There was, however, also a small but steadily growing sector dedicated to the decoration of wares, a function performed in-house by most manufacturers. Most of these enterprises seem distinctly artisanal in character, often comprising single workers, engaged at home or a small adjacent shop as painters, modellers or copperplate engravers. By 1882, however, the firms involved were more numerous and, though still very small compared to large manufacturers, more

[22] *Slater's Classified Directory* (1862); *Keates and Ford's Director* (1872); *Keate's Directory* (1882); *Keate's Gazetter* (1892-3).

substantial. Now more often described as decorating works, the nine such firms in Hanley in 1882 had an average RV of £32, the single largest unit had an RV of £54. Between 1882 and 1914, however, whilst the overall population of auxiliary firms shrank, this sector grew significantly, both in terms of the number of firms and of the size of individual firms. By 1914 there were thirty-four specialist decorating works with a total RV of £1784 in the district, representing thirty-nine per cent of the total population of auxiliary firms and twenty-two per cent of the total RV of the sector. Twelve such firms were to be found in Hanley alone, where their average RV was £62. More significant yet though was the emergence of a small corps of much larger firms within this sector, including the Chromotransfer and Pottery Supply Co. Ltd (RV £200) in Hanley and the Universal Transfer Co. (RV £175) in Tunstall. The assumption must be that these firms were contracted, not only by manufacturers but also by merchants and buyers, to decorate undecorated wares with on glaze lithographic prints.

Yet others similarly indicated that they specialized in lithographic transfer prints, and were thus exploiting a relatively new technological advance that it had initially been feared would undermine both the traditions and the competitive advantage of the Potteries by replacing a hand skill with greater mechanization. The *Pottery Gazette* had noted of this technique in 1880, for example, that 'the printing is done by men, and from it less profit accrues [than from hand-painting by women]. The call for plain printed goods is thus affecting the trade, and some firms will feel it very much'.[23] Thus, a technology that was potentially destabilising for established firms and been absorbed into the capabilities of the district through the institutional innovation of increased specialization by firm. Furthermore, it is yet more significant that the one area in which specialization by firm actually became more pronounced in this period would have had the effect of allowing greater product differentiation, presuming that specialists, through learning and the dedication of their resources, became better equipped to generate the stylistic variations seen as increasingly important in the marketplace.

Finally, it seems possible that some of the growth witnessed in this sub-sector was driven by backward integration from firms involved in retail and distribution. Indeed the largest independent decorating works, located in Fenton, with an RV of £265, was owned by the Co-operative Wholesale Society. Similarly J. Mackee and Sons owned not only a decorating works but also a packing and warehousing site, both located in Fenton again, suggesting a focus on mercantile activities.

The spatial dispersal of the auxiliary sector, detailed in Table 3.2, was as important as its changing size and composition. It might be expected that auxiliary firms clustered most densely where manufacturing firms were most numerous or were smaller, both criteria that apply to Longton for example. However, the status of centrally placed Burslem and Hanley as important nodes

---

23 *The Pottery Gazette*, February 1880, p. 101.

of auxiliary activity was remarkably stable over time. The market for goods and services was district wide rather than articulated Borough by Borough. This picture would be reinforced by inclusion of commercial services, examined in Chapter 5, which were even more concentrated in Hanley.

Table 2.12
Spatial dispersal of the auxiliary firm population, 1913–15

Borough	No. of firms	Total RV (£)	% Total population	% Total RV
Burslem	23	2387	26	30
Hanley	19	2561	22	32
Longton	19	853	22	10
Fenton	12	1279	14	16
Tunstall	9	294	10	4
S-o-T	5	665	6	8
Total	87	8039	100	100

Source: Rate Books, 1913-15.

Clearly then the fortunes of the auxiliary sector reflected not only the impact of general business cycles but also reflected in significant ways changes in the strategies and resources of the manufacturing firms of the district. In some functions the forces promoting specialization by firm declined over time, in others they increased. These processes reflected not only the strategic actions of manufacturers, in making integrating capital investments for example, but represented opportunities for and constraints on entrepreneurs in the auxiliary sector. The mechanisms of this interaction will be studied in greater detail elsewhere in this study and more especially in Chapter 7. We have now however established with some precision changes over time to the structural balances between and within manufacturing and auxiliary sectors in the North Staffordshire pottery industry.

In both the manufacturing and auxiliary sectors success and failure may have been related in the first instance to the skills and resources of individual entrepreneurs but what forces were responsible for the pattern of foundings and failures that, ultimately, shaped the structure of the industry as a whole?

Determinants of business structure

Considering for the moment only factors endogenous to the industry and district, ease of entry may be identified as the primary force shaping industry structure. Ease of entry was related first to the low fixed capital intensity of the industry, associated with very limited mechanization, and, second, to an array of mechanisms present within the district which eased the getting of that capital, fixed and working, which was required. Ease of entry, in combination with a large pool of potential entrepreneurs trained in the productive processes of ceramic manufacture, maintained the steady stream of largely small entrants. Localized sources of working capital then played a significant role in ensuring that, whilst many of these entrants would, in Marshall's words, 'succumb on the way', sufficient numbers would survive and even prosper.[24]

The *Pottery Gazette* captured the route to independent manufacture followed by many thus:

> Almost every factory in Longton is 'bossed' by 'working men-masters'– men who, by dint of hard and unceasing labour, have left the bench for the counting house, the manager's sanctum, or the flying visits of the 'commercial' ... Working men with a few pounds buy or borrow a dozen or so jug moulds and issue into business fully fledged manufacturers 'all of the modern times'– they are their own masters firemen, pressers, throwers, and travellers and so they go on jogging from day to day, seeing, perhaps, in the dim and misty future untold wealth and a comfortable seat by the fireside devoid of every potting care.[25]

Evidence for the low capital requirements of entry firms is largely indirect, but nonetheless convincing. Notices of bankruptcy in the pages of the trade press often contained detail not only of the liabilities and assets of firms but also of their origins and the levels and sources of finance involved. Clearly operating on a very small scale were enterprises such as that of H.B. Preece of the Clyde Works in Burslem, whose creditors met in January 1893. Preece's liabilities amounted to 113 guineas, whilst his assets consisted solely of 'the utensils in the business [which] would not, if sold, realise more than five guineas'.[26] More substantial was the enterprise of Daniel Cotton, another bankrupt, who in had entered into partnership with one Edwin Roberts in September 1892, Cotton investing 100 guineas in the business and Roberts forty-five. By the time the business failed in the February of the following year it had accrued liabilities of 459 guineas. Partnerships were a very common method of acquiring these modest sums and were frequently dissolved, reformulated or supplemented with

---

24 Marshall, *Principles*, p. 263.

25 *The Pottery Gazette*, December 1881, p. 1052.

26 *The Pottery Gazette*, February 1893, p. 127.

additional partners. Chapter 6 will provide evidence of the role of partnerships in the growth a very large and long-lived firm.

Other important sources of entry capital were family and marriage. Typical perhaps were three brother, William, Edward and Albert Brookfield of Longton. In January 1893 the brothers:

> commenced business in Parkhall Street, Longton. [Wm.] put into the business 300 guineas, and his brothers put in sixty guineas each. Twelve months later William Ball joined the firm for the purpose of providing additional capital, and he put into the business 120 guineas, subsequently adding another sixty.

Moreover, William Brookfield, throughout this period, 'also travelled for his father, and got wages in that way'.[27] In another example, Harry Warrilow began in business in 1894 with a loan of 250 guineas from his mother and continued in business, until bankruptcy intervened in 1897, with the aid of a further £350 from the same source. It is not hard to appreciate the marginal and precarious position of these firms. Daniel Cotton, for example, failed on the death of his partner in an accident because he simply 'did not know how the business stood'.[28] These individual details serve also as a reminder that, despite the poverty of the resources with which they were equipped to meet it, each of these tales centres on a purposeful decision, taken perhaps with more hope than calculation but fed by the belief that everyone had the right to at least try their hand.

Localized and informal sources of capital were however also the typical foundation of very successful businesses. One such firm was that of Dunn, Bennett and Co., the result of a partnership between Thomas Wood Bennett and his father-in-law William Dunn.[29] Prior to the formation of the partnership in 1875 Bennett had been in the office of high class earthenware manufacturer E.J. Bodley and Sons whilst Dunn had been in business on his own account, though without conspicuous success. Subsequently the partnership 'prospered because Wm. Dunn was a good practical potter and T.W.B. [sic] was a hard-working imaginative commercial man'.[30] The firm remained an independent family concern until sold to Royal Doulton in 1968 and will be examined in greater detail in Chapter 5. For the moment, the asset structure of this successful and, at the time, rapidly expanding firm is of interest for the light it throws on capital requirements. On registration as a limited liability company in 1890 plant and

---

27 *The Pottery Gazette*, June 1898, p. 742.

28 *The Pottery Gazette*, June 1892, p. 535.

29 Bennett married Mary Dunn, apparently after winning her hand in a fist fight with another suitor, just months before entering into the partnership with her father. E.N.W. Bennett, *The Origin of the Bennetts of Grove House, Cobridge*, (Privately printed pamphlet, 1976).

30 Bennett, *Origin*.

machinery represented 37.7 per cent of gross assets, stock in trade, cash in hand and book debts together 60.8 per cent.[31]

Moreover, the little that entry firms did require in the way of plant and equipment was readily and cheaply available via a ready second-hand market, itself fuelled by the constant turnover in firms, and by the availability of premises for rent. As the *Pottery Gazette* observed in 1892:

> Sales are the order of the day ... sales by auction of working plant and stocks in trade at the various manufactories whose proprietors have either been 'unfortunate' or have taken time by the forelock and have ceased to manufacture for the mere fun of the thing. This is the time that a small manufacturer with a little capital to spate is able to pick up some good bargains in the form of engravings or plant or saggars.[32]

This cycle, which was repeated in other clustered industries, such as cotton, was thus partly triggered by business cycles and in itself contributed to the magnitude of those cycles through the additions made to capacity and output and to the pressure placed on prices. Plant and premises rarely exited the industry permanently, a fact reflected in the fact that the total number of firms in the industry declined only very marginally during the very difficult years of the 1880s.[33]

Entry was further eased by the prevalence of renting and by the ready availability of empty premises within the district. Table 2.13 demonstrates that whilst renting was the most common form of occupancy amongst all firms there was a particularly strong correlation between small firms and renting. Thus, whilst fifty-eight per cent of all firms rented, seventy-eight per cent of small firms rented. Medium-sized firms, on the other hand, were more likely to own than to rent and no large or giant sized firms rented, with the exception of Brown Westhead, Moore & Co., who both owned and rented properties.

Furthermore, analysis of the rate books over time suggests a strong relationship between survival, growth and form of occupancy. Surviving firms were not only likely to grow but also to move from renting to ownership, often of the property that they had originally rented. Moreover, ownership on occasions represented attainment of a 'competence', allowing for retirement. As with plant of all kinds, the trade press carried frequent advertisements for properties available to rent or lease, and again came increasingly to lament the 'temptation'

---

31 *Prospectus: Dunn, Bennett & Co. Ltd., 19 July 1890.* Courtesy of the Pinfold family.

32 *The Pottery Gazette*, November 1892, p. 1023.

33 Farnie has observed that in Lancashire in the early nineteenth century 'The ranks of the employers were swelled during each successive phase of expansion by a new influx of recruits with limited means and were then decimated during the subsequent depression, so creating a market in second hand machinery, facilitating entry by new aspirants and exposing the trade to repeated bouts of over-production and underselling'. Farnie, *English Cotton*, p. 210.

that this represented to those contemplating entering the industry at a time of increasing competitive pressure. Empty factories, paradoxically, represented both one man's failure another's opportunity.[34]

Table 2.13
Form of occupancy by firm size, Hanley, 1882

Size category	Form of occupancy							
	Rented		Owned		Mixed		Total	
	No.	%	No.	%	No.	%	No.	%
Small	32	78	9	22	–	–	41	62
Medium	6	35	11	65	–	–	17	26
Large	–	–	3	100	–	–	3	4
Giant	–	–	4	80	1	20	5	8
Total	38		27		1		66	
% total population	58		41		1			100

Source: Hanley Borough Book, 1882.

Once established, retained profits were the preferred source of funds for further fixed capital investment. Governance structures will be examined shortly, but it can be noted here that registration as a limited liability company was rarely undertaken in the Potteries in order to attract significant investments. Reliance on retained profits has been identified as one factor constraining firms across British industry at this time. However, prior to 1870, the slow rate of mechanization in the pottery industry was determined to a very large degree by technological factors and it is therefore hard to conclude that often informal methods of securing long-term finance had, up to that point, acted as a significant restraint on the growth of either firms or the industry. After 1870, however, technological issues were beginning to be resolved and mechanization was gradually gathering pace, casting continued reliance on traditional sources of investment in a rather more critical light. Perhaps more important than the availability of alternative sources of finance, however, was the willingness of businessmen in the Potteries to make use of them.

[34] Thus, in 1884 it was reported that 'There are no fewer than four manufactories to let in Burslem ... and yet in the face of all this we continually see fresh hands embarking in the enterprise'. *The Pottery Gazette*, April 1884, p. 408.

If the fixed capital requirements of the industry were low, because of limited mechanization, then, for much the same reason, the demand for working capital was relatively high. Limited mechanization was accompanied by a central role for skilled male labour. The industry also demanded a wide range of inputs, amongst which coal was the largest cost item. At the wage of arbitration of 1879, for example, Mr Hammersley of the Brownhills Pottery Co. of Tunstall estimated that in that year wages represented forty-seven per cent of turnover. At the same hearings E.J. Ridgway of Ridgway, Sparks and Ridgway, assessed wages and materials together as representing seventy-six per cent of turnover. Arguing for a reduction in wages, both men were clearly keen to portray wages as a particularly onerous burden. Nonetheless, evidence from other sources suggests that their estimates were not unrealistic.[35] The burden of wages fell most heavily on small manufacturers, who like all firms, were subject to demands for credit from buyers. As the *Pottery Gazette* noted in 1899 the employer 'wants sovereigns at the end of the week. The getting of these has ruined hundreds of small men'.[36] Thus, as in many other industries, working capital was the dominant component of business finance, revealing, as John Wilson argues, 'the tremendous pressure imposed on businessmen by their asset structure'. As a result, 'while few looked outside the firm for fixed investment purposes, they willingly relied on several external sources for working capital'.[37]

The most important of those external sources were highly localized credit circuits, in which almost all firms participated, regardless of size. Locally circulating credit thus played an important role in maintaining not only inter-firm exchange relationships but also the structure of the industry. In turn, just as the very existence of a myriad of small firms was regretted by sections of the industry, so the system and habit of giving credit was identified as helping to sustain the most injurious class of small producers. The following, from 1883, captures the complaint:

> It has been suggested by several manufacturers that the present system of giving credit should not continue. Credit is far too cheap, thereby enabling people to start manufacturing in a small way without enough capital to carry on with. What is the consequence? They have to sell at ruinous prices, thus bringing down the prices of other houses, and after a short time in business ... collapse.[38]

However, as evidence drawn from sources such as bankruptcy cases makes clear, the bulk of this credit was extended by the industry itself. Hawley and Brerton, earthenware manufacturers of the Lichfield Pottery, Hanley, for example, were

---

35 See Chapter 6.

36 *The Pottery Gazette*, December 1899, p. 1393.

37 J.F. Wilson, *British Business History, 1720–1994* (Manchester, M.U.P., 1995), p. 51.

38 *The Pottery Gazette*, January 1883, p. 62.

declared bankrupt in 1890 with liabilities of £425 and assets of £173. All ten creditors were firms or individuals located in the district and active in the industry or its auxiliary sectors. They included other pottery manufacturers, stilt and spur manufacturers and colour makers. The debts ranged in size from £11 to £85, with the majority being for less than £20. No bank was owned any money. In a similar case, seventeen of the twenty four creditors making claims on C.A. Vernon and Co. of Cobridge were drawn from the industry and included highly reputable firms such as Keelings.

Nor was credit a tool relied upon only by small new firms, as was revealed by the bankruptcy of E.J.D. Bodley of the Hill Pottery, Burslem in 1893. The *Pottery Gazette* argued 'that a firm, which, when sold up, realises no more than this, should have been able to carry on business so long, is one of the misfortunes of our long credit system'.[39] As with sources of fixed capital, sources of working capital, in the form of credit for materials, services and limited amounts of sub-contracting, were localized and personal, sometimes emerging from but rarely dependent on the existence of trust promoted by the spatial clustering of the industry. Such credit circuits were of course common to many other British industries in the nineteenth century. Hudson characterized one such system as a 'credit matrix', capturing the way in which credit, for better or worse, bound clustered firms together.[40]

Credit was on occasion supplemented by other sources of working capital, including bank loans and overdrafts. Chapter 6 will reveal the role of the bank in sustaining Mintons Ltd during a period of crisis in the 1880s and 1890s that included severe liquidity problems. Similarly, when Hartley, Arnoux and Fanning, a firm of potter's engineers, failed in 1893 they had an overdraft of £4619 at the National Provincial Bank in Hanley.[41] However, Mintons were a firm of unparalleled standing and other comments in the trade press suggest bankers were not always so accommodating. Thus, when Messrs Fenton and Sons of Hanley failed in 1899 the *Pottery Gazette* felt that the 'chief point of interest is the amount of the bankrupt firm's indebtedness to the bank. One would say that there are few manufacturers in the district with persuasive powers sufficient to get an overdraft of nearly thirty thousand pounds from their bank manager–a class of beings more ready to strain at gnats than to swallow camels'.[42]

Moreover, anecdotal evidence suggests that as competition intensified both within and beyond the district, firms began to experience increasing shortages of

---

[39] *The Pottery Gazette*, February 1893, p. 160. Net assets, after deduction of wages, rent, rates etc., were £3594. Preferential creditors were owed £1084. Ibid., p. 160. For an earlier period see, L. Weatherill, 'Capital and Credit in the Pottery Industry before 1700', *Business History*, Vol. 24 (1982), pp. 243–58.

[40] Wilson, *British Business History*, p. 51–2.

[41] *The Pottery Gazette*, March 1893, p. 249.

[42] *The Pottery Gazette*, March 1899, p.329.

working capital. It was observed in September 1893, for example, that 'On every side one hears complaints of the scarcity of money, and the period of credit demanded by the home trade is ever displaying a tendency to increase. This necessitates a greater amount of capital being at the command of the manufacturer, which is not always practical to obtain'.[43] That traditional methods of finance were at this time becoming less appropriate to changing conditions, and thus potentially constraining the industry, must be considered a possibility.

Business structure and governance

The principal forms of ownership and governance adopted by firms in the North Staffordshire industry throughout the nineteenth century, and indeed for long into the twentieth century, were those associated with personal and familial capitalism. Given that this was true of all firms, regardless of their size and their legal status, the relationship between business structure and governance is not easy to decipher. Certainly, it is not adequate to simply equate personal capitalism with small-scale firms and primitive structures, or with conservatism and a lack of growth. The routes to personal capitalism were almost as numerous and varied as the people following them and the impact of personal capitalism on the growth and development of firms and industries mediated by many factors. To posit a uni-directional line of causality from the retention of personal capitalism to small-scale structures, atomism and conservatism is coming to seem less and less plausible.

Moreover, it cannot be assumed that personal capitalism had the same meaning or importance for those involved. Indeed, there is a strong need for discussions of personal capitalism to become far more nuanced. Acknowledging the differences within personal capitalism as well as those between this and other modes of organization and ownership may aid in understanding the relationship between business structure, governance and business strategy.

One concept with the potential to yield powerful insights in this area is that of the 'competence', advanced by Scranton as a 'phenomenon peculiar to ... proprietary and partnership firms ... one component of a culturally defined alternative to the corporate version of capitalism'.[44] However, the competence may also represent a defining difference within personal capitalism that impacted on the strategies and growth trajectories of firms, leading in turn to outcomes for the structure of the industry as a whole. Evidence suggests that the notion of a personal competence did figure in the aspirations and motivations of small

---

43 *The Pottery Gazette*, September 1896, p. 714.

44 P. Scranton, *Proprietary Capitalism: The Textile Manufacture at Philadelphia, 1800-1885*, (Cambridge, Cambridge University Press, 1983), p.70–1. In this context the term competence refers not to skill but, in nineteenth century usage, to the attainment of a degree of wealth that would permit retirement.

entrepreneurs in the Potteries, and whilst it represented an extension to the very limited time frame of most small businessmen it also recognized that the multi-generational family firm, in which a premium was placed on reputation and stability, was perhaps an unrealistic ambition. And, whilst the trade press might assert that those able to attain an 'easy competence' were few and far between, reconstruction of the trajectories of individual businesses and entrepreneurs throws some light on the existence of such a value system.[45]

Scranton argues that in Philadelphia 'real estate and land purchases were an important element in building a competence', and interrogation of Potteries rate books suggests this route was also followed in the Potteries, perhaps as a cap to the move from renting to ownership outlined above. One example is that of the partnership of William Harrop and T. Worthington, who in 1862 manufactured parian at a small works at Tinkers Clough, Hanley (RV £26). By 1882 both men had retired. Harrop now owned an earthenware and parian factory at Mount Pleasant, Hanley, occupied by Bednall and Heath (RV £31). Worthington owned the adjacent site, occupied by J. Harrop and J. Hall, earthenware, parian and stoneware manufacturers, with an RV of £132. This is a complex picture of modest ambitions fulfilled, limits reached, not least in terms of firm size, and of fresh independent starts by a new generation.[46] The contrast with the picture of personal capitalism at Mintons that will be drawn in Chapter 6 is a powerful one.

For the moment, however, we are concerned only to sketch in broad outline the forms of governance adopted in the Potteries. There was a strong correlation between ownership and management and little development of professional, hierarchical managerial structures. This is perhaps not surprising in an industry composed predominantly of small firms in which upward mobility was the primary source of growth. Moreover, as will be shown in Chapter 4, both prevailing technologies and work practices tended also to promote or protect personal capitalism by minimizing the need to develop complex managerial systems of supervision. Particular managerial specialisms, most notably in accounting, were also slow to emerge, even in the largest firms. Truly multi-generational business dynasties, epitomised by Wedgwoods, may have been the exception and partnerships formed outside the family common, but at the close of the century the family remained central to the management and ownership of firms in all size categories.

There is little evidence of any diminution in this principle in the period under study, even amongst those firms registering as limited liability companies. Registration itself was not common and rarely represented a significant alteration to either the ownership or the management of the business; the majority of such firms remained privately held. In the final two decades of the nineteenth century the trade press reported the registration or re-registration of twenty-two

---

45 *The Pottery Gazette*, December 1881, p. 1052.

46 *Hanley Borough Rate Books*, 1862 & 1882; *Keates Directory*, 1882.

companies in the industry. Fully one half of these registrations took place between 1898 and 1900. The largest share issue was for £120,000 and the smallest £1000. The majority of firms registering were from the Boroughs of Hanley, Burslem and Tunstall, traditionally seen as the location of the biggest and most prosperous firms in the industry. The two Longton firms registering had the smallest and second smallest share issues. It is possible to discern a range of motivations behind registration, but few were concerned with transferring ownership or control or with securing new sources of investment.

For some firms, such as Harrison and Son Limited, registration was a simple act of consolidation. This firm of Hanley based colour makers registered in 1900, capitalized at £50,000 issued in £10 shares, after thirty years of steady but unspectacular growth and the direct involvement of three generations of the family.[47] Moments of dynastic succession were seized upon by other firms as an opportunity to alter the legal status of a firm, as was the case with the venerable but struggling Messrs. William Davenport and Co., registered in 1882 in order to acquire the 'manufactories ... hitherto belonging to Mr. Henry Davenport.'[48] If registration was intended to form part of a rescue package it failed, for the firm was bankrupt before the close of the decade. Less frequently registration helped affect the rationalization of the structure of a business or group of businesses. John Maddock and Son Limited was formed in 1896 with a capital of £75,000 and the object of acquiring:

> as a going concern ... the business of earthenware manufacturer, stilt and spur manufacturer and stone flint grinders hitherto carried on at Newcastle Street, Burslem under the style of John Maddock and Sons, and at the Dale Hall Pottery, Burslem under the style of Maddock and Co.[49]

The signatories included J., J.F., A.H., and R.J. Maddock, all of Burslem, F.W. Llewellyn of Alsager in Cheshire and E.B. and H.B. Allerton of Longton and Blyth Bridge respectively, both in the Potteries. The Maddock family clearly retained a central interest in the firm which, like the overwhelming majority of registered companies in the district, remained privately held.

The interlocking of often prominent local families sometimes meant that apparent transfer of ownership during registration did not in fact represent any real discontinuity. One such case was the registration of James MacIntyre and Co. in 1893, which took place 'in accordance with an agreement expressed to be made between Wm. Woodall of the one part and this company of the other part.' Woodall, a local colliery owner and Liberal M. P. for first Stoke-upon-Trent and then Hanley, was in fact son-in-law to James MacIntyre, who had died in 1868

47 *The Pottery Gazette*, May 1894, p. 7.

48 *The Pottery Gazette*, October 1882, p. 867.

49 *The Pottery Gazette*, March 1896, p. 218.

without a male heir, and already a senior partner in the firm.[50] Of eight initial shareholders four were drawn from the Woodall family, holding between themselves fifty per cent of the shares taken up. For James MacIntyre and Co. registration occurred in the context of a static organizational structure, in which familial control and management remained closely linked, and resulted in no fresh injections of external capital.[51] The fierce defence of family control at Mintons will be examined in greater detail in Chapter 6. In general then, the evidence from the Potteries supports Payne's contention that the 'private limited liability company represented a typical British compromise'.[52] There were, of course, exceptions to the rule that by this approach to governance 'the introduction of new entrepreneurial talent to the board was inhibited'.[53] On registration in 1900 Dunn, Bennett and Co. appointed J. Twells Mogridge, who had previously acted as the firm's agent in London, to the board.[54] However, it is well to remember that companies registering, whether remaining privately held or not, were very much the exception. Personal capitalism dominated the pottery industry.

Conclusion

The function of this chapter, in reconstructing the business structure of the North Staffordshire pottery industry between 1860 and 1914, has been to lay an empirical foundation for the rest of this study. It has been shown that although a number of subtle shifts occurred, the broad outline of industry structure in the Potteries remained relatively stable. Small and medium-sized firms remained dominant throughout in terms of both numbers and weight. There was a weak trend away from small-scale firms but this was not significant and the industry remained very unconcentrated, even though large and giant-sized firms grew both individually and, to a lesser extent, as a population. The growth of both firms and the industry was explored in terms of Marshall's 'trees of the forest' analogy, which was found to be valid for the Potteries. Firms were able to enter the industry at a small scale, to survive and to grow. The majority of large firms had themselves followed this path. The importance of this finding, in its impact on

---

[50] *The Pottery Gazette*, February 1893, p. 6; D. Stuart (ed.), *People of the Potteries* (Keele, Staffs., University of Keele, 1985), p. 145 and pp. 235–236.

[51] A major shareholder was Corbett N. Woodall described as a potter's manager, of Burslem. The assumption must be that he was a manager at MacIntyres. *Summary of Capital and Shares, James MacIntyre and Co., 1893–1900*, Companies House.

[52] P.L. Payne, 'The Emergence of the Large-scale Company in Great Britain, 1870–1914', *The Economic History Review*, Vol. 20, No. 1 (1967), p. 520.

[53] *Ibid.*, p. 520.

[54] Dunn, Bennett and Co., *Prospectus.*

business culture and political economy within the district for example, will be a major motif throughout this study.

Moreover, whilst the number of firms active in the industry also fell in this period this trend too was weak. Firms remained very numerous and the industry very fragmented. It was argued that this fragmentation was largely horizontal, to a great degree because of technological indivisibilties. At the same time as the population of manufacturing firms was shrinking the population of auxiliary firms was contracting even more rapidly, suggesting that vertical integration was being extended and the specialization by firm decreasing, potentially downgrading the importance of intra-district linkages. However, it was also noted that specialization by firm showed a marked increase in some key areas, most especially in decorating, suggesting that some of the considerable burden of achieving product differentiation and stylistic change was increasingly handled at a district level rather than within the individual firm.

However, the fragmentation or atomization of the industry was traced not only to technological issues but also to an array of conditions promoting ease of entry and the proliferation of firms. In turn, fragmentation was shown to have been paralleled in terms of organization and governance by a reliance on what Chandler has condemned as personal capitalism. Thus, though its focus has been empirical, this chapter has begun to hint at the complex and multi-directional lines of causality that flowed between business structure, technology, clustering and the cultural dimensions or attributes of personal capitalism. To a large extent the remainder of this study will be concerned with further unravelling or clarifying those lines and their changing impacts over time. To that end the next chapter will focus on the environmental changes that the Potteries faced in this period, including the timing and impact of business cycles, secular changes in the market for ceramic goods and, perhaps most importantly, the rise of foreign industries and the bases on which they competed.

CHAPTER THREE

Competitive challenges

Introduction

Sidney Pollard has argued that manufactured exports are, 'possibly the key variable in the discussion of the failures of the British economy ... what was significant for Britain was her position as an exporter in a competitive environment'.[1] Observers of the British pottery industry in the late nineteenth century reached a very similar conclusion, urging, in 1892, that 'As an insular and manufacturing nation we feel the fall in exports to be one of vital importance. Our continued existence as a manufacturing and producing power rests largely upon our export trade'.[2] Thus, potters, faced with an increasingly fierce battle for control of export markets from the mid-1870s onwards, identified the rise of foreign industries as perhaps the greatest challenge to the further growth and development of the industry in North Staffordshire. In this judgement they were undoubtedly right. Moreover, it was increasingly recognized, or asserted, that the response of the industry to this challenge had been, at best, lacklustre. In the Introduction to Volume Five of the *Report of the Tariff Commission* it was claimed that whilst:

> it is agreed that the world's use of pottery ware has undergone great expansion in recent years ... the evidence show, however, that the British pottery industry has not only not expanded accordingly, but has failed to keep pace with the home demand [and] the British export trade has remained practically stationary for the last 25 years, while the export trade of the chief foreign competitors has shown great increase.[3]

The Potteries appeared to represent in microcosm a wider 'failure to exploit the opportunities opened up by the new technological style to the same extent as

---

[1] S. Pollard, *Britain's Prime and Britain's Decline: The British Economy, 1870–1914* (London, Edward Arnold, 1989), p. 10 and p. 13.

[2] *The Pottery Gazette*, April 1892, p. 319.

[3] *Report of the Tariff Commission: Vol. 5, The Pottery Industries* (London, King and Son, 1907), para. 2–3.

American and German capitalists [which] exposed British industrial capitalism to increasing competitive pressure'.[4]

This chapter will begin to probe the highly critical thesis advanced by the *Tariff Commission.* What was the export performance of the British pottery industry in the decades of preceding the First World War? To what extent was the domestic market penetrated by foreign competitors? From where did the strongest challenge to Britain's position issue and was that challenge stronger in certain sectors of the industry than in others? Were there correlations between export performance and the changes in the structure of the industry explored in Chapter 2? In uncovering answers to these and other questions we will also begin to probe the bases on which foreign competitors offered their challenge to the Potteries, examining issues such as comparative cost and demand structures and contrasting structural and organizational attributes and strategic alignments.

In attempting to reveal more clearly the competitive landscape of this period we will also be led to ask how potters perceived that landscape. Establishing the nature of the competitive challenges faced by the industry provides one of the key elements necessary to an understanding of the strategic responses offered both by firms and the industry as a whole. However, within any historical context, exploration of the relationship between constraint and strategic response requires caution. Models of the relationship drawn from economics tend to be highly functional. Moss, for example, in a useful conceptualization of the linkages between constraint and response in terms of focus and inducement effects, nonetheless continues to discuss these in terms of 'mechanisms'.[5] It is argued here, in contrast, that any such model must recognize that the nature and extent of any constraint and perceptions of that constraint prevalent in a firm or industry will not necessarily be congruent. Thus, for example, whilst it was recognised in the Potteries that foreign competition was impacting on both foreign and domestic markets, this threat was also played down by some as a result of a belief that there existed a significant quality gap between British and foreign products and that this would continue to prove advantageous in the marketplace. It is perhaps within the perception of a constraint that the more powerful determinant of business strategy will be found.

In *Entrepreneurship and Business Culture*, Mark Casson sets out to replace neo-classical assumptions concerning motivation and decision-making in the economic sphere with 'specific postulates as to how people handle information within a social environment'.[6] It is in the socio-cultural dimension to economic action that both the 'subjectivity of problems' is to be located and the roots of

---

4 R. Lloyd-Jones and M.J. Lewis, *British Industrial Capitalism since the Industrial Revolution* (London, UCL Press, 1998), p. 211.

5 S. Moss, *An Economic Theory of Business Strategy* (Oxford, Martin Robinson, 1981), p. 60.

6 M. Casson, 'Entrepreneurship and Business Culture', in J. Brown and M. B. Rose, *Entrepreneurship, Networks and Modern Business* (Manchester, MUP, 1993), p. 40.

business culture found.[7] For Casson, the subjectivity of problems is a function of how they are defined in terms of both identification and potential solutions. Moreover, Casson contrasts such perceptions with 'the reality of problems'.[8] Attention to the relationship between the competitive constraints facing the North Staffordshire pottery industry and how they were perceived provides, then, a rough map to the handling of information within a specific social environment and an introduction to the business culture(s) of that environment.

Uncertainty, for example, will emerge as a powerful factor in the relationship between constraint, perception and response. Casson identifies 'novel and complex situations where objectives are ambiguous', such as a period of increased competitive challenge, as those in which decision-making becomes both more important and more acute.[9] Similarly, the 'uncertainties of potential competition' is just one of the forms of uncertainty identified by Moss for which evidence can be found in the Potteries.[10] Thus, for the pottery industry, and many other British industries, the last quarter of the nineteenth century was a time when judgements became both increasingly critical and increasingly difficult. In response, the industry entered into a period of intense debate through which there emerged, at points, something close to a collective, if not always coherent voice. These debates echo then Casson's belief that subjectivity is not solely 'an individualistic phenomenon ... But ... can also be collective'.[11]

The extent of the competitive challenge

One perception of the fortunes of the British pottery industry that gained great currency in North Staffordshire, particularly in the 1880s and 1890s, was that it faced nothing short of a crisis. Thus, in June 1883, the *Pottery Gazette* declared, 'the whole commercial world, "Home" and "Foreign", seems paralysed to the core ... We are face to face with a crisis in potting history'.[12] As in the Sheffield metal trades, businessmen in the Potteries 'perceived a growing economic crisis at the local level' during this period.[13] Thus, as Crouzet argues, the concept of the great Depression 'remains valid as a contemporary interpretation of what was experienced', not least in terms of it's psychological impact, despite more recent attacks on its aggregate 'significance and unity'.[14]

---

7 Ibid., p. 35

8 Ibid., p. 35.

9 Ibid., p. 31.

10 Moss, *Economic Theory*, p. 95.

11 Casson, 'Entrepreneurship', p.40.

12 *The Pottery Gazette*, June 1883, p. 559.

13 Lewis, *Growth and Development*, p. 55.

14 F. Crouzet, *The Victorian Economy* (London, Methuen, 1982), p. 62.

We have already identified a concurrent stagnation of exports and a rising tide of imports as principal symptoms of the 'crisis' facing the pottery industry. What does the data tell us about these twin trends in exports and imports? Are the charges levelled by the *Tariff Commission*, and many times previously in the trade press, supported? Immediately striking, after first noting that Britain remained a net exporter of ceramics throughout this period, is the instability in the value of exports in the years 1879 to 1894, that is throughout the period identified as the 'Great Depression'. Considerable growth was achieved at times, most notably between 1879 and 1883 and then again between 1885 and 1889, but steep declines are also evident, the most severe and prolonged occurring between 1889 and 1894. The culmination of this fifteen-year period of fluctuation in 1894 represented a particular nadir, with the value of British ceramic exports lower than at any point since the mid-1870s. The pattern then, at least until the mid-1890s, is one likely to have confounded confident predictions and to have spread uncertainty. Moreover, fluctuation also occurred along many different dimensions; between and within different sectors, different townships within the district and between firms of different sizes. Trade reports were often of a 'strangely contradictory character–some firms flat out–others standing idle'.[15]

After 1894 a recovery was staged. Certainly, falls continued to occur, but the underlying trend was upward. This trend then became more pronounced after 1905 and yet more vigorous after 1909, as British ceramic exports surged to new highs. A growing air of confidence soon found echo in the pages of the trade press:

> Our potters are full of orders at the advanced prices, and looking to the future of our years trade; the anxious period is past as to trade – the next six months at least will not produce a scarcity of orders; and as our commerce is increasing by leaps and bounds, there is no reason why potting should not enjoy a share of it.[16]

The Potteries participated fully in the Edwardian export boom, a development the report of the *Tariff Commission* came too early to fully capture. Thus, between 1900 and 1913 the average annual rate of growth in the value of British ceramic exports was 4.8 per cent, whilst in the economy as a whole during the same period, the average annual rate of growth in the volume of exports was 4.2 per cent.[17]

However, equally clear is the strong and steady upward growth in imports between 1879 and 1903, during which period they grew in value by more than 270 per cent. As we shall see, some potters were clear in their own minds that many of these imports were 'dumped' by foreign industries sheltering behind

---

15 *The Pottery Gazette*, July 1885, p. 816.

16 *The Pottery Gazette*, May 1900, p. 542.

17 Lloyd-Jones and Lewis, *British Industrial Capitalism*, p. 103.

high tariff barriers. Nonetheless, while the growth in imports stalled after 1903, it is clear that import penetration was a very real phenomenon in ceramics in the late nineteenth- century, and that for contemporaries to dismiss the threat as a chimera would have been mistaken. Nonetheless, the *Pottery Gazette* could assert that, whilst 'Germany is making enormous strides ... we fail however to see that there is anything in the policy of Germany to give occasion for alarm to the British producer'.[18]

The proportion of the British domestic markets in the hands of foreign industries is uncertain. Contemporary estimates suggested that exports typically represented between forty and fifty per cent of total UK production.[19] Extrapolating from export figures for 1903, when imports peaked, suggests that the share of domestic markets taken by foreign imports probably ranged from twenty-four to thirty-three per cent in that year. This was certainly far less than the degree of import penetration suffered by an industry such as dyestuffs. Assuming that the ratio of exports to total UK production remained relatively stable, then imports may have declined markedly as a proportion of UK domestic consumption as exports soared in the first decade of the new century. This sense of recovery is reinforced by consideration of the UK balance of trade in ceramics. On an index where 1900 = 100, then in 1905 the balance of trade, which always remained positive, stood at 106, at 168 in 1910 and at 200 in 1913, the last full year of peace.

The picture is then mixed. The Edwardian boom was flattered by very sluggish or even negative export growth in the preceding two decades, during which time foreign imports made gains from which they were not easily evicted. After 1900 the advancing tide of imports may have been halted, but it was not turned back. Moreover, underlying the aggregate figures was a number of important trends. There were significant shifts in the destinations of British exports. Similarly, there were shifts in the origins of imports, and in both domestic and export markets particular sub-sectors displayed varying fortunes.

Taking the first of these issues, the decline in the value of exports to the United States was unmistakable, critical and inexorable. Between 1881 and 1913 the value of exports to the US fell by fifty-two per cent. In 1881 the US took 39.3 per cent, by value, of all UK ceramic exports, but by 1913 just 12.4 per cent. This trend was, of course, largely a result of tariffs. The impact of a specific tariff, in 1883 for example, being immediately obvious in the total export figures. Given the strong growth in exports during the latter years of this period, alternative markets had clearly been found, and these were located primarily in the Colonies.

---

[18] *The Pottery Gazette*, February 1897, p. 181. Similarly, in the following year, it was argued that while 'the cry of German competition would have sufficed for an explanation [of depression] at one time ... it is not good enough now. German earthenware at least is not a very dangerous competitor in our own country, whatever it might be in some of the cheaper foreign markets'. *The Pottery Gazette*, May 1898, p. 615.

[19] *Report of the Tariff Commission*, para. 2.

Trade with Canada, for example, grew by eighty per cent between 1909 and 1913, that with New Zealand by forty per cent. Gains, though they were less dramatic, were also made in Australia, South Africa and India. Indeed, in the 1890s, Australians were regarded as 'the best customers we have, and every means should be taken to keep their custom. While the United States spends annually about two pence per head on British crockery, the Australian spends fifteen'.[20] Nonetheless, this was also a market in which German competition was to grow particularly fierce. Continental Europe, on the other hand, declined in importance as an export market.

Just as the decline in importance of the US was the most marked feature of export markets in this period, so the rise of Germany was the most significant element in the story of import penetration played out from the late 1870s. Indeed, to a very large and increasing degree, imports were synonymous with German wares. Though, as we have already seen, any threat was sometimes dismissed in the North Staffordshire, local attitudes generally mirrored those at the national level, where 'from 1879 ... economic rivalry was seen almost totally in Anglo-German terms'.[21] Beginning in the 1870s, German import penetration became particularly marked from the 1890s onwards. Thus, in 1892, German imports represented thirty-six per cent of total UK ceramic imports but sixty six per cent in 1913. Moreover, between those years, the average annual growth rate in the value of German ceramic imports to the UK was 9.8 per cent. To reiterate, the German 'threat' was a very real one in these years.

Just as German imports to Britain were concentrated in consumer durables, so German pottery imports were also skewed to particular products.[22] Cheap semi-porcelain was particularly important, in ranges such as tea and toilet sets, and china and porcelain also showed growth. Indeed, china manufacturers in the Potteries, located primarily in Longton and Fenton, regularly complained that official returns disguised the extent to which they had borne the brunt of the German import drive. Similarly, considerable growth was seen in the import of German ceramics for use in the electrical and chemical industries, a relatively new sector of the ceramic industry and a supplier of important inputs to two of the key industries of the Second Industrial Revolution. The value of such imports rose by more than seventy per cent between 1909 and 1913 alone. However, neither Germany, nor any other foreign industry, was a serious competitor in tiles or sanitary ware in the UK market. For the British industry to have repelled import penetration in these increasingly important and valuable product categories was undoubtedly a significant achievement.

---

20 *The Pottery Gazette*, February 1898, p. 232–3.

21 P.L. Cotterell, '"Lo, ... Nineveh and Tyre": British Trading Anxieties and Official Reactions, 1870-1929', in D.H. Aldcroft and A. Slaven (eds.), *Enterprise and Management: Essays in Honour of P. L. Payne* (Aldershot, Scolar Press, 1995), p. 277.

22 Ibid., p. 281. Cotterell specifically mentions 'china, toys, prints, pencils and cheap imitations of Sheffield cutlery'. Ibid., p. 281.

British export growth in the Edwardian years was likewise concentrated in particular sub-sectors. Between 1909 and 1913, for example, the value of earthenware exports, long the backbone of British ceramic exports, grew by 37.9 per cent, that of china and porcelain, largely the high-class wares of manufacturers such as Mintons, by 27.7 per cent. More impressive yet, though, was the growth in exports from two relatively new sectors, tiles and sanitary ware. In the same period, the value of exports in these two product groups grew by 85.8 per cent and 81.9 per cent respectively. These figures are suggestive of a considerable restructuring in the British ceramic industry, overwhelmingly concentrated in the Potteries. Opportunities in new product markets were being aggressively exploited. Moreover, in both sectors product innovation was supported by process innovation, most especially with respect to tiles, and by a growth in the size of some individual firms. Most indicative of this trend was the growth of the firm of Thomas Twyford. This firm had even, in 1901, opened a factory at Ratingen, near Dusseldorf.[23]

It is a frequent claim that in the late nineteenth century British capitalism was slow to restructure, failing to shift resources from declining sectors into the technologically advanced industries of the Second Industrial Revolution.[24] But resource reallocations of significant impact could also occur within established sectors. Though an established staple trade, closely identified with the breakthroughs of the late eighteenth century, the pottery industry was, beneath the surface, capable of generating important structural shifts in order to exploit emerging market opportunities. These shifts were, of course, not fully reflected in the overall business structure of the industry, reconstructed in Chapter 2.

Nonetheless, the concurrence of a peak in the total number of firms and an absolute decline in the value of exports in the decade from the mid-1880s, followed by a decline in firm numbers and growth in the value of exports down to 1913, is suggestive. Where failed firms had previously been rapidly replaced, sometimes in even greater numbers, the shakeout that began in the mid-1890s, reflected in rapidly rising number of bankruptcies, bucked this pattern, allowing greater room for firm growth.[25] Certainly, the industry remained characterized by an atomized, small-scale structure, but quantitative and qualitative changes were undoubtedly occurring within individual firms. These included not only Twyfords, but also tile manufacturer H. & R. Johnson, tableware manufacturers Johnson Bros. and Cauldon Ltd. (formerly Brown-Westhead, Moore and Co.) and others. Moreover, each of these firms had been founded by locally born entrepreneurs and, though growing to a size and degree of organizational complexity unprecedented in the Potteries, remained family owned and directed

---

23 Stuart, *People of the Potteries*, p. 212.

24 Most notably perhaps in Chandler, e.g. *Scale and Scope*.

25 The number of bankruptcies per annum rose nearly fifty per cent from 1895 to 1898. *The Pottery Gazette*, October 1899, p.1157.

throughout this period. Regionally oriented personal capitalism did not necessarily imply an inherent absence of dynamism.

The long-term logic of these shifts was not lost on observers:

> A manufacturer who invests capital ... is surely justified in his effort to reap the full benefit of the greater facilities for which he has paid by effecting larger sales at lower prices than can be charged by those who have not his facilities ... In such businesses as the Meakins and Johnson Bros., which have quadrupled themselves in the last ten years , it is certain that some less enterprising firms have had to surrender orders in their favour.[26]

However, others adopted a less sanguine view, arguing that, 'Meanwhile, those who can afford are building new factories with all modern "improvements", with a view to cheapening production and thus securing their share of unprofitable business'.[27]

Clearly, prices were an issue of great moment in the Potteries throughout this period. As was noted in 1886, 'the great depression has been in value more than quantity'.[28] The Potteries were not alone in this experience. Saul, though largely denying the existence of a phenomenon the 'Great Depression', has noted an 'unmistakable' downward trend in prices for the fourteen years from 1873.[29] Complaints that the industry had been made unremunerative through depressed prices were heard consistently throughout the last quarter of the century. In December 1881, for example, prices were said to be 'unsettled'. One year later, it was concluded that although a 'slight improvement' had been shown in the volume of trade, 'the difficulty has been not so much to secure orders, as to obtain fairly remunerative prices'.[30] By late 1883 the situation appeared far more grave, 'prices are simply ruinous. Competition is stalking through the land, leaving a bankrupts trail behind'.[31] As late as 1898, with a tentative recovery underway and confidence beginning to rally, editorial comment in the trade press could still assert that, 'It has been no secret that manufacturer's selling prices of pottery, particularly earthenware, have for a long time been disastrously low ... That something must be done in the direction of improving prices is absolutely necessary'.[32]

---

26 *The Pottery Gazette*, March 1890, p. 233; *The Pottery Gazette*, August 1891, p.733.

27 *The Pottery Gazette*, December 1888, p. 1108.

28 *The Pottery Gazette*, January 1886, p. 40.

29 S. Saul, *The Myth of the Great Depression, 1873-1896* (Basingstoke, Macmillan, 1982), p. 9.

30 *The Pottery Gazette*, December 1881, p. 1036; *The Pottery Gazette*, December 1882, p. 1128.

31 *The Pottery Gazette*, August 1883, p. 955.

32 *The Pottery Gazette*, July 1898, p. 827.

How accurate were the complaints of depressed prices so commonly heard in the last quarter of the nineteenth century? In part, this was an issue of perception. Thus, in the late 1890s, the preceding fifteen years were being compared to the 'the golden age of potting ... those halcyon days' of the 1870s, when 'customers came to us for pots, and thought themselves fortunate is they could get what they wanted, without being too particular about the price ... now we go to the customers and let them dictate terms to us'.[33] As Church has noted, there had prevailed in the 1870s a 'generally optimistic climate of opinion, especially among the business community'.[34]

But these perceptions reflected some underlying truths. As we have already seen the value of British ceramic exports was subject to considerable instability and, though the evidence is limited, it seems certain that this instability extended also to prices. The unadjusted value of ceramic exports reached two peaks in the depression years, in 1882 and 1889, separated by a trough in 1885. After 1899 exports by value again fell markedly, assuming thereafter a pattern of more frequent though smaller peaks and troughs. The declared real value of British ceramic exports adjusted for price, displayed a very similar pattern, peaks occurring in 1883 and 1890. Comparing the two data sets suggest prices had already begun to fall in the late 1870s but then recovered between 1879 and 1883. Between 1883 and 1887, prices either fell or stagnated before a slight rise in 1888 heralded the rapid advances seen in 1889. However, this rally was short-lived, and for the remainder of the century consistent, if unspectacular, falls were relieved by only very modest recoveries in 1894, 1896 and 1900, a pattern consistent with the national picture. Contemporaries had been broadly right to claim that the depression had 'been more in value than quantity'.

Tariffs, profits and strategy

Returning to Pollard's notion of Britain's position within a competitive environment, we can explore the reaction of businessmen in the Potteries to the trends outlined above in relation to three broad areas of concern; political economy, margins and profits and the size, structures and strategies of firms. In relation to each of these issues there was displayed a struggle between inherited conceptions and understandings and the pressures exerted by a changing environment.

The importance of issues of political economy, and of protection in particular, is conveyed by the replies of the *North Staffordshire Chamber of Commerce* to the 1886 *Royal Commission,* which indicated that 'the principal competitors in pottery [are] Germany, France and Holland ... for their home consumption and

---

33 *The Pottery Gazette*, June 1899, p. 669.

34 R. Church, *The Great Victorian Boom, 1850-1873* (London, Macmillan, 1979), p. 11.

for export, and ... the by United States for the supply of its own market'.[35] Thus, competition was seen to emanate overwhelmingly from countries where infant pottery industries were afforded considerable protection. In the late nineteenth century the principal complaint of manufacturers in the Potteries was that they were excluded from important export markets, particularly the United States, where, even American commentators admitted, the pottery industry was 'unusually well protected by tariff legislation'.[36] The cumulative effect of tariffs was such that by the 1920s one American commentator observed that, 'the bulk of our imported pottery should be classified as porcelain. Only earthenware of high artistry and long-established reputation continues to come into our country, although at one time, in the latter part of the nineteenth century, England sent large quantities of earthenware'.[37]

In terms of a simple economic determinism, the pottery industry, as a trade with a strong export orientation, might be expected to have shown an allegiance to Free Trade, and this was broadly so.[38] Certainly, until very late in the century, concerns over import penetration, or over the links between protection and such imports, were aired in the trade press far less frequently than warnings that export markets were being progressively closed to British manufacturers. There persisted a belief that a global system of Free Trade offered benefits, not only to Britain, but also to all nations. Thus:

> In endeavouring to meet the depression in trade we have to consider what are the causes. They are self-evident. It arises from the falling off in demand, and that again is due to the foolish action of some foreign countries which rose [sic] the wall of tariffs, which is even more injurious to them than to us.[39]

It was a further axiom of this position that it was only protection which allowed foreign industries to compete with the Potteries, either in those countries' own domestic markets or in the markets of third countries, such was the 'inherited' superiority of the English producer and product. This issue will be returned to shortly.

However, support for tariff reform clearly grew in the Potteries, or had long existed in a latent form, for in 1907 Volume Five of the *Report of the Tariff*

---

[35] *First Report of the Royal Commission on the Depression in Trade and Industry, 1886: Appendix A.*

[36] H.J. Stratton, 'Technological Development of the American Pottery Industry', *Journal of Political Economy*, October 1932, p. 662.

[37] Ibid., p. 662.

[38] A. Marrison, 'Businessmen, Industries and Tariff Reform in Great Britain, 1897–1914', *Business History*, Vol. 25, No. 2 (1983), pp. 148–178.

[39] *The Pottery Gazette*, October 1894, p. 817.

Commission was devoted to the pottery industry. Attention was now focused firmly on the impact of protection on both export markets and the domestic market, the latter affected by 'dumping' from protectionist countries. A number of witnesses argued that whilst china manufacturers suffered particularly as a result of 'dumped' imports, all sectors of the industry were being punished in export markets, not only as a result of markets being directly closed by tariffs but also in third countries, again through 'dumping'. Here, Germany was identified as the greatest culprit:

> only in a few branches do German manufacturers fail to encroach more or less severely in home, foreign, and Colonial markets. They have made a complete and careful study of these markets, and under the stimulus of a national industrial policy have succeeded in a remarkable degree, and the competition is growing in area and severity.[40]

Witnesses were generally less magnanimous in their estimation of the qualities shown by German manufacturers.[41] All complained of German products being sold at less than cost price, indeed at prices that would not pay for the labour in making a comparable product in Staffordshire. Others identified further unfair practices, including design piracy; 'The Germans wait until they find out which is a success, and then copy it and injure the trade by putting very inferior copies on the market. The competition is not direct, but as soon as there is a cheap copy the good shops will not buy the originals'.[42] Of course, local firms, particularly small start-ups, indulged in similar practices. Rapid set-up times allowed German manufacturers, supported by networks of travellers buying British samples in many markets, to internationalize a problem rooted in the intense seasonality of the trade and furthered, in the Potteries at least, by the interdependence of clustering and ease of entry.

This problem was endemic among some industries batch producing styled and seasonal goods, and as jewellers in Providence, Rhode Island, repeatedly found, the resulting 'price rivalry could readily displace specialists' beloved product competition'.[43] The manufacturers giving evidence to the *Tariff Commission* universally asserted that whilst a tariff would certainly not raise prices in the UK, for 'we should very soon have internal competition to regulate [them] ... we have never been and are not likely to be short of competition', it would stabilise them, preventing 'the cutting to get particular orders which now exists, though that

---

[40] *Report of the Tariff Commission*, para. 31.

[41] The Potteries again justify Cotterell's claim that 'various devices led to German competition being regarded as unfair and underhand in complaints from British exporters'. Cotterell, '"Lo, ... Nineveh"', p. 277–78.

[42] Ibid., para. 36.

[43] Scranton, *Endless Novelty*, p. 111.

cutting rate does not reach the consumer'.[44] Protection was promoted not simply as a defensive tool but also as a way of cementing the industry behind a return to a 'fairer' form of competition based on quality and style.

Nonetheless, despite the claim made by the report that 'Those concerned in the industry ... are practically unanimous as to the need of a change in the British fiscal system', caution must be exercised.[45] The manufacturers prepared to give evidence to the *Commission* were relatively few in number and were not representative of all sections of the industry. As Marrison has asked, 'Can industries always be marshalled into huge, cohesive *blocs* ... It would seem that industries need to be examined for internal divisions along product or market-lines'.[46] Of the thirty-seven witnesses identifiable as being Potteries based manufacturers a clear majority, twenty-one, came from Longton and Fenton, where the manufacture of china for domestic consumption predominated. Just one manufacturer from Tunstall, where the industry was overwhelmingly oriented to earthenware and exports, was prepared to give evidence. This impression is reinforced by an analysis of the product orientations of witnesses. Nearly fifty per cent of witnesses were china manufacturers, twenty per cent earthenware manufacturers. Just seventeen per cent of witnesses were engaged in either sanitary ware or tiles, emerging sectors that, as has been shown, were achieving significant export growth. Moreover, none of the firms represented by witnesses fell into the large and giant size categories, as delineated in Chapter 2.

There were, of course, important differences between manufacturers engaged in ostensibly similar trades. Thus, Mr Enoch Massey, of E. Hughes and Co., Fenton, explained that, 'We keep a class of workpeople that can turn out a great bulk of stuff at a cheap rate, and we can sell it at a cheap rate, but the workmanship and materials are not so high in class and quality as those used and made by Messrs. Moore', that is Moore Bros. of Longton, whose principal, Bernard Moore, also appeared before the *Commission*.[47] But despite these and further differences it cannot be argued that the *Report of the Tariff Commission* provides evidence of widespread support for reform across the industry as a whole. Further, as Marrison has argued, debate over the attitude of businessmen to tariff reform has been 'buttressed by a *belief* (seldom proven) that the great majority of businessmen in [an] industry were of one mind'.[48] Dispute over such a fundamental issue as fiscal reform is clearly significant for the conceptions of deeply ingrained, normative value systems advanced by the industrial district model. Further, the divisions over reform are fairly readily understood in terms of, first, the size structure of the industry and of correlations between structure, product/market orientation and the internal spatial patterning of the district. The

44 *Report of the Tariff Commission*, para. 148 and para. 134

45 Ibid.,, para. 11–16.

46 Marrison, 'Businessmen', p. 159 (emphasis in original).

47 *Report of the Tariff Commission*, para. 124.

48 Marrison, 'Businessmen', p. 158.

Potteries industrial district was not a relatively undifferentiated constellation of 'small' firms, but instead displayed a variegated structure and a concomitant array of interests, economic, political or otherwise.

However, Marrison also advances a further key argument, that:

> economic determinism cannot simply imply that men act of their own self-interest: rather, it must mean that they according to their *perceptions* of what their particular economic interest *is* ... the tariff reform debate was not simply a controversy over short-term economic interests and objectives: occurring in the context of Britain's industrial retardation, it involved fundamentally different perceptions and interpretations of the desirable and likely path of Britain's long-term development over the next 50 or even 100 years. Under such conditions even partners in the same firm might have had different perceptions and made different predictions.[49]

Certainly this statement holds true for the Potteries. Despite its partiality, the report contains many valuable insights into attitudes towards the future development of the industry. Fiscal reform represented a further and very concrete potential point of bifurcation in the developmental path traced by the industry, a point at which choices shaped over many years took on some clarity. Prompted by three decades of growing foreign competition, harnessed to a growing belief that 'Foreign tariffs tend to the efficiency of production in foreign countries', manufacturers in the Potteries turned to the examination of a wide range of issues.[50] These included the impact of competition on prices, margins and profits. Reflection on these issues in turn focused minds on costs and investment and, ultimately on the size, structure and organization of both individual firms and the industry as a whole.

The relationships between competition, margins, profits and costs had earlier been prominent in the very important wage arbitration of 1879. The award of the reduction sought by manufacturers in that year not only created a near obsession amongst unionists with the restoration of 'Hatherton's penny', but had also a tendency to promote attacks on labour costs as an important strategic response to competition.[51] That response was conditioned by the fact that competition, focused on price and occurring in an expanding market contested by new and aggressive competitors, had the principal effect not of reducing sales but of

---

[49] Ibid., p. 150. Indeed, Mr. Herbert Colclough, china manufacturer of Longton and Fenton, claimed that, 'we have sixty firms in the china trade, and there are fifty of them absolutely agreed on the question of fiscal reform. Of the remaining ten, about half of the partners are very favourable, but from the fact that they each have a partner who generally, for political reasons, does not see fit to throw in his lot with us, they have to stand out. *Report of the Tariff Commission*, para. 149.

[50] *Report of the Tariff Commission*, para. 149. Evidence of Herbert J. Colclough.

[51] So-named after Lord Hatherton, umpire at the arbitration of 1879.

squeezing margins. Why was competition seemingly inevitably funnelled towards price and away from differentiation?

Whilst Scranton contends that the bulk New England textile producers, faced with high fixed costs and inflexible systems, ploughed on through depression building stock and maintaining their share of whatever market there was, Lamoreaux has found that in batch and specialty sectors, 'output declined in accordance with demand; prices fell, but not excessively ... ; and the burdens of curtailment were spread throughout the industry'. As Scranton notes, these differences 'suggest lines of inquiry for a parallel review of depression responses by batch and bulk' industries.[52] Similarly, different responses can be observed within the batch sector; the Potteries and Providence, to varying degrees, bucked the trend identified by Lamoreaux, but Philadelphia textiles did not.

Obviously the picture was mixed, many firms did run short time, even in the more buoyant Edwardian years, but they were discomfited by the opportunities lost and lamented the impact on labour, both in terms of its income and its morale.[53] Conversely, the huge inventories built by once proud Davenports in the mid-1880s clearly resulted not from policy but from entrepreneurial failure and a managerial vacuum.[54] But, on balance, the pottery industry was rarely successful in matching production to demand in these years. Certainly relevant is Scranton's observation, of Providence again, that 'Critically important were the low entry costs for new establishments', but any explanation needs to link structural patterns to behavioural patterns.[55] Just as bulk producers were driven to maintain production by high fixed capital costs, so capital structure, and the extensive use of credit in particular, may well prove a key element with regard to the Potteries. Small producers in particular relied on credit from suppliers for a large proportion of their working capital, making them easy prey for 'cutting cash buyers'.[56] At times it seemed as though turning money over, not making a profit, was their *raison d'être.*

---

[52] N. Lamoreaux, *The Great Merger Movement in American Business, 1898-1904* (Cambridge, Cambridge University Press, 1985), p. 26–7; Scranton, *Figured Tapestry: Production, Markets and Power in Phildelphia Textiles* (Cambridge, Cambridge University Press, 1989), p. 116.

[53] All Staffordshire witnesses to the Tariff Commission complained that running below full capacity had become the norm.

[54] T. Lockett and G. Godden, *Davenport: China, Earthenware and Glass* (London, Barrie & Jenkins, 1989).

[55] Scranton, *Endless Novelty*, p. 111. Herbert Colcough argued before the *Tariff Commission*, for example, that 'we have never been and are not likely to be short of competition. Our business is such that it can be soon brought into existence by anyone making an effort to make china and put it upon the market'. *Report of the Tariff Commission*, para. 148.

[56] *The Pottery Gazette*, January 1886, p. 41. The writer added 'To small capitalists the temptation to turn over their money quickly has proved too strong to be resisted, even when the turnover has left nothing to it'.

> The creditors are a good deal to blame, for the reckless manner in which credit is given encourages men to go into business who would not do so if credit were not almost thrust upon them. The evil does not merely end with the loss to the creditors; it is much deeper and reaches further. What is one of the great complaints we hear? "Low prices". And what is the principal cause of low prices. These same small manufacturers.[57]

Equally, others looked to mechanization, undertaken principally by the larger firms and distrusted by many for its deterioration of skills, for a cause. Thus:

> With the increase in the use of machinery there are probably facilities in the Potteries for producing double the amount of earthenware goods being produced. This means that there is a large amount of unoccupied capital in the form of machinery lying idle, which is a constant temptation to its owners to take orders at the lowest possible profit - which often means none. Thus, there is always an element present which is a constant injury to the trade and can only be dealt with by the whole body of manufacturers.[58]

The highly variegated structure of the Potteries ensured that the industry both contained elements of 'too flexible' Providence and, at the same time, was also subject to the pressure exerted by mechanization and, for this industry, historically high levels of fixed capital investment. In other words, the external economies of scope and flexibility generated within the district were being dissipated whilst the internal economies of scale being chased by some individual firms yet remained elusive. Other factors reinforced these basic characteristics to make excess production a constant threat; a fairly high degree of vertical integration, rigidities in a labour market based in annual hiring contracts, custom and reciprocity and, as already indicated, the ease and rapidity with which designs could be pirated.

Whatever its origins, the impact of price competition undoubtedly fell heavily on margins, revenues and the capital available for investment. Thus, during the arbitration of 1879, it was claimed that:

> There are, were the secrets of some offices known, not a few firms of fair standing and promise, who would have been paying as well if doing only half the trade; and some would have saved money if they had turned over

---

[57] 'The Evils of Potting with Insufficient Capital', *The Pottery Gazette*, May 1899, p.552. These were problems of long standing, one correspondent of 1882 had asked, 'Why should the china manufacturers give their goods away in the manner they do? They should consider and ask themselves the question, and not tyrannise over each other with low prices and large discounts'. *The Pottery Gazette*, November 1882, p. 1081. Similarly, 'Credit is far too cheap, enabling people to start manufacturing in a small way without capital ... What is the consequence? They have to sell at ruinous prices, thus bringing down the prices of other houses'. *The Pottery Gazette*, January 1883, p. 62.

[58] 'Trade Notes', *The Pottery Gazette*, August 1892, p. 734.

> less over, for 'cheap lines' have kept the men employed, while the wear and tear of machinery have had to come from somewhere, certainly not from the revenue of trade where it should come from. It is as many say - an unremunerative trade is not worth doing.[59]

The emphasis placed here on the importance of retained income as a source of working and fixed capital is in itself significant. At the arbitration Mr Pinder, of sanitary manufacturers Pinder, Bourne and Co., made a pithy summation of the conditions manufacturers were facing: 'Things [are] going from bad to worse ... and business ... carried on at a loss'. The firm was only keeping going by 'sinking fresh capital'.[60] Complaints of low or non-existent profits surfaced regularly in the following decades. Thus, it was argued in 1887 that; 'bit by bit capital is being swallowed up, and shortly the holders of factories will find that the money invested in their business is returning little or no interest for the amount of care and anxiety that naturally follows a manufacturer's life'.[61]

In the following year one manufacturer, writing anonymously, asserted that 'there is little or no profit left ... not withstanding the cheapened modes of production'.[62] By the close of the century there was a growing acceptance that 'competition is certain to keep profits down to the lowest possible point'. A number of fundamental implications flowed from acceptance of this doctrine:

> Competition, ever growing keener, will cut profits down to the last farthing: wages are not reducible with the same facility as formerly: and tend to become fixed as to a certain minimum; and every possible economy in the way of machinery; of travellers and agents, dead expenses will have to be rigorously cut down. This, of course, means capital, means large turnovers, and large factories. Whether the smaller businesses will be eaten up by the large, or the trust system introduced, remains to be seen, but, except for artistic and special purposes, the small manufactory is doomed.[63]

As the reconstruction of industry structure carried out in Chapter 2 has clearly demonstrated, the demise of the small manufactory was in fact far from imminent. However, there were the stirrings of a reorientation, even if it remained largely theoretical, toward scale and throughput. This reorientation would eventually have ramifications for every aspect of the potting business; technology, investment, labour, prices, marketing and distribution. These realizations had crystallized further by the time of the *Tariff Commission*. Witness after witness concentrated on the links between competition, volume and margins. The argument was forcefully summarised by T.B. Johnson, a Bristol

---

59 *The Pottery Gazette*, October 1879, p.375.

60 *The Pottery Gazette*, December 1879, p. 472.

61 *The Pottery Gazette*, February 1887, p. 177.

62 *The Pottery Gazette*, March 1888, p. 227

63 *The Pottery Gazette*, July 1899, p. 669; *The Pottery Gazette*, December 1900, p. 1248.

based manufacturer with many contacts in the Potteries; 'It is not cheap labour and cheap materials only that is the greatest factor of cheap production, but it is the quantity of production coupled with the efficient use of labour-machinery'.[64] Potteries' manufacturers also advanced this and related arguments. Herbert Colclough, for example, claimed that 'if I could run my factory fully I could certainly reduce my prices and make a much better profit than I can now'.[65] Such thinking certainly represented a departure from that prevalent in the Potteries hitherto, and indicates the importance not only of prices but also of pricing strategy and market orientation.

Evidence on issues of cost accounting and pricing strategy and on the relationship between these issues and markets in the Potteries in the nineteenth century is scant, despite McKendrick's ground-breaking work on Wedgwood in the eighteenth century.[66] Increasing concentration on the production of large volumes of cheap wares implied shifts in the allocation of resources between and within firms and a reorientation of the traditional market focus of the industry, from specialty to standardization. Though there are as yet many competing schema and little consensus, research from a number of fields is increasingly revealing the interdependence of business processes, markets and consumption.[67] Moreover, a number of scholars point to important shifts in the balance of these interdependencies in the period 1880-1920.

Drawing on these, we might posit the historic orientation of the North Staffordshire pottery industry as being towards the 'product concept', in which an emphasis on product quality and distinctiveness predominates. There was an assumption that the products of the district largely sold themselves. Chasing volumes as a matter of strategy, and accepting lower prices as a core element of that chase, would have promoted a shift towards 'the selling/sales concept'. Such a shift had the potential to undermine such intangible resources as reputation and render obsolete existing distribution channels, such as agency networks.[68] Though, as Church and other critics have noted, this schema is simplistic, perhaps with regard to periodization especially, it nonetheless has some broad utility. Moreover, any insights gleaned from it may be refined through incorporation of Tedlow's emphasis on the relationship between sales volume, profit and pricing policy. Thus, the shift from the product concept to the selling concept may be fruitfully associated with the 'key change ... from a search for profitability based on low volume sales and high margins ... to competition based

64 *Report of the Tariff Commission*, para. 183.

65 Ibid., para. 146.

66 N. McKendrick, 'Josiah Wedgwood and Cost Accounting in the Industrial Revolution', *Economic History Review*, Vol. 23, No. 1 (1970), pp. 45–67.

67 R. Church, 'New Perspectives on the History of Products, Firms, Marketing and Consumers in Britain and the United States since the Mid-nineteenth Century', *Economic History Review*, Vol. 52, No. 3 (1999), pp. 405–35.

68 Ibid., p.408.

on high volumes, low prices, low margins and high profits'.[69] Such a shift was fundamental, involving reconsideration of business culture, of shopfloor practice, of technology, of channels of distribution and of inter-firm co-ordination. As Norman Bishnell argued in *Pottery Cost Accounts*, published by the British Pottery Manufacturer's Federation in 1921:

> it will doubtless prove that the organization of factories will develop along lines that will render more adequate costing possible. Indeed works organization and costing are collateral elements of efficiency. It is impossible to have good cost accounts without good organization, and it is impossible to have the best organization without good cost accounts. Few factories have anything that can be called a costing system at all, and probably none are doing all that is at once both possible and advantageous.[70]

Though they appeared but a distant threat in the late nineteenth century, it cannot be denied that many in the industry felt forced into these re-evaluations and viewed them with regret and, on occasion, even distaste.

Impacts would also have been felt in terms of the industry's demand structure, particularly in relation to the centrality of domestic markets, now generally recognized as being in retardation from the 1860s and often characterized as being too small and fragmented to induce manufacturers to chase economies of scale. Furthermore, Wilson argues that in ignoring the 'market-cum-technological environment', Elbaum and Lazonick 'fail to provide the context' in which structural rigidities persisted, and that in many instances the domestic market, its 'size, affluence, rate of growth, level of competitiveness and organisation', provides the 'vital context in which businessmen operate'.[71] Thus, a reliance on domestic markets, accounting for around one half of UK production, may have acted as constraint on the response of firms in the Potteries. However, some qualifications must be introduced. As a consumer good, increasingly marketed by branding, much pottery production was directed at one of the most dynamic sectors of the British economy in the late Victorian period, buoyed up by increases in real wages seen in the Great Depression era. This buoyancy is clearly attested to by the aggressive and successful, interest shown in British markets by Continental firms.[72]

---

[69] Ibid., p. 411.

[70] N. Bishnell, *Pottery Cost Accounts*, (Hanley, British Pottery Manufacturers Federation, 1921), p. 3–4. Bishnell, a cost accountant with Messrs. Doulton & Co. of Burslem, began by stating that, 'Experience has proved that it is impracticable to follow pottery through all its stages allocating expenditure to particular articles or batches of articles'. Ibid., p. 1.

[71] Wilson, *British Business History*, p. 87 and p. 88.

[72] See, W.H. Fraser, *The Coming of the Mass Market, 1850–1914* (Basingstoke, Macmillan 1981), p.193.

Foreign industries

A further fierce debate framed by the rise of foreign competition focused on the size of firms, their governance, management, strategic orientation and their number, foreshadowing the 'rationalization' movement of the 1920s.[73] Thus, having established the extent of the competitive challenge facing the Potteries and noted the impact of that challenge on issues such as margins, profits and strategies, it is necessary to outline the basis of that challenge. That is the competitive advantages enjoyed by foreign rivals. Specifically, did the greater 'efficiency' of foreign manufacturers reflect simply the security offered by tariffs, or did it result from any material or qualitative difference in the scale and modernity of foreign plants, or in their organization and management?

T.B. Johnson was unequivocal in his answer with regard to the United States; 'I went over there in 1897, just after the tariff was raised, and I am firmly convinced that they have no right to make a single ounce of pottery on strictly free trade principles – they can not really compete with us in any way without the tariffs'.[74] It is probable that Johnson's opinion was largely valid. The industry in the United States, concentrated largely in Trenton, New Jersey, East Liverpool, Ohio and, to a lesser extent, in Pennsylvania and elsewhere, bore a distinctly English stamp, inherited from emigrant masters and workmen.[75] This mark was slow to fade in the different commercial, market and even physical environment of North America and led to many transatlantic parallels.

H.J. Stratton, whilst observing that import penetration of the US market was around sixty per cent in 1860 but only fifteen per cent in 1929, claimed that the 'principal factors accounting for the competitive gains of domestic potters were increasing tariff protection and increasing manufacturing skill'.[76] But whilst Stratton felt that 'the former factor reflects no credit upon our potters except as the sustained and increasing import duties reflect effective lobbying', he was also critical of many aspect of the American industry, its organization and technological sophistication.[77] In particular, Stratton, detailing 'some outstanding cases of the laggardness of American pottery managers in adopting new devices and methods' prior to 1914, believed that:

> If one country imitates another and mans its industry with workmen and managers emigrant from the latter, it is not likely to rise above a second-rate position. American potteries occupied such a position during the nineteenth century. Only during the present century has our industry begun

[73] Lloyd-Jones and Lewis, *British Industrial Capitalism*, Chapter 7.

[74] *Report of the Tariff Commission.*, para 181.

[75] M.J. Stern, *The Pottery Industry of Trenton: A Skilled Trade in Transition, 1850–1929* (New Jersey, Rutgers University Press, 1994).

[76] Stratton, 'Technological Development', p. 661.

[77] Ibid., p. 661.

> to take on a native vigor. In the process of transplanting English processes and attitudes in American industrial soil, the undesirable features seem to have taken root more vigorously than the desirable ones.[78]

Research bodies held similar views, the President of the American Ceramic Society admitting in 1900 that, 'It is only too true that we have transplanted the inherited secrets and family monopolies of the English potter and the art is suffering today from the bias and barriers that circumscribe [it]'.[79] With regard to technology, the Bureau of Foreign and Domestic Commerce also contrasted the 'ultra-conservative attitude of the manufacturers' with the 'receptiveness of other leading American industries'.[80] Leaving aside for one moment specific issues of technological diffusion, to which we will return in the next chapter, we may sum up Stratton's evaluation of the management of the American industry. This, he asserted, was typified by a general resistance to change and in particular to scientific research, which condemned American potters to reliance on 'rule of thumb in an industry which severely penalizes such methods'.[81]

American manufacturers were also handicapped with regard to costs, particularly labour costs. A great deal of light was thrown on this issue by the report of Consul Burgess in 1891. Setting out to obtain as 'accurately as possible all the facts and figures entering in the cost of production of the ordinary classes of pottery wares commonly used in the everyday household of the millions, and of which the vast bulk of the output of the Potteries for the American market consists', Burgess compared as closely as possible a new six oven manufactory in the US and North Staffordshire and his figures seem to paint a stark picture of the cost disadvantage under which American firm's laboured.[82] Burgess' final summary table is presented here in Table 3.1. As Burgess commented, 'this shows a difference in favor of the English manufacturer of 88 per cent'.[83]

A further significant finding was that both the fixed capital invested in and working capital required by an American pottery were considerably higher than in the UK, see Table 3.2. Burgess ascribed these differences to a number of

[78] Ibid., p. 668.

[79] American Ceramic Society, *Transactions*, Vol. 2 (1900), p. 19. Quoted in Stratton, 'Technological Development', p. 669.

[80] *Cost of Production in the Pottery Industry*, U. S. Bureau of Foreign and Domestic Commerce, Miscellaneous Series, Vol. 21 (1915), p. 194.

[81] Stratton, 'Technological Development', p. 675. Stratton's final conclusion was tariffs must have 'had a bearing on' American laggardness and that 'advocates of tariff protection for infant industries ... searching for a good supporting case for their arguments ... would be unlikely to choose this one'. Ibid., p. 676.

[82] W. Burgess, 'Staffordshire vs., American Pottery', *Reports of the Consuls of the United States*, Vol. 37 No.s 132–135 (Washington, Government Printing Office, 1892). Burgess estimated that his hypothetical six oven works would have a RV of £337, placing it firmly in the medium-size firm category, p. 48.

[83] Ibid., p. 63.

factors, including; climatic conditions in America, the cost of building materials and labour, the cost of plant and other utensils, the absence of renting in America and the need for a warehouse, given the very important fact that American firms, unlike their English brethren, manufactured largely for stock.

The result, Burgess believed, was that 'opportunities present themselves [in Staffordshire] to men of small capital which are not to be found in the United States'.[84] These conditions clearly impacted on the strategies of firms. 'Persons or firms doing business [in Staffordshire], requiring to carry little or no stock and receiving prompt cash payment for their product, are enabled to turn over their capital many times to the Americans' once or twice in the course of a year'.[85]

Table 3.1
Total cost of the product of a six-oven pottery in England and the United States, 1891

Description	England ($)	United States ($)
Labour	26,865	61,727
Materials	28,930	47,628
Interest	4855	9840
Taxes	550	1450
Utilities	840	985
Total	62,040	116,630

Source: Burgess, 'Staffordshire vs. American', p. 63.

Table 3.2
Comparative capital requirements in the United States and Staffordshire

Description	English ($)	American ($)
Invested in plant	67,100	84,007
Invested in working capital	30,000	80,000
Total	97,100	164,007

Source: Burgess, 'Staffordshire vs. American', p. 47.

84 Burgess, 'American vs. Staffordshire', p. 47.
85 Ibid., p. 47.

Conditions looked ripe for prompting American manufacturers towards volume, throughput and mechanization, bringing in train a rise in firm size, but this trajectory was only slowly adopted. Data on the size structure of the American industry are scarce, but estimates made by American consul Edward Lane in the early 1880s suggest that American potteries were significantly smaller that the English counterparts, with average workforces of 14.5 and 164 respectively.[86]

Nor, did high labour costs, as we have already seen, prove to be a spur to mechanization in this case. Instead, not withstanding the aid given by tariffs, conditions in the US pushed manufacturers towards price competition. Indeed, one English observer noted that, 'the prices of ... ware are very low in relation to the cost of labour in the United States'.[87] Given limited mechanization and low skills relative to North Staffordshire, the majority chased volumes through 'speed ups' and by neglecting quality. Serving the bottom end of the market was the key motif of the industry's strategic orientation. In particular, 'Ohio's speed demons and shops [were] geared only to cheap, shoddy output'.[88] The Americans, without mechanizing to a level beyond that found in the Potteries, developed methods of 'quantity manufacture more suited to a mass standardised market, than the English emphasis on small batches, variety and quality'. The American firm, instead of 'working at a slow speed to produce a small quantity of ware with as much as ninety per cent of firsts, as ... in Staffordshire, ... turned out from thirty five to 140 per cent greater production, but was content with as little as sixty per cent firsts'.[89]

The American industry seems to have been under conflicting tensions, having an atomistic small-scale structure rooted in the district-like environments of Trenton and East Liverpool, but ill-equipped to genuinely compete on the basis of skill and differentiation and, simultaneously, wary of mechanization. As Scranton's work has shown, specialty production and proprietary capitalism rarely formed a straightforward path to industrialization.[90] The one area in which American firms were more successful than those in Staffordshire was in building intra capital and inter-capital/labour institutions able to stabilize wages and prices, learning after 1900 to 'reject unproductive competition in an unstable economy'.[91]

These tensions over orientation were eventually to be resolved. As Stratton demonstrates, a process of technological catch up began after 1914, whilst Stern

86 'An American View of the Potteries', *The Pottery Gazette*, May 1883, p. 451–2.

87 Ibid., p. 451–2.

88 Stern, *Pottery Industry*, p. 123. This statement is however disputed by Bill Gates in his review of Stern's study, *Business History Review*, p. 119.

89 F. Thistlethwaite, 'The Atlantic Migration of the Pottery Industry, *Economic History Review*, Vol. 11, No. 2 (1958), p. 274.

90 Scranton, *Endless Novelty*.

91 Stern, *Pottery Industry*, p. 223.

documents a 'conjunctural transformation' of industry structure between 1921 and 1923, induced by a successful federal anti-trust suit and backward integration into the sanitary sector by national plumbing supply firms.[92] Some individual firms also shaped innovative strategies and production regimes. At the Homer Laughlin China Company, for example, 'mass production succeeded precisely because it was not thoroughgoing Fordism ... [but blended] continuous-flow techniques with Staffordshire methods'.[93] Nonetheless, we can conclude that Johnson's original judgement must stand. Prior to 1914 the American industry could not have offered serious competition to the Potteries without the protection afforded by tariffs.

German, French and other continental manufacturers, on the other hand, did have one very decided advantage over Staffordshire, labour costs. Evidence presented to the wage arbitration of 1879 again forms an excellent introduction to the cost structure of the industry. Mr Pinder, of Pinder, Bourne and Co., for example, claimed that whilst wages had represented thirty per cent of turnover in 1873 by 1879 they represented forty per cent. Mr Hammersley of the Brownhills Pottery Co. traced a similar steady rise in wages as a proportion of total costs, from 31.4 per cent in 1873 to 47.1 in 1879. Finally, E. J. Ridgway, of Ridgway, Sparks and Ridgway, calculated wages and materials as a combined proportion of turnover rising from 68.25 per cent in 1876 to 76.25 per cent in 1879. Both Mr Ridgway and Mr Hammersley also estimated that selling prices had fallen in the region of twenty per cent in the same period.[94]

Clearly the comparison with 1873 was carefully chosen, Britain having experienced a 'spectacular' price inflation between 1870 and 1873.[95] Indeed, that inflation, rather than any actual rise in wages, may account for the increased proportion of wages to total costs and turnover experienced in the 1870s. Moreover, evidence suggests that the prices of most materials were either stable or actually fell throughout the greater part of the last quarter of the century.[96] Nonetheless, more significant than trends in the relative weight of various costs, was the fact that labour costs formed such a significant element in the cost of production. The industry was vulnerable to competition from low-labour cost countries, more especially so when those emergent industries, unhampered by a

---

92 Stratton, 'Technological Development'; Stern, *Pottery Industry*, p. 5.

93 R.L. Blaszczyk, '" Reign of the Robots"', p. 906.

94 'The Arbitration in the Earthenware Trade', *The Pottery Gazette*, December 1879, p. 472.

95 Church, *Victorian Boom*, p. 16.

96 It was claimed in 1898 that 'Coal also, in spite of rumours of difficulty, shows if anything a downward tendency, and, upon the whole, manufacturers are now obtaining materials more cheaply perhaps than at any time in the past half century'. *The Pottery Gazette*, January 1898, p. 88. Further detailed evidence on cost will presented in Chapter 6, a case study of Mintons.

traditional respect for skill or by craft unionism, were more aggressive in the pursuit of mechanization.

Potters understood fully that wages in Germany, France and other countries, Japan especially, were lower than in Staffordshire. In January 1886 it was noted that German and French firms 'have a great advantage over us in the cost of labour', whilst in 1892 it was claimed that 'the manufacturer of British products has been, and still is, handicapped in the price of labour to an alarming extent as compared with his confrère in other nations'.[97] More surprisingly, it was argued in the following year that, 'not only are wages much lower [on the continent] than with us, but the cost of the management is reduced to a minimum, and does not represent, as it does in England, a considerable percentage on the finished article'.[98] This claim, confounding received wisdom that British personal capitalism minimized managerial structures and costs, urges consideration of the strategies, scale and sophistication of the continental industries.

However, judgements were confused then, and remain difficult now. Though at times appearing to dismiss the threat posed by Germany, the trade press had also long recognised that German firms in particular could present significant qualitative and quantitative differences to their counterparts in the Potteries. Thus:

> Another point is that German makers are mostly wealthy men to commence with, who adopt every mechanical means for cheapening the cost of production – steam batters, jollies, patents of every description that money can buy or skill devise, are brought into requisition to keep the trade in their own country.[99]

The difference in technologies being pinpointed, vital in allowing German manufacturers to reduce costs, was seen as related to differences of structure and culture which meant that German firms were larger and more heavily capitalized than those in Staffordshire. The relationship between structure, developmental pattern and competitive position was stated even more explicitly, and lent important temporal and spatial dimensions, when it was acknowledged that, 'Our prestige is fast evaporating before the encroachment of German and French houses', these competitors having 'started from the point already reached by the Staffordshire makers and profiting by the experience gained by the latter are able at one bound to almost eclipse their opponents in cheap goods'.[100] There is a sense here of that dynamic identified by Marshall when he claimed that 'even a little obstinacy or inertia may ruin an old home of industry whose conditions are

---

97 *The Pottery Gazette*, January 1886, p. 43; *The Pottery Gazette*, March 1892, p. 233.

98 *The Pottery Gazette*, June 1893, p. 533.

99 *The Pottery Gazette*, February 1886, p. 200.

100 *The Pottery Gazette*, June 1886, p.696.

changing; and ... the opening out of new sources of supply ... may quickly overbear the strength which old districts have inherited from past conditions'.[101]

Two decades later witnesses to the *Tariff Commission* were again claiming that German firms were larger and more heavily capitalized and mechanized, and that they were so because of the 'security' afforded them by protection. So whilst Enoch Massey of Fenton may have declared that 'we have about the finest factories in the world; there is nothing finer than the best equipped factories in the Potteries', others were certainly less confident.[102] T.B. Johnston, for example, asserted that:

> The great thing they have, and it is borne out by what a young German chemist told me, is better organisation, larger works and more machinery employed for moving goods all the way through. In England there is nothing of that kind, it is all done by hand. In Germany there is greater division of labour in the works and larger works. Machinery can be put in on a larger scale. The foreigner, with the help of his tariff, makes on a larger scale to start with.[103]

We are returned again to the question of strategic orientation. Manufacturers in the Potteries remained determined to sell on reputation, quality and differentiation, whilst German firms pursued volume and sold on price. This then appears to be a classic example of English strategic inertia in the changing competitive environment of the Second Industrial Revolution. Moreover, as Chapter 6 will demonstrate, even a 'high-class' producer such as Mintons was far from immune from the new competition, the firm's products losing out to cheap German semi-porcelain in many Continental markets from the late 1890s. Further, a British consular report of 1906 argued that there could be 'no doubt that [the] remarkable development in the export trade of German ceramic ware ... has been largely due to the constant efforts made towards increasing the quality of goods produced'. In support, the report adduced evidence showing that whereas the average value of German ceramic exports in 1891 was twelve shillings per cwt, by 1900 the figure had increased to eighteen shillings per cwt.[104]

However, caution is still required. Were German plants really larger? Was the strategic path charted by firms like Mintons destined to remain an anachronism?

---

[101] Marshall, *Industry and Trade*, p. 287.

[102] *Report of the Tariff Commission*, para. 133. T.C. Moore similarly claimed that, 'We have manufactories that are as up-to-date as any on the Continent. Most of the improved machinery on the Continent for the cheap production of pottery has been obtained from our own district', Ibid., para. 107.

[103] Ibid., para. 180.

[104] *Memorandum on German Ceramic Industries and German Trade in Ceramic Products*, Miscellaneous Series of Trade Reports No. 653 (1906), Cd. 2683–17, p. 7.

Did no English firms follow the path German firms appeared to pioneer and exemplify?

Certainly there were some very large firms in Germany, France and other Continental countries. Professor Thomas Thorpe, touring Continental factories with regard to the lead question early in the twentieth century, found Petrus Ragout & Cie, of Maastricht, to employ 2,100 hands and La Societe Ceramique, also of Maastricht, 1,300. In Germany Villeroy and Boch employed 6,000, a figure unprecedented in the Potteries. However, this enormous workforce was dispersed across six factories, four producing china and earthenware, one terra cotta and one glass. The largest of the pottery works, that in Dresden, employed 1,500, a figure matched in several establishments in the Potteries.[105] Thus, it is not at all clear that plant, as opposed to firm, sizes were significantly greater in Germany than in North Staffordshire. On this measure at least, German manufacturers do not seem to have achieved significant new levels of scale.

Nor is it clear that firms such as Villeroy and Boch were any more representative of the German industry than Johnson Bros. were of that in Staffordshire. The consular report of 1906, using data compiled by the German Pottery Trade Association, suggests that the average establishment workforce in the German ceramic industry stood at seventy-two in 1898. However, the figure was much higher in particular sectors, notably those leading Germany's export drive. Thus, the average establishment workforce in porcelain was 181 and in earthenware 310. The report went on to conclude that:

> whilst the total number of hands employed in the German ceramic works in 1898 largely exceeded the total number employed in 1882, the total number of works had considerably diminished in 1898. This circumstance proves that the German porcelain and pottery manufacturers had come to the conclusion that in order to cope in profitable manner with the increasing demand as well as in order to meet foreign competition successfully, it appeared judicious to concentrate their efforts by reducing the number if smaller works and carrying on the work in factories established, wherever possible, on a large scale.[106]

Clearly the German ceramic industries were undergoing a degree of structural change in this period, though the mechanisms underlying that transformation remain unclear.

However, Kinghorn and Nye's work, summarized in Table 3.3, appears to demonstrate that average establishment size, measured by employment, in ceramics in this period was higher in the UK than in Germany, France or the

---

[105] T.E. Thorpe and T. Oliver, *Report on the Employment of Compounds of Lead in the Manufacture of Pottery, their Influence upon the Health of the Workpeople with Suggestions as to Means Which Might be Adopted to Counteract their Evil Effects*, C. 9207, p. 17–18 & p. 25.

[106] *Memorandum on German Ceramic Industries*, p. 5.

United States. Moreover, when the smallest plants are excluded, German plants were consistently smaller than those in France.

As Kinghorn and Nye comment, these 'quite surprising' results underline 'the inadequacy of current understanding of the evolution of industry structure and its relationship to the legal and institutional environment'.[107] Assumptions as to the comparatively small-scale structure of British industry have been too readily made in the past. Thus, whilst the UK pottery industry had a small-scale structure compared to some other UK industries, (establishment size was greater in textiles for example, but smaller in paper and leather and equal in chemicals), from an international perspective its structure was relatively large-scale.[108]

Table 3.3
Establishment size measures: ceramic industries, 1904

	France	US	Germany	Britain
A. Average number of workers per establishment				
	18	29	21	42
B. Average number of workers in establishments employing > 20				
	112	67	63	–
C. Average number of workers in establishments employing > 50				
	190	112	144	–
D. % of workers employed in establishments employing > 50				
	63	85	55	–

Source: Kinghorn and Nye, 'Scale of Production', p. 99.

[107] J.R. Kinghorn and J.V. Nye, 'The Scale of Production in Western Economic Development: A Comparison of Official Statistics in the US, Britain, France and Germany, 1903–13', *Journal of Economic History*, Vol. 56, No. 1 (1996), p. 110.

[108] Kinghorn and Nye, 'Scale of Production', p. 99. William Woodall, of James MacIntyre & Co., visiting the '"Kannenbacherland", or county of potters', centred on Höhr in the Rhineland, found the district to have around fifty ovens, 'and these belong to almost as many master employers. The factories are therefore small in size, employing often less than a dozen workpeople ... In general appearance the factories ... suggest a comparison with the small potteries that might have been built in Staffordshire in the far away pre-Wedgwood days'. W. Woodall, 'Potters in Rhineland', *English Illustrated Magazine,* (1890), p. 854–6.

Of course, these figures say relatively little about what went on inside firms, the technologies used and the ways in which they were deployed. Nonetheless they form a useful corrective to any assumption, perhaps as prevalent in the Potteries of the late nineteenth and early twentieth centuries as amongst economic historians today, that firms in Germany, and indeed the US, were typically larger. The case for the greater efficiency of the German ceramic industry in this period, or for the ossification of industry structure in the Potteries, remains unproven.

Potters identified other advantages enjoyed by German firms, beyond those of tariffs and low labour costs, and other areas of strategy in which they displayed greater energy or innovatory capacity. Material costs were thought roughly comparable across all European industries, but it was conceded that German firms gained very significantly from much lower freight rates, both within Germany and internationally. German sales and distribution and technical education were all also held to be significantly superior, views which could shade into complaint. J. Ridgway, for example felt that although 'the system of commercial travelling on the Continent is not superior to that in this country ... the Germans are exceedingly pushing in their methods of business'. Herbert Colclough, however, did admit that 'Commercial travelling is better in the case of foreign countries than our own because there is a greater security or a greater chance of getting orders, and hence the traveller's expenses are more easily paid'.[109]

Enoch Massey argued with regard to technical education that that available in Britain 'is not by any means the best suited to our trade', but that in Germany 'it is very much more complete and to the point. The branches of education are made to correspond with the needs of the district. There is always an affinity between the education given and the branch of manufacture carried on in the district'.[110] However, as was also true with regard to comparisons of industrial structure, some caution is required. A consular report of 1904 examined the four dedicated ceramic schools in Germany, but found that German potters could be very reluctant educationalists. At Höhr, for example, 'the local industries were at first opposed to the school, considered it unnecessary, resented any attempts to interfere with their methods of manufacture, neglected the school when opened and contributed nothing towards the expenses of building, equipment and maintenance'.[111] At Landshüt too 'for a long time the attitudes of persons engaged in the pottery branches of the district was one of indifference to the

[109] *Tariff Commission*, para. 156 and para. 147. See also evidence of T.C. Moore, para. 108.

[110] Ibid., para. 128.

[111] *Technical Instruction in Germany: Report on Special Technical Schools for the Ceramic Industries*, Miscellaneous Series of Trade Reports No. 615 (1904), Cd. 1767 Vol. xcvi, p. 9.

school'. Whilst, by 1904, this had ceased and 'even small manufacturers have sent their apprentices and journeymen to the school', it remained true that:

> hitherto it has been the state and the municipal authorities who have first recognised the advantages accruing to the industry from such a school, and not the manufacturers themselves. I have noticed this tendency several times in Germany in the case of minor industries. It forms by no means a general rule, as the larger and more scientific an industry is the greater the cry for adequate technical instruction.[112]

The case for the conservatism of German potters seems as credible as that for manufacturers in Staffordshire. Thus, despite the very real and severe nature of the threat posed to the Potteries by the growth of the German ceramic industry, the basis of that threat, its foundations, are as yet far from clear. As in many other areas of international comparison, further detailed empirical work is required in order that prevailing assumptions can be either verified or abandoned.[113]

Conclusion

This chapter has set out to explore the competitive challenges faced by the North Staffordshire pottery industry, especially in the period after the mid-1870s. It has been shown that those challenges, largely in the form of the rise of foreign industries, were real, substantial and of profound and lasting impact. Export markets, foreign and Colonial, became much more contested. This was reflected not in absolute decline but in greater instability and, as critical, stagnation or actual falls in prices. This pattern was not reversed until after 1900, thereafter the Potteries participated vigorously in the Edwardian export boom. Recovery was associated with the onset of a period of structural change in the industry, during which the total number of firms fell and average firm size grew. Perhaps even more marked than the increasingly competitive nature of export markets was the penetration of domestic markets by foreign manufactures, an almost unknown phenomenon previously, and whilst this penetration was also halted after 1900 it was never reversed. The competitive environment facing the North Staffordshire pottery industry had undergone a permanent alteration, to which difficult adjustments were required. Price was becoming as, or even more, important than quality and differentiation, old lines of market segmentation were being eroded.

This altered landscape caused businessmen in the Potteries to seek for causes and for answers, to look to their own firms and industry and to those of competing nations. Here we must invoke Casson's notion of the 'subjectivity of

[112] Ibid., p. 22.

[113] See, for example, M. Eason, 'Business, Training and Education: Sheffield, c. 1880–1940', (Unpublished Ph.D, Sheffield Hallam University, 1997).

problems'. Doing so, our attention is drawn to the emphasis placed by potters on foreign tariffs, their own profits and the scale, organization and strategies of their own and competing firms, both within the district and beyond. There was a tension between the urge to seek explanations in factors within the control of local firms and businessmen and in those outside their purview. Were existing strategies, and their concomitant technologies and organizational forms, to be permanently or only temporarily eclipsed? Answers to these questions were uncertain. Germany, for example, was one moment dismissed and at the next deeply feared. This uncertainty was understandable. Germany, and France, Holland and the United States were, as competitors, difficult to weigh and assess, no matter how stark the returns of the Board of Trade. The next two chapters will explore, respectively, responses the competitive challenges outlined here in the areas of production and distribution. It is hoped, going forward to those explorations, that they are informed by a sense of the ways in which strategies and responses emerged not from any simple optimizing instinct, but from a difficult process of reflection on existing strategies and capacities; that is from the developmental path elaborated in the Potteries for more than a century.

CHAPTER FOUR

Machines, masters and men

Introduction

The changing competitive environment facing pottery manufacturers from the 1870s onwards was complex in its impact on production strategies and technologies. Mechanization, in particular, presented a vexed question in which factors other than the technological often played a central role. Certainly, it was recognized that the competitive challenge offered by Continental and American producers represented a powerful spur to mechanization and that the:

> very cheap rate at which the Continental china is produced, should warn every potter that his only chance of a prosperous trade is to encourage that trade by cutting down expenses and the cost of production, until the foreign element is driven from the field.[1]

At the same time, however, unrelenting competition and wafer-thin margins and profits appeared to sap remorselessly the confidence and enterprise of some in the district. Towards the close of our period of study, manufacturer after manufacturer clamoured to complain to the *Tariff Commission* of the brake placed upon investment by foreign competition and uncertain demand. T.C. Moore, for example, described how:

> In the foreign countries competing with us trade is carried on a large scale. Those manufactories which I have visited (and I have visited most of the important potteries throughout Europe, and have investigated their methods of manufacture) were selected by me for some special excellence or merit, and were of the very first rank, and accordingly well up-to-date. That is the reason they capture the market to a great extent; but if we had the security they have there are plenty of people in our district who would invest capital in the same manner. We have large concerns in the potteries and people who are prepared to furnish any amount of capital when they can see that that it is going to be productive of good results.[2]

Herbert Colclough presented the yet blunter and more pessimistic argument that 'the utter hopelessness of the present condition of things renders it altogether

---

1 *The Pottery Gazette*, November 1880, p. 717.

2 *Tariff Commission*, para. 107.

improbable that anyone will put money into a business that they know they are going to lose by'.[3] He continued, 'the great point in the whole matter is that if one can only secure sufficient trade ... one is never afraid to spend money in order to bring oneself up to date ... If you have not that, a spirit of hopelessness pervades all trades and tends to check enterprise'.[4] Both Moore and Colclough argued that any restraint on the development of the industry came not from an insufficient supply of capital but of confidence.

Nonetheless, by the time of the *Tariff Commission*, the industry had experienced some three decades or more of increasing competition, during which period unprecedented levels of investment had undoubtedly occurred. As the trade press had noted in 1888, 'the puzzle that occupies most minds here [is] the fact that despite bad trade and adverse reports from all sides, factories continue to be built'.[5] Similarly, in 1891, it was observed that 'many alterations and improvements have been made in the past twelve months ... New plant has been laid in many factories and new ones have been built. This speaks well for the confidence which capitalists and manufacturers have as to the future of British pottery'.[6] Thus, in meeting this apparent contradiction, we are faced with two tasks. First, with attempting to chart how and to what extent the industry reshaped its productive processes during this period, particularly in terms of mechanization. Second, with exploring the attitudes toward mechanization of those, owners and workers, affected by the process.

It will be argued that prior to 1914 the progress of mechanization in the pottery industry was gradual, uneven and partial, inhibited by the structure and the culture of the industry. The primary determinants of this pattern will be sketched and its implications explored, in particular it will be argued that the mechanization that did take place was of limited effectiveness in meeting the competitive challenge outlined above.

The chapter will first introduce the basic productive processes in pottery manufacture before outlining the timing, extent and sources of process innovations, the pattern of their diffusion, and the forces shaping that pattern. Attention will then focus on the impact of mechanization, particularly in terms of its effect on cost structures, on the other resources employed by firms, especially human resources, and on implication for the structure of the industry and the strategies of firms.

---

3 Ibid., para. 147.
4 Ibid., p. 149.
5 *The Pottery Gazette*, July 1888, p. 640.
6 *The Pottery Gazette*, January 1891, p. 36.

The progress of mechanization

Pottery manufacture had by the mid-nineteenth century long been subject to an extensive and still evolving division of labour. Since Wedgwood, the industry's innovatory impulses had been expressed primarily in organizational rather than technological terms. It has been claimed that the pottery industry is 'so varied that no "flow diagram" can represent what goes on at different times or places ... Sequential arrangements may vary ... There is thus no "logical sequence"'.[7] Nonetheless, four basic stages may be identified in most examples of pottery manufacture, each subject to further sub-division. These stages are, first, the preparation of the body, involving the conditioning, purification and mixing of clay and a wide range of other materials, such as the bone found in bone china, to form either a plastic body or liquid slip from which wares are formed. Second, the forming of the ware, regarded by many manufacturers and workers in the late nineteenth century as both the most difficult and controversial stage in relation to the question of mechanization, as the traditional and totemic thrower's wheel was progressively supplanted by the jolly and by casting. Third, the firing of the wares, and, fourth, the decoration of the ware, again employing many different techniques, from hand-painting and gilding to lithographic printing.

Whilst the precise sequence in which these operations were performed may have varied, particularly in relation to firing and decorating, they were very difficult to physically separate, it being impractical to transport fragile semi-finished wares between sites or firms. Therefore, largely regardless of firm size, the vast majority of firms in the Potteries were vertically integrated and occupied single sites. Thus, the 1908 description of potbanks, as the works were known, as 'functionally separate workshops' should not be read a suggesting that these workshops were independent either of each other or the firm. The workers, with their highly developed and specific skills, may have stayed within their shops, but each pot had to pass through the hands of all. In this respect at least, pottery manufacture was not comparable to many of the cutlery 'factories' in Sheffield, where the 'little mesters' often effectively worked for themselves. Mechanization thus had to occur within a highly sub-divided yet integrated process requiring careful co-ordination.

The first and last of the four stages of production were the first to undergo any degree of mechanization. Celoria notes that the preparatory sub-process known as wedging 'could be fully mechanized ... by the first third of the nineteenth century'.[8] Indeed, the preparation of the many necessary materials, by crushing and grinding, had long required some machinery, and many different types of mill had been adapted from other uses, powered initially by water and

[7] F. Celoria, 'Ceramic Machinery of the Nineteenth Century in the Potteries and in Other Parts of Britain', *Staffordshire Archaeology*, Vol. 2 (1973), p. 13.

[8] Ibid., p. 13.

increasingly in the nineteenth century by steam. As will be shown in a later chapter, specialized firms were carrying out some of these processes by the mid-nineteenth century. However, with firms increasingly naming and promoting their own variations on standard bodies, such as the so-called granitewear from which much common tableware was fashioned, the preparation of the final body was generally carried out, amidst some secrecy, by each firm on its own premises from semi-processed materials.

However, generalizations about many aspects of mechanization in the industry are now extremely difficult to make. Some cases of invention may be pinpointed fairly accurately, but the processes of innovation and diffusion are often more obscure. There are several reasons for this. First, there is a shortage of documentary evidence, particularly lacking in this respect being the papers of the various potters' engineers responsible for the design and manufacture of many machines.

The mechanization of the pottery industry was also particularly uneven, both within and between firms. The industry did not, as Whipp rightly notes, conform easily to any simple core/periphery model, in which core firms were large, stable, innovative and deployed best practice techniques and peripheral firms were small, transient and characterized by poor practice. Chapter 6 will demonstrate the relatively limited extent of mechanization at the very large and long-lived firm of Mintons for example, where growth was predicated on economies of scope rather than of scale. Similarly, in 1883 US Consul Edward Lane observed that Wedgwood's famed Etruscan works were 'worth a visit. They are quaint and old-fashioned in appearance [and] are precisely the same as when Wedgwood, in the fullness of his powers, directed the industrial forces and produced perfect and beautiful work'.[9]

A further complication is provide by the contradictory nature of contemporary assessments of and attitudes towards the progress of mechanization. Thus, whilst it was asserted by one commentator in 1892 that, 'This is the machine age, particularly in the Potting trade ... Machinery is constantly being applied ... and this mechanical aid has become essential in order that the demands made upon the potter may be met with rapidity', another, writing in the same year, felt that, 'There are many articles of pottery which it is almost impossible to make except by the hand labour of the hollow-ware presser'.[10] As late as 1908 William Burton, Chairman of the *Joint Committee of the Pottery Manufacturers of Great*

[9] *The Pottery Gazette*, May 1883, p. 451–2. Similarly, Consul Schoenhof observed in 1886 that, 'One still sees in the same factory with steam power and other appliance of the most improved pattern, boys turning the wheel for the potter', whilst as late as 1908 H. M. Superintending Inspector of Factories J.A. Redgrave noted simply that in the Potteries 'there are all kinds of places'. *The Pottery Gazette*, July 1886, p. 813; *Truck Acts Committee, Final Report*, Vol. 3 (1908), p. 38.

[10] *The Pottery Gazette*, September 1892, p. 830; *The Pottery Gazette*, August 1892, p. 718.

Britain, could still claim of potting that 'it is a very complicated trade, and an old trade in which the handicraft still survives, perhaps more than in any organised trade in the country. Machinery for performing many of the operations attendant upon the production of pottery ... has been very slowly introduced into our trade'.[11]

Nonetheless, so long as the qualifications introduced above are borne in mind, it is possible to propose a broad framework for the mechanization of the industry.[12] W.H. Warburton, with a lifetime's experience as a working potter and unionist, suggested in 1931 that the 'Industrial Revolution', defined as the replacement of manual skills by machinery, 'began for the Potteries in the 1870s, with the preceding twenty years as an introductory period'. Of this preparatory period, Lamb notes that all innovations, most notably the greater use of steam power, essentially 'complemented human skills without replacing them. Throughout the industry the skilled hands of the craftsmen ultimately fashioned and shaped the wares'.[13] Further, Warburton was careful to place an emphasis on the gradual nature of this process, commenting that 'the displacement of the hollow-ware presser by the jiggerer and the caster was taking place roughly during the fourteen years preceding the European war'.[14] Nonetheless, no matter how incremental diffusion had been, Burton, when asked in 1908 if best china tea saucers were still hand-thrown answered 'very few are now'.[15] Thus, the period 1870–1914 emerges as the most significant phase in the mechanization of the industry, though the process had far from run its course by the latter date.

A reading of the trade press supports this periodization. Debates over the importance and implications of mechanization and reports of firms re-equipping old factories and building new ones appear with increasing frequency in the pages of the *Pottery Gazette* from the late 1870s and during the 1880s in particular. Moreover, this period was also marked by the emergence and growth of a dedicated and localized sector of firms, styled potters' engineers, designing

---

[11] *The Truck Acts Committee, Final Report*, Vol. 1 (1908), p. 42.

[12] Difficulties in accurately gauging the progress of mechanization are not restricted to the pottery industry. Church has commented of the boot and shoe industry in the 1880s that though 'the pace of innovation was faster than it had been hitherto ... we cannot establish this quantitatively and must rely on the observations of contemporary trade commentators'. R. Church, 'The Effect of the American Export Invasion on the British Boot and Shoe Industry, 1885–1914', *Journal of Economic History*, Vol. 28 (1968), p. 230.

[13] Celoria, 'Ceramic Machinery', p. 11; A. Lamb, 'The Press and Labours Response to Pottery-Making Machinery in the North Staffordshire Pottery Industry, *Journal of Ceramic History*, Vol. 9 (1977), p. 1. This point is also stressed by Warburton.

[14] W.H. Warburton, *The History of Trade Union Organisation in the North Staffordshire Potteries* , (London, Allen & Unwin, 1931), p. 196.

[15] *The Truck Acts Committee, Final Report*, Vol. 4 (1908), p. 275.

and making plant for the industry.[16] Many of these firms, including the largest and most important, William Boulton and Co., began life as general engineers, ironfounders and smiths. As late as 1867 Boulton's advertisements in local trade directories described the firm as 'Engineers, Iron and Brass Founders, Manufacturers of Every Description of Ironwork for Potters, Colliery Proprietors, Paraffin Oil Makers, Brick and Tile Manufacturers, Builders etc.'.[17] That Boulton, described by the novelist Arnold Bennett as a 'lone and wonderful genius', had not yet specialized in the design and manufacture of pottery machinery by this date is clearly significant when, by 1898, the trade press could claim that there was no, 'branch of the of the potting industry Boulton and Co. have not materially assisted with some specially-designed mechanical contrivance for the saving of labour ... enabling the trade to compete successfully with their previously better equipped continental competitors'.[18]

The transformation of Boulton's firm in the years between 1870 and 1900 clearly suggests a quickening in the pace of mechanization experienced by the industry. These developments are also in sharp contrast to those associated with the Sheffield cutlery trades, which were not able to support a similarly specialized engineering sector in the nineteenth century. Taylor argues that cutlery 'provided insufficient stimulus for engineers to design and manufacture machines, the demand for which would have been too small to justify development'.[19] Like Platts of Oldham, and other textile machinery manufacturers, Boulton also went on to develop an export trade, T.C. Moore describing how:

> Most of the improved machinery on the Continent for the cheap production of china has been obtained from our own district. In one of the most up-to-date places visited, I was rather surprised to find some machines which I had not seen in our district; I asked the proprietor whether it was his own inventive genius that had suggested these, and he first of all tried to claim some credit for them but ultimately admitted that they came from Staffordshire-from the very people who supply our own.[20]

---

[16] The original jiggers developed by local manufacturers Wall and Ridgway in the 1840s were made at the Manchester works of Whitworth. Lamb, 'The Press and Labours Response', p. 1.

[17] *Keates & Ford's*, (1867).

[18] Boulton was born in Newcastle-under-Lyme in 1825 and died in 1900. He began business as a ironfounder in 1852 in partnership with Benjamin Brough, the firm moving to premises on Navigation Road Burslem, still occupied in the 1980s, in 1856. Between 1860 and 1897 Boulton took out twenty three patents for machines connected to the industry and in the mid-1880s employed in the region of 150 hands. He was a Methodist, Liberal and Country Magistrate. Stuart, *People of the Potteries*, p. 42–3; *The Pottery Gazette*, March 1898, p. 349.

[19] S. Taylor, *Tradition and Change: The Sheffield Cutlery Trades, 1870–1914* (Unpublished Ph.D., Sheffield University, 1988), p. 38.

[20] *Tariff Commission*, para. 107.

Unfortunately, whether the more rapid adoption of this unspecified machine on the Continent was an isolated incident is not known, as also is the extent of the export trade carried on Boulton and other Staffordshire engineers.

However, the role of the potters' engineers as a source of technological innovation is significant not only for the light that it throws upon the growth of the parent industry. First, the highly localized growth of this engineering sector conforms to a Marshallian model of industrial districts, in which agglomeration lead to the clustering of suppliers in step with the growth of localized markets for important inputs. For Marshall, the 'high automatic organisation' of clustered industries was 'in great measure due to the fact that their plant is made in their own districts, with constant intercommunication between machines makers and machine users'.[21] Certainly, in the Potteries, a collaborative relationship between engineers and manufacturers was felt to be largely beneficial, though not as common as it might be. For example, a new clay press, developed jointly by the manufacturing firm of G.W. Turner and Sons and an engineer called Renshaw, provoked the trade press to commend and call for further such collaborations:

> many manufacturers might offer valuable suggestions concerning the improvement of the machinery used in the trade so as to facilitate and increase the work executed by it. It is for the manufacturers to know the requirements of their machinery, to see the shortcomings of it, and so by their practical knowledge to suggest alterations and improvements to their engineers. It is by such co-operation the engineer, with his skill, works out the beautiful machinery of the day.[22]

Evidence from the catalogues of William Boulton and Co. makes it clear that the firm, though endeavouring to make and supply standard designs, operated very often in the role of consulting engineers. The introduction to a catalogue of 1902, for example, notes that 'We make also modifications of the machinery shown here, to suit particular conditions or site, which is quite impossible to describe ... quotations with drawings and full particulars, will be given when require, meeting any special enquiry'.[23] Moreover, both a 'quantity of the general, and a number of the special, Machines are always kept in stock'

The impact of potters' engineers such as Boulton was then quite different to that of the American owned British United Shoe Machinery Co. on the boot and shoe industry. In the 1890s the market power of this much larger firm, and perhaps its lack of intimate local roots, enabled it use restrictive leasing contracts

[21] Marshall, *Industry and Trade*, p. 603.

[22] *The Pottery Gazette*, May 1880, p. 270.

[23] Boulton & Co., *Catalogue*, 1902. The firm asked that 'To avoid all delay ... all enquiries should be as full as possible and should express the exact nature of the work to be done by each machine, or should give detailed specifications for our guidance. Where, however, any of the Machines specified herein meet all the conditions of the inquiry it is sufficient that parties wishing us to tender for the same should refer simply to the distinguishing number'.

to virtually impose standardized and fully integrated lines of machinery on the shoe manufacturers of the East Midlands, leading to a more far reaching transformation of productive processes in that industry than was achieved in the Potteries in the same period. Instead, the situation approximated to that in Lancashire, where, Mass and Lazonick have argued, the localization of the capital goods industry 'meant that ... machine design was geared towards the technological requirements' of the district, and in particular to the 'complementary capabilities of its labour supplies'.[24] In North Staffordshire too labour supplies were very strongly rooted in the locality, often resistant to change and central to the existing resource bases of all firms. However, these arguments begin to impinge on discussion of the forces shaping the diffusion process, which is to follow shortly.

In order to further explore the mechanization of the industry the diffusion of two specific machines will be explored in more detail. The jigger and the jolly were perhaps the most important of the machines being diffused through the industry in the late nineteenth century, in both practical and symbolic terms. Ultimately the industry, both in Britain and elsewhere was to be truly revolutionized not by the jigger and the jolly but by changes in firing methods, and in particular the abandonment of the characteristic periodic or intermittent bottle oven in favour of continuous or tunnel kilns. However, these were essentially twentieth-century developments, though foreshadowed around the turn of the century.

In the late nineteenth and early twentieth centuries though, the closely related jigger and the jolly acquired a dual significance, practical and symbolic, because they impacted on those stages of the manufacturing process, the forming or shaping of wares, where the wages, skills and status of workers were both high and where mechanization seemed least likely to manufacturers and workers alike. The jigger and the jolly had the potential therefore to do much to alter the cost structures prevalent in the industry, whilst at the same time also weakening its cherished claim to remain as much a craft as an industry. Their gestation, through innovation and diffusion, was a long one, but this did not notably ease their path towards eventual acceptance.

By the 1870s and 1880s neither the jigger, used in the making of flatware (that is plates, saucers etc.), nor the jolly, used in the making of hollow-ware (bowls, cups etc.), could be considered of recent invention. The origins of the jigger, in particular, can traced to the 1840s, when first John Ridgway in 1840, Charles Mason in 1844 and, finally, Copeland and Garrett in 1847 attempted to introduce the machine into North Staffordshire. These attempts were defeated as much by technical shortcomings as by the concerted opposition of the unions.[25] The

[24] W. Mass and W. Lazonick, 'The British Cotton Industry and International Competitive Advantage: The State of the Debates', *Business History*, Vol. 32 No. 4 (1990), p. 13.

[25] Celoria, 'Ceramic Machinery'.

machines seem next to have appeared in the Potteries in the 1860s. In 1880 Godfrey Wedgwood described how in 1863:

> Mr Ragout-one of the largest houses on the Continent ... presented him with a jolly, telling him that they used it in his works, and that a man could be taken off the roads and taught to use it in two months. He [Wedgwood] showed it to his men but they would have nothing to with it.[26]

Progress remained slow and in 1879 Mr Pinder of the firm Pinder, Bourne and Co., claimed that jigger/jolly, his definition being imprecise, was still 'only adopted to a very limited extent, the houses using it being almost entirely engaged in the American trade'.[27] It is not surprising that mechanization of the forming processes should have first gained a toehold in this sector of the trade, which consisted principally of large volumes of common earthenware tableware. However, despite the claims made by Ragout to Godfrey Wedgwood, the limited effect of these machines in displacing skilled labour must again be reiterated. Thus, in 1884, A 'Staffordshire Potteries Supplement' to the *Illustrated London News* was quite accurate in describing the jigger as a 'modification of the potter's wheel', and to note that it occupied 'an intermediate position [marking] the transition which is slowly being made from he simplest position of pure handiwork by the introduction of mechanical contrivances'.[28]

Nonetheless constant improvements were made to these machines and the sophistication of some examples increased rapidly. Boulton's' Double Automatic Jigger and Jolly, for example, recipient of the Highest Award for Potters' Machinery at an International Inventions Exhibition in 1885, was described in the maker's catalogue as 'self-contained and automatic'. Boulton commended his patented design as capable of producing 5–6000 thousand articles a day and reducing wear and tear on moulds. However, in reporting this new machine, the trade press also noted its initial sales, and these are evidence of a cautious approach to the installation of new plant. Just one had gone to Mintons and further two to the Hanley firm of Powell, Bishop and Stonier.[29] A more thorough-going adoption of new plant was most likely either where the firm was young, as in the case of the Empire Porcelain Co., whose new factory for 600 hands was equipped only with steam driven jiggers and jollies and contained no traditional wheels, or where an old firm built entirely new premises.[30]

---

26 *The Pottery Gazette*, December 1880, p. 794.

27 *The Pottery Gazette*, December 1879, p. 472. Pinder & Co. had themselves first installed jollies in 1874.

28 *The Illustrated London News*, 'Staffordshire Potteries Supplement', 30 August 1884, p. 201.

29 *The Pottery Gazette*, September 1885, p. 1074.

30 *The Pottery Gazette*, May 1898, p. 589. An example of the latter strategy was that of Worthington & Sons, a Hanley based firm that grew from small to medium-size between 1862 and 1882, who in 1886 'fitted up a large shop with a full complement of steam jiggers and jollies'

Though eventually triumphant, the diffusion of the jigger and jolly was thus slow and uneven, Given the long resistance to 'jollying' in the region and the fact that the workers directly affected were amongst some of the most highly unionised in the industry it is no surprise that the reappearance of the jigger and the jolly from the 1870s should have aroused suspicion and resentment amongst sections of the workforce. Unions identified appeals to notions of 'the trade' as their most promising line of attack, the union paper the *Potters' Examiner*, for example, argued in 1887 that both machines were:

> a waste of time as well as of material, and can only, where used, prove detrimental to the production of good and sound ware, and thereby lower the fame of the Staffordshire Potteries in the renowned production of the finest and choicest ceramics in the whole wide world.[31]

However, the organized resistance to machinery seen in the 1840s did not reappear in the 1870s. Instead, resistance typically took the form of either individual refusal to work the machines or disputes over the adjustment of piece rates, a vital issue in the reception of mechanization that will be explored in depth shortly. The most salient point is that the very prolonged diffusion process experienced by the jigger and jolly, some four decades or more from the 1870s, cannot be ascribed solely, or even largely, to worker resistance. If employee resistance alone did not inhibit the spread of these and other machines, then what other factors influenced the pace of mechanization in the industry?

Technological pathways

Thus, we have a picture of a gradually unfolding and locally generated pattern of technological innovation and diffusion. The most salient characteristic of this pattern was not so much its slowness, slow though it was, but its partial nature, both within and across firms. Staffordshire did introduce new technologies, indeed its engineers were responsible for pioneering many of them, but it did so in a very piecemeal fashion.

This pattern suggests a number of questions. Did the small-scale and atomized structure of the industry in North Staffordshire constrain investment in manufacturing, an argument central to the critiques of both Chandler and Lazonick and Elbaum. To what extent may such a structure be equated, in turn, with a business culture at root inimical to or, at best, ambiguous about

---

in order to 'turn out their orders better and with quicker dispatch'. *Hanley Borough Rate Books*, 1862 and 1882; *The Pottery Gazette*, February 1886, p. 206.

[31] Lamb, 'Labour and Press Responses', p. 6.

mechanization?[32] However, these questions also beg to what extent, if at all, the pattern of diffusion of new technologies in North Staffordshire represented a 'failure' on the part of the region's manufacturers? In particular, it is not clear either that businessmen in Staffordshire forewent significant efficiency gains in not diffusing these technologies more rapidly and completely, or that they were diffused more rapidly and completely in competing nations.

These questions may be addressed by invoking and elaborating on notions of 'path dependency', the argument that the 'stock of technological knowledge at any given time can only be understood by a systematic investigation of the earlier history out of which it emerged'.[33] In the context of an industrial district there may be a need also to explore the extent to which any stock of technological knowledge was embedded in a localized paradigmatic understanding of the relationship between technology, industry structure, markets and strategy. Equally important may be an assessment of the forces effecting contemporary judgements on the continued validity of such a paradigm. In other words, the path dependency of process innovation was not only technological in nature, but was also cultural. Mental horizons, as much as technological horizons, were moulded by the past conditions from which they emerged.

However, it is important to avoid a rigid determinism, either technological or cultural. The frames of reference employed by Staffordshire potters when weighing options for technological change should not be dismissed automatically as the expression of a blind, inherited conservatism. Instead, the possibility that they represented a reasoned assessment of the appropriate fit between technology, structure and strategy must be considered. The working out of the range of possible technological pathways was a process in which actors actively participated, directed not only by the technological knowledge available to them but also by their own interests and identities as businessmen and potters.

Certainly, at a purely technological level, the technologies being diffused in the late nineteenth century represent a clear case of path-dependency. The jigger and jolly were clear outgrowths of the basic and ancient wheel, though increasingly differentiated from it in terms of construction, operation and impact. The machines called jiggers and jollies in the mid-twentieth century may have been very different beasts, but even they emerged only very slowly from a protracted sequence of sub-innovations and modifications.[34] Moreover, that sequence was worked out largely through a pattern of learning-by-doing, occurring *in situ*, and through the 'constant communication' between manufacturers and engineers. These machines, despite the outcry they sometimes provoked in both the trade and unions press, were essentially familiar to both

---

[32] N. Rosenberg, *Exploring the Black Box: Technology, Economics and History* (Cambridge, Cambridge University Press, 1994), p. 10.

[33] Ibid., p.10.

[34] Blaszcyzk, '"Reign of the Robots"'.

masters and men. They required no new sets of knowledge, particularly no new order of scientific knowledge, and thus chimed with rather undermined the education many manufacturers had received 'at the bench'. Even where a manufacturer had not risen from such a background but had instead emerged from a dynastic family capitalism, experience and practicality were cherished over more formal sources of learning. The following exchange took place between William Woodall, M.P. for Burslem and senior partner in the firm of James MacIntyre & Co., and Godfrey Wedgwood:

> Let us, without making it particularly personal, take a typical potter who has a large and successful business. Is he, as a rule, a man who has had anything like a scientific training especially adapting him for that business?
> I do not know of any such man who has had any special education. Some of them have had the advantage of the ordinary public school and university education, but by the greater number have not.[35]

Moreover, Wedgwood clearly viewed this state of affairs as appropriate to the needs of the industry, for he continued; 'the people who do succeed in our business are men who have risen from the bench'.[36] This attitude was typical of those towards technical education for both workers and manufacturers. Given the demands made of both masters and men by the production process and prevalent systems of training, often rooted in familial employment patterns, education beyond the workplace was often held to be superfluous:

> By technical education is meant a theoretical and practical knowledge of manufacture. But how far a theoretical education may be of practical advantage to an artisan in some branches of potting may be doubtful. It is true such knowledge would enlarge the mind and ... fit the artisan better to fulfil his as a citizen, but it is questionable if it would make him a better workman. It is without the sphere of such an operator to improve the form of pattern if his manufacture ... Theory to such a one must be but a luxury.[37]

Such attitudes persisted and were scattered throughout the evidence presented to the *Tariff Commission*. Bernard Moore, for example, noted that 'There is too much tendency to exaggerate the value of what is called scientific training. The potting methods, however, imperfect they may be, have been arrived at as a result

---

[35] 'The Technicality of Potting', *The Pottery Gazette*, May 1885, p. 560.

[36] Ibid., p. 560.

[37] 'Technical Education and Potting', *The Pottery Gazette*, January 1884, p. 49. Others both noted and appeared to regret such attitudes, arguing that 'few are the manufacturers who appreciate the value of experiments. For the most part they rely upon the experience of the past'. 'Thoughts on Potting', *The Pottery Gazette*, December 1883, p. 1137

of experience ... *Practical* knowledge of chemistry is required'.[38] Enoch Massey, Fenton based china manufacturer, on the other hand, explained how 'I made my son apprentice to our firm to teach him his business, believing that the potter is best who has worked his way up from the bottom'.[39]

The notion of path-dependency clearly has some affinities with the notion that in an industrial district the mysteries of a trade are somehow 'in the air', internalized and passed from one generation to the next. Indeed, the continuation of the existing stock of technological knowledge in the Potteries was propagated and furthered by clustering, which lowered barriers to entry, ensuring many manufacturers came from the essentially artisanal background outlined above. Clustering also led to the recruitment and training of young workers through networks of kinship. For some proponents of the industrial district model this special 'industrial atmosphere' leads to the culturing of an 'innovatory milieu'. Langlois, for example, claims that 'innovation ... is a matter of rapid trial-and-error learning'. Crucially, 'the variation that drives an evolutionary learning system ... depends, in effect on outbreeding [and] the ability to engage in rapid-trial-error learning can sometimes be an external economy ... of the system as a whole'.[40] Langlois explicitly links this argument to clustering, arguing that in Silicon Valley this system-wide 'learning effect went beyond the background culture however. It included the proclivity of engineers to hop jobs and start spinoffs, creating a pollination effect and tendency to biological differentiation that Marshall would have appreciated'.[41] But these arguments do not establish on any theoretical basis the assumed relationship between clustering and innovatory ferment. Langlois believes, quite plausibly, that any systemic learning effect 'depends on people being on different wavelengths'. But it is equally plausible that actors in clustered industries are in fact far more likely to be on the same wavelength as one another than not. That would certainly be a logical conclusion to derive from the emphasis placed on shared and tacit knowledge and value systems in many district studies, both theoretical and empirical. It would also be a conclusion congruent with resistance to external sources of knowledge; represented by a lack of engagement with technical education and by the idealization of learning-by-doing evinced by potters.

Certainly some cross-pollination may have occurred within the system. The relatively few potters' engineers active in the district obviously worked with very many different manufacturers and may have acted as important nodes for the

---

[38] *Tariff Commission*, para. 118 (emphasis added). Moore, perhaps the leading Potteries based researcher into glazes, bodies and firing techniques of the late nineteenth and early twentieth centuries, was not university trained. A. Dawson, *Bernard Moore: Master Potter, 1850–1935*, (London, Richard Dennis, 1982), p. 7.

[39] *Tariff Commission*, para. 128.

[40] R. Langlois, 'Creating External Capabilities: innovation and Vertical Disintegration in the Microcomputer Industry', *Business and Economic History*, 2nd Series Vol. 19 (1990), p. 95.

[41] Ibid., p. 101.

exchange of technical information, whilst manufacturers also communicated with one another. It was reported in 1881, for example, that 'Messrs Barker Bros. Commence building their new premises during next week. The workshops will be fitted with modern appliance for the rapid production of earthenware, repeated visits for the purpose of gaining accurate information having been paid to the leading manufactories of the district'.[42] Leaving aside for one moment the notoriously guarded and secretive attitude of many in the Potteries, it must be noted that even when such communication took place it tells us nothing about how much that was *new* was learnt. Indeed, Llobrera *et al.* argue that very strong local networks can act to restrict actors' access to 'nonredundant information', that is information they themselves do not already have.[43] The pool of technological knowledge available to the Potteries was relatively small and not regularly replenished by fresh streams.

Of course there were those with more open minds. T.B. Johnston, noting how 'a thoroughly good German chemist in general pottery and colouring as well as in bodies and glazing called on me this morning ... anxious to come into the works', continued; 'We have got the empirical knowledge but we want the chemical knowledge. For the last 10 years I have been urging that the best reserve fund we can make would be to have a chemist in our place constantly experimenting on research work ... We are bound to have scientific chemists if we are to hold our trade'.[44] Johnston found though that 'my partner does not quite see it in the same light when we have argued the thing out. The fact is, he says, we cannot afford it'. Johnston was, however, a Bristol potter. He also felt bound to acknowledge that:

> There is no doubt that Staffordshire is the place to manufacture, because of the labour. The skilled labour has been there for generations, and the Staffordshire pottery, beyond doubt, is the best in the world, and I see the difference in my workmen when I go to Staffordshire. The way they handle the clay in Staffordshire is absolutely different.[45]

The respect felt for the inherited, path-dependent strengths collectively possessed by Staffordshire, in the shape of a highly skilled workforce, is obvious, and Johnston's openness to the need for trained chemists may have reflected, in part at least, a feeling of isolation from the those strengths.

At a purely technological level then the mechanization of the industry in the late nineteenth century grew out of and was shaped by prior technologies and by

---

42 *The Pottery Gazette*, April 1881, p. 327.

43 J. Llobrera, D. Meyer and G. Nammacher, 'Trajectories of Industrial Districts: Impact of Strategic Intervention in Medical Industrial Districts', *Economic Geography*, Vol. 76 No. 1 (2000), p. 72.

44 *Tariff Commission*, para. 176–7.

45 Ibid., para. 175.

the sources of technological knowledge available to both manufacturers and workers. Those sources of knowledge were not only path-dependent, that is historically patterned, but also space-dependent, that is spatially patterned by prolonged clustering. However, the path-dependencies shaping the innovatory process were not simply technological. Instead, technological horizons were just one component in a wider set that linked strategy, firm, industry and market. These views were perhaps widely enough held, in the Potteries at least, to have constituted a paradigm. J. Ridgway captured many of the most important elements of that paradigm thus:

> it is very often said that foreign countries are better equipped and better trained and that their manufacturers are more up-to-date. I very much question that. In many cases it proceeds from the wrong method of comparison. For instance a man goes down to a large place in Dresden, employing perhaps 3000 hands and erected within the last twenty years. Then he goes to some old factory producing very high class goods in the Potteries, and he compares one with the other, and immediately jumps to the conclusion that the Englishman is old-fashioned and the foreigner is very go-ahead. But the old rule holds good. If you wish to compare, compare things of the same order. To a producer of high-class goods, e.g. a 5-guinea plate–and a near neighbour of mine is constantly selling 5-guinea plates–the amount of saving that can be effected in a great many of these mechanical appliances, would be nothing in the value of that plate or in a trade of that kind. But if you are turning out plates by the thousand at 2s. a dozen, then it does make a difference.[46]

These arguments explicitly recognize the interdependence of technological choices, the size and age of firms and strategy, particularly in terms of market orientation. Thus many Staffordshire firms at least attempted to pursue strategies based on niches, differentiation and flexibility, strategies to which unit prices, throughput and internal economies of scale were not decisive. Indeed, until at least the late nineteenth century, the growth of the very largest firms in the Potteries, such as Mintons, had been largely a function of attempts to capture economies of scope and to secure the capabilities, especially in design skills, central to those economies. Naturally, few firms matched Mintons in the development of such capabilities, relying instead on the more contested external economies of scope and flexibility generated by the district as a whole, but their strategies were nonetheless closely related to those of their most prestigious brethren. Moreover, maintenance of these strategies was clearly a matter of choice on the part of manufacturers. Those choices may have been structured by

---

[46] Ibid., para. 157.

the historically moulded resources of firms and industry, but choices they remained, predicated on an understanding of the region's strengths.[47]

The creative capacities of the Potteries were then best and most forcefully expressed through product rather than process innovations. To be sure, as we will shall see, much of this innovation took the form of a ferment of relatively minor stylistic variation, easily copied and rarely giving a firm sustained competitive advantage in the market place. Even firms making very considerable investments, largely in the form of salaries for well paid artists and designers, often found themselves vulnerable in this respect. But on occasion a new shape or pattern or a simple but clever product idea embodying a new function or quality could be the making of a firm. Dunn, Bennett & Co., who successfully identified and exploited a niche in hotelware, did so on the basis of a series of simple but effective patented products. Their story will be explored in more detail in a later chapter, setting out how product strategy was matched by marketing strategy.

The greater status accorded to product innovation than to process innovation was further reflected in the relatively greater openness shown to foreign trained designers than to formally trained chemists and ceramists and the greater enthusiasm for art education than for technical schools. Schools of Art were first established in Hanley and Stoke-on-Trent in 1847, the latter known as the Minton Memorial Institute in acknowledgement of the support of Herbert Minton, and in Burslem in 1853, renamed the Wedgwood Institute when re-housed in 1873.

Important to any wider notion of path-dependency is the degree of fit between strategies, shaped by the history of firms and the industry and embodied in the fragmented, small-scale structure of the industry, and the technological innovations represented by the jigger and the jolly. These machines undermined neither strategies nor firms. Capable of being either hand or steam powered, easily, quickly and cheaply adapted to make new products, relatively simple, robust and inexpensive, quickly amortized by making reductions from the pieces rates of workers operating them, they did not demand either that firms be large or chase volumes in order to employ and make effective use of them. They could be, and were, introduced in a piecemeal fashion, one or two machines at a time.

It might be argued that this degree of fit, the great extent to which new technologies emerged from and were congruent with existing technologies,

---

[47] Thus, it has been argued; 'Does Britain still have a place in pottery production ... ? Grim though this latest news has been, there are certain unique selling points. The "Hand Crafted in England" stamp is a key part of top brands; cheap labour competitors cannot replicate that. There are also some parts of the production process where the British have skills that are not often matched elsewhere - hand-painting for example'. Interestingly, this assessment was made as recently as 1998. *The Independent*, 11 December 1998, p. 19. Conversely, an 'excessive' mechanization was seen as undermining those strengths. Thus, 'the unfortunate thing about machinery is that its effect is to equalize the quality of goods. When hand labour was the rule, there was never any question about English pottery being the best made in the world'. *The Pottery Gazette*, May 1888, p. 430 and July 1896, p. 538.

capabilities and strategies of firms, should have led to a much quicker and more complete diffusion throughout the industry. However, for all the protestations of both the trade and union press, their very lack of radicalness may have induced what appears in retrospect to have been an overly cautious approach on the part of employers and employees. In short, it was not clear what, if any, decisive advantages their use conferred on firms in return for the erosion of skills, however slight, they seemed to imply.

Lloyd-Jones and Lewis, building on Rosenberg, have argued that the 'speed with which techniques are innovated from the basic innovation to the subsequent diffusion will depend on upon a series of modifications and adaptations', the sub-innovatory timescale becoming stretched as the technique or machine in which the innovation is embodied 'goes through innumerable minor modifications and alterations in design'.[48] The timing and duration of the sub-innovatory process will be effected heavily by technological factors, as was certainly the case in the Potteries. The jigger, first innovated in the 1840s, was still undergoing significant evolution in the 1940s. Lloyd-Jones and Lewis go on to suggest that 'given a trajectory of improvement, uncertainty concerning the time path of sub-innovations may well effect entrepreneurial expectations', expressed in relatively cautious attitudes.[49] Elbaum too has argued that diffusion will be slower the 'smaller the prospective efficiency gains', and that 'gradual and evolutionary' technological change may cause firms to make 'suboptimal investment decisions which result in a relatively slow rate of technological progress'.[50] All these arguments are clearly germane to the experience of the pottery industry in the second half of the nineteenth century.

However, Lloyd-Jones and Lewis argue further that the effects stemming from uncertainty may be heightened in an industry whose 'structure is characterised by large numbers of small-scale firms operating in a highly competitive environment'.[51] These arguments prompt consideration of two further issues in relation to the process of technological change; the impact of industry structure and the importance of the wider competitive environment, including not only that offered by the Potteries industrial district but also that generated by competing nations. To what extent was the rise of foreign competitors likely either to galvanise manufacturers in the Potteries or to increase the uncertainty they already felt with respect to mechanization?

As the last chapter demonstrated, judgements as to the size and modernity of Continental firms were, and remain, difficult. In reality the picture was probably as mixed as it was in the Potteries. Some German ceramic firms were highly artisanal in nature, deploying traditional techniques and serving limited domestic

---

48 Lloyd-Jones and Lewis, *Manchester and the Age of the Factory*, p. 87.

49 Ibid., p. 87.

50 B. Elbaum, 'The Steel Industry Before World War One', in B. Elbaum and W. Lazonick (eds.), *The Decline of the British Economy* (Oxford, Clarendon Press, 1987), p. 62–3.

51 Lloyd-Jones and Lewis, *Manchester and the Age of the Factory*, p. 87.

markets, others were very large and used all available technologies.[52] For Stratton, writing in the 1930s, the single most important difference between the industry in Germany, on the one hand, and in the United Kingdom and the United States on the other, was the much readier acceptance in Germany of the need for '"laboratory control" ... both the existence of a testing laboratory and the presence of scientific habits of mind'.[53] As evidence of this Stratton cited the much more rapid diffusion in Germany of the Seger Cone. Invented by German ceramist H. A. Seger in the 1880s, this simple device allowed for more precise control over the firing process.[54] In Staffordshire, control over this crucial process, in which hundreds or even thousands of pounds worth of wares could be spoiled, was traditionally the responsibility of the head ovenman who, using only experience and the naked eye, judged the heat of an oven from the colour of its flame, a classic example of reliance on rule-of-thumb.[55] But the Seger Cone was shortly made available in the Potteries, imported by Harrison & Son Ltd. of Hanley, manufacturers and suppliers of colours, glazes, enamels, lithographic prints and flint and stone. Given the claim that they held 'large stocks always ready for prompt delivery', we may presume that the cones were not only available but also used.[56] In a parallel but reverse trend, German manufacturers were continuing to recruit important personnel from the Potteries at the turn of the century.[57] Moreover, we have already seen that technical education was not so readily accepted by all German manufacturers as later propaganda has sometimes suggested.

Perhaps most important were the perceptions of foreign competitors prevalent in the Potteries. We saw in the last chapter that commentators frequently stressed the modernity of Continental firms and the strengths this gave them in markets for cheap mass produced goods, exactly the markets where Staffordshire's reputation for quality and differentiation counted for least. However, this was just one side of the picture. Other commentators felt there were sufficient grounds for declaring that; 'The cry of German competition would have sufficed for an

---

52 Reporting on the contrasting fortunes of two German firms, *The Pottery Gazette* argued that 'the reasons were not really far to seek – the one was working on an economical and thrifty concern, the other was hard put to it to keep up an old and ill-arranged concern afloat. Abroad, as at home, those concerns which are most fully equipped with labour-saving devices, or which are looked after personally by thoroughly capable and saving men, are the last to feel the pressure'. *The Pottery Gazette*, January 1901, p. 62.

53 Stratton, 'Technological Development', p. 674.

54 Ibid., p. 666.

55 In a parallel example, at Sheffield steel firms 'rule of thumb methods enabled workers "to determine when the steel was satisfactory and to judge the carbon content and hardness of a fractured ingot ... simply by looking at it"'. Lloyd-Jones and Lewis, *British Industrial Capitalism*, p. 115.

56 *The Pottery Gazette*, February 1901, p. 221.

57 *The Pottery Gazette*, January 1901, p. 63. Ceramists and chemists were also far from unknown in the Potteries

explanation [of depression] at one time, but it is not good enough now. German earthenware at least is not a very dangerous competitor in our own country, whatever it may ... be in some of the cheaper foreign markets'.[58] A very similar judgement was offered in an article, entitled 'Germany Over-Estimated', which argued that:

> Germany is making enormous strides, and notably in those manufactures in which superior knowledge, technical skill, and the agency of the expert in chemistry or other sciences can be brought to bear. We fail, however, to see that there is anything in this policy of Germany to give occasion for alarm to the British producer.[59]

The clear inference was that pottery was not an industry in which either 'technical skill' or the 'expert in chemistry' played any really decisive role. Certainly, it would have been difficult to find in the Potteries of the 1890s many who would have agreed with Stratton's claim, made in the 1930s, that pottery was 'an industry which severely penalizes' rule-of-thumb methods.[60]

Less important than the validity of these assessments is the basis on which they were offered. What they tells us is that, from the perspective of the Potteries, the threat posed by Germany and other competing nations was as yet inchoate, the case for the mass-production and mass-marketing in ceramics essentially unproven and consumer preferences unresolved. Just as new technologies had as yet far from invalidated the old, so the economic foundations of a regime of specialty production did not appear to have been swept away by a tide of cheap, undifferentiated goods. In this uncertain context, it made much sense to adapt new technologies to better expedite existing strategies than to attempt to radically reconfigure the orientation of firms and district. The paradigm outlined above was not obviously made obsolete either by new machines or new competitors.

Moreover, the threat of foreign competition first became apparent during a marked downturn in the business cycle, a downturn severe enough and prolonged enough to register forcefully with manufacturers and to induce considerable uncertainty. This uncertainty not only constrained the investment behaviour of some in the Potteries, it also led to reflection on the impact of mechanization on the balance of supply and demand. For some, mechanization was a potent source of over capacity, placing unwelcome pressure on the structure of the industry. Slowly, it became a 'half-recognised fact that production has outrun consumption, and that at any cost the demand must be increased so as to provide sufficient food for the capacious jaws and stomach of modern machine supported supply'.[61] Thus, whilst:

---

58 *The Pottery Gazette*, November 1893, p. 993–5.

59 *The Pottery Gazette*, February 1897, p. 181.

60 Stratton, 'Technological Development', p. 675.

61 *The Pottery Gazette*, July 1899, p. 833.

> it is probable that there are sufficient pottery operatives, enough works and ample machinery and material to turn out fifty per cent more crockery ... yet the moment an exceptional and temporary demand arises new works are put in hand, new machinery laid down and foolish and unnecessary capital sunk, which hangs like an Old Man of the sea round the neck of the trade when things return to their wonted level.[62]

Mechanization thus appeared to exacerbate the problems of overcapacity caused by the ease with which the industry could be entered.

But if mechanization, through the levers of over capacity, higher volumes and lower margins, was eventually to force a period of restructuring on the industry, had a fragmented, small-scale structure previously inhibited the innovation and diffusion of new technologies in the Potteries? That is certainly the charge levelled by Chandler, Elbaum and Lazonick against British manufacturing industry generally in this period.

Lazonick and his associates equate economic development with 'effort-saving technological change' and its utilization, in part through 'processes of ... organisational innovation'. Thus, they argue that in a number of British manufacturing sectors a 'fragmented industrial structure' imposed 'organisational constraints on the development and utilisation' of new technologies.[63] In particular, market co-ordinated structures of 'vertically specialised firms' tended to become locked into a reliance on 'traditional technologies', systemically inhibited from realising the advantages of newer, high-throughput technologies.[64] But the pottery industry was not vertically specialized to a significant degree. Manufacturers in the Potteries did not face the problems of co-ordination imposed on Lancashire by the historic separation of spinning and weaving. Any issues of co-ordination that followed on from greater mechanization, and there certainly were some, were largely internal to firms.

Nonetheless, Lazonick *et al.*, though concentrating more on the structure of industries than the size of individual firms, do also emphasize the 'number of firms competing with each other at each vertical level'.[65] Horizontal competition imposes not problems of co-ordination but of uncertainty, creating disincentives to capital investment. Thus, from a Chandlerian perspective, the fragmented nature of British manufacturing industry in this period was intimately bound up with its small scale relative to competing nations, and America in particular. In

---

[62] Ibid., p. 833. Other ill effects were attributed by some to machinery. It was observed, for example that, 'it appears strange ... that the cheapening of production by the introduction of machinery should have the effect of decreasing profit. Such, however, has undoubtedly been the case'. *The Pottery Gazette*, January 1893, p. 49.

[63] Mass and Lazonick, 'The British Cotton Industry and International Competitive Advantage', p. 9, p. 26 and p. 51.

[64] Ibid., p. 51.

[65] Ibid., p. 50.

America, by way of contrast, the growth of firms and of their organizational and technological complexity was associated with the emergence of oligopolistic market structures. Certainly, horizontal competition was intense among the more than two hundred firms located in the Potteries. Did horizontal fragmentation impose then a constraint on the more complete diffusion of new technologies? In order to address this issue it is necessary to note that the Chandlerian critique, with its strong emphasis on internal economies of scale, is of most relevance where technological changes clearly dictated that individual firms achieve interdependent step changes in their levels of throughput, market-share, capital intensiveness and size, leading to oligopolistic competitive environments. To that extent Chandler's work is technologically determinist and of limited relevance in the context of the Potteries, where the technological processes being diffused in the late nineteenth did not mandate any such epochal break with established structures and strategies. A perspective on the path-dependency of technological change casts a subtler light on these issues than the Chandlerian narrative, which is essentially one of entrepreneurial failure, of the failure to recognize the potentialities embodied in new technologies.

Eventually, the continuous or tunnel kiln was to usher in and hasten far more radical change in the structures of both pottery firms and pottery industries around the world. H.J. Stratton enumerated the reasons why the tunnel kiln was so slow to diffuse in America despite the cost savings it offered. First, tunnels kilns were far more costly to build than conventional bottle kilns. Second, 'its large capacity ... robs it of flexibility and makes it unfit for a small pottery with a fluctuating output. ... potential savings will go unrealized if the kiln is not kept constantly in operation'.[66] Third, it involved changes in firing methods beyond the reach of the stock of technological knowledge possessed by most firms and manufacturers. Finally, Stratton was convinced by 'strong evidence of technological laggardness, in the absence of which the foregoing difficulties would have been overcome long since'. His conclusion was that, almost wholly through the agency of this technological development, 'the small pottery appears to be doomed ... Most of the picturesque processes of manufacture and the medieval managerial attitudes will not survive the change'.[67] This analysis serves equally well in the context of an exploration of the impact the kiln would eventually have on the British industry. However, despite being experimented with throughout the nineteenth century, the tunnel kiln was everywhere a child of the mid-twentieth century.[68]

---

[66] Stratton, 'Technological Development', p. 673.

[67] Ibid., p. 673–4 & p. 675–6.

[68] In a study of the pottery conducted by B.R. Williams in 1958, considerable emphasis was again place on the importance of the tunnel kiln. Williams argued that 'the new methods of production have given a greater incentive to apply principles of costing and flow production. With adequate costing there is a tendency to reduce the number of shapes and decorations in production at any one time. This increased standardization is likely to bring a much greater

Mechanization, men and work

A broad outline of the progress of mechanization in the North Staffordshire pottery in the late nineteenth century has now been sketched and the forces shaping that pattern introduced. In particular, it has been argued that a version of the notion of path-dependency, elaborated to establish its cultural and spatial dimensions and the inter-relatedness of technological and strategic frames of references, is best able to illuminate innovatory process in the Potteries. These arguments may be strengthened by an examination in detail of the impact of mechanization on existing working environments and practices. The process of integration was characterized more by compromise between manufacturer and worker than by conflict and was both a further cause and a significant outcome of prolonged and uneven patterns of diffusion. In essence, a very gradual process of mechanization created a self-reinforcing mechanism, a negative feedback, which limited the impact of those process innovations that were made by firms.

Evidence as to the actual impact of mechanization on the cost structures of firms in the industry in this period is limited and ambiguous. Moreover, contemporaries argued fiercely over the impact of mechanization, and these arguments occurred not only between capital and labour but also within capital. Typical was the observation, made in 1893, that, 'It may be fairly questioned, however, whether having abandoned our old methods we have made the best of the new ... Having sacrificed so much for the cheapness of production, have we made-too little - or too much - of all or any of our new devices'.[69]

Evidence presented at the important wage arbitration of 1879 allows these doubts to be seen more clearly. Certainly, this evidence suggests mechanization could improve the earning potential of workers. Manufacturers argued, in the words of Pinder, Bourne & Co., that through mechanization 'the masters were put to a very large outlay, and the men ... much more benefited by it that they were'.[70] This claim finds some support in average net earning figures compiled in 1881. These data suggested that hollow ware pressers earned on average £1 13s 7d per week and hollow ware pressers working with jiggers £2 8s.[71] Behind

---

attention to selling what is produced, rather than to producing whatever distributors ask for ... (and) greater attention to economies that can be achieved from long-runs on a few lines'. B.R. Williams, 'The Pottery Industry', in D. Burn, *The Structure of British Industry: A* Symposium (Cambridge, Cambridge University Press, 1958), p. 325 and p. 320. See also Blaszczyk, '"Reign of the Robots"'.

[69] *The Pottery Gazette*, November 1893, p. 999.

[70] *The Pottery Gazette*, December 1879, p. 472. Pinder claimed that the introduction of the jolly by his firm in 1874 had led to a 'very large rise of 6s 7d, or over twenty five per cent' in weekly wages for plate makers. Similarly, at the arbitration of 1880 E.J. Baxter of the large Hanley firm of Clementson Bros., claimed that the 'new modes introduced had been of service to the workmen and with machinery they could get more money that they could under the old system'. *The Pottery Gazette*, December 1880, p. 794.

[71] *The Pottery Gazette*, January 1882, p. 57.

this difference in net earnings lay differential rates of pay for hand and machine assisted labour. At Wedgwood, for example, the piece rates in 1880 for making a 7" muffin, a small plate, were 2s 6d by hand, 2s by hand jolly and 1s 10d by steam powered jolly.[72] Though the unions vociferously disputed the manufacturers' claims that workers could earn more on machines, it is clear that mechanization had at least the potential to increase the productivity of labour and to reduce unit costs.[73] Thus, the report of the *Truck Act Committee* of 1908 stated unequivocally that in the pottery industry mechanization had given 'the worker increased power of production'. This conclusion was based largely on the evidence of J.A. Redgrave, H.M. Superintending Inspector of Factories, who, pressed on the basis for and implications of differential rates of pay for hand and machine work, answered thus:

> Question 659: What we are anxious about is the comparison. Take the manual worker first of all? - His out put is less.
> Question 660: Then he goes to where there is steam power; his output is more and his piecework is subject to a deduction? - Yes.[74]

Qualified confirmation of this conclusion was supplied by the *Census of Production* of 1907, which estimated that the gross output (by value) per person in potteries with a source of power was £112 p.a. and £88 p.a. in works without a source of power.[75]

However, on their own evidence at least, pottery firms seemed unable to translate this potential for increased productivity and lower unit costs into increased profitability. For, as one manufacturer noted in 1888 there was little or no profit left in the industry, 'not withstanding the existing cheapened modes of production'. As in the Sheffield cutlery trades, the 'question of wages in relation to relative unit costs became of major concern to ... businessmen faced with competitive pressures and falling profit margins.'[76] In order to explore the limited impact of mechanization the notion that the path to mechanization had to be negotiated will be developed, drawing in part on Whipp's concept of the

---

[72] *The Pottery Gazette*, December 1880, p. 794. Also significant of course is the fact that Wedgwoods actually employed all three methods of working in making this one product.

[73] The counter claims of workers and unions were too persistent to be dismissed out of hand. A member of the Hanley lodge of the National Order of Potters wrote to the *Staffordshire Knot* in 1885 to argue that due to mechanization the 'workman was ... required to sacrifice a part of his wages to defray the cost of working machinery that was ... the employers' own property, instituted with the express intention of cheapening production and without perceptibly increasing the workman's earnings'. Reprinted in the *Pottery Gazette*, May 1885, p. 559.

[74] *Truck Acts*, Vol. 1, p. 42 & p. 39.

[75] *Census of Production in the United Kingdom, 1907: Final Report*, p. 751. It must be remembered however that the presence of a power source says very little about the processes and machines in use in a works.

[76] *The Pottery Gazette*, February 1888, p. 227; Lewis, *Growth and Development*, p. 88.

'recomposition of skill across time', but also considering issues of business strategy and business culture.[77] These tools will be used to reconstruct the positions from which workers and manufacturers entered into both specific and more generalized processes of negotiation over mechanization.

First, both employers and employees, encouraged by the gradual way in which mechanization had occurred, consistently sought to minimize any resultant disruption. Though capital and labour sought to preserve different things from disruption, the net effect was to allow the survival after mechanization of long established work practices and arcane and complex systems of payment.[78] New machines and techniques had to adapt themselves to the rhythm of existing practices and workforces rather than vice versa. Second, and closely related in origin and effect, the unfolding pattern of mechanization did little to alter the composition of the workforce. In particular, manufacturers were afforded little scope for replacing skilled and highly paid male labour with cheaper semi and unskilled labour, particularly that of adult females and male and female adolescents.

Third, because mechanization tended to be uneven within individual firms and impacted with varying weight upon different elements of the production process, it rarely improved throughput, even where that was the aim of its introduction. Indeed, mechanization was often as likely to cause bottlenecks as to eliminate them. Moreover, because the jigger and jolly, even when steam powered, could be employed as the basis for either batch or throughput production, economies of scale were made yet less likely when such machines were introduced in a piecemeal fashion into the established resource bases, organizational structures and market-orientations of firms. Finally, in the increasingly competitive environment of the 1880s and 1890s, a potential reduction in the cost of production was often seized as an opportunity to enlarge (or simply maintain) market share through price-cutting. Indeed, mechanization was seen as further complicating the balance between capacity, demand and price, already disturbed by the rise of foreign competition. However, overarching all of these constraining

---

[77] Whipp, *Patterns of Labour*, p. 4. Indeed, generally, Whipp places considerable emphasis on worker autonomy in the pottery industry, identifying a 'constant interplay between the abilities of owners to define, demonstrate and control the nature of a job or task in detail', and concludes that the industry does not fit models of 'the capitalist labour process involving the necessary degradation and homogenisation of labour'. Ibid., p. 4 and p.22.

[78] An important comparata is supplied by Joyce's work on differeing textile regimes in Lancashire and West Yorkshire. In West Yorkshire, as in the Potteries, an industry possessing a small-scale and fragmented business structure began to mechanize in the late nineteenth century and exhibited a 'unique prolongation of the craft relationship between master and man ... gradual mechanisation and the intimate nature of the local valley life' ensured that 'the modern factory inherited many of the characteristics of the social relations of small-scale and quasi-craft production'. P. Joyce, *Work, Society and Politics: The Culture of the Factory in later Victorian England* (London, Methuen, 1982), p. 166–7.

factors, conditioning even the extent to which they were identified as imposing constraints, were the cultural attributes of both workers and manufacturers.

Mechanization must be seen as far more than a narrow technical issue dependent on the progressive solution of a series of technological blockages. An indication of the breadth of the concerns aroused by mechanization is contained in the belief that 'just as machinery has crushed, and is crushing the skilled artisan, so it is crushing out the small manufacturer'.[79] Thus, mechanization was understood to hold implications not only for the classes of skilled labour most directly affected but also for the organizational structures, principles and even existence of firms, of classes of capital and, perhaps more distantly, for the structure of the industry as a whole. These realizations hung over manufacturers as they moved, however hesitantly, towards mechanization. Their responses were determined, as we have already argued in general terms, by two broad forces; that is by the existing resources, structures and strategies of their firms and by the business culture(s) of both firm and district. These claims will now be examined in more detail and related to the internal workings of firms.

With regard to the first of these factors, the typical organizational structure of firms in the industry, that is independent personal capitalism, was supported, to a very large degree, by existing work practices. Those practices were, in turn, rooted in the human resource endowments of the district. Both owner/managers and workers, through what may be termed the demography of work in the Potteries, possessed particular, closely overlapping and complementary bodies of knowledge and skill that were highly specific to existing practices. Moreover, due to the prolonged clustering of the industry, these attributes were highly generalized or thickly supplied throughout the district. In turn, further characteristics of the workforce, not only its skills but also the ways in which it was recruited, trained and disciplined enabled management to stay very light, both in terms of size and intervention. This promoted the retention of the personal capitalism in which the small-scale business structure of the industry was rooted.

Thus, the highly sub-divided yet vertically integrated production process of pottery manufacture had not led to the evolution of correspondingly sophisticated management structures marked by division and specialization.[80] Instead, the

---

[79] *The Pottery Gazette*, May 1899, p. 552.

[80] In a typical partnership one partner would be responsible for production issues and the other for commercial aspects. In small-scale firms such arrangements probably often represented the full extent of the management. In medium-sized firms similar structures would again have predominated, though perhaps supported by a small clerical staff. Only in the very largest firms did a notably larger management structure displaying some divorce from ownership emerge, but even this was limited. At Mintons, for example, there were in the 1880s four non-family managers. These structures were reflected in demographic data. The 1871 Census for Burslem, the location of many firms, some of them large, records a total of 160 clerks and fifty one managers, a proportion of whom must have worked in other industries, including the important transport and retail sectors. Similarly, the Census of Production of 1907 enumerated 3862 salaried

division of labour had encouraged gang-working, sub-contracting and an important role for the family in the recruitment, training and disciplining of the workforce, explored in depth by Whipp and Dupree.[81] Through these systems much of the day-to-day regulation of work, particularly its pace, was allowed to reside in the hands of key workers.[82]

Through these practices, management responsibility for supervision and discipline was lessened, potbanks being described in 1908 as 'places by themselves with hardly any supervision ... the ordinary discipline of the factory or the machine shop is not brought to bear on them'.[83] At the same time, the payment system known as good from oven shifted much of the onus, and also the financial penalties, for the vital issue of quality control onto key workers.[84] The result was that, as Whipp asserts, 'workgroup independence ... was strong', and that 'Owners were generally tolerant of workgroup identity ... Workgroup employment lifted the burden of detailed management of production off the shoulders of the owner'.[85]

In turn, the Potteries to a considerable degree bucked Garside and Gospel's contention that 'the importance of subcontracting began to decline from the late nineteenth century onwards' under the impetus of factors that included foreign competition and the concomitant need to introduce 'new machines and methods of working' requiring 'more direct forms of management'.[86] This array of priorities and practical realities does much to explain why owners were often, at best ambivalent about technological developments likely to undermine existing practices and thus to create demands on management beyond the scope of

workers in the ceramic industries, 5.7 per cent of a total workforce of 68,186. It cannot be assumed that all salaried workers occupied management positions.

81 Whipp, *Patterns of Labour*; idem., '"The Art of Good Management": Managerial Control of Work in the British Pottery Industry, 1900-1925', *International Review of Social History*, Vol. 29, Pt. 3 (1984), pp. 359–85; Dupree, *Family Structure*

82 William Burton, in his evidence to the *Truck Acts Committee*, said of the head slipman, 'when you have a man in that position you do your best to keep him ... because so much depends on him'. *Final Report*, Vol. 3, p. 275.

83 Whipp, *Patterns of Labour*, p. 55.

84 'Good from Oven', whereby central pieceworkers, e.g. throwers, pressers and those operating jiggers and jollies, were only paid for their work if the wares emerged as 'firsts' from firing, a stage of the process over which they had no control, was a source of controversy in the industry throughout the nineteenth century. In 1872 Mintons became the first to abandon the practice, instituting payment by 'good from hand'. Very few firms followed their lead, however, and at the Martinmas negotiations of the same year the manufacturers announced a lockout and submitted the issue to arbitration, a process decided in their favour by umpire T. H. Davenport. The policy was again the cause of a trade dispute in 1908 and was not finally abolished until 1919. Burchill and Ross, *A History*.

85 Whipp, *Patterns of Labour*, p. 66.

86 W. Garside and H. Gospel, 'Employers and Managers: Their Organizational Structure and Changing Industrial Strategies' in C. Wrigley (ed.), *A History of British Industrial Relations, 1875–1914* (Brighton, Harvester, 1982), p. 102.

traditional organizational structures and the resources of family firms and partnerships. Examples close at hand appeared to bear out this threat. For example, a manufacturer noted in 1888 how 'Many of the great houses of this trade have laid down a large amount of capital in alterations, machinery etc. ... The conditions resulting from these changes entail a considerable outlay in management expenses'. As a warning the writer served up the example of the long-established and prestigious firm of Davenports, whose 'burdens in large capital and ... great cost of management have killed them'.[87] Little matter that the firm was more likely killed by the incompetence of its management, a horror of overweening and expensive bureaucracies was real enough. Moreover, interlinked systems of management and labour were resistant to change, the complex nature of the industry being, as Lewis has observed of the Sheffield cutlery trades, 'deeply entrenched in the economic and social relations between capital and labour'.[88]

However, this suspicion of, or even opposition to, the emergence of professional managers, paralleling resistance to the employment of trained chemists and other technologists, arose not simply out of practical issues or the inertia of established institutions but also had a cultural dimension. That is, it was not only that change was feared but also that the status quo was positively valued. First, manufacturers valued the status associated with independent ownership, not only for themselves but also for their family, past, present and future, for whom the firm was, in some sense, held in trust. Manufacturers had to negotiate not only with the workforce during the process of mechanization but also with themselves over their priorities. Thus, a natural uncertainty over the new demands that mechanization might place on management was reinforced by a common antipathy to the encroachment of 'black cloth uselessness' on the domain of personal capitalism.[89]

Buttressed by the tenets of populist laissez-faire political economy, the value placed on independent manufacture bore a distinctly moral quality. One example in the trade press, entitled 'Small Factories', argued that:

> The most healthy form of work is what a man does on his own responsibility. The deposition of the handloom by steam power has lessened the number of master and increased the number of servants in an inordinate degree; a few big heads and a multitude of weak "hands" are the order of the day. Monster mills and gigantic concerns threaten to dissipate the useful middle classes of comfortable and independent men.[90]

---

87 'The Condition of the Potting trade', *The Pottery Gazette*, 1888, p. 227.

88 Lewis, *Growth and Development*, p.94.

89 'Failures in the Potting Trade', *The Pottery Gazette*, March 1893, p. 251. This correspondent too felt that redundant layers of management 'must be nearly wiped off the face of the ... industry'. Ibid., p. 251.

90 'Small Factories', *The Pottery Gazette*, November 1889, p. 735.

Equally, many feared the 'degrading' impact of mechanization on the quality of the wares made in Staffordshire. To make good wares was perhaps as important as independence.[91] Thus, manufactures had to uphold not only their own reputations but also that of the district and dialogue had to be entered into over the values, priorities and traditions of the district. The Potteries industrial district was not only a locus of exchange and transactions but also of tradition, reputation and assumed common understandings.[92] We will have occasion in this work to question the strength and homogeneity of those forces, but there is no doubt that they existed and played a central role in generating powerful notions of a legitimate and, conversely, an illegitimate trade. In this framework, the most deleterious actions were those which undermined reputations for quality. These notions applied not only to specific instances of opportunism but to actions damaging to the industry as a whole. In turn, these frameworks informed attitudes towards mechanization; which ranged from the pessimistic, 'there are many articles of pottery which it is almost impossible to make except by the handlabour of the hollow-ware presser', to the plainly hostile, 'the future of English pottery rests with the artisan, for whilst machinery has done much, and will do more, there will always be pottery demanded that only the ... workman can supply ... which must maintain the prestige of our manufacture'.[93]

There was much in common in the attitudes of labour and employers towards mechanization in the Potteries. Workers too feared the loss of status independence, reputation and skills, of which they believed themselves, with considerable legitimacy, to be the custodians. It was these attributes that they sought to defend, as far as possible, from the slowly encroaching tide of mechanization. It was vital to the central and most powerful of the unions of the Potteries, fragmented along craft lines, that craft status and high levels of pay be maintained in the face of new processes and technologies. So, whilst outright opposition to new modes of production was rarely mounted after the 1870s,

---

[91] Some manufacturers seem, by the turn of the century, to have believed that years of competition and mechanization had borne fruit in the form of an inferior workforce. Enoch Massey, for example, told the Tariff Commission that 'The English workman leads all workmen in pottery, there is no doubt about it, though at present he is deteriorating; he is getting into a careless, slipshod method of working owing to the depression in the trade which somehow reaches the man'. *Tariff Commission*, para. 126.

[92] Blaszczyk provides an interesting inverse example, where a lack of commitment to a district helped propel innovation. At the Homer Laughlin China Co., the Aarons, Pittsburgh financiers made a big difference; 'Whereas many pottery owners never looked beyond the boundaries of East Liverpool for solutions to managerial and technical problems, the Aarons, with their ties to a wider midwestern manufacturing district, abandoned this parochialism. Instead, they searched broadly through American business practice, selectively adapting modern manufacturing methods-including those pioneered by big businesses', Blaszczyk, '"Reign of the Robots"', p. 870.

[93] *The Pottery Gazette*, August 1892, p. 718; *The Pottery Gazette*, November 1886, p. 6.

unions were concerned to defend both their ability to regulate some aspects of work and to ensure that workers were not disadvantaged by the type of plant with which they worked. Thus, the uneven mechanization of the industry provided a powerful spur for the unions to bargain aggressively in the interest of achieving parity for members working in different firms and under very varied conditions. It had, for example, been noted in 1880 that:

> There are large firms in the Potteries where there is every necessary mechanical appliance ... Exactly the same wages are paid ... to workmen on such a 'bank' as are paid to employees of other firms where there are not all the improvements of modern machinery introduced, and where all sorts of circumstances render it impossible for the men to do so large an amount of work. Thus one industrious man may get several shillings less than other industrious man.[94]

Thus, when proprietors committed and attached to the managerial structures and strategies outlined above met with determined trade unions, both often made compromises designed to ensure the continuation of practices dating back a century or more. Management in the Potteries, as in the Sheffield cutlery trades, 'saw the long-standing tradition of piece rates and related deductions for power and rent as conducive to the resource base of the firm', a resource base which typically encouraged firms in both industries to compete on the basis of quality, differentiation and scope.[95]

This is a salient point, for it suggests that the stance of managers and owners cannot be condemned as merely idiosyncratic or arbitrary but must be understood as reflecting, in part at least, an appreciation of Staffordshire's genuine strengths. Those strengths were dependent on the relationship between skill and product diversity. The point is reinforced by comparison with the Homer Laughlin China Company, in the mid-twentieth century America's largest and most technologically sophisticated pottery firm. At Homer Laughlin, Joseph M. Wells, a perceptive admirer of the industry in Staffordshire, whilst instigating dramatic technological innovations, recognized that 'preserving certain British pottery traditions went hand in hand with the decision to preserve [the firms] diversified customer base'.[96] As the trade press warned the industry in starker terms, many of

---

94 *The Pottery Gazette*, January 1880, p. 35.

95 Lewis, *Growth and Development*, p. 109. The parallels between Sheffield and the Potteries are strong with regard to mechanization. Indeed, the *Truck Acts Committee* deliberately and explicitly discussed the two district in tandem, because the 'origin and growth' of these trades was 'an interesting chapter in industrial history' displaying many similarities. Both industries were 'Originally ... handicraft trades, practised by the workers in their homes or in separate tenements'. *Truck Acts*, Vol. 1, p. 42.

96 Blaszczyk, '"Reign of the Robots"', p. 906. Blaszczyk concludes that the Homer Laughlin example 'suggests that the models of batch production and mass production are not

the districts capabilities might be eroded by an 'excessive' mechanization, or that through mechanization 'the inherited and acquired skill of the English operative, which used to be reckoned our main advantage over other potters, now counts for nothing. The inevitableness of it should not be allowed to hide from us this important fact'.[97]

It is now possible to examine in detail the transition to machine work in the Potteries and to suggest how the path traced above circumscribed mechanization as a cost-reducing measure. Crucial to this issue is the concept of continuity, introduced to the *Truck Act Committee* of 1908 by factory inspector Redgrave:

> Question 675: As you have explained the system it is to a considerable extent ... a survival? - It is a survival of the old system when a man took his gang of boys and girls and his candle to the potbank; he took a lump sum and paid his boys and girls and paid for his candle and everything. Now these things are provided for him, and he gets what the workmen themselves have accepted as the equivalent.[98]

W.H. Burton reiterated the point, with specific reference to the introduction of new methods and machines:

> The consequence [of slow mechanization] is that the method of payment, which has remained unchanged for about a century and a half, has been adjusted in this way, that whenever a fresh method, or a fresh process, or even a fresh method of employment, has been introduced, instead of making it there and then a question of wages the manufacturers and operatives have agreed that the former should make a deduction for whatever new process or method of work was introduced.[99]

The institutions of labour relations thus displayed considerable rigidity, and such was the power of the trend to compromise that even entirely new tasks were accorded a position within the old piece rate payment systems. Elements of this rigidity were drawn out in the summation of the *Committee*. Some issues were remarkably prosaic:

> A revision of the piece-rates would be inconvenient. Many of the piece-rates did not lend themselves readily to alteration, dealing as they did with fractional sums ... the system of making fixed deductions accordingly sprang up as the most convenient was by which to arrive at a fair

exclusive categories', a valuable insight when charting the strategies steered by some firms in Staffordshire. Ibid., p. 911.

[97] *The Pottery Gazette*, May 1888, p. 430: *The Pottery Gazette*, March 1896, p. 211.

[98] *Truck Acts*, Vol. 1, p. 40.

[99] Ibid., p. 42.

> equivalent for the facilities provided by the employer which the workman had previously to provide for himself.[100]

It was also felt that 'attempts to revise rates might have involved disputes between master and man'. Furthermore, as well as trying to avoid costly disputes, manufacturers no doubt also saw maintenance of the system of deductions as a means by which to shift some of the capital costs of mechanization onto labour. Even the pro-capital trade press noted of the introduction of batting machines, which displaced unskilled labour previously employed under sub-contracting arrangements, that; 'the cost is so little that a very small percentage of the price paid for the work would have compensated for the price of the machine. But instead of adopting this reasonable course, reductions have been made by some manufacturers ... that will pay for the cost of the machine in a few months'.[101]

Moreover, the process by which adjustment and deductions were arrived at involved a tortuous degree of repetition, for 'localised and informal bargaining was widespread and almost certainly the most common means of experiencing industrial relations for a potter'.[102] As the trade press noted in 1900; 'there is probably no industry in the world so concentrated, and yet so chaotic in respect to prices and customs'.[103] Clustering, it seems, did little to salve the effects of a fragmentation that inhibited the resolution of these fundamental problems.

Equivalence, a word alighted upon by Redgrave in 1908, was the core ideal striven for in negotiating these difficult transitions. Piece rates in the Potteries were paid according to 'counts' of ware, either of 'dozens' or 'scores'. A dozen, though, rarely comprised twelve pieces of ware or a score twenty. Each of the many different products made by most firms, and the different sizes in which most products were in turn made, were paid for according to different counts. Thus, for a very large and complex piece a dozen, the 'count' by which the worker was paid, might consist of only a single piece, for a small simple item however a dozen could total many more than twelve pieces. Thus, there was a multiplicity of different piece rates, reflecting the large and diverse product ranges produced by most factories and their commitment to serving highly differentiated markets and customers. As a further complication, piece rates were very frequently, as we have seen, not round, easily computed sums.

These varied counts and their associated rates had grown out of the need to express in monetary terms the two primary characteristics of work in the pottery industry; skill and sheer physical labour. Many jobs required both great dexterity and judgement and very considerable muscular strength and endurance under difficult conditions. Whilst it is clear that few tasks within the industry were entirely revolutionized through mechanization during this period it is also clear

100 Ibid., p. 42.

101 *The Pottery Gazette*, May 1885, p. 559.

102 Whipp, *Patterns of Labour*, p. 147.

103 *The Pottery Gazette*, May 1890, p. 557.

that the skill levels and effort demanded by many tasks were altered by innovatory machines and techniques. Yet the core ideal of equivalence ensured that both methods and levels of payment continued to be derived from assessments of the levels of skill and effort involved that were very long-established, arrived at under different conditions and increasingly anachronistic.

It was in this way that control over and the realism of the relationship between labour and reward under new modes of working or with new technologies became lost and blurred to both master and man. Though a general judgement is and was difficult, because of the fragmented nature of both payment and negotiation systems in the Potteries, it is probable that in many cases not only the net wages that key workers were able to earn but also the contribution of wages to unit cost were thus maintained after mechanization.

The survival of payments inappropriate in both the method by which they were calculated and the actual levels at which they were set was largely due to the gradual nature of mechanization, continually postponing confrontation with the question of the implications mechanization held for the skill, status, effort and reward of workers. Moreover, this postponement occurred in the context of interdependent institutions, within both capital and labour, displaying deep-rooted cultural bonds to the status quo. These arguments clearly relate to and deepen the notion of path-dependency, but they also warn that it is a tool for explaining rather than exonerating actions. These were outcomes that, with hindsight, were clearly imperfect, if unintended.

The gradual and partial progress of mechanization had also tended to minimize alterations to the composition of the workforce. Skilled male labour remained in place in the clay shops where wares were formed. In those shops, unlike in some aspects of decorating, there was no real 'process of deskilling [that] went hand in hand with the introduction of a gendered division of labour'.[104] A fundamentally unreconstituted workforce also reinforced the technological barriers to realizing reduced unit costs outlined earlier.

Mechanization did not lead to a reconstitution the workforce in the Potteries for two broad reasons. Firstly, extending to different departments to varying degree and with varying speed, mechanization did little to re-order the sub-divided work process in which the traditional and highly hierarchical workgroup consciousness of working potters was embedded. Though some of its content had changed the basic organization of work, and much of its detail, remained relatively unscathed, as did, at its centre, the gang, often based in kinship networks and with the skilled male at its head.[105] As Burton admitted in 1908, the sub-employment of family members was 'very often the case to this day'.[106]

---

[104] R.L. Blaszczyk, 'The Aesthetic Moment: China Decorators, Consumer Demand and Technological Change in the American Pottery Industry, 1865-1900', *The Winterthur Portfolio*, Vol. 29 (1994), p. 138.

[105] See Joyce, *Work, Society and Politics* and Whipp, *Patterns of Labour*.

[106] *Truck Acts*, Vol. 1, p. 42.

Moreover, it was not only the position of groups or classes within labour that remained unchanged after mechanization but also that of specific individuals. Reflection makes it clear that the system of deductions examined above had sprung up for the very reason that the same operative was in place before and after the introduction of jiggers, for example, and demanding compensation. Details of an important court case demonstrate the extent to which the stance adopted by workers were by shaped by more than simple straightforward economic rationales. The case between Frederick Chesters and the firm of W.H. Grindley of Tunstall was described as 'an important decision affecting potters' and occurred because:

> At the time [employment] contract was entered into, all the work done by the flatpressers was by hand ... the plaintiff worked for the defendants until September 20, 1882, when the latter substituted steam machinery for hand work and gave notice ... that he would be required as a flat presser to work by steam machinery at certain rates. The plaintiff refused ... whereupon the defendant refused to find him work by hand, having, in fact, none to give him.

The judge found in favour of the plaintiff, but noted that 'although the prices for working by ... machinery were less, the amount of work which could be done was greater and therefore it would have been better ... to have accepted the change.[107]

Second, mechanization rarely, if ever, caused real deskilling. Operatives were not turned into mere machine-minders. The persistence of skill justified and aided the actions of the male craft worker in defence of his status against what were viewed as the interdependent threats from mechanization and female labour. Certainly, the substitution of female for male labour was both feared and demonized by the craft unions, which generally excluded women from membership. The following complaint is from 1885:

> On the first acquaintance of resistance on the part of the workman to any injustice offered him, he is told to get another situation, and then the crowning evil is wrought, the girl or woman who formerly was his attendant takes his place at the bench. This great fact cannot be denied, and it is the result of years of scheming and planning on the part machinists and manufacturers for their own special aggrandizement ... it is degrading our handicraft and its workers.[108]

---

[107] *The Pottery Gazette*, January 1883, p. 65.

[108] Member of Hanley Lodge, National Order of Potters, 'Machinery and Its Operation In Potting', Reprinted from the *Staffordshire Knot* in *The Pottery Gazette*, May 1885, p. 559. This piece provoked a stinging rebuke, which began 'I hate all machinery, and would, if I were in the Union, do away with it ... I hate the spade, this is a machine'. The letter was signed 'Idiotic' of Hanwell Lunatic Asylum. *The Pottery Gazette*, June 1885, p. 692.

Manufacturers' motives in replacing male workers with women seemed clear enough; 'there is a great outcry being made against the introduction of further female labour where hitherto males have been employed. The innovation is said to have been made in order to cheapen production'. Clearly innovative resource responses to new competitive challenges need not always involve mechanization.[109] As well as being cheaper (journeywomen were typically paid the rates set for male apprentices), the employment of women had the potential to encourage and facilitate both further mechanization and recomposition of the workforce by weakening the position of the male dominated craft unions.

However, it is far from clear that the claim, made in 1883, that; 'In the potting trade of this district women's labour is superseding the labour of men to an extent unprecedented in the history of the trade' can be uncritically accepted.[110] Though the number of women working in the North Staffordshire pottery industry did increase throughout the second half of the nineteenth century, both absolutely and relatively, the position of women workers is open to some question.

Correlating various estimates of the female proportion of the workforce reveals broad agreement on the direction of this trend. These figures are presented in Table 4.1. The element of fluctuation underlying the slight upward trend is probably realistic, as women's labour, generally occupying a more marginal position than that of men, showed greater responsiveness to trade cycles. That the nineteenth century peak for female employment occurred in the early 1870s is congruent with that supposition. Do these figures, though, tell us anything particularly forceful about the composition of the workforce and its relationship to skill and mechanization. Without more detailed information and analysis it cannot safely be assumed that these increasing numbers of female workers were occupying hitherto more highly paid male positions or that they were more likely to be employed to use innovatory technologies such as the jigger and jolly. Their relationship to and effect on the resource mixes and cost structures of firms is at best uncertain and evidence suggests that direct female for male substitution as a result of mechanization, though not unknown, was limited.

---

109 *The Pottery Gazette*, February 1884, p. 176.

110 *The Pottery Gazette*, June 1883, p. 559. The writer, not a trade unionist, continued; 'such cheapening and degrading of labour has generally the effect of improving the position of capital'.

Table 4.1
Female labour as proportion of total workforce in the North Staffordshire pottery industry

Date	%
1834	37*
1851	36*
1861	31**
1864	38*
1871	40*
1881	38**
1901	44*
1907	41***

Source: * R. Hall, 'Women in the Labour Force: A Case Study of the Potteries in the Nineteenth Century', *Occasional Papers*, No. 27, (Department of Earth Science, Queen Mary College, University of London, 1986); ** J. Sarsby, *Missuses and Mouldrunners: An Oral History of Women Pottery Workers at Work and at Home* (Milton Keynes, Open University Press, 1988); *** *Census of Production* (1907).

Sarsby, following Dupree, is surely right to assert that 'the increase in the proportion of the labour force made up of women and girls in the 1870s ... was related to the Factory Acts, which reduced the availability of child labour', the proportion of child labour in the workforce falling from seventeen per cent in 1861 to twelve per cent in 1871.[111] This suggests that many women entering the industry in the last quarter of the nineteenth century, that is as the jigger and jolly were diffused, did so as assistants to men. Indeed, Sarsby goes so far as to suggest that it was not until the 1870s that 'the stereotype husband and wife-attendant emerged'. For some women, such positions did provide a route to skilled, traditionally male positions, as it had done for male youths in the past. Sarsby provides interesting anecdotal evidence of this process, but her examples date from the period during or after the upheavals of the Great War.[112] Moreover,

[111] J. Sarsby, *Missuses and Mouldrunners: An Oral History of Women Pottery Workers at Work and at Home* (Milton Keynes, Open University Press, 1988), p. 21. Sarsby quotes the Mayor of Hanley, who, in giving evidence before the *Royal Commission on the Working of the Factory and Workshop Act* of 1875, claimed that 'because of the requirements of the Factory Act the supply of boys has been narrowed, and the workmen had been obliged to get female labour'. Ibid., p. 21.

[112] Sarsby, *Missuses and Mouldrunners*, p. 21 and p. 22. It is perhaps also a mistake to assume that women were more docile and compliant workers, or less conscious of craft status and traditions. Sarsby gives the example of a Mrs Gregory, who began her working life in 1929 as a mouldrunner and graduated to bowl-jollying. Mrs Gregory later 'gave up work when her machine was automated; she refused to become, as she put it, "a slave to that machine"'. Ibid., p. 22.

analysis of employment data contained in the Census of Production of 1907 demonstrates the failure of women to rise through the skilled based hierarchy of the pottery firm, as might have occurred if women had begun to colonise in significant numbers previously male sections of the trade from the onset of mechanization in the 1870s. The majority of salaried workers in the industry were shopfloor employees who, through long service and the status that accrued to skill, had risen to privileged supervisory positions.[113] In 1907, women represented a far smaller proportion of these upper echelons of the workforce than they did of the overall workforce. The figures are ten and forty per cent respectively.

Thus, it is hard to conclude that the last quarter of the nineteenth century saw any significant displacement of the male workforce with cheaper female labour working new technologies. Male craft workers had, of course, reason to overstate what they perceived to be a threat to their position in both the factory and the home. Mr Pinder, a manufacturer, had some justification in levelling the charge of hypocrisy at them at the arbitration of 1879, noting that whilst the men now objected to the employment of women 'because it was too hard for them, [they] had not always been so sentimental'.[114]

That the partial and gradual mechanization of the industry may have created new imbalances in the productive process must also be considered in any attempt to assess the nature and effectiveness of the resource responses offered by firms the Potteries to a changing competitive environment. As has already been stressed, varying degrees of mechanization occurred not only between but also within firms. American Consul Schoenhof, for example, discussing 'Improved Methods of Manufacture' in 1886, observed that:

> The works show by their construction, in the additions, annexes etc., that they are of gradual growth. Even the machinery and working methods employed show the gradual growth. Improvements and new appliances, while rapidly introduced now, do not at once displace all old tools. While some remind us of the time of the Pharaohs, others in the same factory bear the stamp of the greatest era of invention and are models of ingenuity. One still sees in the same factory with steam and other appliances of the most improved patters, boys turning the wheel for the potter.[115]

---

[113] *Census of Production*, p. 745. That women in the pottery industry typically left paid employment when starting a family would however also militate against promotion to salaried positions.

[114] *The Pottery Gazette, December* 1879, p. 472. Pinder may well have been thinking of batting out, an extremely laborious task often performed by women and children, in making these comments. Batting machines were at this time progressively replacing manual batting, but whilst these machines could impact on the pace of work performed by skilled males such as flatpressers, they did not impact on his skills.

[115] *The Pottery Gazette*, July 1886, p. 813.

Whilst such situations might in part be explained by the need, given the heterogeneous markets served by the industry, to maintain a core of skilled workers, it is also clearly not indicative of a fully evolved and interlocking mechanization. Some did advocate a more thorough going and rational approach. William Boulton, the potters' engineer, for example, urged in his Catalogue of 1902 that;

> We cannot too strongly emphasize the importance of having a Plant correctly arranged for the production of the best possible goods ... with the utmost economy of power, fuel, and labour. We supply plans of complete plants ... these plans will be suited to the particular circumstances of the case as to site etc., and as a result of our long experience in erecting plants of all sizes, the purchase of our machinery is assured a compact and, at the same time, economical plant.[116]

However, with most new entrants to the industry being small in scale, established firms bearing heavy fixed costs in existing infrastructure and the built environment of the district increasingly crowded, the opportunities Boulton received for building from scratch new and carefully planned works were relatively few. Indeed, most small new firms were only able to enter the industry because of the ready availability for rent of old premises, often vacated by failed firms.

Conclusion

This examination of technological change in the Potteries has highlighted the way in which mechanization was experienced as a gradual, uneven and incomplete process. In part this pattern may be attributed to considerable technical difficulties. However, this can serve only as a partial explanation. Instead, we must look also to the structure of the industry and, more particularly to the existing resources, technologies, strategies and cultures of individual firms and the wider industry. Mechanization was seen to hold unmistakable long-run implication for each of these attributes of the industry, whilst, at the same time, emerging from and being shaped by them. In particular, the organizational principle on which most firms were based, that of personal or familial capitalism was as at 'risk' from an extensive and far-reaching mechanization as skilled hand labour. Aided by the fact that mechanization was driven by a relatively weak technological logic, interdependent processes of technological and institutional change were slow and cautious. At the same time, uncertainty concerning the cost and productivity gains to be had from mechanization fed back into doubts

---

[116] Boulton, *Catalogue*, 1902.

about both its value and wisdom that were rooted in the quasi-craft culture of the industry and district.

However, caution need not equate with conservatism. Instead, it should be acknowledged that attitudes to mechanization in Staffordshire were powerfully shaped by a legitimate assessment of the district's strength relative to its competitors. Moreover, we should not lose sight of the fact that during this period many firms did press forward with a range of resource responses. The years 1870–1914 were the most significant yet in terms of the development of production technology in the industry. Some firms in Staffordshire participated in this wave of change as fully as did those of any other country. This speaks well of the vigour and determination of the entrepreneurs of late nineteenth century Staffordshire. If the business culture and the backgrounds of these men lent to them a certain caution then it also made them defiant in the face of the challenge offered by foreign competition. The trade press was right to note that despite depression; 'wherever we travel in the pottery towns of North Staffordshire we observe alterations ... of old factories, new ones being built and machinery of the newest type being placed. Such actions speak louder than words, and seem to emphasise ... that there is yet a great future before the British potter'.[117] In turn, these changes led many firms to consider other aspects of their organization and business strategy. Most obviously, change in the way products were made pointed to changes in the way that products were sold. It is to this issue that we turn in the next chapter.

---

[117] *The Pottery Gazette*, October 1893, p. 899.

CHAPTER FIVE

Selling the wares

Introduction

Marketing strategies based upon differentiation and focus were generic amongst firms in the Potteries, complementing batch production technologies and strategies, and aligning the region's industry with those specialty sectors surveyed by Scranton.[1] The dimensions along which manufacturers could attempt to distinguish themselves from competitors were numerous, and the scope of the district's productions was immense. Most obviously firms could concentrate on the production of either earthenware or china, but other bodies were also important. These included parian, stonewares, majolica, basalt and jasper. These bodies could be applied to a myriad of products; dinner and dessert services, tea sets, toilet sets, jugs, cheese and fruit dishes, electrical and chemical wares, door furniture, casters, statuary and other ornamental wares, beer sets and mugs and a vast range of trinkets, 'toys' and brooches. Numerous decorating techniques added further variation. In turn, manufacturers could choose to focus on particular geographical markets and, of course, wares were made in varying 'classes', that is to a range of quality standards and prices.

Firms of all sizes, ages and structure exploited these possibilities in the search for a distinctive position in the market place. Thus, Llewellyn Jewitt recorded how J. & G. Vernon Bros., who were in business in Burslem between 1880 and 1889, produced earthenwares specifically for the South American, West Indian and Mediterranean markets.[2] Nor, despite the harsh criticisms aired in the trade press, was quality exclusively the preserve of the largest, oldest and most famous houses. Jewitt, for example, commended F.J. Emery, occupant of the Bleak House Works Burslem from 1880 to 1894, as making 'the higher and better classes of services for exportation to the United States', wares characterized by 'soundness of body and superior quality of glaze'.[3] Even the two very transient firms who occupied the Peel Works, Longton in the 1880s had managed to produce china of 'more than average excellence ... [much] richly gilt'.[4]

---

1 Scranton, *Endless Novelty*.

2 Godden, *Jewitt's Ceramic Art*, p. 27.

3 Ibid., p. 25.

4 Ibid., p. 90.

However, amongst these comments, Jewitt frequently observed that some now forgotten firm made the 'usual' or 'ordinary' classes of wares. Clearly, there was much produced in North Staffordshire that was of no particular note, and some that was poor or shoddy. Thus, we are reminded of Scranton's exploration of the great degree to which such strategies varied in their operationalization and success across and within different specialty sectors. How firms different in terms of their age or size or structure met the conflicting pressures exerted by these marketing strategies, the capabilities they mandated and the rewards with which they met will be the principal themes of this and the following chapter. This chapter will focus on the institutions of marketing and distribution through which marketing strategies were realized and customers reached. The chapter will begin, however, with three brief case studies, fleshing out the complex interactions between district, technology and markets and introducing a discussion of the factors operating to mould, at a generic level, marketing strategies in the Potteries. The following chapter will consider the resources and capabilities demanded by the strategies outlined here. Particularly important in this respect were design capabilities, reflecting the ability of firm and district to generate differentiation as society became increasingly 'aestheticized' and taste democratized.[5]

Three case studies

However, any barriers constraining firms from shaping effective marketing strategies were not binding, and 'some firms proved capable of challenging successfully a given set of constraints'.[6] There were firms in the Potteries able to derive a creative energy from the tension between tradition and change that the industry was experiencing in the late nineteenth century. Their attempts to forge innovative paths in the market place were, though, rarely dependent on organizational change or process innovation.

Taking our cue from Porter's elaboration of three basic generic marketing strategies, differentiation, focus and cost leadership, we can identify an intense degree of differentiation as the aim of the Art or Studio potteries formed by leading firms such as Doulton, Wedgwood and Copeland in the last two decades of the nineteenth century.[7] These studios, often wholly owned by large parent

---

5 Blaszczyk, 'The Aesthetic Moment'.

6 M. Kirby, 'Institutional Rigidities', p. 642.

7 Porter defines differentiation as 'seeking to establish a distinctive product or reputation in the market that will command a premium in the market', *Competitive Strategy*, p. 120. The so-called Studio Pottery movement is closely associated with the later nineteenth century, however firms such as Wedgwood had since the late eighteenth century blended large-scale production of mid-range goods with limited runs of more expensive wares, and even spectacular one-offs, such as the Portland Vase.

companies, produced very low volumes of high quality decorative wares, often drawing their aesthetic inspiration from the latest developments in the art world, Clearly marked as the work of a single, identifiable artist or craft worker, these products were the very antithesis of the mass of common tableware produced in the district and commanded premium prices.[8] Thus, it can be argued that the Studio Potteries sought to exploit a niche market for wares of the very highest quality that was progressively being reinforced by the mechanization of both the domestic and foreign industries.

The appeal that these wares were intended to have may be discerned by a reading of an advertisement of 1886, in which W.T. Copeland and Sons, successors to Josiah Spode, 'the most successful manufacturer of the Japan style of decoration', announced that they:

> continue to produce these Japans from the original pattern books of Spode, and by precisely the same methods as employed by him. These Japans are executed entirely by hand, thus securing the spirit and fancy of the design and brilliance of colour – qualities wanting in the mechanised and heavily tinted copies produced by imitators who print their designs.[9]

This advertisement emphasizes three interlocking attributes that Copelands believed their Japans to possess, and around which they thus oriented their marketing. These attributes were derived from the firm's resources and history. First, the product was explicitly associated with one of the most renowned names in the industry, Spode. Second, the connection to Spode was reinforced by the claim that not only the design of the wares but also their methods of manufacture had remained unaltered, legitimizing Copelands' appropriation and exploitation of the Spode name. Third, emphasis on the importance of continuity with the past is accentuated by advantageous comparison with imitative products made using modern production methods. The claim on Spode's reputation could not be made lightly and required that Copelands possess an appropriate resource base.

Thus, though in control of the firm for over three decades, and successful not only in negotiating the transition from Spode's ownership but also between

[8] Typical was Minton's 'Secessionist Ware'. Designed by Louis Solon and launched in 1902 this range was highly imitative of the work of the Vienna Secessionists, such as painter Gustav Klimt. The Arts and Crafts Movement was another important influence, at least at an aesthetic level, though the trade press was often hostile to other aspects of William Moriss' doctrines. Thus, the *Pottery Gazette* added a fifth 'canon on the hand making of pottery' to those advanced by Morris, suggesting that 'finally, when you have asked for these qualities from the potters, and even, in a very friendly way, boyvotted them a little until you get them, you will of course be prepared to pay a great deal more for your pottery than you do now, even for the rough work you may have to take. I'm sure that won't hurt you, we shall only have to have less and break less and our incomes will be the same'. Clearly, there were limits to the craft culture of the Potteries. *The Pottery Gazette*, March 1883, p. 268.

[9] *The Pottery Gazette*, January 1886, p. 3.

generations within his own family, William Taylor Copeland continued to view the Spode name as having considerable commercial value. However, the production of wares such as the Japans was just one element of a complex strategy reliant on a number of factors that other, particularly younger, firms would find it hard, if not impossible to replicate.[10]

A highly vaunted market position was matched by direct selling methods that protected the firm from both market shocks and district centred labour unrest. At the wage arbitration of 1879, one witness explained why both Mintons and Copelands had not joined other manufacturers seeking a wage reduction. It was claimed that whilst, 'Mintons might sell staple goods, as dinner sets etc., ... these were purchased almost exclusively by the aristocracy; [therefore] their goods did not take the place of other manufacturers in the shops; and Copelands were virtually their own retailers in London'.[11] For both firms, marketing strategies brought a stability that made easier the maintenance of the skilled human resources on which firm and strategy were dependent. This emphasizes some of the ways in which such strategies were embedded in and an expression of the firm's sum of capabilities. The chain of causation suggested in Scranton's observation that 'the choice between variety and volume had strong technical correlates built into the structure of production', is perhaps best viewed as bi-directional.[12]

However, Copeland's production of such exclusive wares took place in the context of a very large firm also doing a volume trade in a wide range of product, particularly useful domestic wares in the firm's own 'ivory body'. Jewitt again effectively conveys the sheer scope of the firm's output:

> Of the productions of this firm it is manifestly impossible to give even a résumé. The bare enumeration of the different articles in porcelain and earthenware would occupy many closely printed pages. For breakfast, dinner, dessert, tea, and toilet services the firm ranked among the very highest in order of merit. Services were produced both in china and earthenware, and in every variety of ornamentation - in china from the simple gold or coloured lines and borders, and in earthenware from the

---

[10] William Taylor Copeland's father, also William, was in partnership with Josiah Spode, whilst W.T. was himself partner to Josiah Spode II from 1824 to 1827 and in 1833 acquired the Spode factory from the executors of Josiah III. The firm initially continued as Copeland and Garrett (late Spode), Copeland's principal traveller having been taken into the partnership, and subsequently as William Copeland (late Spode) between 1847 and 1867, in which year W.T. took in to partnership his four sons, the firm becoming known as W.T. Copeland and Sons. In 1970 the firm reverted to the title of Spode Ltd., under which name it continues to trade from the site of the original factory.

[11] Burchill and Ross, *A History*, p. 127.

[12] Scranton, 'Diversity in Diversity', p. 38.

> commonest printed patterns, to the most profuse and lavish relief and painting.[13]

It is not clear whether the most exclusive products were intended to be profitable in their own right or to function as a form of advertising, reinforcing a firm's reputation monopoly. Nor is it clear that they often yielded significant competitive advantage. Achieving such marked differentiation was costly, even for the largest of firms, and was, by definition, unlikely to generate a significant volume of sales. It will be shown in the next chapter that Mintons often found it hard to make a profit on wares that were expensive to make in terms of both labour and materials. Copelands also appear to have suffered in the difficult conditions of the 1880s and 1890s. The RV of their premises contracted from £1552 to £1000 between 1879 and 1898, though the firm survived and remains an industry leader. Where firms did not have the financial and productive resources available to firms such as Copelands the production of Art pottery could very easily precipitate failure. One such example is that of W.H. Turner, who 'during three years expended £12,000 on the production of art pottery, and to do this had borrowed money from many different people', only to become bankrupt in 1896.[14]

However, whilst it was hard for younger firms to trade on the kind of 'reputation monopoly' conferred by longevity, they were often also less hidebound by tradition, and it proved possible for an enterprising firm to create very different forms of niche market.[15] An excellent example is that of Dunn Bennett and Co., whose success in the late nineteenth century stemmed from the entrepreneurial drive, vision and skills of its founding proprietors and the formulation of a strategy combining both differentiation and focus. This firm, founded in the mid-1870s, had by the turn of the century established a commanding position in the market for specialty wares for hotels, restaurants and other caterers, railway companies and shipping lines. The firm began as a partnership between Thomas Wood Bennett and William Dunn in 1875, in which year Bennett also married Dunn's daughter, Mary. Bennett had previously worked for earthenware manufacturer E.J. Bodley and Sons, whilst Dunn had been in business on his own account at the Boothen Works, Hanley, where the new partnership initially remained. The firm began relatively small, the premises on Brook Street, Hanley having an RV of £217 in 1882. However, the firm prospered and the firm moved to larger premises at the Royal Victoria Works, Burslem in 1886 or 1887. By 1914, the factory's RV stood at £405, reflecting capital investment. The growth of the firm may be attributed not only to interlinked product and marketing innovations, which will be discussed shortly,

---

13 Godden, *Jewitt's Ceramic Art*, p. 110.

14 *The Pottery Gazette*, November 1896, p. 132.

15 Farnie, *The English Cotton Industry*, p. 193–4.

but also to its embeddedness in local networks of kinship. The partnership secured financial backing from Enoch Colclough, uncle to Bennett's wife and member of an ancient potting family. Colclough was a sleeping partner from 1877, became active on the retirement of Dunn in 1900 and was bought out by Bennett in 1905. The business remained an independent family firm until taken over by the Doulton Group in 1968, though Frank Bennett, grandson of the founder, remained Managing Director thereafter.[16]

Success, from the 1880s onwards, was built on simple but effective product innovation combined with carefully targeted marketing and, eventually, forward integration into distribution. In travelling frequently for the firm, particularly in the United States, Bennett noted that heavily used hotelwares quickly developed unsightly chips. A thickened or rolled lip under the rim of plates acted to transfer shocks, and thus also chips, to the back of plates, where they were less visible. The idea was successfully patented and immediately identified by the partners, using their existing knowledge of the market, as having a particular appeal for hoteliers and other institutional caterers. From the 1890s they concentrated exclusively on these markets. Whereas previously their ironstone china had been advertised merely as 'adapted for hotels, restaurants, clubs, public institutions etc.', the firm began to style itself 'Specialists in the manufacture of Crockery ... for Hotels, Clubs, Steamship and Railway Co.s and caterers generally'.[17]

The firm produced a full range of the ceramic goods required by any hotel, catalogues detailed as many 500 products and variants, but the 'Patent Unchippable Surface Plate' formed the bedrock of their trade. The economic benefits to their target customers of harder wearing crockery were obvious and were stressed in advertisements, one catalogue of the early twentieth century claiming a 'saving of fifty per cent'. The firm did not, however, compete on price but on quality, contending that 'We do not profess to sell at the lowest prices; We do however give the best value'. Advertising material also stressed that the plates were of 'smart appearance' and in no way 'heavy or clumsy'. These and other qualities of the firm's products were said to be guaranteed by 'scientific methods of manufacture in which only the very best materials and the most highly skilled workmanship are used', and by a depth of 'experience and enterprise not shown in the same direction by any other firm'.[18]

Again, as at Copelands, pronounced differentiation was being claimed for a product, clearly there could be many different categories of 'exclusivity'. Production of the patent plates, standing at 12,000 units per week in 1895,

---

[16] *Hanley Borough Rate Book*, 1882; *Burslem Borough Rate Book*, 1914; *Keates and Ford's Directory*, 1882; Bennett, *Origins*.

[17] Dunn, Bennett & Co., *Catalogue*, 1890; idem, *Advertisement*, c. 1898–9 (All Dunn Bennett & Co. material held by the Pinfold family)

[18] Ibid., *Advertisements*, c. 1900 and c. 1910.

expanded rapidly, reaching 25,000 units per week in 1898 and 50,000 in the first decade of the new century.[19]

The firm's advertisements offered numerous further inducements to purchase; free samples and quotes, free engraving of copper plate badges so wares could carry the names and livery of hotels and companies, renewal and matching services, and monthly accounts. The firm clearly aimed to provide a quality service alongside a quality product. Sales were increasingly channelled through a showroom established in London c.1890 and, after 1900, through agencies in Australia, Hong Kong, India, Egypt, Italy, South America, New York and Canada. Advertisements frequently carried news of medals won at international exhibitions and specialist catering shows, and testimonials from both customers and trade magazines, such as *The Hotel*, *The Caterer* and *The Caterer and Hotel-keepers Gazette*. The result of this close attention to a defined niche market was considerable customer satisfaction and loyalty, such that one journal declared:

> few firms have deserved so well of the catering trade as Dunn, Bennett and Co. For they have devoted all their time and energies to the trade for many years, and are at present time probably the largest manufacturing firm of chinamen making specially for the Hotel and Restaurant business in the world.[20]

Further product innovations followed, all evidence of the same close attention to the needs of their customers. First, the unchippable surface principle was applied to meat and vegetable dishes, and sunken knobs and handles introduced so that items would 'stack well ... saving considerable storage space, and there are no projections to knock off'. There followed the "Perfecto" Tea and Coffee pot, promised neither to drip nor chip, and the "Safety" Shape Cup and Saucer, designed for ship board use. Finally, in 1900, the firm:

> struck out a new decorative idea by transferring to ... plates hotel views ... A view of the hotel occupies the central portion of the plate, and around the rim is an elegantly designed border in excellent taste. Hotels ordering such specially designed ware secure an advertisement of a rather novel nature.[21]

Not surprisingly, the firm met with imitators and competitors and warned customers to ensure that they were receiving the genuine article, though there is no evidence of legal action being taken in defence of either brand names or patents.

---

[19] Ibid., *Advertisement*, 1898; *Catalogue*, 1910.

[20] Quotation from *The Caterer and Hotel-keeper's Gazette*, 15/5/1909, carried in Dunn, Bennett and Co., *Advertisement*, c. 1910.

[21] Ibid.

Dunn, Bennett and Co. represent a very successful example of niche marketing, but there is reason to consider them exceptional. Whilst there remained much scope for process innovation in the pottery industry, distinctive product innovations of the kind on which this firm was built, embodying a new functional quality, were far more elusive. As will be shown later, the degree of differentiation that could be achieved through mere surface decoration was low and often transient. Moreover, the industry's largest market, for common tableware, was vast and lacked the more easily defined needs and more readily accessible customers of the hotelware trade. True niche markets in which there were few competitors were rare. Instead, many firms were unable to clearly define their customers and achieved only limited focus. Rarely did this approach make them as successful in the competitive battle as Dunn, Bennett and Co.

In turn, around 1910, the firm, building on its established position in a niche market and the focused strategy through which that position had been elaborated, became one of the first in the industry to bypass all intermediaries and sell direct to the final consumer. Retaliatory action by dealers and wholesalers caused great difficulty in the first year of this policy but thereafter receded and success continued to intensify for this already vigorous firm.[22] However, the firm was aided in this strategy by the nature of its market and thus their example was again of limited relevance to other firms striving to strengthen their market position. Whilst Dunn, Bennett and Co. had developed a sophisticated marketing strategy the majority of firms were less well placed to innovate.

Marketing strategies based on differentiation and focus were perhaps most appropriate. However, entrepreneurial flare was not limited to these fields. There was also emerging a class of firms deploying best practice production techniques and aggressive selling tactics, willing to enter the competitive, price sensitive mass-markets into which foreign industries had made the deepest incursions. Economies of scale were as yet far from decisive in pottery, but such strategies represented the beginnings of a move towards the pursuit of cost leadership. One firm taking this path was the Empire Porcelain Co. Founded in 1896, this firm's original factory on Elgin Street, Shelton had by 1898 already 'proved too small in capacity for their extended business', leading to the construction of entirely new works housing 600 hands. The firm's strategy was forcefully stated by manager Harold Emery:

> Our business is to make such goods as have been imported in to this country, and we prove that we can make them as cheap here as they are made on the Continent. We are competing in France, in Germany, in Belgium and in

[22] Interview with Peter Bennett, 2/9/1996.

> Norway. We have permanent agents there, and enter into direct competition with the foreigner with just such goods as were imported from him.[23]

In order to pursue this strategy the making shops on the first floor of the new factory were fully fitted up with steam jollies and automatic batting machines, powered by a thirty-two h.p engine. The firm's physical resources were then very different to those of a firm such as Mintons, where, even in the 1880s, steam powered making machines were rare. The firm also employed Helzel's patented continuous kilns, moving the firm's productive orientation closer to that of a throughput industry.[24] The Empire Porcelain Co. was a firm in which marketing and resource responses operated on one another in sequence as the business expanded very rapidly in the first few years of its existence.

However, the firm still placed a clear emphasis on the quality of the workforce they employed. Emery asserted that, 'One British workman [is] equal to two foreigners ... Why? Because [he is] a vastly better man physically and mentally. He is well fed and therefore more capable ... and the Empire pays ... accordingly'. Exposed again is the tension between tradition and the pressure for change, exerted by a shifting competitive environment, that lay behind Dunn, Bennett's claim to manufacture using both 'scientific methods' and the 'most highly skilled workmanship'.

Determinants of marketing strategies

The prevalence of marketing strategies emphasising differentiation and quality was an outcome of a confluence of forces arising in technologies, endowments of resources and industrial structure and their rootedness in the history of a particular place. That is, in the 'industrial atmosphere' of the Potteries, which had not been 'quickly acquired' and was 'not easily to be had elsewhere'.[25]

Thus, though both Dunn, Bennett and Co. and the Empire Porcelain Co. were able to accommodate conflicting forces of tradition and change within innovative strategies, Emery's description of his firm's resource base was indicative of a genuine dilemma facing most firms in the Potteries. Skilled labour, central to productive capabilities of firms in the Potteries, was more expensive than for their Continental competitors. In the context of international markets increasingly sensitive to price, the relatively high wage costs associated with North Staffordshire, in part an historical product of clustering, represented a real constraint. Either deskilling, lower prices and reduced profit margins had to be

---

[23] *The Pottery Gazette*, May 1898, p. 1003. The Empire Porcelain Co. was acquired by Qualcast in 1958 and closed in 1967 after it had failed to yield adequate profits. Gay and Smythe, *The British Pottery Industry*, p. 48.

[24] Ibid., p. 1003. The factory cost £10,000 to build and £5000 to equip.

[25] Marshall, *Industry and Trade*, p. 287 & p. 284.

accepted or consumers had to be persuaded to pay more for British goods. Thus cost constraints might be tackled through marketing strategies that conveyed the greater value added by the highly skilled labour generated by the district, hence the emphasis on quality.

However, such marketing strategies were related not only to the resources of firms in the district. Account also has to be taken of the craft-oriented culture of both labour and capital in the Potteries. Broadly, many within the industry were uncertain of and feared the direction in which mechanization and market forces were driving them. They lamented the erosion of skill and the imposition of standardization, pressures exerted by the nature of the competition offered by foreign industries. These developments may have appeared to have created scope for an even greater differentiation of Staffordshire wares. In fact, conversely, continued falls in selling prices seemed not to increase the elasticity or the segmentation of markets for ceramic goods but instead acted only to devalue all wares in the eyes of consumers. Mechanization, with its tendency to equalize products and costs, was seen as undermining the basis for differentiation. Machinery was 'unfortunate' because it worked to 'equalize the quality of goods. When hand labour was the rule there was never any question about English pottery being the best made in the world'.[26]

Craft-consciousness was rooted in the history of the district, and in its small-scale personal capitalism. Thus, changing conditions held implications not only for the products firms made and how they sold them, but also for the structure of individual firms and the industry as a whole. The small independent family firm has been implicated by Aldcroft, Elbaum and Lazonick, Kirby and others in the failure of British to integrate forwards into distribution and selling, and commentators in the Potteries also identified such firms with disappearing market conditions and orientations.[27] It seemed inevitable that, 'Competition, ever growing keener, will cut down profits to the last margin; ... this of course means capital, large turnovers and large factories'. The only question remaining unanswered seemed to be 'Whether the small businesses will be eaten up by the large, or the trust system introduced ... but, except for artistic and special purposes, the small manufactory is doomed'. Specialty production, it was predicted, could not remain the dominant paradigm amongst the majority of firms.[28]

Scale, though, was not the sole structural determinant of the relationship between firms, their products and markets. Governance was also held to be

---

[26] *The Pottery Gazette*, April 1899, p. 459; idem, July 1896, p. 538.

[27] Aldcroft, 'The Entrepreneur'; Kirby, 'Institutional Rigidities'; Elbaum and Lazonick, *Decline*.

[28] *The Pottery Gazette*, November 1900, p. 1248. In 1885 it had been asserted that in the future, 'profit will not so much depend on the produce of a few article, but upon them many ... The small manufacturer and limited capitalist will not in the future be able to devote his attention so much to general goods as to specialities'. *The Pottery Gazette*, July 1885, p. 783.

important. Whilst it was admitted that the 'principle has not yet been extensively applied' to the pottery industry, changing conditions, it was argued, would lead to the emergence of business structures that conflicted with the interests and values of the district's personal capitalists. The practices and priorities of public limited liabilities were singled out for comment, echoing attacks made by some sectors of the cotton industry on the Oldham Limiteds during the *Royal Commission* of 1886:

> The extensive promotion of companies with limited liability has drawn a very large amount of capital into trade, and the holders of this capital being numerous, and with small individual liability, are satisfied with small profits. Private manufacturers ... are therefore compelled by the competition of these limited companies to accept smaller profits also.[29]

Again, a host of interlinked implications for production and marketing strategy flowed from this analysis. But the new competitive conditions impacted not only on margins and turnover, but also on status. Thus, though it is important to stress that mechanization and foreign competitions underlay the uncertainty with which the future was viewed, culture undoubtedly complicated the setting of marketing strategies in response. Examining the standardizing effect of pottery machinery of the period, and thus its impact on the marketing strategies of what were essentially specialty producers, reveals the influence of culture. Standardization, it was argued, conflicted with the maintenance of levels of workmanship that were more consistent with the organizational form of personal capitalism and necessary to differentiation strategies. If these levels were defended then:

> the operative will still be in possession of their inherited and acquired skills, and the profits of the masters will be a tribute from the world at large to their knowledge and conscientiousness. But if, on the other hand, the trade is trading on the reputation of British goods, and cheapening production by the use of inferior materials, machinery and women labour, and less coal, then success, such as it is, will probably be of short duration, and the lookout for the next generation of makers without reputation and workmen without skill is anything but promising.[30]

Notable here is both the link between reputation and ways of trading and an emphasis on the collective nature of both reputation and skill. The 'cultural centrality of the firm to the lives of proprietors' demanded the maintenance of standards. At the heart of these attitudes lay a craft pride, a belief that, 'the true potter will always be an artist; but the manufacturer, who caters for the number of

---

[29] *The Pottery Gazette*, January 1886, p. 41.

[30] *The Pottery Gazette*, June 1895, p. 440.

people rather than the artistic few, will ever be driven to bow to the god of cheapness'.[31]

Did mechanization necessarily imply standardization and deterioration in quality though? Certainly, advertisements for, and reviews of, new models of the jigger and the jolly placed much emphasis on their capacity both to increase and regularise production. In 1882, for example, Boulton exhibited in Burslem new jollies, which for 'perfection of machinery and perfect simplicity, stand unrivalled'. The reviewer, an anonymous 'practical potter', was certain the machine would allow an 'immense saving', but he was more impressed by their capacity for making 'more perfect work ... wares made by [these] new jollies will be equal thickness, even weight, and consequently of exact measure'.[32]

However, though these machines made possible greater standardization and a higher volume of production, they compelled neither. Relatively simple machines, little more than jigs making for accuracy of shape and dimension, they needed more than mere minding. Faster than hand throwing and pressing they did not, however, depend upon long runs of identical wares in order to be economic. Most importantly, in terms of the scale, speed and standardization that they implied, and hence also their impact on marketing, they did not need to be powered by steam, and were thus as viable in the smallest workshop as in the most modern factory.[33]

Appreciation of these issues can be heightened by reference to a definition of craft work proposed by David Pye. Focusing not on technology but on the relationship between forms of work and their outcomes, Pye argues that craftsmanship is simply work 'using any kind of technique or apparatus' in which 'the quality of the result is not predetermined ... the quality of the work is constantly at risk during the process of work'. In contrast, in the 'workmanship of certainty', which is always found in quantity production, and ... in its purest form in full automation', the 'quality of the result is exactly predetermined before a

[31] Scranton, *Figured Tapestry*, p. 100; *The Pottery Gazette*, July 1894, 575. Similar attitudes were to be found in other British industries, including those of more recent origin. Lloyd-Jones and Lewis, in work on the British bicycle industry, claim that, 'In the specific British form of personal capitalism there is a particular focus on the culture of respectability and reputation of the firm. Emphasis is frequently placed upon the quality of the product, of the product being worthy of the company name'. R. Lloyd-Jones and M.J. Lewis, 'Regional Business Networks in Historical Perspective: The British Bicycle Industry, 1870–1914', *Business History, Theory and Practice: Proceedings of the Conference on Business History and Theory*, (Glasgow, Centre for Business History in Scotland, 2000), p. 150.

[32] *The Pottery Gazette*, November 1882, p. 1032.

[33] In 1896, Boulton noted that his best selling products were those for 'the driving of jiggers, throwing wheels, lathes and other machines by means of an endless band', suggesting many manufacturers may have acquired such machines before a source of motive power. Asked if many manufacturers employed this drive system Boulton replied, 'yes, most works of note now utilize it', implying that many outside that top stratum did not. *The Pottery Gazette*, September 1896, p. 809.

single saleable thing is made'.[34] Pye specifically associates the workmanship of certainty with 'standardisation', but also allows that there are 'intermediate form[s] of workmanship'. Thus, on a continuum of practices that runs from pure workmanship of risk to pure workmanship of certainty, the late nineteenth century saw the ceramic industry shift somewhat away from risk towards certainty. But the balance was not tipped in favour of a thoroughgoing standardization.[35] The relationship between mechanization, standardization, markets and marketing was unresolved, allowing room for cultural doubts about change to take root.

The gradual nature of change in ceramic making technologies further complicated the reformulation of marketing strategies. Economies of scale were not yet sufficient to encourage the pursuit of mass-production, cost leadership and mass marketing. At the same time, however, as the Mintons case will demonstrate, the effectiveness of strategies predicated on differentiation seemed increasingly uncertain and the focus on quality unrewarding. Some entrepreneurs, such as those at Dunn, Bennett and Co., did react decisively in this uncertain environment, but many others found themselves '"stuck in the middle", lacking clear direction' and proceeding by cautious adaptation.[36] Indecision was further heightened by a craft culture that promoted the belief, as expressed by Pye, that 'there is something about the workmanship of risk, or its results ... that has been long and widely valued'.[37] The argument, advanced in 1888, that replacing the wheel with the jolly was 'undoubtedly a retrogression, brought about by keen competition, and the desire to avoid the risk and care required in the production of thrown and turned ware', depended for its force and meaning on just such a craft-oriented valuation of risk and uniqueness as desirable qualities.[38]

The institutions of marketing and distribution

If potters in the late nineteenth century seemed unsure of how to present themselves and their products to the world then they also expressed a growing sense of dissatisfaction with the institutions of marketing and distribution on which they relied, complaining that 'there must be something wrong with the medium of exchange, or with the intermediaries between' producer and

[34] D. Pye, *The Nature and Art of Workmanship*, (Cambridge, Cambridge University Press, 1968), p. 4.

[35] Ibid., p. 5–7.

[36] M. French, 'Structure, Personality and Business Strategy in the US Tyre Industry: The Sieberling Rubber Company, 1922–1964', *Business History Review*, Vol. 67, No. 1 (1996), p. 247.

[37] Pye, *Nature and Art*, p. 6–7.

[38] *The Pottery Gazette*, May 1888, p. 430.

consumer'.[39] As this suggests, there was little forward integration, but what structures were in place and how had they emerged?

Lorna Weatherill has demonstrated that a sophisticated, hierarchical and disintegrated institutional structure had emerged to distribute and market ceramic wares in Britain by the close of the eighteenth century.[40] As Weatherill argues, 'The mechanics of the pottery trade were complex and the middlemen fulfilled a vital role in the development of the industry', linking the producer to a nascent consumer society both in the capital and throughout the provinces[41]. Weatherill traces the emergence of networks oriented around London, the capital's centrality emerging from the role of the original 'chinamen' in the importation of Far Eastern porcelains and by its position as an arbiter of taste and seat of wealth. These networks comprised metropolitan wholesalers, shops and factory warehouses, and provincial wholesalers and shops, large and small, located in secondary centres, such as Bristol, and increasingly more peripheral urban sites. Also important were occasional auctions and a mass of itinerant peddlers and packmen, some associated with factories, the majority independent, linking producer to consumer. Weatherill concludes that, 'Sales outlets ... seem to have been adequate to sustain the growth of the industry and do not seem to have inhibited expansion at any time'. Weatherill attributes much of this efficiency to the network-like attributes of the system:

> Correspondence and personal visits ... had a more general significance, for it was through these personal contacts that the trade was knitted together into a framework of people who knew one another and who could discuss and influence the development of the industry. It was along these lines within the distribution networks that information about new products and consumer preferences could be channelled.[42]

---

[39] *The Pottery Gazette*, May 1894, p. 436.

[40] L. Weatherill, 'The Business of the Middleman in the English Pottery Trade Before 1780', *Business History*, Vol. 28, No. 3 (1986), pp. 51–76. See also, A. Eatwell and A. Werner, 'A London Staffordshire Warehouse - 1794-1825', *Journal of the Northern Ceramic Society*, No. 8 (1991), pp. 91–124.

[41] Ibid., p.71.

[42] Ibid., p. 68 and p.63. However, neither the efficiency of these networks nor the always wise apportioning of trust may be assumed, as is revealed by the story of Elijah Cotton, who operated as a pottery merchant in Edinburgh in the early decades of the nineteenth century. Cotton was himself Potteries born and in 1805 married the daughter of David Wilson, described by the *Staffordshire Advertiser* in that year as 'an eminent manufacturer' in Hanley. Cotton's brother Benjamin was an important local merchant in clays and other inputs and a further relative was probably an agent for Davenports. These local roots seem to have served him well, for several manufacturers extended him considerable credit, Wedgwood in excess of £250 and Mintons more than £450. However, though Elijah was bankrupt in 1811, many of these manufacturers continued to trade with him and with his brother Stephen, a merchant in Glasgow. In turn, Stephen was bankrupt himself in 1819, owing nearly £800 to a total of ten Staffordshire manufacturers. The single largest debt was of £217 owed to Bourne, Barker and Bourne.

Here Weatherill traces the growth and development in the eighteenth century of those institutional structures which, in Wilson's words, ensured that throughout the nineteenth century transaction costs were 'heavily skewed in favour of external dealing', providing 'little incentive for British manufacturers to internalise marketing and distribution'.[43] The result was that the pottery industry, like many others in Britain, 'remained committed to disintegrated structures', foregoing the potential advantages of greater co-ordination and encouragement to mass-produce claimed by Chandler for forward integrating American corporations.[44] However, Weatherill's article deals only with distribution within the UK. Before examining in detail both the operation and the impacts of these marketing structures in the second half of the nineteenth century, we also need to briefly examine the methods and structures first adopted and evolved by potters for the penetration of foreign markets, for, as we have already demonstrated, exports were central to the growth and prosperity of the industry.

Here we may identify two basic approaches, though their characterization is necessarily rather crude, that emerged during the late eighteenth and early nineteenth centuries. Again, all firms, large and small, old and new, were reliant on a structure of intermediaries. However, a small corps of older, long-lived firms was more successful than the mass of smaller, newer and more transient firms in embedding these intermediaries in network-like structures exhibiting relatively high levels of trust.[45] Following a variety of routes, some firms were able to broaden and deepen the information channels that linked them to growing foreign markets, most especially in the United States. By contrast, the majority of firms in the Potteries were reliant on a range of structures, and actors, displaying more market-like attributes in which trust and loyalty were weaker and information flows, in both directions, far less rich.

Moreover, Elijah was bankrupt for a second time, owing a total of £2303 to twenty-one Potteries' firms. £416 was owed to Machin & Co. of Burslem alone. J. Turnbull, 'Staffordshire Potters and Scottish Merchants', *Journal of the Northern Ceramic Society*, No. 9 (1992), pp. 115–22. As Turnbull notes, this case reveals 'the considerable credit which trading at such a distance entailed', p. 121.

[43] Wilson, British Business History, p. 91.

[44] Kirby, 'Institutional Rigidities', p. 638. Such issues persisted. An article in the *Pottery Reviews* in 1944 argued that whilst the 'functions of manufacturing and selling should be separate, though co-ordinated', the industry would after the war have to be 'ready to tackle the job of selling in bulk and manufacturing in bulk-for the two functions must be synchronised to be fully successful'. However, the journal recognized that a significant barrier existed in the form of 'those orders calling for a hundred different sets in a hundred different patterns ... This of course is largely a matter for the agents and travellers ... and it needs to be emphasised that salespeople are paid by, and therefore representatives of, the factory and not buying agents for the customers. No longer will it be sufficient for them to point to an impressive aggregate total of orders secured; the order must be of a character such as will individually show a profit'. 'Exports in 1945 and After', *The Pottery and Glass Trades Review*, March 1944, p. 142 & p. 145.

[45] Throughout this work we adopt Casson's definition of a network as a 'set of high-trust linkages connecting a set of entities'. Casson, 'Analysing Regional Business Networks', p. 10.

Building on ongoing and sustained relationships with both British and American merchants, and indeed on formal partnerships with British merchants, most famously in the case of Wedgwood and Bentley, a handful of manufacturers were able to build impressive distributive structures and export records. From relationships with merchants firms moved onto establish either directly owned outlets or formal agency agreements, particularly on the Eastern seaboard of the US. These arrangements facilitated the flow of information about the level and composition of foreign demand and eased payment, important in the relatively hazardous environment of the early nineteenth century.

Several features of these developments and the way they unrolled are of interest. First, action was often distinctly co-operative as Staffordshire entrepreneurs collaborated with one another in building institutions for the distribution of their wares. Thus, both formal and informal arrangements between manufacturer and merchant, or manufacturer and manufacturer, were rarely exclusive, instead linkages tended to be multi-lateral. John Ridgway, for example, visiting Liverpool in September 1822, noted in his diary a visit to 'my friend Messrs. Morral and Watson: attended to Messrs. Booths business with them'. Similarly, Adams and Sons used their Liverpool warehouse not only to conduct their own export trade but also that of several other 'leading ... manufacturers', Similarly, in the 1810s, Keeling and Mayer, described as manufacturers and agents of Shelton in the Potteries, were placing orders from America, routed through Liverpool merchant William Lees, with at least five other local firms.[46]

Similar strategies were being operated at the mid-century. Thus, when George Meakin first visited New York in the summer of 1854 he called immediately on fellow Staffordshire man John Maddock, who introduced him to valuable contacts in the American commercial community. In turn, in the 1870s, Meakins introduced Wedgwood's new traveller to their New York representative, who advanced cash as well as contacts. Wedgwood's man acknowledged himself 'very much indebted ... for advice and help in various ways'.[47] This co-operation was fostered by the way in which pottery merchants and dealers clustered on Pearl and Water Streets in New York, recreating the clustering of the industry in the UK.

As these examples suggest, Staffordshire manufacturers could be very active travellers, purposively seeking out opportunities for expanding their trade, drawing on a range of often-intangible resources to support their endeavours. Joseph Clementson, for example first travelled to the new world at the encouragement of his former employer, Ridgway, and then went on to develop an

---

46 N. Ewins, '"Supplying the Present Wants of Our Yankee Cousins ... ": Staffordshire Ceramics and the American Market, 1775–1880', *Journal of Ceramic History*, Vol. 15 (1997), p. 77–8. Moreover, whilst in Boston in 1822 Ridgway again attended to Booth's business and to that of another Longton manufacturer, Bailey and Batkin.

47 Ewins, '"Supplying the Present Wants", p. 94–5.

extensive trade with Canada. Clementson's prominent role in Methodism in the Potteries played no small part in this, the journeys enjoining missionary work religious and commercial. Clementson naturally made important contacts that were built on in subsequent visits. Thus, Henry Alcock, visiting Canada in 1839, wrote to Clementson, his employer, in the following vein:

> Mr Harris of Toronto has been building and Mr Turner (of Montreal) thinks any accommodation you may be able to afford him may be done with safety and will not be thrown away. Mr Wilson and Mr Hales of Kingston are as good men as can be, [and] if you can agree terms will be extensive Customers.[48]

The need to 'accommodate' merchants highlights the centrality of credit to much foreign trade and, hence, the importance of warranted trust. In turn, Francis Clementson, eldest son of Joseph, moved to New Brunswick, Canada in the 1840s, establishing an independent import business. Francis remained in Canada for twenty-five years and the business continued after his death until the close of the century. Manufacturers proceeded cautiously then as intra and inter-firm learning occurred, trust accrued and institutional developments unrolled in an evolutionary manner with the formation of credible information channels, leading to a progressive extension of the geographical scope of trade.[49]

Those who did not travel themselves either relied on the support and aid of fellow manufacturers, as already shown, or strove to formalize relationships with American importers. Such agreements tended to emerge from prior histories of ad hoc but repeated transactions and foreshadowed the development in the later nineteenth century of the kind of agency agreements studied by Nicholas.[50] In Chapter 7 we will examine one such agency in greater detail.

In summation, there was a clear pattern to the growth of institutional structures linking the district to international markets. In part, we may relate this to growth in the scale of exports. Directly owned foreign offices especially incurred cost independent of the volume of trade done. Their establishment required a minimum level of involvement and it is no surprise they first appeared in the crucial and dynamic markets of North America.[51] However, a number of

[48] P. Halfpenny, 'Joseph Clementson: A Potter "Remarkable for Energy of Character"', *Northern Ceramic Society Journal*, 5 (1984), p. 194.

[49] However, trust could yet prove misplaced. Thus, when, in 1840, Clementson tried to encash a draft for £150 sent by the aforementioned Hales he found that the 'said Bill cannot be accepted for want of advice'. Halfpenny, 'Joseph Clementson', p.198.

[50] S. Nicholas, 'The Overseas Marketing Performance of British Industry, 1870-1914', *Economic History Review*, Vol. 37, No. 4 (1984), pp. 489–506; idem, 'Agency Contracts, Institutional Modes and the Transition to Foreign Direct Investment by British Manufacturing Multinationals Before 1939', *Journal of Economic History*, Vol. 43, No. 3 (1983), pp. 675–686.

[51] See, E. Collard, *Nineteenth Century Pottery and Porcelain in Canada* (Montreal, McGill University Press, 1967).

other factors had also proved important. First, it should be emphasized that in progressively building and refining these structures potters often took the lead and displayed considerable entrepreneurial drive and vision, both in their appreciation of the importance of commercial intelligence and in their determination to find effective means of gathering it.

Second, whilst potters actively strove to extend the scope and reach of the networks in which they were involved they did so in an incremental fashion that built on and exploited local foundations with which they were familiar and in which they had confidence. Kinship, co-religion and personal knowledge enabled them to breach the boundaries of the district. These forces made co-operation a common occurrence, emphasizing the continued importance of local networks as the basis for expansion. Even in an international setting, who to trust remained locally defined, at least in part. Thus, powerfully rooted local networks, as those of the Potteries undoubtedly were, were not necessarily insular. Instead, trust could form the basis of effective decentralized institutional structure able to gather information and co-ordinate markets, even across considerable distances. However, these developments occurred largely within a relatively restricted cadre of relatively large, well established and well known firms, a factor that may be related not only to the greater financial strength of such firm but also to their principals' identification and interaction with one another within the local setting.

How then were smaller and often newer firms integrated into national and international markets? Two important archives provide detailed insights into many aspects of this question. The first relates to the firm of Cork, Edge and Malkin and consists of more than three hundred letters written to the firm by merchants and other customers, both in the UK and many foreign locations, in the years 1863 to 1867.[52]

A number of the general characteristics of this correspondence are of note. First, the number, diversity and heterogeneity of the firm's mercantile and retail contacts is striking. The evidence, which is almost certainly not complete, suggests that exports were handled entirely by merchants, both UK based exporters, overseas importers and multinational partnerships, such as S.

---

[52] The firm, located at the Newport Pottery, Burslem, traded as Cork and Edge (1846–60), Cork, Edge and Malkin (1860–70) and then as Edge, Malkin and Co. Ltd. (1870–1902). Jewitt lists their productions as dinner ware, jet, enamelled lustre, other fancy goods and 'all the ordinary ware for the home and foreign markets'. Godden, *Jewitt's Ceramic Art*, p. 14. In later years the firm also made tiles using a patented process. The firm was embedded in a matrix of personal relationships. James Malkin married Joseph Edge's daughter Annie and their son, Sydney, was taken into the business before, in 1894, leaving to go into business with his own brother, Elijah. Benjamin Cork, Joseph Edge and Sydney Malkin all fulfilled a variety of roles in local politics and voluntary and charitable organizations. Certainly the Edge and Malkin families also shared an allegiance to Wesleyan Methodism. Joseph Edge had interests in local utility and transport companies. Stuart, *People of the Potteries*, p. 84 and p. 146.

Greenshield and Son of Montreal and Liverpool.[53] At least twenty-five merchants are represented in the correspondence, located in London, Manchester, Liverpool, Bristol, Hull, Glasgow, St Malo, Paris, Lubeck, Hamburg, Christiana in Norway, New Brunswick, Montreal and Toronto in Canada, and Boston. The importance of London and Manchester merchants is notable. It has been assumed in the past that Liverpool merchants were dominant in the Potteries' export trade, but this was not true with respect to Cork, Edge and Malkin. The destinations of wares were rarely specified, but included; New Brunswick, Montreal and Toronto, Boston, New York and Cincinnati, the Levant, Dominica, Bermuda, Puerto Cabello, Bombay and the Windward Coast of Africa.

In contrast, the domestic trade was handled far more directly, the majority of such correspondents, who numbered more than thirty, being engaged in the retail and wholesale trade in glass, china and other fancy goods. Most of these were located in the Southwest, where the firm's traveller, Mr Hawley, seems also to have focused his energies.

Perhaps yet more interesting though is the nature of the information transmitted by correspondents and the light that this throws on the relationship between manufacturers and intermediaries. Here a number of salient themes stand out immediately and we will again deal first with export markets. Striking here is an overwhelming emphasis on issues not of design but of price and, above all else, lead times. Indeed, the correspondence conveys most powerfully the intense time pressures faced by manufacturers and, correspondingly, their need to be able to respond with considerable speed. Moreover, merchants often expected to be able to call-off orders for immediate delivery at some unspecified point in the near future, shifting the burden of stock-keeping and control onto the manufacturer and heightening the risk associated with any potential cancellation. Thus, C.W. and W. Gray, of London, wrote with an order in October 1864:

> Please to get up for T.A.T., well ... and as cheap as possible. But neither these or the other order on hand from us should be sent up until we again write (although they should be proceeded with at once) our present vessel being full.[54]

---

[53] SD 1204/36. *Letter from D. Greenshield* , Montreal, 16 February 1866. In this instance orders were conveyed directly by the Montreal branch, the Liverpool branch handling shipping and remittances. The letter contains interesting evidence of the importance of buyers visits and of the way in which clustering created opportunities, noting that 'You were kind enough to say to our enquiry from one year or so ago when in England that you would supply us with the "Blue Marino" ware such as Mr Godwin, with whom we had an account, use to make', Godwin was in business in Longport in the Potteries between 1834 and 1866.

[54] SD 1204/12. *Letter from C.W. & W. Gray, London*, 19 October 1864. Gray, a very frequent correspondent, always specified how the wares were to be marked on the bottom, for example T.A.T, almost certainly the initials of the importer in the destination country. Hence, Cork, Edge and Malkin were hampered in attempting to develop any prominence or 'brand awareness' through this trade.

Similarly, Greenshields wrote from Montreal in March 1866 that 'the goods would be better with you until an opportunity offers to ship'.[55] However, more common were demands for immediate delivery. Thus, J. Good wrote on 15 April 1865 ordering goods to be marked 'Brough Chapel' and to be delivered to Hull by 28 April, adding that 'the customer must be conciliated on this point [delivery]'.[56] Later that year Gray sent further orders for 'immediate execution ... an opportunity will offer [to ship] in fourteen days and we trust you will have no difficulty in putting them up by that time'.[57] Clearly, Gray expected that the firm would have to actually make these wares.[58] On occasion, such exhortations were accompanied by a more coercive tone. For example, an unidentified merchant in Hamburg wrote early in 1866 both to complain of the quality of wares he had received but also place a further small order that the firm was to 'forward immediately. I wish to have it in four weeks, in this case you may be sure to get afterwards a much larger one'.[59]

However, the intense time pressure may not have been related only, or even primarily, to seasonal fluctuations in demand, as much of the literature on specialty trades might suggest. On only one occasion is the importance of delivery linked to seasonality, when William Harris of London wrote with 'a small order for you from my son, Edwin Harris, Toronto'. Harris explained that quick delivery was imperative because 'Jelly Cans are only wanted at a certain season and if they arrive in Toronto (too late) when the season is over they have to be kept on hand until next year, it is not like any other sort of good which is saleable all year round'[60]. A far more pressing issue for merchants was the opportunity to ship. Thus, attention is focused on information lags. Communication between UK based merchants could be rapid and frequent, Gray wrote to Cork, Edge and Malkin concerning a single order on the 25th, 27th and 29th of September 1864 for example, but was likely considerably attenuated by the distance between merchants and their foreign correspondents. In compensation, communication and time pressures were greatly compressed at the point of the manufacturing link in the distribution chain.[61]

---

55 SD 1204/39. *Letter from Greenshields & Son, Montreal*, 23 March 1866.

56 SD 1204/22. *Letter from J. Good Jnr.*, 15 April 1865.

57 SD 1204/26. *Letter from C.W. & W. Gray, London*, 29 August 1863.

58 In 1866, Gallet of St. Malo asked for an order to be sent 'with least possible delay', adding that 'I don't think this will be very difficult for during my stay at Burslem I noticed that your warehouse was plenteously stocked'. However, this is the only such reference to filling orders from stock. SD 1204/35. *Letter from Gallet, St. Malo*, 14 February 1864.

59 SD 1204/20. *Letter, Hamburg*, 6 March 1866.

60 SD 1204/97. *Letter from Wm. Harris, London*, 15 February 1867.

61 SD 1204/8-10. *Letters from C.W. & C. Gray, London*, 25 September 1864; 27 September 1864 and 29 September 1864. International trade had many perils. In spring 1864, for example Gwyer & Son of Bristol suspended an order when Gwyer Jnr. failed to arrive home, as expected, 'by the next African mail'. SD 1204/4. *Letter from Gwyer & Son, Bristol*, 25 April 1864.

The other principal concern of merchants facilitating the firm's export trade was prices. Merchants, however, did not ever specify the price they wished to pay. Instead there was an unwavering insistence that orders were sent in the hope 'that the very best will be done for our friends in point of price', or that a small order be sent 'as soon as possible on best terms for cash'.[62] On occasion these requests shaded into demands for hidden discounts. Thus, B.A Grauthoff and Co., London, only confirmed one order 'on the understanding that extra cash discount not named to Mr Panthes be allowed to us'.[63] Cork, Edge and Malkin were clearly reluctant to grant this favour, for within days Grauthoff had written again to express their:

> regret to hear that you do not see the advisability of allowing a premium to the Agents. Most of our friends in the Potteries do and reap the benefit by having other of our friends introduced to them, which it won't be against our interest to bring to you.[64]

Here we see the merchant attempting to exploit both informational asymmetries and the clustering of the industry. Certainly concern over price far outweighed concern over design and, for Cork, Edge and Malkin at least, there is cause to doubt the extent to which differentiation could or did form the foundation of a firm's marketing strategy.[65] Moreover, on those several occasions when a merchant suggested that perhaps some wares 'you will no doubt be able to procure for us if not manufactured by yourself', no preference was ever expressed as to whom Cork, Edge and Malkin should source from.[66]

What does this correspondence reveal of the inter-firm relationships involved? Much important information is missing. For example, whilst many relationships were sustained throughout the four years covered by the archive, there are few clues as the length of relationships, their relative importance to Cork, Edge and Malkin, or of how they were formed. There is some evidence that relationships could begin through entirely speculative enquiries, unmediated by any social process and untroubled by distance or a lack of face-to-face contact. Both

---

62 SD 1204/8; SD 1204/88. *Letter from J.H. Greene & Inglis, Commission & Forwarding Agents, Oldhall St., Liverpool*, 24 December 1866.

63 SD 1204/45. *Letter from Grauthoff & Co., London*, 1 May 1866.

64 SD 1204/47. *Letter from Grauthoff & Co., London*, 5 May 1866.

65 It was very rare for specific patterns or designs to be requested. More typical was Gray's instruction that goods be 'of cheap description and of the staple usually supplied for our mark'. Similarly, Elwell & Sons, simply requested a quantity of goods 'suitable for North America - we leave the matter in your hands'. SD 1204/25. *Letter from C.W. & C. Gray, London*, 29 August 1865; SD 1204/42, *Letter from Elwell & Sons*, 4 April 1866.

66 SD 1204/56,. *Letter from C.W. & C. Gray, London*. 24 August 1866. The extent of inter-trading between Potteries' manufacturers is largely unknown. Certainly, Cork, Edge and Malkin not only sourced from but also supplied other firms. See SD 1204/209. *Letter from G.L. Ashworth Bros., Hanley*, 26 July 1867.

Schuster Bros. of Manchester and Gwyers of Bristol, apparently without introduction, wrote offering opportunities in the Levant and Africa respectively.[67] The latter was certainly pursued. However, whilst the correspondence contains no evidence of serious opportunism, nor does it suggest that these were especially high-trust relationships governed by notions of reciprocity and the identification of mutual ends and gains. Where the relationship between trust, the district and intermediaries is made explicit, particularly in the use of other district manufacturers as a source of references, the temptation to overestimate the depth, utility and importance of trust should be resisted. When Longton manufacturers Holland and Green wrote to Cork, Edge and Malkin concerning a Mr Hassel of Christiana, Norway, who 'gives us you firm as a reference', asking that they should 'kindly say ... if you consider him respectable and trustworthy', there is no reason to assume they had in mind anything more than an essentially negative definition of trust. In other words, that Mr Hassel was not known to default.[68]

Instead, the exchange of information appears highly functional and businesslike, with disclosure of information kept to a minimum. Gray, for example specified neither the full identity of customers nor their location. At best, merchants did not see reducing information asymmetries as part of their role, at worst, they occasionally used them for their own ends. No great premium was attached to reputation or familiarity. Moreover, many merchants, like Grauthoff, no doubt had many 'friends' in the Potteries. Overall, the impression that Cork, Edge and Malkin were largely dependent on merchants, as a class, is unmistakable.

However, paradoxically, whilst this cannot be meaningfully characterized as a high-trust environment, it does not seem to have been an environment in which transaction costs were high. Orders were simple, negotiation all but non-existent, terms and conditions readily understood and the mechanisms for remittance well established and reliable.[69] Importantly, these characteristics hold as true for a merchant placing a first order with Cork, Edge and Malkin as they do for Gray and others who placed repeated orders over a number of years, suggesting a generalized learning process, rather than one specific to particular inter-firm relationships.

The correspondence from domestic customers is certainly less rich than that concerned with exports. Nonetheless, it is significant, not least because it reveals

---

67 SD 1204/150. *Letter from L. Schuster Bros. & Co., Manchester*, 4 May 1866.

68 SD 1204/149. *Letter from Holland & Green, Longton*, 4 May 1866. In a mirror image of this letter, Charles Smith of the Wholesale and Retail Glass and China Warehouse, Weymouth, sent an order, adding 'you can hear of me at Wedgwoods, Mintons, E.J. Ridgway, Davenports, Hammersley, Copeland (and more)', certainly an impressive list of referees. SD 1204/121. *Letter from C. Smith, Weymouth*. 12 April 1867.

69 The most common source of dispute or misunderstanding were the goods themselves. Whilst this is not surprising, given the vagueness of many order, it does not seem to have jeopardized relationships.

the extent to which the firm dealt directly with large numbers of retail customers, both via the post and through employment of a traveller. The archive contains correspondence from more than thirty domestic customers, the majority of them engaged in both retail and wholesale trade. The extent to which they bought from Cork, Edge and Malkin in order to act as wholesalers to retail-only outlets is not clear, but some orders were very small, often for quantities of wares worth only a few pounds.

Though unintermediated these relationships may well have been more troublesome than those with merchants, a large number of letters being concerned with complaints and quibbles over delivery and payment. Difficulty in extracting payment from customers was clearly a serious problem and whilst the sums were rarely large they might in aggregate represent a significant drain on a small firm. Again, transaction costs seem low, but the risks were greater, both from deliberate opportunism and from incompetence and misfortune. Thus, Parker and Baldwin, of Knutsford, wrote in 1867 to argue that:

> We are very sorry you cannot [send] the goods, part of our order, till we [pay] the remaining portion of cash owning. We would rather cancel the order altogether as we have before stated that it is extremely inconvenient to obtain money in the present time and we have no desire to get in a quantity of goods we cannot pay for ... We really have not got the money to pay.[70]

Here the firm faced two potential sources of loss, from goods delivered but not paid for and from goods made and then cancelled.

The second archive to throw light on the relationship between smaller firms and the institutions of distribution are the diaries, covering the years 1851-1860, of pottery exporter John Hackett Goddard of the partnership of Goddard and Burgess, of Longton, in the Potteries, and New York.[71] Again, we first reconstruct the broad pattern of this trade. In the ten years covered by the diaries Goddard channelled orders from the United States to at least thirty-six, mainly small firms. Of these, however, nearly eighty per cent probably received orders in four or fewer years, one third in only one year. Most firms also received orders some or all of their orders in non-consecutive years. Just two firms, Walley and Bootes, both of Burslem, received orders in all ten years.

It is hard to argue on this evidence that Goddard sought sustained, long-term relationships with his suppliers. The pattern of trade suggests inter-firm relationships mediated more by the market than by notions of reciprocity. Detailed evidence reinforces this characterization. Goddard's own position and

---

70 SD 1204/130. *Letter from Parker & Baldwin, Knutsford*. 29 April 1867.

71 The diary is held privately by the Goddard family, still resident in North Staffordshire. Unfortunately, access to the diary is currently denied. See Ewins, '"Supplying the Present Wants ..."'.

role was shaped jointly by his partnership with Burgess, integrated by weekly transatlantic communication, and by his own knowledge of the district's producers. Goddard then acted to filter the information conveyed to him from America to manufacturers. Goddard supplied manufacturers with a range of information, including advice as to what they might make. This, however, often went hand in hand with encouragement to copy the shapes and patterns of other local manufacturers, both firms Goddard did business with and others with whom he had no connection. For example, in 1853, when Goddard urged Walley to make a pattern very similar to one produced by Bailey of Longton, who also supplied Goddard, Walley surreptitiously attempted to question Bailey's engraver. Goddard, alarmed by this crude industrial espionage, was quick to ascertain that 'Walley has seen Bailey who is satisfied that I have not improperly told him [Walley] anything of his [Bailey's] patterns'.[72]

This strategy was sometimes accompanied by the division of single orders amongst several manufacturers, reinforcing Goddard's ability to bargain by giving credibility to any threat to switch, whilst also buttressing information asymmetries. On the other hand, as we have already seen with reference to Cork, Edge and Malkin, manufacturers did on occasion subcontract work supplied by Goddard to other firms, sometimes doing so without his prior knowledge or agreement.[73] Such strategies were part of a wider attempt by Goddard to foster dependency amongst his suppliers, of which ready cash payments and exclusive agreements to export to the United States through him were central props. Goddard's use of cash was certainly a boon to small, financially insecure firms, but it also gave him a powerful lever. Agreements to deal only through Goddard on the other hand, not only guaranteed his command of a given productive capacity but also limited manufacturers' access to alternative sources of information about and from the market. In particular, he was concerned to prevent direct contact between manufacturers and his own customers in the US and even tried to extract commission on the rare occasions such links were established.[74]

Agreements binding manufacturers to Goddard were in no way reciprocal however, though buoyant demand could strengthen a manufacturer's hand. Thus, in 1855, Walley, though allowing Goddard and Burgess exclusive sale of his wares in New York, refused to entirely give up the Anglo-American house of

---

72 Ewins, '"Supplying the Present Wants ... "', p. 110.

73 Thus, in December 1852, Goddard noted, 'drove to see Bootes respecting Fell's goods ... it turns out that they did not make the goods but that Godwins of Cobridge did. They said that as a matter of course we must be protected from loss, but what does this mean? The goods ... must not be shipped until some terms have [been] come to with Godwins'. Ewins, '"Supplying the Present Wants ... "', p. 119.

74 Similarly, it was noted, on their failure, that Dawson and Hancock, merchants of New York, Philadelphia and London, had a number of firms 'mainly or exclusively depending on them for the supply of orders'. *Staffordshire Sentinel*, 3 October 1857.

Dawson and Hancock.[75] Clearly, competition between merchants could go some was to inhibiting their individual power. Indicative of this is the failure of a proposal, floated by importer George Hammersley in 1853, to apportion US markets amongst a select group of merchants.[76]

However, most significantly, negotiations with manufacturers, including those with whom Goddard had sustained relationships, were overwhelmingly price-oriented. Moreover, important elements of those price-based negotiations remained deliberately hidden from view. Thus, even when purportedly working in unison to raise export prices, manufacturers were secretly allowing the discounts demanded by Goddard and, as we have seen, other merchants. In March 1854, for example, Goddard recorded that 'Livesley have agreed to execute Sheridan's order upon the terms [offered] but they will not quote them'. In general, the diaries suggest wide discrepancies between the discounts allowed to Goddard and official lists agreed and published by the *Potteries Chamber of Commerce*.[77] Finally, if Goddard acted as a valve, information flow was largely uni-directional, his partnership not being in any way concerned to promote the name or brands of firms supplying them. The failure to establish clear identities in foreign markets hindered moves toward direct selling for such firms, if their name literally did not matter then reputations could not be forged.

It is hard to characterize Goddard's relationships with firms in the Potteries as networked based. Even when sustained over time high-levels of trust and information sharing did not necessarily emerge. Moreover, the use of cash rather than credit eliminated a mechanism through which the fortunes of merchant and manufacturer might have become interlinked. Instead, past, present and future actions were dissociated, structuring Goddard's supply base as a series of essentially discrete bilateral institutions.[78] In the majority of relationships, underpinned by information asymmetries, arms-length, price-based and, at times, surreptitious interactions ruled. These were relationships to which power was more salient than trust, the information supplied by Goddard was low-cost, but its utility uncertain. In turn, these characteristics inhibited the emergence of the collaborative behaviour displayed by larger firms in the first half of the century. Intra and inter-regional networks remained fragile in the small firm sector.[79] In contrast to the large firm sector, unrestrained entry and exit hindered the

---

[75] Ewins, '"Supplying the Present Wants ... "', p. 123.

[76] Ibid., p. 123.

[77] Ibid., p. 120.

[78] G. Dei Ottati, 'Trust, Interlinking Transactions and Credit in the Industrial District', *Cambridge Journal of Economics*, 18 (1994), pp. 529–546.

[79] Indicative of the importance of merchants to small firms is the proportion of resident merchants located in Longton, where a plethora of small shops clustered. In 1867, of the eleven merchants located in the Potteries, seven were to be found in Longton, in 1882 the figures were six out of fourteen. Conversely, in both years, no merchants were located in Tunstall, home to a number of larger firms concentrating on the North American markets. *Keates & Ford's Directory,* 1867 and 1882.

emergence of the coherent, high-trust networks amongst small producers that might have discouraged opportunism amongst themselves (largely in relation to prices) and circumscribed the power of Goddard to rule through market discipline. In turn, few of the firms supplying Goddard went on to build more direct links with export markets and those that were able to do were those whose relationship with Goddard had been the most sustained.[80]

However, Goddard's role cannot be ascribed easily to any individual lack of embeddedness within a district milieu, for he was locally born and well integrated into social and political networks in the district.[81] Thus, his obituary in the *Pottery Gazette* described Goddard as a 'leader in politics, a large merchant, an alderman and magistrate, there are but few to take his place and none to excel him in the estimable traits that make a public man, a very giant among men'.[82] Either Goddard resisted inculcation in a district-level moral economy of norms and values, delimiting the boundaries and balances between collective and self-interest, or such an economy was weak or segmented. Thus, his civic and institutional role integrated Goddard into elite networks in the Potteries, emphasizing how in any region or industry it may be possible to identify multiple business networks, whose interests will not necessarily be aligned. Goddard's strategies were then related not only to information asymmetries but also to the highly competitive structure of the industry and, as a corollary to that structure, to a fragmented notion of 'the trade'.

Throughout the last quarter of the century it is probable that the majority of firms remained largely dependent on a range of intermediaries, not only resident merchants but also buyers and jobbers who arrived in seasonal influxes. The spatial clustering of the industry made it worthwhile for buyers to come and view samples, bargain and place orders. Clustering also promoted a somewhat fevered atmosphere in which rumours about styles, prices and terms accepted could circulate.[83] Some industries were able to turn clustering to goods effect. At Grand Rapids, in the United States, furniture manufacturers launched in 1878

[80] T. & R. Boote, of Burslem, with whom Goddard placed orders in each year from 1851–1860, is the principal example of such a firm, Edward Boote acting as the firm's American agent by the 1880s. Ewins, '"Supplying the Present Wants ... "', p. 126.

[81] However, Goddard's otherwise warm obituary in the *Pottery Gazette* described him as 'to all intents and purposes a Longton man'. The qualification may relate to his father's birth in Glossop, Derbyshire. *The Pottery Gazette*, March 1882, p. 293-5; *Census Returns, Longton*, 1851.

[82] *The Pottery Gazette,* March 1882, p.293-5. Goddard was also prominent in important local associational activities, sitting on the committees of the North Staffordshire Chamber of Commerce and North Staffordshire Exchange in the 1870s.

[83] Thus, reports that manufacturers were 'busy executing the order which the Americans have left' were typical. *The Pottery Gazette*, June 1882, p. 542. Scranton is surely right to note that what is missing from 'standard theories of how markets should work when there are many buyers and sellers', are the pressures exerted by temporal and spatial compactness. Thus, 'when sixty per cent of a year's trade is compressed into ten weeks, and makers are compressed into two pairs of adjacent districts, individual buyers can rule'. Scranton, 'Diversity in Diversity', p. 84

expositions which 'gradually drew scores, then hundreds of outside firms as exhibitors ... and thousands of retail buyers as clients'. In time, these 'collective efforts ... solidified direct selling, wrecked wholesaling, and facilitated collaborative price defences'.[84] In 1883 Staffordshire potters were urged in the same direction:

> strike out at new markets, cut at foreign competition, plan scheme and invent, bring out native talent by offering prizes for new bodies, new glazes, new styles, new decorations, etc., organise a trades exhibition, make it an annual affair, and great and lasting good will undoubtedly accrue therefrom.[85]

However, as with so many calls for collaborative action in the Potteries in this period, the idea was still born.

Instead, there was an intensification of a sense of unease, focused on the impact on prices, and reputations, of the relationship between small firms and buyers. Crucially, the weak position of small firms, individually and as a sector, was seen to impact on *all* firms. Thus, the *Pottery Gazette* claimed in 1886 that:

> mushroom firms ... who, having no good name to lose, and not much capital to lose either, are reckless in their dealings, caring only to send out something and to get ready money for it quickly ... All this is very detrimental to the best interests of the trade ... depraving the tastes of manufacturers, dealers and consumers alike.[86]

Dealers and merchants, working with the grain of clustering and exploiting cash hungry manufacturers, were able to play firm against firm. Hence, in 1885, whilst 'the very best houses have been phenomenally slack, the small producers ... have been able to keep their ovens going regularly'. A twofold reason was identified:

> These smaller makers have a decided advantage over the larger ... Their expenditure, in comparison, is so much less and as a rule the labour they employ is cheaper if less efficient. Most of them are obliged to turn over money quickly, and hence it is just now that they get so well patronised by the ready money dealers.[87]

---

[84] Ibid., p. 56.

[85] *The Pottery Gazette*, March 1883, p. 263.

[86] *The Pottery Gazette*, January 1886, p. 43.

[87] *The Pottery Gazette*, November 1885, p. 1246. Here the issue was worsened by the Christmas rush. Scranton notes that in the American jewellery industry also 'Jobbers demanded punishing trade terms and played makers off against one another to enhance their advantages'. Again the blame was laid at the door of 'mushroom' firms. Scranton, 'Diversity in Diversity', p. 83.

The same critique was reiterated the following year, the trade press commenting that 'we do not know of any industry so much at the mercy of the ruthless "cutting" buyer for cash ... To the small capitalists the temptation to turn over their money quickly has proved too strong'. At the same time, others were squeezed by the push for dealers to insist on ever-longer periods of credit; 'on every side one hears complaints of the scarcity of money, and the period of credit demanded by the home trade is ever displaying a tendency to increase'.[88] But these pressures not only depressed prices, they also conflicted with quality oriented marketing strategies. 'Mushroom firms' were 'reckless in their dealings' not only because of their financial weakness but also because they had 'no good name to lose'. In this context, a manufacturer making expensive investments in design capability could not reliably capture 'premiums' for either creativity or skill.

The picture is then mixed. Wilson's argument that transaction costs had over time become skewed towards disintegrated structures in distribution has considerable merit. Cork, Edge and Malkin, for example, had few opportunities to break out of dependence on mercantile networks. At the same time though, their incentives for so doing were also slight. This last point indicates the value of a network-based analysis. The majority of firms were not in a position to build network-like structures. The contrast with those firms more successful in this direction serves to reinforce the emphasis placed by Casson on leadership and entrepreneurship in regional business networks, and in particular on the metropolitan entrepreneur or merchant who 'specialises in coordinating international trade' and 'who [is] the true entrepreneur'.[89] At the same time, merchants such as Goddard or those servicing Cork, Edge and Malkin should not be condemned out of hand for their unwillingness to build more co-operative links with local manufacturers. As Nicholas argues, 'the merchant house overcame the high information costs of transacting, allowing small manufacturers to compete in the international market'. Similarly, Broadberry and Marrison have demonstrated that 'external economies of specialisation associated with the merchant-converter system' persisted well into the twenthieth century and 'slowed the shift of comparative advantage to low wage countries'.[90]

However, pressures on prices continued into the new century, not withstanding the beginnings of a recovery in export volumes. E. Hughes and Co. of Fenton, for example, complained of the 'undercurrent which now exists to take special order at cut rates'.[91] However, institutional developments had also undoubtedly occurred. In part, these were in response to structural change in the wholesale and retail sectors. *The Pottery Gazette* presciently sketched elements

---

88 *The Pottery Gazette*, January 1886, p. 40; idem., September 1896, p. 714.

89 Casson, 'Analysing Regional Business Networks', p. 30 and p. 34.

90 Nicholas, 'Overseas Marketing Performance', p. 506; Broadberry and Marrison, 'External Economies of Scale'.

91 *Tariff Commission*, para. 302.

of these changes as early as 1884 in a comment worth quoting at some length. Noting that 'sharp competition will not now admit of ... intermediate profits, the long and devious journey of articles from producer to the ultimate consumer is much shortened', the journal continued to identify the prime movers:

> First, in the gigantic co-operative societies, and again in the addition of glass and china departments to nearly all large drapery and furnishing establishments. The retail trade is drifting out of the hands of the glass and china dealers, properly so called, and into the hands of large capitalists who combine almost every retail business in one house. Whatever may be said about these unlimited emporiums there is no denying that they have one immense advantage over smaller dealers. An advantage not only on account of the better terms on which they can buy, but because in the extensive field at their command for selling they are enabled to dispose, and quickly too, of a variety of articles, good, bad and indifferent, that a small dealer would often find very dead stock. Their rapid turnover admits of a small profit'.[92]

These developments would, in the twentieth century, eventually alter selling methods in many industries. At the same time, whilst for many small firms there had been little change in the institutional structures linking them to markets since the 1850s, others had moved toward the formal agency system earlier adopted by larger firms and described by Wilson as 'the vital marketing innovation of the era'.[93]

Nicholas, in assessing the marketing performance of British manufacturing firms, argues that the 'choice of the particular institutional mode adopted depended on the nature and frequencies with which transactions occurred and the degree to which durable transaction-specific investments were incurred'. In this analysis, the switch from the use of merchant houses to direct agency representation typically occurred as 'transaction frequency increased' and 'brand name loyalty differentiated products'.[94] Moreover, Nicholas claims that 'Direct representation was not restricted to large or best-practice manufacturers. Irrespective of firms size or product line the basic agency contract was surprisingly uniform'.[95] Evidence from the Potteries both supports and qualifies these arguments. Certainly the spread of the agency system amongst the district's manufacturers was not restricted to large firms and did coincide with a greater awareness of the advantages of branding throughout the industry.[96] However, the

92 *The Pottery Gazette,* January 1884, p. 47–8.

93 Wilson, *British Business History*, p. 91.

94 Nicholas, 'Overseas Marketing', p. 497–8.

95 Ibid., p. 498.

96 A snapshot taken in 1885 reveals this development unfolding. In that year the *Pottery Gazette* published a list of pottery agents and showrooms in London. The list details outlets for seventy-six firms served by fifty-six different agents. As this suggests some agents represented

causal mechanisms are ambiguous and in some instances the move to branding may have followed rather than led to the adoption of direct representation. Certainly, at an earlier date, it was the mercantile structures that Cork, Edge and Malkin had supplied which had constrained any move to branding. Moreover, it is not clear that direct representation always helped to 'avoid conflicts of interest between competitors by specifying exclusive and sole marketing arrangements'.[97] Here again differences may have been oriented around firm size and age. Exclusivity seems to have been more successfully enforced by the largest and most prestigious firms, as suggested by the report of 1902 of Currall and Strasser, Mintons' agents in Germany. In Hamburg, for example, one previously important customer had begun to confine its 'business in English goods as far as possible to Wedgwood (for whom Mr Schmidt's nephew travels) and to Copelands for whom they act practically as agents', whilst in Vienna another customer had become 'bound to Brown-Westhead', another large Potteries' firm.[98]

However, amongst smaller or newer firms, relationships with agencies displayed many of the same weaknesses as those between manufacturers and Goddard half a century earlier. Interesting in this respect is the evidence of Herbert Colclough, a Longton manufacturer who introduced himself to the *Tariff Commission* thus: 'I attempt to manufacture for the million. I attempt to reach that class of trade that which buys largely ... and I am always seeking orders in bulk'.[99] These strategies bought Colclough into direct competition with continental manufacturers, in both domestic and international markets. Colcough first described how in the:

> home trade we do a good deal now by direct dealing with senders of orders, the trade is done usually by the introduction of agents and travellers in the first case, and repeat orders when the connection is established. We deal direct with both retail and wholesale traders.[100]

---

multiple makers, often with complimentary specialisms (say one manufacturer a piece of china earthenware, china and majolica). The firms represented included many relatively small, new firms, such as Banks and Thorley, majolica manufacturers of Hanley (RV £100, 1882). The twenty firms representing themselves were generally large, such as Copeland, Minton and Doulton; some, however, were much smaller, such as the familially connected firms of John and Thomas Bevington or the two Longton shops, W. Hines and Spencer and Stanway, who shared an address. Similarly fraternal was the strategy of Worthington & Sons and W. Harrop & Co., successors to the single firm of Worthington & Harrop, both represented by R. Green. Finally, as in the Potteries, agents clustered together in a few streets and buildings in Holborn. *The Pottery Gazette*, January 1885.

97 Ibid., p. 498.

98 M.Mss 1331, *Report of Currall and Strasser*, 1902.

99 *Tariff Commission*, para. 137. Colcloughs were a medium-sized firm with an RV of £260 in 1913. *Longton Borough Rate Book*, 1912–3.

100 *Tariff Commission*, para. 139.

In a market such as Australia though Colclough relied on agents. However, the agreements entered into by the firm with agencies differed from those described by Nicholas in one important respect, Colclough was unable to insist on exclusivity.[101] He described how:

> I arranged with an Australian firm to represent me in Australia last year, and naturally made an effort to insert a clause in the agreement excluding he sale of German china by the firm that was selling mine and they said "If you insist on that, we shall drop the matter altogether, we sell more German china than English", I was anxious to make the arrangement with this house so I had to drop the clause. I had similar experience previously; there is no chance of getting a decent house to represent us without submitting to that.[102]

Clearly, the competitiveness of German makes contributed to this situation, but so did the structure of the industry in North Staffordshire. Colclough noted that increasingly:

> customers ... see there is no difficulty about procuring what their requirements in small supplies, and the order have been reduced in volume for the last few years on account of the ease with which they can get anything they want. The orders are more in number now, but very much smaller ... on account of the ease with which they can replace anything they sell.[103]

In other words, the highly competitive structure of the industry allowed agents to parcel out demand in much the same way that Goddard had done. Logically, this strategy implied continued intense time pressures. Moreover, the alignment of agents' interests with those of manufacturers must have been cast in doubt. Other firms were obliged to except agencies on terms similar to those faced by Colcough and these often become conduits for information that inevitably forced down prices in Staffordshire. Disclosing detailed information on the design and cost of competing German lines handled by the same agents must have had the effect of encouraging manufacturers in the Potteries to match those prices or lose orders. Thus, the New Zealand agents of one firm openly noted:

> We send you ... a sample cup and saucer of a [German] make that has been selling in this neighbourhood very well, and should like you to get

[101] Many small firms would have been lucky to engage an agency on any terms. Typical was the following advertisement; 'London - A well known, established house, having a first class wholesale connection ... is open to accept COMMISSION AGENCIES. None but large manufacturers [will] be treated with'. *The Pottery Gazette,* January 1885.

[102] *Tariff Commission*, para. 140.

[103] Ibid., para. 144.

> us out something like it; but it is only fair to say that no earthenware teas are now selling well, as the foreign china can be landed at the same price.[104]

Agency representation may have reduced the costs of transacting in international markets, but their performance, particularly in terms of promoting the interests of manufacturers, could vary significantly depending on the nature of the inter-firm relationships of which they were a formal embodiment. As in the past, small firms were constrained when trying to mover towards high-trust relationships with intermediaries and the extension of the networks in which they participated. Isolated from fellow manufacturers and occupying a weak position relative to buyers, small firms remained as bound within the region at the close of the century as they had at its mid-point, weak information channels between both fellow manufacturers and manufacturers and intermediaries conditioning their position.

Conclusion

As was true also of technological change, the marketing strategies of firms in the Potteries were shaped by a range of factors, not least of which were their existing resources and technologies, structures and cultures, the diversity of the products that they made and the markets that they served, and the existence of well established and specialized institutions of distribution in both domestic and international markets. Again, though, the district was not unimportant. Reputation was a collective as well as an individualized phenomenon, and was threatened, in part at least, by the intensity of competition fostered by clustering. Further pressure was also exerted by change in the market place, originating both in a nascent reconfiguration of the retail and distributive sectors and in the strategies of foreign competitors.

These forces could urge manufacturers in conflicting directions. Structures and resources, at the level of the firm and the industry, compounded by culture, made it difficult for firms to compete on price and volume or to integrate forward. Intermediated exchange, however, often made the maintenance of premium prices difficult and, even after the shift towards direct agency representation, could be unsympathetic to attempts at differentiation or could undermine claims as to the quality of Staffordshire wares. At the same time, the rise of foreign competition was reshaping markets in ways many were suspicious of and individualized priorities worked against collaborative actions that might have either built more robust networks for marketing or defended prices and reputations. The majority of firms were too small to build such networks

---

[104] Ibid., para. 264–5.

themselves and too weak to resist the demands of buyers. Thus, they found, as did firms in other specialty sectors, that 'marketing was the weakest link in their struggle to create a surplus'.[105]

That the industry was apparently 'committed to selling traditional goods in traditional markets', and that it was 'even further behind the times in her selling methods' than in her productive processes, cannot then be ascribed simply to managerial shortcomings.[106] Moreover, success was far from unknown. Dunn, Bennett and Co., and others, carved out and defended highly profitable niches and moved towards a fuller forward integration, whilst others, large and small, developed the system of agency representation found in other manufacturing sectors. Some firms proved themselves 'capable of challenging ... a given set of constraints'.[107] Furthermore, the claim of 'Made in Staffordshire' retained much of its cachet. That it did so urges detailed consideration of business structures and cultures at the level of the district. However, before that challenge is accepted, we will explore further the capabilities mandated by the strategies outlined here.

[105] Scranton, *Figured Tapestry*, p. 135.

[106] Kirby, 'Institutional Rigidities', p. 640.

[107] Ibid., p. 640.

CHAPTER SIX

Keeping stock and keeping up

Introduction

Stock-keeping and design do not seem to be closely related functions, yet for specialty sectors they are bound together by the intersection of time and fashion. The marketing strategies and institutional structures outlined in the preceding chapter, mandating flexibility and the ability to respond quickly, placed considerable burdens on manufacturers. Inevitably tensions were set up by the pressure to satisfy occasional demand with great alacrity, suggesting some degree of stock-holding, and the relentless march of fashion and obsolescence. The link between stock-keeping and design is then temporal, time remorselessly eroding the design and monetary value of stocks held for too long. As shall be shown in the case of Mintons, styled goods rapidly depreciated in value but producing to order led often to slow delivery, cancelled orders and the loss of goodwill. As the trade press warned at the signs of a revival in colonial markets in 1894, 'continued efforts at production must be put forth or with the approaching expansion ... orders will be kept on the books too long, and may drift in to other channels'.[1]

On the other hand, holding stock also placed demands on a manufacturer's capital structure, demands that were heightened by flows of orders and cash that were often irregular and unpredictable. This chapter will therefore examine, firstly, the extent to which manufacturers held stocks, their attitudes towards stocks and the capabilities needed and, secondly, the provision of design capabilities. Crucial here will be the balance between such provision at the level of the firm and at the level of the industry. In other words, were design skills largely firm specific, potentially conferring considerable competitive advantage, or were they generalized throughout the region?

Keeping stock

Consul Burgess claimed in 1892 that the American manufacturer:

---

1 *The Pottery Gazette*, December 1894, p. 973.

> must carry a large and assorted stock, so as to be ready at a moment's demand to fill his orders. A like order given by the same customer to an English manufacturer would not be expected to arrive within 2 or 3 months and would be patiently waited for. In the handling of English goods the merchant anticipates his wants. He it is who carries the stock goods, and it is his, and not the English potter's, capital that is locked up in stock goods. The consequence is that the American potter must, and does, manufacture for stock, while the English potter manufactures on orders.

The result, Burgess notes, is 'a large additional outlay of capital on the part of the American, as compared with the English, manufacturer'.[2] However, as we have seen, not all merchants were prepared to wait patiently for two or three months, and nor is it true that Staffordshire firms only manufactured to order. Inevitably some stocks were held. Some of the difficulties that resulted from this may be attributed to the distance from markets created by indirect selling, leading to an unpredictable flow of orders, but they were undoubtedly exacerbated in many instances by the loose control exercised by management over many aspects of production and by the inadequacy of managerial and clerical structures.[3]

Evidence of the extent to which firms held stocks is often contained in bankruptcy notices, which dissaggregated the assets of failed firms. Stocks commonly represented a significant proportion of gross assets. At E.F. Bodley, a Burslem firm that failed in the early 1890s, for example, stocks represented fifty-seven per cent of gross assets and an astonishing 297 per cent of the value of the firm's plant. At the venerable firm of Davenports stocks also continually rose in value in the years leading up to collapse in 1887. Thus, in the financial year 1881–2, when profits of £6997 were made, stock, at the factory and the Liverpool warehouse, totalled £17,642. In the following year profits decreased but the value of stocks now topped £20,000. By 1885, with the firm plunged into loss-making, stocks at the factory alone were worth more than £13,000.[4]

Clearly, these examples relate to firms facing an exceptional moment in their histories, that of failure, and it is not clear to what extent the high levels of stocks held were normal or related directly to failure, as either cause or effect. No doubt they were both, at least in part. Whatever the exact balance though, there can be no mistaking either the burden such stock levels must have placed on an already

---

2 Burgess, *Staffordshire vs. American Pottery,* p. 42.

3 For the American pottery and glass industries the growing buying power and direct dealing of mass merchandisers such as department stores and mail order firms, together with the instigation of annual show by manufacturers associations, did much in this period to make more orderly the cycle of seasons and, with that, the design process. R.L. Blaszczyk, *Imagining the Consumer: Design and Innovation from Wedgwood to Corning* (London, John Hopkins University Press, 2000).

4 Lockett, *Davenport*, p. 30–1.

struggling firm or the impression of a management unable to co-ordinate supply and demand at a critical time, the firm 'chasing [its] tail in a downward spiral'.[5]

However, there is also no doubt that successful firms held stocks, though perhaps at lower levels. Thus, on registration in 1899, Dunn, Bennett and Co. held stock valued at £4687, or a much more reasonable sixty-five per cent of the value of plant. Even so, stocks still formed a significant component in the firm's asset structure, representing one quarter of the gross total.[6]

That firms did hold often very considerable quantities of stocks, even when prospering, does not imply though that they always wished or aimed to. In August 1880, for example, in the face of a collapse in all but the American markets, without which 'there would be scarcely anything to do', the trade press reported that 'those houses whose capital has allowed them have been adding to stock, and have resigned themselves to the fate having to continue to do so'.[7] Two points emerge from this comment. First adding to stock was clearly not seen as a chosen strategy but as one into which firms were unwillingly forced by the state of the market. Strategy was dictated rather than under their control and was unlikely, in such circumstances, to be viewed in a positive light. Second, producing for stock was recognised a capital hungry practice viable only for larger or less pressed firms, another reason why smaller firms, unable to hold substantial stocks, had to consider almost any order, no matter what it paid, in order to maintain production and cash-flow.

These factors account, at least in part, for why the industry viewed producing for stock as a burden, its fate during periods of slack trade. Such attitudes also speak to the capabilities of most firms, and in particular the rudimentary management control systems and book-keeping practices of the majority. Effective and efficient production for stock requires that the firm is able to marshall and co-ordinate two separate information flows; the first concerned with the amount and, in an industry characterized by wide product ranges, the composition of stock held, and the second with the level and, again, the composition of demand in the market place. That all firms in the Potteries possessed the management skills and resources to control these information flows, regardless of the quality of information supplied by buyers and agents, must be open to doubt. Typically, in the absence of trained and dedicated specialists, these complex and demanding tasks fell to the proprietary capitalist. As late as 1900 complaints were being voiced as to the 'elementary conditions of

---

5 Scranton, *Figured Tapestry*, p. 163. Scranton made the comment of Schofields, a Philadelphia firm whom, despite declining sales, 'still had to keep getting goods out in order to secure cash for wages and bills'.

6 *Registration Prospectus of Dunn, Bennett & Co.*, 1899. The valuations were prepared by potter's valuer Spencer Lawton, who, perhaps significantly, went on to join the Board of the newly formed firm. The firm's books were examined for the same prospectus by P.H. Pope of Tunstall and showed an average profit of £2,935 p.a. for the years 1896–8.

7 *The Pottery Gazette*, August 1880, p. 400.

book-keeping [in] the trade' which were such that it 'practically defied finding out ... whether the manufacturers had made any profit or loss'. More specifically, stock-taking was discussed in 1896 as though it were generally an innovation of recent origin:

> Many firms have been taking stock, a custom which appears to be much more general than was the case a few years ago ... it is to be feared that even now there are quite a considerable number of potters who think stocktaking a loss of time and money, or who carry out the work in a very imperfect manner.[8]

Such procedures were part of the baggage of rountinization, which few in Staffordshire had wholeheartedly embraced.

There were, however, yet more fundamental reasons for the aversion to holding stock displayed by potters, for they recognised that the practice clashed with both their orientation towards markets and consumers and their production strategies and technologies. The pottery industry served markets that were not only heterogeneous in terms of taste, price and even cultural context, but which were also subject to rapid change over time, sometimes occurring not on a yearly basis but on a bi-annual or even shorter cycle. Demand in such markets, and with it the value of a product, was 'often time critical'.[9] Holding stock not only tied up capital and space but also left manufacturers vulnerable to changes in fashion that could rapidly devalue the productions of even the most astute and design conscious.

There was then a dilemma in which the scant enthusiasm of the industry for producing for stock may be located. It was a strategy into which they were sometimes forced by both unpredictable demand and their own weakness relative to buyers and merchants, but which, at the same time, was far from wholly suited to the nature of the markets they served. Moreover, if anything, growth in the demand for staple tableware, where needs were more easily predicted, was outpaced by that for fancies, novelties and ornamental pieces of all qualities as a taste for consumption and display spread throughout society.[10] It is not surprising then that, in common with other specialty sectors, that the 'holding of final goods was avoided' by potters, or even that some had a 'horror of running stock'.[11]

Of course, manufacturers could attempt to stay ahead of the game, but the inevitable contradictions between the need to hold some stocks, given the resources a firm needed to do so effectively, and the variegated demand structure

---

8 *The Pottery Gazette*, October 1900, p. 1139 and February 1896, p. 133.

9 Scranton, 'Diversity in Diversity', p. 29.

10 See Blaszczyk, *Imagining Consumers*, for an excellent exploration of these issues in the American context.

11 Scranton, 'Diversity in Diversity', p. 30; idem, *Figured Tapestry*, p.8

faced by the industry was forcefully captured by the *Pottery Gazette* in an article of 1886 entitled 'Changes in Pottery Art':

> On even a small factory now the patterns, shapes, bodies and colours grow in number with amazing rapidity, and it is next to impossible for the potter to keep of them a large stock, supposing that it would be judicious thing for him to do.[12]

Expressed perfectly here are the temporal dimensions and pressures inherent in the struggle to co-ordinate design and production with the dictates of an emerging consumer society.

This dilemma could be partially met through a variety of strategies. One would be to manufacture for stock a relatively limited number of different undecorated blanks, or shapes, to be differentiated through the application of a wider range of motifs and patterns as and when orders arrived. This policy was, moreover, increasingly facilitated by technological and structural change. Important here are the introduction of lithography, and, in particular, the growth of an independent decorating sector, as outlined in the reconstruction of the structure of the industry in Chapter 1. These changes together reduced the costs of differentiation, smoothed and lengthened time-frames and shifted the burden of what Blaszczyk has called 'aesthetic risk'.[13] Such a policy would be especially attractive to firms that had increased their capital intensity during the wave of re-equipping and factory building which had swept the district from the 1870s through to the 1890s. But these were not perfect solutions and firms needed to ensure they possessed some capability to respond to or even predict the vagaries of taste.

Keeping up

Design, as a central element in the business strategies of specialty, batch producers needs careful consideration then. Important are its precise role, cost and method of fulfilment. Design historians, with a good understanding of the design process, have tended to be critical of the standards of design prevalent in British consumer and fashions goods industries in the nineteenth century. This reaction has been conditioned by the precepts of Modernism, themselves derived from the negative reactions of the Cole group and of Ruskin and Morris to the Great Exhibition of 1851, and by a poor understanding of the conditions and constraints under which business firms operated, and of their priorities. Their thinking may be considered a sub-clause of the entrepreneurial failure thesis;

12 *The Pottery Gazette*, October 1896, p. 1161.

13 Blaszczyk, *Imagining Consumers*, p. 39.

British businessmen, often reflecting their artisanal roots, were crass and uncultured and paid little attention to either aesthetic developments or the role that design might have played in selling their goods. Similarly, in the past, wary business and economic historians, with a few exceptions, such as Chapman on printed textiles, have tended to steer clear of design as both a business function and as a factor in the fortunes of firms and industries.[14]

More recently, scholars have begun to explore the complex linkages between production, design and consumption and their nexus in the business firm. As we shall see, such an approach is necessarily implied, though often latent, in the flexible specialization literature. Others, such as Blaszczyk, have begun to address this issue more directly. Central to Blaszczyk's work is the claim that consumer goods producers in late nineteenth-century America, recognized and exploited the fact that 'design and development was an interactive process that took places at the intersection of supply and demand'.[15] In short, firms did not impose taste on markets and consumers but instead let themselves be guided by them. Blaszczyk characterizes this process as one 'best facilitated by seasoned fashion intermediaries experienced in the task of imagining consumers':

> Although few took merchant partners like Bentley, most manufacturers relied heavily on feedback from *fashion intermediaries*, astute consumer liaisons whose jobs entailed studying markets, evaluating tastes and making product recommendations. Identifying these fashion brokers as the primary agents of innovation turns the canon of design history inside out and back to front.[16]

The same might also be said to be true of much of business history. Nonetheless, questions remain about how the process of 'imagining' the consumer is translated into the creation of concrete products. For some industries, these questions may prove as important as those concerning the sources of purely technological innovations. Blaszczyk derives from her study of the pressed and cut glass sectors in America a framework of analysis that depends on identifying the location of 'aesthetic authority', and this may well prove useful.[17] Equally important, however, are questions concerning the centrality of design and design skills to competitive advantage. That such an advantage exists and is significant is, for example, largely assumed in the concept of flexible specialization offered

---

[14] S.D. Chapman, 'Quantity versus Quality in the British Industrial Revolution: The Case of Printed Textiles', *Northern History*, Vol. 21 (1985), pp. 175–192.

[15] Blaszczyk, *Imagining Consumers*, p. 13.

[16] Ibid, p. 12–3.

[17] Thus, Blaszczyk argues that; 'The pressing trade bestowed aesthetic authority on the mechanics responsible for building its molds; the cutting business saw design as a job best shared by workshop proprietors, cutters and engravers, and china merchants. In pressing, the creation of beauty pivoted largely on a craft skill; in cutting it rested on the tripod of entrepreneurial, artisanal and retail competence'. *Imagining Consumers*, p. 16.

by Sabel and Zeitlin. Sabel and Zeitlin define flexible specialization in terms of the 'flexible use of multipurpose or universal machines and skilled labour to make an ever-changing assortment of semi-customised products'. They ascribe to this approach attributes such as efficiency, a lack of rigidity in product and process development leading to a technological dynamism and, above all else, heightened responsiveness to consumer demand. In terms of the implications for the relationship between firms, industries and markets, they argue that flexible specialization is an advantage where industries serve 'highly differentiated' markets that demand that products be 'constantly altered'.[18] Thus, they argue that flexible specialization enables industries and firms to respond to and benefit from fashion led markets; creating, seeking out and exploiting pockets of and shifts in taste.

Encouraged by their focus on regions and districts, Sabel and Zeitlin search for an enabling 'institutional framework' supportive of flexible specialization at these broader levels and not at that of the firm. Returns to flexibility are also conceived of in terms of the industry as a whole in this schema, for example through the effect of a reputation for quality or for originality attaching as much to the region as to specific firms.

Certainly, to a degree, design capabilities were generalized throughout the Potteries, an effect of both specialization by firm and the inter-firm movement of key workers, but potters viewed designs and design skills in highly proprietorial terms. This fierce proprietorialism, though it was not easily defended from piracy, naturally reflected the terms of competition under which firms were understood to operate. Design skills, though to an extent generated by the district, were not a public good. How and to what extent then were individual firms able to realize the ideal of market-sensitive flexibility?

It is probable that most potters understood their markets in terms akin to those proposed by Sabel and Zeitlin, and that they strove to turn this to their best advantage.[19] However, it is not so clear that the majority of them 'revelled' in satisfying a highly variegated demand, as Tweedale claims Sheffield cutlers did.[20] Despite the apparently standardizing direction in which production processes were beginning to trend, wider societal forces were increasing the attention that had to be paid to the needs, tastes and pockets of markets segmented along the lines of class, gender and nation. Thus, it has already been shown that

---

[18] Sabel and Zeitlin, 'Historical Alternatives', p. 133 & p. 144.

[19] The importance of this realization might not always have been so widely appreciated. In 1889 the trade press noted that 'care is now being taken by English potters to manufacture goods especially suited to the markets for which they are intended'. *The Pottery Gazette*, June 1889, p. 425.

[20] G. Tweedale, *Steel City: Entrepreneurship, Strategy and Technology in Sheffield, 1743–1993* (Oxford, Clarendon Press, 1995), p. 53. Tweedale claims that cutlery manufacturers 'thrived on economies of flexibility and opportunism, tailoring their production to fill highly specific niches in the market'. Ibid., p. 12.

Staffordshire potters conceived of the 'American notion of fine effect' as a predilection for things made with mechanical exactitude and rapidity. But this rather blunt characterization, offered in the 1880s, also had an aesthetic dimension; 'Bright colours, odd shapes, peculiar decoration, are the things most eagerly sought for by the Transatlantic cousin'.[21] These 'imaginings' were, however, never static and by the 1890s, as competition continued to increase, this somewhat crude caricature of Yankee vulgarity was being supplanted by another. As a token of this it was noted that 'a good sign from the United States is a growing demand for more expensive goods, which speaks eloquently of the increased purchasing powers in that country'.[22]

This need to tailor products to particular markets was also overlain by a general restless striving after novelty that was, in turn, supplemented by the opportunities offered by historic events, such as Queen Victoria's Diamond Jubilee in 1897.[23] The market was seen as being insatiable for novel products and effects, to the extent that constant, though often very superficial and purely decorative, product innovation was seen by some as being of greater importance to the future of the industry than process innovation. At the height of a trade depression in 1883, manufacturers were being advised that it would be better 'to spend money in preparing fresh novelties for the spring trade instead of pushing out in other directions for remunerative orders', whilst in the early 1890s it was felt to be of some concern that nothing startling in the way of novelties ... has made its appearance during this year ... the general conditions of business tend to eliminate originality'.[24]

The response of both individual firms and the wider industry to this search for fresh designs and 'novelties' with which to catch the eye of the consumer was regularly commented upon in the trade press. Indeed, if we are searching for those 'fashion intermediaries' identified by Blaszczyk as critical to the vitality of specialty sectors, then none may have been more important than the trade press. As a conduit for fashion intelligence the trade press operated in two directions, presenting manufacturers' latest patterns to buyers and alerting manufacturers of trends adopted by their competitors in Staffordshire and elsewhere. For many it must have been a more reliable, and certainly a more comprehensive, source of information than those merchants and jobbers with whom they had direct contact.

---

[21] *The Pottery Gazette*, February 1882, p. 157. See also Collard, *Nineteenth Century Pottery and Porcelain*, and Ewins, '"Supplying the Present Wants ... "', for further discussion of how potters sought to adapt their products to North American markets.

[22] *The Pottery Gazette*, June 1895, p. 440.

[23] The trade in commemorative wares, celebrating a panoply of different events, was an important one, though it could rarely rescue a bad year, as in 1897 when it had to 'be confessed that on the whole the Jubilee year has been very much a failure from our trade point of view'. *The Pottery Gazette*, December 1897, p. 1404.

[24] *The Pottery Gazette*, September 1883, p. 855; *The Pottery Gazette*, January 1896, p. 49.

The trade press was also a relatively cheap source of information, but even so the costs of keeping up with increasingly intense fashion cycles remained considerable. As the *Pottery Gazette* itself conceded in 1880; 'the result of the persistent demand for something novel has been an increased cost of manufacturing, reaching in some case a considerable amount'.[25] The costs incurred were twofold. Direct costs were incurred in terms of wages paid to designers and decorators, amongst the most highly paid members of the workforce, but there were also considerable opportunity costs for management, arising from the need to devote time to the monitoring of information from the marketplace.[26] The constantly shifting demands of highly variegated markets, to which the vitality of flexible specialists is tied, was thus seen as draining. Crucially, those demands could also appear fickle as well. The sense of frustration with a fashion led consumer market is clear in a comment issued in 1886:

> Beautiful as were many of these patterns, the public taste was to fitful to be satisfied with them for any length of time ... Our modern potter has to speculate largely. If he hits the market he may have a run with a certain article or class of goods, and make a good return. But this is not so often done as may be imagined.[27]

Thus, fashion was seen by many in the pottery industry as a costly and fairly superficial commodity that was unlikely to yield significant and lasting advantage to many firms. Observing that 'there has been no striking novelty brought out by the trade this year', the trade press lamented that 'it is difficult to see where any absolute and valuable novelty is to be looked for'. [28] Genuine differentiation was an elusive quality for all but the most prestigious of firms. Moreover, tight clustering, facilitating rapid imitation and outright piracy, further exacerbated an attitude that, in turn, fed back into and reinforced fears of standardization, reduced originality and declining quality rooted in the ongoing process of mechanization.

It was as though potters were not confident in design, and yet this attitude seems to sit uncomfortably alongside an emphasis on quality in many marketing strategies. To a considerable degree, however, the emphasis on quality pertained more to the actual making of the ware's rather than to the originality or competence of their design. To many, the highest expression of the potter's craft

---

[25] *The Pottery Gazette*, December 1880, p. 791. Similarly, Scranton found occasions when the return of Philadelphia firms 'to "striving ... after new effects" increased their costs'. *Figured Tapestry*, p. 154.

[26] For an indication of the potential cost of design activity see Bernard Moore's claim that forty models 'had cost me £400 or £500'. *Tariff Commission*, para. 121.

[27] *The Pottery Gazette*, October 1886, p. 1161. Moore, for example reckoned that; 'Out of 7 or 8 designs the probability is that only 2 or 3 are a success'. *Tariff Commission*, para. 121.

[28] *The Pottery Gazette*, January 1897, p. 98.

was to be found in good workmanship applied to the best materials. Moreover, these were factors which potters felt they understood. Uncertainty over design, its role and worth and how it should be approached stemmed from the concrete experience of trying to adapt to the inconstancy of the market. In contrast, the particular understanding of quality dominant in the Potteries, which did have a legitimate foundation in the human resources of the district, was familiar, buttressed by a constructed image of the Potteries that was built out of and rich in historical resonances.[29] The conception of quality prevalent in the Potteries may be considered an example of those 'collective subjectivities' identified by Casson, and is a reminder that the relationship between skill, flexible technologies and markets are marked by cultural as well as technological or economic dimensions and will thus vary from sector to sector.[30] This attitude was not without its critics though, one warning that; 'to make good ... china body does not mean all that is necessary for success'. The implication was that prevalent attitudes imposed a narrow outlook that relegated the importance of satisfying genuine consumer needs and preferences.[31]

As already noted, ambivalence about design and fashion was further fuelled by the constant problem of design piracy, a persistent feature of other specialty sectors.[32] Scranton highlights turnaround and set-up times as important to the degree to which an industry will suffer from this problem, equally apposite though is his emphasis on the possibility that industries may be '*too* flexible and spatially compact'.[33] Bernard Moore discussed piracy in some detail before the *Tariff Commission*, and he too emphasized temporal factors:

> If the cheaper imitations can be found in time they can be stopped, but unfortunately they get distributed all over the country and a comparatively small alteration will be quite sufficient to nullify the registration. It is difficult to bring it home to the person issuing the article, as it passes through many hands. As a rule it is too late and the damage is done ... The competition is not direct, but as soon as their is a cheap copy the good shops will not buy our originals.

---

[29] For skill levels of Potteries workers see T.B. Johnston's observation that; 'There is no doubt that Staffordshire is the place to manufacture, because of the labour. The skilled labour has been there for generations, and the Staffordshire pottery, beyond doubt is the best in the world, and I see the difference in my workmen when I go to Stafforshire. The way they handle the clay in Staffordshire is absolutely different'. *Tariff Commission*, p. 175. For separation of the concepts of 'design' and 'quality', see the claim that though 'the decoration of our productions ... [is] not always of such as a character as to command the market ... For quality and durability Staffordshire productions will hold their own in any market'. *The Pottery Gazette*, p. January 1893, p. 43.

[30] Casson, 'Entrepreneurship and Business Culture', p. 40.

[31] *The Pottery Gazette*. January 1896, p. 47.

[32] See Scranton, *Endless Novelty,* chapter 5.

[33] Ibid., p. 110.

Moore's final comment demonstrates how piracy not only impacted on the sale of a specific product, but also shifted the broader terms of competition, downgrading differentiation and upgrading price. For Moore, in his own words 'exclusively [a] high class china' manufacturer, piracy was a constant, destabilizing threat: 'We have our own designs and make according to them, and in this connection we suffer enormously from unfair competition'.[34]

However, just as potters disliked holding stock but could not avoid doing so, provision had to be made for design, no matter that the vagaries of fashion were distrusted. However, before design provision is discussed it is necessary to introduce a qualification. In many instances, the term 'design' retained in the late nineteenth century the limited meaning that had emerged during the earliest stages of industrialization, when both aesthetic traditions and the unified tasks of conception and execution were disrupted by new productive processes and new forms of work. A vacuum came into being in the process of making things. The task of formulating how industrial products were to be designed had to be worked through. The task was a fundamental. The very role of industrial design, its scope, approaches and the training of its practitioners all had, in effect, to be invented. This innovatory process, like that for many instances of technological innovations, occupied an extended time-frame and was far from complete at the close of the nineteenth century. In the mean time the vacuum was filled by a more limited conception of design as the application of 'art' to the surface of an object. This understanding of design was perhaps first expressed in the report of Ewart's *Select Committee on Art and Manufacture* of 1836 and then propogated through the system of provincial branches of the Normal School of Design, themselves an outcome of that report.[35] It was thus a preoccupation with surface decoration to which many potters referred when they spoke of design and which governed their conception of the role of design within their business.

To a considerable degree this conception fitted well with prevalent technological horizons and market orientations. For firms serving bottom and mid-range markets, techniques such as transfer printing, and later lithography, allowed a degree of differentiation to be achieved relatively cheaply, a multitude of patterns being applied to a limited number of shapes.

---

[34] *Tariff Commission*, para. 121. Moore had little faith in design registration, for a variety of reasons. Thus, he noted that 'At one time we were bringing out quite 500 or 600 designs in a year. We register our successes; to register everything would be throwing money away ... We only register in England, and it is not much use when it is done'. Ibid., para. 120-1.

[35] The local Schools of Design undoubtedly had an impact on design practice in the Potteries, many designers, both well-known and anonymous attending the classes they offered. Opinion on the utility of design education was however mixed. One contribution on 'Technical Education' in the trade press asserted that 'schools of design ... have not educated the workmen, nor even the masters', but Bernard Moore felt that 'Designing and the art part of our work is a very important branch, and there the technical training has done a great deal of good'. *The Pottery Gazette*, January 1896, p. 47; *Tariff Commission*, para. 119.

Design provision was extremely variable in the Potteries. The largest firms were able to employ art directors, charged not only with producing designs themselves but also with overseeing the work of a design team, including artists and modellers. In Blaszczyk's terms, it was with the art director that 'aesthetic authority' rested in such cases. Moreover, in this context, the phrase is genuinely meaningful. First, art directors were charged with and responsible for achieving an artistic excellence which, second, was central to the firm's whole strategy. In turn, they were generally given the resources necessary to this end.

In the late nineteenth century many art directors were foreigners, though those working under them were almost exclusively local and trained in the region's schools of design. At Mintons alone Arnoux, Boullemier and Solon came from France and Jahn from Germany. It was as though the district, though certain of its potting prowess, was less confident of its artistic skills and in particular of its understanding of artistic developments in Continental Europe. Thus, it was perhaps hoped at Mintons that the employment of men such as Boullemier and Solon, both of who had worked at the factory at Sèvres, would serve to heighten the firm's prestige. What is clear is that the firm took design seriously, devoting considerable resources to it and integrating design personnel into the management of the firm and its governance structure. A handful of other firms followed suite, whilst at Wedgwood, continuing a tradition established in the eighteenth century, links were forged with a series of prominent and progressive metropolitan designers, including Christopher Dresser, Walter Crane and William de Morgan.[36] Moreover, the longevity of this cohort of firms had allowed them to amass unparalleled repositories of patterns and shapes on which to draw. In time, particularly in the twentieth century, these repositories came to shape to a large degree the design strategies of such firms and to define for consumers their images as ones in which tradition was uppermost. Indeed, as early the late nineteenth century, Wedgwoods were already principally famed for the production of wares a century old in design.

However, such formidable artistic teams could be recruited and maintained by only the very largest and most prestigious firms. For the rest of the industry, design provision was achieved through a variety of means, including both direct employment and contracting out. In the majority, whilst there may have be no designated 'art director', it was true that, as in Trenton, New Jersey, 'the job of deciphering the wants, needs, and desires' of consumers 'fell into the hands of

---

[36] Other prominent examples include C.F. Hürten who, born in Cologne and previously employed at Sèvres, worked for Copelands between 1859 and 1897, whilst Lessore, again from Sèvres, came to the Potteries in 1858, first to Mintons for a brief period, and then forging a long standing connection with Wedgwoods. However, it is notable how frequently Jewitt, for example, chooses not to name any artists when describing even the most prominent firms, including those he commended for their artistic excellence. Most artists in the Potteries were essentially anonymous.

practical men like the china decorator Jesse Dean'.[37] However, unlike in Trenton before the mid-1870s, contracting out for all decorating functions was probably unknown and the decorating shop was an integral part of every 'bank' in the Potteries.[38] The atmosphere of a typical decorating shop is wonderfully captured in the tour of his works given by Henry Mynors to Anna Tellwright in Arnold Bennett's *Anna of the Five Towns.* It is worthwhile first establishing the market position of Mynor's firm, based in a medium-sized but well-ordered, three-oven bank. Mynors would '"sooner do as I do than make swagger ware for a handful of rich people" ... [he] was in fact always very enthusiastic concerning the virtues of general markets. He had no sympathy with specialities, artistic or otherwise. He found his satisfaction in honestly meeting the public taste. He was born to be a manufacturer of cheap goods on a colossal scale'. However, this did not mean that Mynors could ignore the desire for embellishment, the satisfaction of which desire began in the printing shop:

> where, by means of copper-plates, printing-presses, mineral colours and transfer-papers. Most of the decoration was done. The room was filled by a little crowd of people - oldish men, women, and girls, divided into printers, cutters, transferrers, and apprentices. Each interminably repeated some trifling process, and every article passed through a succession of hands until at length it was washed in a tank and rose dripping therefrom with its ornament of flowers and scrolls fully revealed. The room smelt of oil and flannel and humanity; the atmoshpere was ... languid ... Contiguous with the printing-shop was the painting-shop, in which the labours of the former were taken to a finish by the brush of the paintress, who filled in outlines with flat colour, and thus converted mechanical printing into handiwork. The paintresses form the *noblesse* of the banks.[39]

Finally, they visit the lone girl applying 'band-and-line', whose work 'represented the summit of monotony; the regularity of it hypnotized the observer, and Mynors himself was impressed by this stupendous phenomenon of absolute sameness'.[40]

Several points may be drawn out from this description, not least the resources devoted to decoration. Notable too is how the filling in of printed patterns is used to create a similitude of 'handiwork', satisfying the desire of the mass-consumer

---

37 Blaszczyk, *Imagining Consumers*, p. 55. As Blaszczyk notes many firms 'could afford to pay only one person as an all-round design expert - typically the china decorator. This person served as an artistic jack-of-all-trades under one of several titles ... chief decorator, head decorator or art decorator'. Ibid., p. 57.

38 Blaszyzck claims that from the early to mid-1870s Trenton's 'pottery managers became frustrated with delays associated with the outside contract system. To protect themselves against design priacy, to cut costs and to expedite output, potteries established on-site facilities for china decorating. *Imagining Consumers*, p. 75.

39 A. Bennett, *Anna of the Five Towns* (London, Penguin Books, 1969), p. 120–1.

40 Ibid., p. 121.

for some of the aesthetic pleasure available to those able to afford Mintons' finest products. No less striking is the co-presence of creativity and monotony. However, perhaps most important is the absence of an identifiable 'designer'; indeed during the whole tour the reader is introduced directly to only one worker, Eli Machin; 'the engineman, the oldest employee on the works, a moneyed man, and the pattern of reliability'.[41] If 'aesthetic authority' did rest with one person at these works, it was not of sufficient weight to distinguish that person from his or her fellow workers. Instead, design decisions would in such works very often have been taken by the proprietory capitalist, able to fulfill this role only because very often 'design meant keeping abreast of new patterns, glazes and bodies, and being able to respond to market demands in a competitive business. It did not necessarily mean creating new patterns and shapes'.[42]

Certainly, skilled operatives in the decorating shops were important to the realization of this task and many, male and female, fulfilled in the rather circumscribed way outlined above some of the functions of the designer. Indeed, work in the decorating shop was the most common form of design training in the Potteries and the most frequently travelled path to work as a designer.[43] Young painters and paintresses graduated from the simplest tasks executing the designs of others to positions of greater responsibility, which may have included producing original designs.

However, we should be cautious in claiming that many possessed anything worthy of the description 'aesthetic authority', in relation either to the governance of the firm or, more importantly, to the determination of strategy. The position occupied by the majority of in-house decorators was often ambiguous. Though often considered rather superior by other workers and immediately distinguished from others by the lack of grime that attended their labour, they certainly remained for the most part shopfloor employees and not management. The uncertain and incomplete separation of the essentially different roles of designer and decorator in the Potteries indicated not only a hesitant committment to the commercial value of a planned and progressive design policy but was also likely, in conjunction with on-the-job training at the hands of experienced older workers, to result in a great deal of imitative work which built only slowly on traditional forms and patterns. Indeed, even the normally bullish trade press was forced to concede that; 'the manufacturers of this district are unfortunately imitative rather than creative' in terms of decoration.[44] This tendency was exacerbated by a lively second hand market in designs and design tools, including moulds and engraved copper plates, some decades old. These would have been particularly attractive to the small and increasingly burdened

---

[41] Ibid., p. 118.

[42] Buckley, *Potters and Paintresses*, p. 18.

[43] Most pupils attended Schools of Design in the evening. Hence, education was essentially a supplement to on-the-job training.

[44] *The Pottery Gazette*, August 1881, p. 665.

management typical of many firms in this period as they strove to cope with consumers demanding ever more novelty at lower prices. If inherited designs connected a firm to one more illustrious, then so much the better. Undoubtedly, that was the rationale behind an advertisment placed by Wengers, suppliers of colours and glazes, which announced that the firm 'having bought the printing copper plates of Messrs. Davenports Co. and other firms is prepared to *sell* or hire [them], and to *match the colours* and supply *the shapes* used with the ... patterns'.[45]

It was asserted above that decorating shops were integral to all English potbanks, nonetheless it is also clear from evidence contained in rate books and trade directories that there had long existed an ancillary design sector of independent china decorators, modellers and copper plate engravers. However, this ancillary trade was more artisanal than artistic in its background and tenor, certainly before the final decades of the nineteenth century. They were artisanal in so far as their prime skill, and pride, lay in the execution of a difficult craft rather in aesthetic originality. Most frequently they were either single workers or one or two family members operating from workshops at their residential addresses and displaying poor survival rates. Thus, atypical was copper plate engraver Henry Toft who operated a workshop on Upper Cliffe Bank (RV £9) and workshop and house on Thomas Street (RV £8), both in Stoke-upon-Trent, and survived in business from at least 1886 until 1898. The role of such craftsmen was essentially reactive, furnishing manufacturers with quick and cheap copies of currently fashionable styles and patterns. Certainly they did not match 'the air of prosperity at the three-storey brick workshop of china decorator Jesse Dean [that] impressed visitors to Trenton' in the early 1880s.[46]

However, just as American potters began to bring decorating under their own roofs and control, heralding decline for Dean and his like, so the scale and scope of the ancillary decorating sector began to undergo a significant transformation in North Staffordshire. As Chapter 2 outlined, this sub-sector grew in relative and absolute terms as other auxilliary trades declined between the 1880s and 1914. Two features of this growth were particularly striking; the size of some individual firms (and of the average firm) and their exploitation of the relatively new technique of chromo-lithography. As Blaszczyk argues, such firms, which 'employed staff artists ... made decals to manufacturers' specifications and guaranteed not to sell those designs to competing potteries', were eventually to 'eclipse china decorators as the pottery industry's embellishing experts'.[47] The

[45] *The Pottery Gazette*, February 1888, p. 185 (emphasis in original). Davenports, an old and much respected firm, had failed the previous year.

[46] Blaszczyk, 'The Aesthetic Moment', p. 121.

[47] Blaszczyk, *Imagining Consumers*, p. 86. The success of English and German lithographers in dominating the market amongst American potters deserves mention. The vast majority of lithographs applied to American pots in the early twentieth century were European imports.

appeal of lithography was neatly captured in an advertisement of 1901, which asked manufacturers; 'Do you want to give a filip to your trade? Then get the newest and artistic transfers. The best and most up-to-date patterns are produced by The Chromo Transfer Co. Ltd.'.[48]

The growth of this new sector had a number of foundations. Some were well-established firms that had diversified, often from the supply of potters' materials such as colours and glazes. We have already seen how Wengers sought to integrate a more complete design service with the sale of colours (see note 45 above). Another interesting example is provided by the firm of Harrison and Son Ltd., Hanley. After displaying modest growth in the 1870s this firm staked out a significant presence in a number of related fields. Following registration in 1900 the firm operated on six separate sites, each dedicated to a particular function; offices were located on Bath Street, underglaze colours manufactured at the Phoenix Chemical Works, enamel colours at the Providence Works, glazes at the Victoria Mills, flint and stone at the Boundary Street Mills, and, finally, lithographs were designed and printed at the aspirationally named Tintoretto works. Truly, this firm could claim to offer a one-stop service capable of meeting the decorative demands of most manufacturers.[49] Others, such as the Co-operative Wholesale Society, appear to have integrated backward from distribution and retailing. Whatever the origin of these firms, however, their strengthening presence marked a departure for the Potteries, and whilst they would not have been patronized by the likes of Mintons they did represent a valuable resource for the many firms which, as we have seen, felt increasingly hard-pressed by the market's desire for novelty and by the costs and risks that seemed to be associated with providing it.

Related, though exceptional, was the career of Bernard Moore, who early in the twentieth century positioned himself as perhaps the first genuine design consultant to the industry in North Staffordshire. Moore was a third generation potter and at a young age took over the St Mary's Works, Longton, of which his father had been sole proprietor until his death in 1867. In 1870 Moore was joined by his younger brother Samuel and the pair quickly established a reputation for the quality of both the make and design of their bone china wares, a reminder that there were always small firms willing and able to strive towards these ends. However, for reasons unknown, the firm closed in 1905, an event reported with regret in the trade press, for; 'the loss, both to the china trade and to the town of Longton, will be a heavy one, for the business has for many years enjoyed a

---

[48] *The Pottery Gazette*, January 1901, p. 22.

[49] Thomas William Harrison, born in Essex, first worked at and then took over the colour works of John Gerrard in Bath Street. This site, the Phoenix works, had an RV of £12 in 1862, £38 in 1872 and £62 in 1882. Thomas was later joined by at least one son, Sidney Thomas, and on registration in 1900, by which date Thomas was fifty seven, the firm was capitalized at £50,000 in £10 shares. Stuart, *People of the Potteries*, p. 113–4, *Hanley Borough Rate Books*; 1862, 1872 and 1882. *The Pottery Gazette*, January 1901, p. 221.

world-wide reputation for its artistic productions'.[50] In the same year Moore opened new workshops on Wolfe Street, in Stoke-upon-Trent. However, this was a quite different enterprise from that in Longton, for Moore manufactured no wares but only decorated those supplied by others. As Aileen Dawson has commented 'to break away so completely from the manufacture of mass-produced bone-china domestic ware which was in every way typical of the Victorian tradition' was a 'remarkable ... decision'.[51] Moore had become an independent china decorator of the very highest class.[52] However, his role was somewhat different to that earlier fulfilled by Dean and others in Trenton. Though Moore's blanks came firms such as Wedgwood, Minton, Copeland and the Crown Staffordshire Porcelain Co., Moore was no subcontractor. Instead, the wares carried his own mark, not those of the above manufacturers. The wares that emerged were exquisite but pricey, the target of wealthy private collectors, galleries and museums. In this way, Moore's workshop at Wolfe Street foreshadowed the so-called Studio Pottery movement far more than it proposed a viable way forward for volume production in the Potteries.

Of greater significance for the wider industry though was Moore's further role as chemist and consultant, 'his deep interest in the behaviour of clay and glazes in both industrial and craft production [being] the mainspring of his life'.[53] Here Moore not only directly helped numerous local firms but also paved the way for both a more scientific investigation of materials and their properties and potentials but also planted in potters' minds the realization that chemists had a valuable role to play in the industry.[54] Chemists certainly allowed potters to better understand and gain greater control over the production process, particularly in relation to firing, but they could also greatly enlarge the range of decorative effects available. Their impact was far from purely utilitarian, and this was particularly true of Moore who, as much as any other figure, embodied that amalgam of artistic and commercial endeavour so strong in the Potteries. Understanding the position of design in the industry in North Staffordshire requires an understanding of how excellence and quality were seen as the sum of

---

[50] *The Pottery Gazette*, June 1905, p. 674.

[51] Dawson, *Bernard Moore*, p. 20.

[52] Moore employed and trained a considerable cohort of designers and paintresses at Wolfe Street, some of whom at previously been employed at the original factory in Longton and the majority of whom were Potteries born. For details see Dawson, *Bernard Moore,* Chapter 6.

[53] Ibid., p. 88.

[54] Changing attitudes to the importance of employing chemists cannot be attributed solely to the influence of Moore. Wedgwood, for example, had employed William Burton as chief chemist between 1887 and 1897. Also important was the appointment as Lecturer at the Pottery School, Tunstall in 1904 of Joesph Mellor, who held a doctorate in chemistry from the University of Manchester. Moore worked as a consultant for at least eighteen firms in North Staffordshire. Dawson, *Bernard Moore*, Chapter 8; Stuart, *People of the Potteries*, p. 54, p.151–2 and p.158–9.

a constellation of different attributes, a stance summed up in Frederick and George Rhead's praise of Moore:

> In the Potteries today is one potter who has done something to redeem Staffordshire from the charge of indifference and decadence - Bernard Moore - a potter in the truest sense of the world. He is master of all the resources of the potter's craft, and his work alone shows Staffordshire still capable of coping with the potters of France. It is technically triumphant, and it is quite delightful ... to find in his showroom a case of pottery - perfect in colour and artistic feeling - which he will not sell, but prefers to retain for mere pride in its accomplishment ... In potters like Mr. Moore there is hope.[55]

In this context, design was never likely to become a slave to sales.

Conclusion

The locus of 'aesthetic authority' is then hard to locate. It shifted both from firm to firm and over time. As we saw in the previous chapter many merchants were rarely interested in functioning as 'fashion intermediaries' and many manufacturers lacked the skills or contacts to tackle the role with confidence. Some firms had generated over time the attributes and resources necessary to the task, but their generally large scale is worthy of emphasis. Indeed, Marshall himself had noted this as a particular feature of the pottery industry, commenting that; 'in the pottery trade ... the small manufacturer cannot even afford to make experiments with new patterns and designs except in a very tentative way. His chance is better with regard to an improvement in making things for which there is already a good market'.[56] In other words, the average potter should hope only to follow rather than to make fashion. As both cause and symptom of this the roles of art director and decorator were rarely disentangled or 'aesthetic authority' properly bestowed upon an individual. By the eve of war in 1914, however, structural change had started to alter this situation, with the innovation of chromo-lithography being accommodated through specialization by firm.

The advocates of flexible specialization and the historians of batch industries have been right to insist on the importance of issues such as novelty and to balance more evenly our appreciation of the impact of supply and demand factors. Moreover, Blaszczyk in particular has performed ground-breaking work in exploring how firms themselves attempted to perform the difficult task of matching production to consumers' desires. Nonetheless, caution still needs to be

---

[55] F. Rhead and G. Rhead. *Staffordshire Pots and Potters* (London, Hutchinson, 1906), p.

[56] Marshall, *Principles*, p. 234. Hobson makes essentially the same observation, see *Evolution*, p. 131–2.

exercised. Staffordshire potters frequently found divining what the customer wanted, or might buy, to be a vexed question that cost them money and time. Away from the upper echelons, and despite the real and widespread pride in being part of the Staffordshire tradition, there is little sense of that revelry in creativity held to be characteristic of flexible batch producers selling fashion goods and consumer durables. The time pressures exerted on production and stock-keeping by changes in fashion further heightened ambiguity over design. Co-ordination of batch production was no easy seamless job, instead manufacturers often felt harried by the complexities that seemed to inevitably accompany their chosen production and marketing strategies.

Thus far we have examined in turn how in the last quarter of the nineteenth century change had occurred in the structure of the North Staffordshire pottery industry, in its competitive environment, in its technologies and how these changes had been expressed through strategic orientations and adjustments. In the following chapter we will focus on the interaction and impact of these forces in the context of a single firm, Mintons.

CHAPTER SEVEN

Strategy, structure and culture: Minton Ltd.

Introduction

In this chapter a case study approach will provide an opportunity to explore competitive constraints and firm strategy, structure and culture. Particular emphasis will be placed on the response offered by Mintons, one of the district's oldest and most illustrious firms, as the competitive environment shifted in the last quarter of the nineteenth century. It will be shown that at Mintons business strategy followed on from existing organizational structures and cultures. This interpretation stands in contrast to Chandler's model, in which structure follows strategy, and sits more easily with Church's classic study of the Midlands hardware firm Kenricks. More specifically, Church's conclusion that at Kenricks, 'The existing structure and organization were taken as parameters rather than as variables' has much relevance also to the practice of personal capitalism at Mintons.[1] Thus, the case study will be informed by Casson's proposition that very often, in assessing business strategy and performance, 'It is the quality of the culture ... which is crucial'.[2]

By 1851, when international acclaim was accorded to its display of wares at the Great Exhibition, the firm of Mintons, founded in 1796 by Thomas Minton, was firmly established as one of the largest and most prestigious in the Potteries. The firm was in a position to exploit a 'secure' and 'old established market connection' and a carefully nurtured 'reputation monopoly'.[3] However, the competitive environment in which Mintons operated was to change considerably in the final decades of the nineteenth century as patterns of demand changed and new competitors emerged, both at home and abroad. The challenges faced by the firm in this period therefore form an important element of the context in which strategic response, and its performance, is to be

---

[1] R. Church, *Kenricks in Hardware: A Family Business, 1791–1966* (Newton Abbot, David & Charles, 1969), p. 325.

[2] Casson, 'Entrepreneurship and Business Culture', p. 43.

[3] Farnie, *The English Cotton Industry*, p. 193-4. In arguments very relevant to the example of Mintons, Farnie suggests that such characteristics offer firms an 'effective way of limiting competition' and, conversely, that competition tends to be most sever where products are 'undifferentiated ... and therefore unsubstitutable', p. 192–3.

considered. The firm's business records make it possible to examine the effectiveness of its strategies in those years and to demonstrate that both structure and strategy were marked by considerable stability, even as performance declined. However, it is necessary first to trace the emergence of a strong company culture, informed by the firm's history and its proprietorial and managerial structure, in order that an assessment may be made of the influence of business culture over business strategy.[4]

Strategy, structure and culture

By the late nineteenth century narratives about and within Mintons, such as those of Rhead, Jewitt and Stringer, already priviliged a belief in the pursuit of excellence and extolled the skills necessary to its capture.[5] Strategy was concentrated on the production of wares of the very highest quality selling at premium prices in both domestic and foreign markets. Herbert Minton, son of the founder and in control of the firm from 1836 until his death in 1858, has been described as having a 'driving ambition....to attain international recognition that the wares of Minton and Co. equaled those of the great continental ceramic houses'.[6] This ambition may be said to have been realized and the firm acquired the highest of reputations. Colin Minton Campbell wrote to his mother describing the impact made by the firm at the Great exhibition with obvious pride:

> The reputation of Mintons is second to none, only Sèvres is a remote contender, and that is a government manufactory, grant aided annually to the tune of £12,000. Uncle [Herbert Minton] sought out and courted by all. He escorted the Royal Family and the Prince and Princess of Prussia through the building ... and the Queen presented him to the Princess ... as the manufacturer of that beautiful desert service.[7]

---

4 Rowlinson and Procter point out that some historians ' equate[s] path dependence with culture. Lipartito maintains that, "Introducing history, is already a half-step toward a more cultural model'. M. Rowlinson and S. Procter, 'The Culture of Business History and the History of Business Culture', *Business History, Theory and Practice: Proceedings of the Conference on Business History and Theory* (Glasgow, Centre for Business History in Scotland, 2000), p.46.

5 Any discussion of business culture is necessarily difficult, for, as Kono suggests, 'corporate culture is an intangible asset'. T. Kono, 'Changing a Company's Strategy and Culture', *Long Range Planning*, Vol. 27, No. 5 (1994), p. 85.

6 P. Booth, 'Herbert Minton: Nineteenth Century Pottery Manufacturer', *Staffordshire Studies, (1991)*, p. 65.

7 M.Mss. 17, *Letter from Colin Minton-Campbell to his mother*, 14 May 1851.

The firm had acquired this privileged position by developing an appropriate resource base, and in particular by employing many talented artists, designers and decorators. Registration as a limited liability company in 1883 confirmed the central position of design personnel and policy in the management and strategies of the firm.[8] The company was similarly enlightened in its attitudes to the employment and working conditions of the entire workforce and may be described as a model of nineteenth century paternalism. Thus, at a functional level, the company culture set out to inculcate in the workforce a sense of familial loyalty. Herbert Minton's obituary in the *Staffordshire Advertiser* claimed, for example, that:

> As an employer he was well served because he was greatly beloved; and he was greatly beloved because he was no hard, tyrannous task master, grinding pecuniary wealth and conventional grandeur out of the unappreciated and ill-requited toil of slaves; but he was just generous and good.[9]

Here we may note a further particularly potent element of what may be described as the Minton mythology; that making money was not the principal purpose of the firm.[10]

The firm paid well, took the lead in sweeping away restrictive conditions of employment, earned the approval of the unions and avoided disputes.[11] However, the workforce were expected to respond with loyalty and hard work, the family taking the lead in providing models of such virtues whilst also acting as a guarantee of the firm's good name in the market place. The figure of Herbert Minton, in particular, became with time a slate onto which could be enscribed eulogies to the virtues of duty, work, charity and Christianity.[12]

---

[8] Art Director Leon Arnoux was made a partner on registration of the firm in 1883. He and other artists, such as Solon, were very well paid and lived at highly desirable addresses at The Villas, Stoke-upon-Trent

[9] *Staffordshire Advertiser*, 3 April 1858, quoted in Booth, 'Herbert Minton', p. 66.

[10] Whilst the historian must beware claims that companies pursued 'higher' goals than mere profit, it is nonetheless worthwhile to consider Rowlinson and Procter's reminder that, 'As oral historians have warned, "puncturing legends" by revealing them to be invented runs the risk of failing to recognise that "myth is a fundamental component of human thought'. Rowlinson and Procter, 'The Culture of Business History', p. 52.

[11] In 1845 the union paper *The Potter's Examiner* had taken care to distinguish the 'good employers, Ridgway, Minton and Copeland' from the 'grovelling Spoil-Trade makers ... the little men as they are known', while in 1866 union leader William Evans testified before the *Select Committee on Master and Servants* that 'I do not know of a single [prosecution] by Mintons' for the breaking of yearly bonds. Finally, in 1872, the firm became the first in the industry to discontinue the despised custom of 'good from oven'. As a result of this and other actions the firm did not become involved in the disputes of 1882 and 1890. Burchill and Ross, *History of the Potters' Union*, p. 46, p. 15, p. 126 and p. 129.

[12] See Booth, 'Herbert Minton'.

The emphasis on artistic excellence and the good treatment of the work force had allowed the firm to move towards the development of a stable resource base of skilled workers capable of producing an output spanning both top-end and mid-range goods. As with many of its other features, experiments in productive techniques and, more especially, decorative techniques and new ceramic bodies had been established as an element of company culture by the activities of the proprietors prior to 1850.[13]

However, in the late nineteenth century the firm found itself facing the apparent trap of serving only a dwindling luxury market. Increasingly, it seemed that the firm's strategies did not isolate it from deteriorating trading conditions, which impacted as forcefully on Mintons as they did on any other firm in the Potteries. From 1887 until the end of the century the firm made continuous losses and in the early 1890s acute financial crisis made failure a very real possibility. The nature of these difficulties and their relationship to the firm's structure, culture, and strategies will all be explored. Several questions flow from this line of enquiry. Did Mintons cling 'in a changing world, to methods and types of organization which had been formed in the days of her supremacy'?[14] If so, why and was it wrong so to do?

Certainly, it may be argued that the company culture, and the strategies which it informed, were in part a cause of the firm's problems; but they also gave to the firm, its workforce and owners an impressive tenacity. However, rather than viewing 'culture' as a further determinant of success or failure, we instead perhaps to recognize that, 'Culture may be constitutive. It may define the permissible limits of thought and actions, including even notions of rationality'.[15] Thus, it was culture that made meaningful the 'irrational' behaviour of John Fitzherbert Campbell, favouring survival over profit

---

[13] In relation to process innovation, for example, Herbert Minton had in 1840 been instrumental in the purchase of a half share in Richard Prosser's patent from pressing tiles from powdered clay, a process augmented by further patents taken out by Minton and James Naysmith in 1851. In turn, in 1863, Colin Minton-Campbell invented and patented a stove for drying unfired wares and in 1873 patents were issued for the 'Minton down draught oven', an invention that Minton strove to exploit through licensing agreement with firms in the Potteries and abroad. Celoria, 'Ceramic Machinery of the Nineteenth Century', p. 43. For detail of the licensing of the down draught oven see M.Mss. 958–63, 970, 975–6, 1003–21 and 1086. Product innovations were legion, but perhaps the most significant in the second half of the nineteenth century were the introductions of majolica and pâte-sur-pâte.

[14] D.H. Aldcroft, 'The Entrepreneur and the British Economy, 1870–1914', *Economic History Review*, Vol. 12, No. 1 (1964), p. 125.

[15] K. Lipartito, 'Review of A. Godley and O. Westall (eds.), *Business History and Business Culture*', *Business History Review*, Vol. 73, No. 1 (1997), p. 127. Discussing alternative approaches to business culture, Rowlinson and Procter argue that, 'From a functionalist point of view the most important question is: "what function does culture fulfil in the organization?" Whereas the "fundamental question" for symbolic interpretivism is: "What is the meaning of the organization to its members"'. Rowlinson and Procter, 'The Culture of Business History', p. 45.

maximization, without which collapse may well have occurred in 1894. Thus, the influence of a company's history cannot be characterized simply as 'the restraining dead-hand of ... past achievement'. Instead, as Lloyd-Jones and Lewis have demonstrated of personal capitalism in the Sheffield metal and metal-making trades of this period, the 'tenacity of this form of business organization suggests that it was not in its nature incapable of meeting the challenge of increased competition'.[16]

Thus, culture bears on the question of entrepreneurship in the context of British personal capitalism in the late nineteenth century. As Westall observes, culture may provide a 'different perspective on ... themes explored in recent works in British business history [which] have revolved around the emphasis on family capitalism in Britain and the delayed transition to the large-scale managerial corporation'.[17] The charge commonly laid against British entrepreneurs is that they were complacent or risk and growth averse. Explanations of the influence of such cultural dispositions amongst owner/managers turn, at least in part, on a belief that leaders, and founders in particular, are able to to shape or engineer corporate cultures.

However, this perspective may often over-estimate both the power of founders and leaders to shape cultures and the long-term stability of the effective meaning of any such cultures. It will be shown that in the 1880s and 1890s Mintons perhaps lacked a leadership able to recognize that 'some of its assumptions were no longer valid'.[18] Thus, in comparison with the activities of the firm's founder, the behaviour of Colin Minton Campbell and his son John Fitzherbert Campbell in the latter half of the century was more 'managerial' than 'entrepreneurial', seeking stability before growth.[19] In particular, Colin Minton Campbell, perhaps unwittingly, presided over the transformation of the company culture into a 'sacred cow'.[20] In contrast, his son, though willing to save the firm, adopted an almost rentier stance towards the company. The passage of time, involving the accretion of history, stories and myths, inevitably changed the meaning for members of a culture that had remained, nominally, the same over a considerable period of time. An apparently basic concept such as 'excellence' was necessarily altered by the development of reputation and status undoubtedly acheived by the firm. Moreover, as will be

---

[16] T. Veblen, quoted in Aldcroft, 'The Entrepreneur', p. 114; Lloyd-Jones and Lewis, 'Personal Capitalism and British Industrial Decline', p. 373.

[17] O. Westall, 'British Business History and the Culture of Business', in A. Godley and O. Westall (eds.), *Business History and Culture*, (Manchester, Manchester University Press, 1996), p. 31. See also; R. Church, 'Ossified or Dynamic? Structure, Markets and the Competitive Process in the British Business System of the Nineteenth Century', *Business History*, Vol. 42, No. 1 (2000), pp. 1–20.

[18] Schein, *Organizational Culture*, p.2.

[19] H. Livesay, 'Entrepreneurial Dominance in Businesses Large and Small, Past and Present', *Business History Review*, Vol. 63, No. 1 (1989), pp. 1–21.

[20] Lloyd-Jones *et al.*, 'Culture as Metaphor'.

shown, the meaning that the organization held for different members, even amongst the highest echelons of the Minton and Campbell families, could be strikingly divergent or conflicting. Caution is necessary in claiming homogeneity within a corporate culture.

Returning then to the question of the links between business culture, personal capitalism and the claimed structural and strategic ossification of the British manufacturing economy, it can only be noted that the example of Mintons offers no easy lessons. With respect to this question, it is vital to stress that the firm exhibited considerable growth for much of the nineteenth century and was highly innovative in terms of product development. As is increasingly recognized, the role played by product innovation in driving economic growth has hitherto been neglected in favour of a fascination with process innovation.[21] In the long-run the firm was successful and dynamic. However, a commitment to personal capitalism had effects other than those seen on business culture. As in other regions and sectors, a regime of personal capitalism at Mintons powerfully influenced the evolution of managerial and governance structures. That evolution will now be sketched.

Thomas Minton, the firm's founder, may be viewed as a Schumpeterian entrepreneur, aggressive, growth oriented and with the 'drive and dynamism ... of the classical industrial revolution', and it was he and his son Herbert who did most to shape the structure and direction of the business.[22] The firm's market orientation was based on his personal skills as an engraver. This background meant that Thomas Minton prioritized product over process, unlike the majority of manufacturers inculcated in the craft values of the workbench. Though he did not undertake a craft apprenticeship, as his father had done, it was commonly attested that Herbert too showed a keen appreciation of and involvement in design at the company.[23] At the same time the firm's commercial development was forged through a series of partnerships, though the family was careful to retain control.

Born in Shrewsbury in 1765, Thomas Minton was apprenticed as an engraver at Thomas Turner's Caughley China Works at Broseley. He moved to the Potteries in 1789 and worked as an engraver and designer at Bridge House in Stoke-upon-Trent, during which time he produced a number of popular patterns for Josiah Spode I. According to John Thomas, it was upon becoming a master engraver in 1793 that Minton decided to begin manufacture himself

---

[21] M. Berg, 'Inventors of the World of Goods', in K. Bruland and P. O'Brien, *From Family Firms to Corporate Capitalism: Essays in Business and Industrial History in Honour of Peter Mathias*, (Oxford, Clarendon Press, 1998), pp. 21–50.

[22] Aldcroft, 'The Entrepreneur', p. 114.

[23] Booth claims that, 'Herbert was acquainted with many artists and sculptors, many of whom visited the factory ... The benefit to the workforce, especially the modellers and painters was to heighten interest in art and to encourage talent'. Booth, 'Herbert Minton', p. 82.

and 'like Spode ... who appointed a practical potter ... to manage [his] pottery, Minton the engraver made Joseph Poulson the manager of his new factory', Poulson having previously been a manager at Spode.[24] Clearly Thomas Minton had quickly and effectively integrated himself into the highly localized business networks of the district. The extent to which later members of the family and management were integrated in local socio-economic elites wll be highlighted in Chapter 9. Poulson was made a partner in 1797 and shortly after William Pownall, a Liverpool merchant, also became a partner, the firm trading as Minton, Poulson and Pownall until 1809, by which time Poulson had died and Pownall retired. The partnership with Pownall paralleled that of Wedgwood with Bentley and demonstrates that Thomas realized beautiful wares were as nothing without sales.

Thomas Minton's sons, Thomas Webb and Herbert, entered the partnership in 1817, but Thomas Webb withdrew to enter the church in 1823 and Herbert also left, in 1828, and was not to return until his father's death in 1836.[25] On his return, Herbert's first partner, John Boyle, was again from outside the family, but this partnership was short-lived and during its dissolution in 1841, which was attended by considerable difficulties, Herbert revealed a capacity for aggressive business techniques. Boyle noted in September 1841 that the relationship between the two men had deteriorated 'to the extent of personal abuse'. Even Herbert's nephew and successor, Colin Minton-Campbell, was moved to complain in 1852 that 'our worthy uncle has been very difficult'.[26] Immediately after ending the partnership with Boyle, Herbert formed another, with his wife's nephew, Michael Daintry Hollins. His own nephew, Colin Minton-Campbell, entered the business in 1849. On Herbert's death in 1858 Minton-Campbell and Hollins continued in partnership together until 1863, though again dissolution was not easily achieved, disputes as to the right to produce certain wares not being settled until the early 1870s or without recourse to the law.[27]

Thus, across a series of partnerships spanning some sixty years, the Minton and Campbell families proved themselves determined to maintain direct personal control of a firm that had grown very considerably during the same period. The firm had, like others in the district, begun life in a small way, but a strong commitment to personal capitalism had not acted as a constraint on growth and the Potteries had proved itself 'capable of producing large firms of national and international repute'.[28] Given this history it is no surprise that the

---

24 Thomas, *Rise of the Staffordshire Potteries*, p. 15.

25 Ibid., p. 16 and p. 19.

26 M.Mss. 227 *Diary of John Boyle* (entry dated 11 September 1841); M.Mss. 18–20 *Letter from Colin Minton-Campbell to his Future Wife*, September 1852.

27 M.Mss. 279, *Minutes of an Exchange between M. D. Hollins and Minton & Co.*; M.Mss. 280, *Memorandum of Terms: Hollins and Minton & Co.*

28 Lloyd-Jones and Lewis, 'Personal Capitalism and British Industrial Decline', p. 372.

commitment of the Minton and Campbell families to the firm did not diminish in the second half of the century. This continuing commitment was demonstrated in both the governance and the managerial style of the firm. No extensive managerial hierarchy was developed. Instead there emerged a small body of managers drawn from outside the family, each with a broadly defined functional role. The cohort of managers that were to serve under the stewardship of the family in the last quarter of the century, comprising Leon Arnoux, Art Director, George Leason, manager at Stoke, P. Holdcroft, manager at Walbrook, and W. Hawley, manager at Great Portland St., were all in place by the mid-1870s.[29] Moreover, Leason, who was apprenticed to Mintons at the age of thirteen before becoming journeyman and then foreman, is evidence of managerial dynasticism, his father having played an important role in the firm in the 1830s and 1840s.[30] Such forms of managerial recruitment and training were certain to produce managers fully imbued with the company culture.

Governance was equally tightly controlled. The incorporation of the firm as a private limited liability company, styled Mintons Ltd., in September 1883 did not weaken family control and is further confirmation of the conclusion of Payne and others that the adoption of corporate status by British firms 'initially did nothing to disrupt the familial nature of British business organization'.[31] The shareholders were; Colin Minton-Campbell, Thomas William Minton, Herbert Minton, Herbert Minton-Robinson, L. Arnoux, G. Leason and Alfred Reynolds, the last two described respectively as potters' manager and manager of printing process. Very soon afterwards Leason was nominated a director of the company, but the other managers did not follow him and the Board of Directors was composed almost entirely of family members.[32] T.W. Minton, H. Minton and H. Minton-Robinson were all appointed as managing directors in September 1884, the latter, who had only entered the firm in the autumn of 1883, was made Company Secretary at the same time, a post he was to occupy until his death in 1923.[33]

The reliance upon family members to fill managerial posts and directorships, however, represented a potential rigidity. Given the absence of sons the succession of 1858 was handled smoothly, but the determination with which family control was maintained, both then and subsequently, offers

[29] M.Mss. 43–4, *Address of the Minton staff to Colin Minton-Campbell,* 16 November 1876.

[30] Stuart, *People of the Potteries*, p. 138.

[31] P. Payne, 'Family Business in Britain: An Historical and Analytical Survey' in A. Okochi and S. Yasuoka (eds.), *Family Business in the Era of Industrial Growth: Its Ownership and Management* (Tokyo, Tokyo University Press, 1984), p. 172–3.

[32] M.Mss. 233, *Certificate of Incorporation of Mintons Ltd.*, 22 October 1883.

[33] M.Mss. 235, *Memorandum of Nomination of G. Leason as Director by John Fitzherbert-Campbell*, 26 October 1883; M.Mss. 238, *Epitome of Documents Compiled by S. Herbert Cooper, Solicitor*; M.Mss. 54, *Address of Minton Staff to Herbert Minton-Robinson on His Entry into the Firm*, 5 November 1883; Stuart, *People of the Potteries*, p. 183.

evidence of the very great extent to which, as Casson suggests, the supply of entrepreneurs is 'organized with reference to cultural subgroups', in this case the family.[34] In such patterns of recruitment the cultural affiliations of candidates (i.e. membership of the family) are at least as important as their attributes in determining selection and may lead to future problems. Bias can cause:

> considerable inertia ... when a particular group begins to dominate a particular industry (or firm) favouritism recruitment may make that group difficult to dislodge. This can be a serious difficulty if environmental change alters the role requirements, so that the culture is no longer appropriate given the different kinds of judgment now required.[35]

Similarly, Schein notes that 'Once cultures exist they determine who will or will not be a leader'.[36] A strong company culture offers no guarantee that leaders able to recognize that some or all of the culture's basic assumptions have become inappropriate will necessarily emerge.

Comparisons serve to highlight the conservative style of governance at Mintons. Unlike the cases of Wills (1893), Pilkington (1894), or the re-registration of Courtaulds in 1904, where in each case 'growth was the spur', neither the incorporation of Mintons in 1883, or re-registration in 1892, took place in a context of 'sustained growth and the need to secure its financing'.[37] Indeed, in the case of Mintons reregistration and accompanying financial reconstruction are best understood as an example of crisis management.[38] The initial act of incorporation, however, taking place against a background of a stable resource and product base, minimal investment, and static or declining sales, must be seen as a symbolic act of consolidation.[39]

More generally, the example of Mintons provides evidence that the 'the transition from small to large, from entrepreneur-dominated to manager-dominated enterprise' characteristic of this period required neither the separation of ownership and control nor organizational development.[40] Profitability returned in 1902 and, despite a run of losses in the 1930s, the firm remained an independent family business until it was bought by the Doulton

---

[34] Casson, 'Entrepreneurship and Business Culture', p. 43.

[35] Ibid., p. 44

[36] Schein, *Organizational Culture and Leadership*, p. 15.

[37] Gourvish, 'British Business and the Transition to a Corporate Economy', p. 24–5.

[38] For comparisons see: R. Lloyd-Jones and M. J. Lewis, *Raleigh and the British Bicycle Industry: An Economic and Business History, 1870–1960* (Aldershot, Ashgate Publishing, 2000), Chapter 4.

[39] Gourvish, 'British Business and the Transition to a Corporate Economy', p. 24. Family considerations may have played some role, Colin Minton Campbell was in his mid-50s at the time of registration and died shortly afterwards, in 1885.

[40] T. Gourvish, 'British Business and the Transition to a Corporate Economy: Entrepreneurship and Management Structure', *Business History*, Vol. 29, No. 4 (1987), p.21.

group in 1968. Given the caveats entered above, the company culture maintained many familiar traits throughout the twentieth century. Thus, a recent history of design and production at Mintons over the last two hundred years, written by the company archivist and curator, declares that at Mintons 'art and invention were never sacrificed for financial considerations'.[41]

As has been briefly indicated, culture, resources and strategic orientation were tightly interdependent at Mintons. The depth of this interdependence is demonstrated by the fact that during the arbitration of 1879, at which manufacturers sought and won a wage reduction, Mintons stayed aloof because, in the words of one witness, though 'Mintons might sell staple goods, as dinner sets etc., ... these were purchased almost exclusively by the aristocracy; their goods did not take the place of other manufacturers in the shops'.[42] As Scranton claims, 'the choice ... between variety and volume had strong technical correlations built into the structure of production'.[43] How were these correlations expressed at Mintons in the late nineteenth century?

To a very large degree the firm's resource base displayed the same stability as its structure and governance in the latter half of the century. At the time of the Great Exhibition Minton, Hollins and Co., as the firm was then known, had a workforce of 1500. In 1882 the workforce stood at 1565.[44] Correlating the composition of the workforce of 1882 with an inventory of the firm's fixtures completed for January 1884 demonstrates that the limited growth that had occurred had been extensive rather than intensive. Fifty per cent of the workforce of 1882 were either artists, designers or decorators, some of the most highly paid manual occupations in the industry. Potters, those responsible for forming the wares, where mechanization was to have the most impact in reducing the labour costs in the industry, formed just seventeen per cent of the workforce.[45] The firm's existing human resource balance meant that even full adoption of the most advanced techniques of the day would have had a limited impact on costs, but the evidence points to a cautious approach to mechanization within the firm.

The inventory of 1888 lists a total of 172 forming machines, comprised of a combination of whirlers, jiggers and throwing wheels. Jiggers, the most advanced of these machines, numbered just twenty six, or fifteen per cent of the total. Even more significantly a very similar number, only twenty seven, of

[41] J. Jones, *Two Hundred Years of Design and Production at Mintons* (Shropshire, Swan Hill Press, 1995), p. 7.

[42] Burchill and Ross, *History of the Potters' Union*, p. 127.

[43] Scranton, 'Diversity in Diversity', p. 38.

[44] M.Mss. 50, *Address to John Fitzherbert Campbell*, 6 July 1882.

[45] Ibid.

all machines were steam powered.[46] Moreover, this inventory did not capture the firm at the bottom of an investment cycle, for it was taken four years after an auditors' report of 1879 had noted that 'The charge for Repairs and Additions to Buildings and Machinery for the past few years has been exceptionally heavy'. The auditors, Deloitte, Dever, Griffiths and Co., also noting that 'we are informed by Mr. Leason that the works are now in excellent order and that a large saving may be expected under this head'.[47] Certainly, significant investment in plant virtually ceased for some years after this. In no one year between 1883 and 1893, for example, did spending on new machinery represent more than one per cent of total expenditure.

It will later be shown that an inability to control costs, particularly labour costs, was to dog the firm throughout the 1880s and 1890s and, as was true of also of structure and governance, Mintons resource base may have been subject to some rigidities at this time. This potential rigidity would have been reinforced by the reciprocity of employer/employee relations. Thus, much like high class Sheffield cutlers such as George Wostenholm and Sons, Mintons found any move down-market difficult and unappealing.[48] When external pressure began to mount from the mid-1870s the firm did not exploit any potential for diversification it may have possessed but retreated instead to a reliance on its core values. Undoubtedly, the resource base of the firm was congruent with a strategy of diverse and premium specialty production and a culture that favoured excellence, but it also inevitably shaped the responses the firm was able to make to any challenges that arose.

Attention to resources directs attention to the extent to which the firm drew on the competencies and external economies available in the surrounding district. Generally, as both Marshall and Hobson observed, large firms in the Potteries grew more through the internalization of economies of scope than of scale and were less reliant than the majority of firms on the resources generalized throughout the district. In terms of localized economic linkages, Mintons was relatively unembedded. Broadberry and Marrison have stressed skilled labour as a particulary important source of external economies in the Lancashire cotton industry. Naturally, Mintons drew on the local populace for by far the greater part of its workforce. But even here we must introduce a note of caution. As has been demonstrated, a cohort of key workers central to the

---

46 M.Mss. 1235, *Schedule of Inventory of Fixtures and Articles in the Nature of Fixtures and About Certain Manufactories, Works and Premises at Stoke-upon-Trent, Staffordshire, Belonging to Colin Minton Campbell*, 1 January 1884.

47 M.Mss. 503, *Report on Accounts to 11 August 1879.*

48 G. Tweedale, 'Strategies for Decline: George Wostenholm and Son and the Sheffield Cutlery Industry', *Transactions of the Hunter Archaeological Society*, Vol. 17 (1993). See also; Lloyd-Jones and Lewis, 'Culture as Metaphor' for the case of Raleigh, whose 'committment to quality ... made it difficult for the company to reposition itself in the market-place', p. 115.

competitive advantages enjoyed by the firm were recruited not only from outside the district but even from outside the country. Second, recruitment and employment practices, not only of Mintons but also of other leading firms, combined with low mobility within the region amongst workers, led to the formation of a highly segmented local labour market. At all levels, many of Mintons labour needs were met internally. The firm's relatively weak integration into local resources and competencies must also have played its part in conditioning strategic options and responses. This conclusion will be enhanced by comparison with the responses offered by small, more networked firms, detailed in Chapter 8.

Challenge and its impact

Thus, any analysis of the response offered by Mintons to the fresh challenges offered by the late nineteenth-century must be framed by an understanding of the interdependencies between strategy, structure, resources and culture. Central here, for example, was the belief that the firm's higher quality goods not only embodied the company culture but were also more profitable per unit. These beliefs and strategies were encapsulated in an internal memorandum of 1890, which attempted to assess and account for the differences in the firm's performance in the years 1884 and 1890. Thus, this document asserted that 'The greater the value of a piece, the more profit is put on'. In turn, pride was expressed in the fact that 'The company still produces patterns equally as rich and good as in 1884 and still supplies as large or larger a proportion of (i.e. the great bulk of) the highest priced ware now sold in the trade'.[49] In other words, the quality of the firm's products had not declined and, *within* a specific market segment, its market share had not been eroded.

These statements of basic strategic principles, producing high quality wares targeted at the top end of the price range and bearing high margins, framed further analysis of the firm's performance. The problem faced by the firm was that, while 'the sales and prices, and the profit put upon all goods is practically the same in both years [and] practically the same quantity of ware has been ordered and sold in each year', these sales had yielded £32,000 revenue in 1890 than in 1884. Thus, it was concluded that 'The demand for the richest decoration has therefore decreased ... [and] the profit on the extra £32,000 worth of decoration ordered and supplied in 1884 has of course not been realised in 1890'.[50] In short, it was reasoned that the firm's difficulties were entirely related to demand conditions, particularly as they affected those

[49] M.Mss. 240, *Memorandum*, 1890. This document was probably written by company secretary Herbert Minton Robinson.

[50] Ibid.

products which most clearly defined and represented the reputation of the firm in the market-place. Speculation as to the cause of the decline in demand for the 'richest decoration' was not entered into.

The silences in the 1890 memorandum are as significant as what was said. Most important was the complete failure to discuss any alternative strategies in the light of these apparently far reaching conclusions, implying a very strong belief that the defects in demand conditions that had been identified would prove to be temporary. It was on this belief and on the strength of the company culture, supported by the enduring framework of personal capitalism, that the future of Mintons rested in the closing years of the century. No change in strategy was to be countenanced. Indeed, on the basis of a series of proposed one-off and piecemeal economies, an estimated minimum profit of £3864 was forecast for 1891.

However, Mintons' auditors, Deloitte, Dever, Griffith and Co., had been expressing doubts about the firm's market orientation since the late 1870s. Their report on the accounts of the year to August 1877 noted that; 'Assuming that no ware is made which does not [make] profit, it is clearly desirable that (to fully occupy all the machinery and plant) as much business as possible should be done, especially in the wares which are believed to produce the best results.[51] In 1878, which had 'to bear the double disadvantage of increased expenditure and decreased production', the firm was again urged to consider:

> the question as to which class of ware it is most profitable to manufacture. With reference to this latter question we must point out that the statistics in our possession relating to the output from the different ovens, shew an increased production of china and a decrease in the quantity of earthenware manufactured and this may in some measure attribute to the unsatisfactory result.[52]

The firm chose not to heed this advice. The 'comparatively favourable' result achieved in 1877 the accountants felt 'doubtless arises from the decrease in the sale being entirely in the Gilt China-probably the least profitable part of your manufacture'. Nonetheless, the proportion of sales of Gilt China to all sales rose from twenty continued to rise, from nine per cent in 1883 to thirty two per cent in 1893 for example, and consistently represented around ten per cent more of the total value of sales made than the next most significant product type. In the same ten year period the production of earthenware lines such as Stoneware, Majolica and Cream Coloured, which the auditors had recommended be expanded, was either discontinued or shrank as a percentage of total sales.[53] These trends were consistent across the period. In 1894, when a

51 M.Mss. 501, *Report on Accounts to 11 August 1877.*

52 M.Mss. 502, *Report on Accounts to 11 August 1878.*

53 M.Mss. 501; M.Mss. 1328, *Annual Summary Book No. 1.*

loss had been recorded for the previous eight years, the accountant's concern was again focused on the balance of wares made by the firm; 'The decrease in the sale of expensive articles included under the head of "China" may probably have been expected owing to the bad times but that Earthenware etc. ... should have become reduced to their, at present, insignificant figure is certainly alarming'.[54]

Clearly, the auditors felt that sales in luxury markets were bound to suffer in the prevailing market conditions, but the alarm over falling earthenware sales was particularly heightened because 'not withstanding the reputation of the firm ... competitors must have found means of securing a large amount of business which based on the importance of the works should undoubtedly' have been retained by the firm. Not only was the focus on quality wares proving insufficiently profitable but it appeared that it was also beginning to fail as a marketing strategy. The power of the firm's 'reputation monopoly' to sell less prestigious mid-range wares was weakening as the competitive environment changed and, as will be shown, customers, both at home and abroad, began to complain of a tangible deterioration in standards of both manufacture and service.

These shifts in the balance of the types, values, and profitability of wares made by the firm took place against the background of an overall decline in sales, static and rising costs, and, less consistently, falling prices. All of these trends first emerged in the mid to late 1870s, though the company was still making profits at that time. The indications appeared then to point to a secular rather than a merely cyclical shift in demand conditions, whether presaged by changes in taste or in the competitive environment. However, for the time being, judgement must be reserved as to the clarity of these signal and, more importantly, as to their interpretation within management at Mintons. We have already stressed the uncertainty induced by change in the structure of the industry at both the local and international and that long-term trends were, at best, inchoate.

Deloitte, Dever, Griffith and Co. were assiduous in providing detailed annual audits of the accounts, which were generally noted to be in good order, and in warning of the consequences of what they found. Indeed, though the performance of the firm was deteriorating, Mintons may not be included in the judgment that; 'Ignorance seems to have been a common failing in the direction of British enterprises'. The directors did not make decisions 'without adequate information or even without any awareness that such information was desirable'.[55] In addition to the annual audit, the management also had recourse,

---

[54] M.Mss. 246, *Report on Accounts to 11 August 1894*.

[55] Coleman, 'Failings and Achievements', p. 3. For a fuller discussion of the relationship between Mintons and the auditors see; A. Popp, 'Specialty Production, Personal Capitalism and Auditors' Reports: Mintons Ltd., c. 1870–1900', *Accounting, Business and Financial History*, Vol. 10 No. 3 (2000), pp. 347–69.

from 1883, to an Annual Summary Book which carried detailed information on all aspects of the firm's finances. In particular, the relationship between each element of expenditure and the value of wares manufactured and sold was calculated with considerable detail. Occasional comparative exercises, such as the memorandum of 1890 already referred to, were also carried out with the aim of identifying specific problems. Only once, in a letter of 1885, did the accountants make reference to serious 'accounting difficulties between Stoke and Walbrook [the London showroom] due to lack of co-ordination'.[56] However, perhaps crucially, such costing and accounting procedures that were in place at the firm did not allow either the management or the auditors to calculate the profitability of individual product lines. What, in detail, did the information flows that were marshalled show?

Deloitte, Dever, Griffith and Co. reported that in 1877 there had been a 'great falling off in sales as compared with the previous years' and, although costs had been managed well, it also appeared 'that the ware sold did not realize such good prices', as was demonstrated by the figures presented in Table 7.1.[57] Though, in the same year, net profit on the wares manufactured showed a 'satisfactory advance' (to 8.2 per cent from 7.4 per cent in 1876), this report concluded with a negative assessment of the results, tellingly couched in relation to the firm's reputation; 'we do not consider that the result is commensurate with the large amount of business done and the high position of the firm'.[58]

Table 7.1
Sales, costs and profits, 1876–77

	Net sales (£)	Cost of goods sold	Gross profit (£)	% on cost of goods sold
1876	12,569	10,598	1971	18.5
1877	9543	8791	752	8.5

Source: M.Mss. 501.

If falling sales had been accompanied by reduced costs in 1877 the same was not true in the following year. A detailed analysis of expenditure showed under almost every head an increase as a percentage on the value of the ware manufactured. The result was a reduction in profits of £8411. The auditors were frank in their judgment, concluding that the increase in expenditure was

[56] M.Mss. 526, *Letter from Deloitte, Dever, Griffith and Co. To Mintons Ltd.*, 29 May 1885.

[57] M.Mss. 501.

[58] M.Mss. 501.

'entirely unwarranted as, with the exception of the standing charges, the cost should be in proportion to the production'.[59] The figures for 1878 were in fact worse than they first seemed, for they had been buoyed up by a 'considerable ... reduction of stock', which had masked the fact that behind falling sales lay a reduced output. These adverse movements in sales and output became more obvious the following year, as is demonstrated by the figures presented in Table 7.2. Though the reduction in output was regarded as serious, a lost opportunity for profit-making, criticism was again focused largely on costs in 1879.

Table 7.2
Sales and output by value, 1878–79

	Sales (£)	Output by value (£)
1878	123,935	116,998
1879	115,753	115,607

Source: M.Mss. 503, *Report on Accounts to 11 August 1879.*

Thus, though down on 1878, costs in 1879 were still four per cent up on 1876-7, when a larger trade had been done, and despite the fact that:

> nearly every article of consumption is costing less than in 1876–7 and the price of wages is also lower, under these circumstances instead of an increase of 4% we should look for a reduction, and we therefore trust to find that a serious improvement in this respect will be perceptible in the current year.[60]

In 1880, though output rose in value, sales again fell and costs continued to show real rather than merely relative rises. Some of these increases the auditors were simply 'at a loss to understand', such as the extra £700 spent on bone when the sales of the china, into which bone went, had fallen by £3750.[61] By the early 1890s near continuous falls in sales for a decade and a half meant that, irrespective of expenditure, it had become 'quite impossible for the sales to stand the fixed charges and show anything but a loss ... it seems clear to us that nothing but loss can result unless means are found to materially increase the sales'.[62] Falling sales were increasingly exacerbated by a heavy burden of bad

---

59 M.Mss. 502.
60 M.Mss. 503.
61 M.Mss. 504, *Auditors' Report*, 1880.
62 M.Mss. 246.

debts and extended credit given to customers, against which the firm was warned as 'providing them with working capital, which you can ill afford to do, and which causes you to be deeper in debt at the bank than you otherwise would be, at a considerable cost for interest'.[63] Clearly, costs must form an important element in this story. Statements appended to the report on the accounts of 1894, summarizing net sales and the percentage of each expense on ware manufactured, form a useful introduction to the question of costs. Their contents are collated and presented in Table. 7.3.

Table 7.3
Percentage costs relative to output by value, 1884–94

Item	1884	1892	1893	1894
Materials	26.3	33.3	22.5	31.3
Wages and salaries*	47.8	52.1	49.9	53.2
Models, moulds and engravings	3.1	4.1	3.8	4.3
Rent	3.8	1.7	1.6	2.0
General expences**	4.0	6.0	6.0	7.0
Discounts and allowances	5.4	5.0	5.1	4.9
Bad debts	0.2	0.3	0.2	1.9
Output by value (£)	132,290	88,775	90,775	75,148
Net sales (£)	132,972	87,824	97,273	75,367
Profit at Stoke (£)***	13,801	–	810	–
Loss at Stoke (£)***	–	1822	–	3529

Source: M.Mss. 246, *Report on Accounts to 11 August 1894.*
* Includes directors remuneration
** Includes travelling, commission, taxes, insurance etc.
*** Does not include cost associated with the London showroom. Thus, taking into account results at Walbrook, the firm made a net profit of £11,000 in 1884 and a loss of approximately £1000 in 1893.

Most striking is the very heavy contribution of wages and salaries to costs and the strong correlation between rises in both this figure and of that for materials and either reduced profit or actual loss. These figures were not exceptional, a *Summary of Wages and Salaries* (which excluded directors

[63] M.Mss. 509, *Auditors' Report*, 1898.

remuneration) shows that for the ten years from 1884 to 1893 the percentage of wages on wares manufactured never fell below forty-six per cent and rose as high as fifty five per cent in 1885, a year in which profits fell by £9000 in comparison with 1884.[64] Behind these relative increases wages and salaries actually showed a steady reduction in real terms. Thus, wages and salaries were reduced by £12,220 between 1884 and 1890 (from £61,234 to £48,293) but because the tendency, first apparent in the 1870s, for wages and other expenses to fall less rapidly than either sales or output had persisted, these reductions represented a relative rise of 1.4 per cent.[65]

Though the accounting systems in place at Mintons do not allow unit wage costs to be calculated the conclusion must be that they were rising at this time. Furthermore, because few, if any, of the other costs of manufacture showed significant relative decreases it was profits that were inexorably squeezed.

The heavy burden placed on the firm by labour costs must be traced back to the firm's resource base, already explored, and thus to the focus on the production of high quality goods, i.e. quality remained a 'core' value of the company. In turn, the failure to reduce costs is testament to the commitment of the firm to that focus as both a strategy and as a central plank in the company culture. However, the question must also be raised as to how easy this strategy would have been to reverse, given the firm's relative lack of integration in to the competencies and economies of the district. More integrated firms certainly possessed greater flexibility, at least in the short-run.

High labour costs were not the only penalty for these commitments however. Design materials and designs sourced outside the company, not withstanding the firm's own very strong art department, all proved costly. In the 1880s expenditure on models, moulds, engravings, copper plate and designs, was consistently in the region of eight or nine time greater than that spent on new machinery.[66] Typical of these costs was that arising from the agreement made with sculptor Adolphe Megret in July 1884 'relating to the copyright of his statue "Aurora", Minton's production of the same, their payment to him of a royalty of 7.5 per cent'; whilst an extension to J.L. Hughes patent for ornamenting china, first purchased by the firm in 1863, was obtained

[64] M.Mss. 513, *Summary of Wages and Salaries*, 1883–91; M.Mss. 321, *Profit and Turnover from Accounts*, 1875-1920. Profits are pre-tax, after charging Debenture and other interest and depreciation, but before dividends.

[65] M.Mss. 513.

[66] M.Mss. 513. For example in 1884 a total of £4177 was spent on models and moulds, engravings, copper plates and designs, whilst £498 was spent on machinery. In 1891 the respective figures were £3863 and £656. Indeed, in this period, more typically was spent on the repair of machinery than on the purchase of new machines.

in 1877 because Minton's were able to prove that the technique was 'valuable but not yet remunerative'.[67]

The London showrooms at Walbrook, demanded by the market profile and clientele of the firm, also proved to be a near constant drain on the firm in these years. Again these problems, some of which undoubtedly resulted from poor co-ordination and faulty pricing policy, first began to emerge in the late 1870s. Thus, in 1878, it was noticed that much of the increased cost of conducting Stoke business in London was 'due to the loss resulting from an increased stock of patterns etc., these being charged to Walbrook at full prices but taken into stock there at a discount of fifty per cent'. At the same time, 'The stock and debts [are] very heavy, the former representing more than a year's net sales and the latter about six months sales'.[68] Later, Walbrook was responsible for nearly one quarter of the £6000 loss made in 1894; 'the increased cost of conducting Stoke business in London' that year 'owing to the absence during the past year of sales being effected there on which extra profit could be made, the ordinary sales realizing little more than the price charged for the ware at Stoke'.[69] Nonetheless, it was felt that the showrooms had to be maintained as the public face of a company with an international reputation.

Generally, even though the firm's primary response to deteriorating performance was not to change broad strategy but to trim costs wherever possible, expenditure on all forms of marketing tended to hold up throughout this period. Though Deloitte, Dever, Griffith and Co. had noticed in 1879 that there had been 'in the past two years....a considerable reduction in the cost of travelling and travellers commission', spending under these heads actually increased both absolutely and relative to production in the 1880s.[70] Expenditure on travellers stood at £2097 in 1884 and grew steadily to £2915 in 1890, though this sum represented an increase of only 1.22 per cent on the value of the ware made. Indeed, in 1898, Deloitte, Dever, Griffith & Co. thought travellers' expenses 'worthy of your attention with a view to [their] reduction ... without sacrificing the efficiency of representation'. Expenditure on advertising, pattern sheets, and photography also held up fairly well until it fell to significantly lower levels in 1899 before beginning to climb again after the turn of the century.[71]

---

[67] M.Mss. 688; M.Mss. 697–700. Mintons paid £1000 for the rights to Hughes' patent, in three installments between 1862 and 1865. In 1870 a further £600 was paid for a second patent and Hughes himself employed on a salary of £200 p.a. for five years to oversee the utilization of his patent.

[68] M.Mss. 502.

[69] M.Mss. 246.

[70] M.Mss. 503.

[71] M.Mss. 513; M.Mss. 240; M.Mss. 509 and M.Mss. 1328. The sum spent on patterns sheets, advertising and photography typically averaged £300–£400 in this period, though as much s £660 was spent in 1884, £160 more than was spent on machinery in the same year.

Given the commitment of the firm to its established market position maintaining expenditure in these areas was undoubtedly necessary. Indeed, Kono has argued that 'strategies which aim to increase short-term profits but which undermine the corporate culture of the company, will impede the creation and implementation of successful strategies in the next period'. In particular a negative strategy which attacks core capability 'may cut costs but it may damage the corporate culture'.[72] However, a refusal to cut cost did not guarantee the effectiveness of the firm's marketing strategies.

It has already been shown both that the volume of sales fell in the 1880s and 1890s at that Mintons were less able to realize a profit on those sales that were made. If sales paid less well because costs fell insufficiently, then a range of factors lay behind the declining volumes. Some, such as a decline in the quality of the wares and service provided, may be traced to the firm, others to the market. The report of 1902 made by Currall and Strasser, the firm's German agents, provides a wealth of information on the difficulties encountered in some Continental markets, whilst also suggesting the development of an agency system gave Mintons flows of information from the market at least as adequate as those concerning financial performance.[73]

The agency certainly appeared energetic. In 1902 visits were made to numerous established customers in a total of thirty cities and towns in 1902, twenty two in Germany, five in Holland and Belgium, two in Switzerland and one in Hungary. Moreover, a further seventeen cities in Germany, Switzerland, Poland and Czechoslovakia were visited 'experimentally but without result', and an exhibition held in Berlin was attended by many of the dealers visited during the year and by others from Moscow, Riga, Stockholm and Copenhagen.[74]

Currall and Strasser's report concluded with some general remarks, which form a useful introduction to developments in these markets. Almost all indicators were unfavourable. Currall and Strasser began by noting that the 'trade becomes increasingly difficult every year', not only for Mintons but for

---

72 Kono, 'Changing a Company's Strategy and Culture', p. 85.

73 M.Mss. 1331, *Report of Currall and Strasser*, 1902. Beyond the maintenance of the London showroom, Mintons did not integrate forward. However, as Nicholas has argued, 'there was no general rule that branch selling and production were more efficient than the agency system'. Moreover, given that 'the major innovation in selling over seas after 1870 was the control by manufacturers of the channels of distribution ... exercised through an agency network based largely on local firms appointed as direct representative', Mintons participated in an innovation widespread in British manufacturing in this period. Contracts between firm and agent normally specified vigorous travelling promotion and advertising, requirements apparently met by Currall and Strasser Nicholas, 'The Overseas Marketing Performance of British Industry'. However, agencies could be problematic, with monitoring and enforcing the fulfillment contracts difficult. Thus, an un-named South African agency proved singularly unsuccessful for Mintons in the early years of the twentieth century.

74 M.Mss. 1331.

all participants. These difficulties were rooted in increased competition 'owing to the growth of native industries and to the cheapness of French china and English semi-porcelain'. Though the agents believed that 'Nothing but your general excellence of design enables us to do any business', for example the 'new "Secessionist" ware' had been found to be 'greatly in the prevailing taste and ... capable of adding very appreciably to the total returns', it was still clear that reputation alone would not completely insulate the firm from the effects of cheaper competitors.[75] That even a firm such as Mintons had become vulnerable to competition from cheaper goods of lower quality represented something of sea change.

This problem was worse in some markets than in others. Currall and Strasser found for example that 'generally our class of ware is a bit too high in price for Belgium, which market is very much overdone by the lower grade earthenware and semi-porcelain'. These changes in the markets favouring makers of large quantities of cheaper wares were further exacerbated by the behaviour of some dealers in deliberately excluding English goods. Mintons was, however, also failing itself. In addition to complaints from customers the agents themselves noted that wares 'ought to be more systematically modelled so as to have greater uniformity of shape', and were forced to complain, with reference to the valuable "Secessionist" range, that 'we had no drawings or illustration of this ware during the whole of our journeys right up to September'.[76]

These problems led directly to orders being lost. In Berlin, for example, though A. Westheim 'favours English goods', P. Raddatz & Co. were 'falling off greatly in their purchases from England, pushing German makers more and more, very difficult to get them to take up new patterns'. Similarly, in Vienna Haas & Czisek had 'Given up English goods altogether being sole depot for certain Austrian and German makers'. In Stuttgart the firm of Haersklin, previously a customer for Mintons, was found to have joined a group, including others in Frankfort, Mannheim and Nurnberg, forming a 'syndicate holding the monopoly in their respective towns for "Hutschneider A Earthenware"-to the practical exclusion of English-business therefore....limited to matching'. In Budapest it proved 'impossible to get orders ... sale of English goods declining' in general. The spread of exclusive agency arrangements was not confined to Continental manufacturers. In Hamburg one firm had begun to confine its 'business in English goods as far as possible to Wedgwood (for whom Mr. Schmidt's nephew travels) and to Copelands for whom they act practically as agents', whilst in Vienna it was 'very difficult to induce' one customer 'to take up new dinner ware-he being particularly bound to Brown-Westheads'.[77]

---

75 Ibid.

76 Ibid.

77 Ibid.

If the concentration upon the top end of the market was beginning to restrict sales, then it also exposed the firm to greater criticism when standards were not maintained and encouraged the firm to persist with unrewarding customers thought to be prestigious in some way. Thus, C.F. Otto Muller of Carlsruhe, though he was 'faddy and cannot buy largely', was carefully solicited because he 'Numbers the Grand Ducal Court of Baden amongst his customers [and] is therefore valuable to us'. More importantly though, Muller was just one customer whose orders were very slow in arriving, making him 'Well displeased as customer'. One firm in Hanover was 'much incensed at late delivery ... would buy nothing at present ... ware not having given satisfaction'. Late delivery meant that another in Berlin missed the 'Xmas season entirely and the spring season in part. Customer was greatly incensed at this ... which had the effect of stopping all further purchases for the year'. Clearly prompt delivery was crucial in a fashion industry marked by considerable seasonality. Even C. Hansch & Co., also of Berlin and 'one of the most satisfactory of the Continental customers ... always fairly open to take up new' patterns, considered himself 'not at all well treated by yourselves in matter of deliveries'.[78] It must have been well known to Mintons that prompt delivery was of key importance to their business and it is difficult to attribute this problem to anything other than managerial failings.

Even more serious for a firm relying on reputation as the mainstay of its marketing strategy was that customers had begun to express 'great dissatisfaction with quality of goods recently supplied'. Though not expressed in reduced costs, fifteen years of trading at a loss does seem to have had an adverse impact on the firm's resource base, rendering it less appropriate to the strategy of concentration on high quality goods. Most vociferous of these complainants was P.A.W. Philippona of the Hague, who wrote to Currall in November 1902 after an order went unfilled. The agents felt the letter worth quoting at length in their report:

> Mintons is going down, their ware is second rate lately. I had much annoyance with their goods. Two large sets had to be returned for bad gold and those new in line are worse; not only the gold is bad but the glaze is rough. The new patterns ... brought were very nice ... and I could not resist buying them. But now I get word they cannot be supplied as not sufficient has been sold to pay the engraving expenses. This is a bad sign.[79]

Such complaints were indeed a bad sign, but they also point to the difficulties in co-ordinating supply and demand inherent in industries making specialist and fashion items and in which orders precede manufacture,

---

[78] Ibid.

[79] Ibid.

difficulties largely avoided by makers of mass-produced, standardized goods. As has been shown, such problems were common to the whole of the pottery industry but were particularly pressing for a firm such as Mintons, for whom expensive materials and high quality workmanship represented potentially greater added value when sales were realized but greater loss when stock went unsold. Inevitably, the firm could not afford to produce the full range of goods it sought to offer and thus incurred further costs. Not only was goodwill lost but direct costs were also incurred, though a copperplate engraving had not been made in this case the original design had been.

The auditors had long counselled against both holding excessive stock and late delivery but solutions were not obvious. In the auditors report of 1877 for example both an increase in stock, representing a 'possible loss by ... change of fashion', and 'the length of time which very often elapses between the receipt of orders and the delivery of goods', through which 'the firm must suffer', were criticized. Often though the two aims of reducing stock and prompt delivery simply conflicted.[80] The sword was two edged. When stocks fell too low or production could not precede orders, such orders as were received might be either filled late or not at all, but excessive stock showed a strong tendency to depreciate in value through a change in fashion. Furthermore, holding stocks of finished wares complicated pricing policy and auditing. In a letter of September 1889 Deloitte, Dever, Griffith & Co. warned Peter Holdcroft, manager at the Walbrook showrooms, where stock tended to accumulate in bad years, that:

> Profits are made on the sale of goods, not on the manufacture ... if the present increase in selling prices results from, and represents any increased cost of production in the past year, it would of course be right to value the stock accordingly, otherwise we should say that the only sound method would be to money the stocks at old prices, leaving any benefit resulting from your prices being raised to be shown when the goods are sold. The result of increasing the price of the stock when you increase the price to your customers ... is to show a fictitious profit and fictitious profits should not be shown.[81]

This examination of financial performance, production costs at Mintons and of the changing market conditions that the firm faced has clearly demonstrated that a strategy of quality production was expensive, demanding of both management and workforce alike, and increasingly ineffective. What, then, were the responses made by the firm to its problems in this period?

---

[80] M.Mss. 501.

[81] M.Mss. 550, *Letter from Deloitte, Dever, Griffith and Co. to P. Holdcroft, Walbrook*, 4 September 1889.

Response: resilience or inertia?

Mintons' initial response to these difficult times may be broadly characterized as directed to holding course in an attempt to ride out the storm, with costs being reduced or at least contained wherever possible. However, existing resources, managerial structure and company culture, all contributing to a strategic focus on the production of fine and expensive wares, foreclosed on fundamental attempts to reduce costs, and the savings that could be made were necessarily piecemeal and ineffective in turning the firm around. For example, the memoranda of 1890 principally looked for salvation in a projected saving of £258 on travelling expenses and commission in 1891 and of £900 on managers salaries in 1892, realized by cutting Thomas Minton's salary by £300 and by the retirement of Peter Holdcroft, manager of the London showroom.[82] Similarly the Report of the Directors of August 1892 noted a reduction of £675 in costs 'consequent on Mr. Arnoux's retirement and Mr. Minton's removal to London' and hoped that the year '1892–3 will feel the benefit of these and other reductions more fully'.[83] Furthermore, directors salaries, which had risen from £2050 in 1884 to £2200 in 1891 fell steadily throughout the 1890s and by 1899 stood at only £700.[84] Dividend payments had long since collapsed from ten per cent in 1883–4 to 2.5 per cent in 1884–5 and suspension the following year. Eventually though it was to become obvious that such savings as had been made were inadequate and that a more thorough going response was needed if the firm was to survive.

Unwilling to countenance market reorientation, and with it a restructuring of the firm's resource base, Mintons underwent a financial reconstruction intended to ease the most pressing burdens. The reconstruction in 1892 was combined with financial sacrifice by the owners and directors. It is clear from the actions taken then and subsequently that both governance and managerial style were, if possible, to be spared change.

Though Colin Minton Campbell had confided to his future wife as early as 1852 that he was 'almost prepared to leave this place' if things did not improve, the previous year not having been 'a good one financially', the third quarter of the century had been generally profitable for the company and, as we have seen, problems did not become acute until the late 1880s.[85] The severity of the situation was perhaps first explicitly recognized in 1890, initially in the memorandum already referred to, and then in a note written by John Fitzherbert Campbell on the fifth of September, giving notice of a 'special general meeting

82 M.Mss. 240.

83 M.Mss. 245, *Report of the Directors*, August 1892.

84 M.Mss. 513; M.Mss. 1328.

85 M.Mss. 18–20.

to be called after the ordinary general meeting to consider the financial problems of the firm and pass a resolution thereon'.[86]

The 'special' general meeting, held in January 1891, led to an agreement between Campbell and Mintons Ltd whereby Campbell, as principal shareholder in the firm and owner of the premises that it occupied, was to accept, first, a reduction in the rent from £5000 to £3000 for the year 1890–91 and, second, four per cent interest on debentures numbered 25–48 and five per cent on debentures numbered 49–80. The agreement cited a lease of thirty years, dated 1 January 1884, between Colin Minton Campbell and the Mintons Ltd., and the issue on the 2 of January 1884 of debentures to the amount of £40,000, numbered 1 to 80, to fall due at 12 August 1893 and bearing interest at six per cent p.a.[87]

Thus, these rather more substantial savings on rent and interest due on debentures were added to the ad hoc and piecemeal savings already outlined. However, these remedies were still inadequate and in early 1892 a memorandum 'embodying terms for the reconstruction of Mintons Ltd.' was prepared and presented to the directors for their consideration. The memorandum proposed that the company be liquidated and a new one, bearing the same name, formed to purchase its business, property and assets and to take over all responsibilities. The new company was to have a nominal share value of £99,000 divided into 13,332 shares of £7–10. 11,300 of these shares were to be fully paid up and the rest remain unissued. Crucially the new shares were to be 'distributed ... among the members of the old company in proportion to their holdings in that company'.[88] The reconstruction explicitly sought to preserve the ownership and governance of the firm and did not seek new sources of capital. It is also clear that re-registration in 1892 did not take place in a context of 'sustained growth and the need to secure its financing'. The re-registration of Samuel Courtauld and Co. in 1904 may, as at Mintons, have 'followed a decade of difficulties ... a decline ... in sales and a writing-down of capital' but was also 'inspired by the decision to move into artificial silk', but no such innovation or diversification may be associated with re-registration at Mintons.[89]

Instead, the intended 'practical effect' of the restructuring was 'that the capital of the old Company would be reduced by twenty-five per cent [standing] at the formation of the new company at £84,750'. Moreover, the memorandum shows that Campbell was willing to further forego his returns from the company by, first, accepting the debentures of the new Company for

---

[86] M.Mss. 234, *Agenda Book*, 20 October 1884–18 April 1902.

[87] M.Mss. 239, *Agreement between John Fitzherbert Campbell and Mintons Ltd.*, 20 January 1891.

[88] M.Mss. 241, *Memorandum Embodying Terms for the Proposed Reconstruction of Mintons Ltd.*

[89] Gourvish, 'British Business and the Transition to a Corporate Economy', p. 24-5.

£40,000 in substitution for the existing debentures of that amount in the old Company and to reduce the interest on the new debentures from six per cent to four per cent; second, by again reducing the rent charged against the old Company from £3000 p.a. to £1500 p.a. and, third, by wiping out all arrears of rent and interest owing to him on the 1 February 1892, amounting to some £9000. Whilst it was anticipated that none of the firm's creditors would raise any difficulties Campbell also agreed that if the bank demanded securities he would deposit with them debentures equivalent in value to the overdraft.[90] These proposals were quickly agreed and put into effect, the Articles of Association of the reformed Mintons Ltd. being issued on 29 April 1892.

The Report of the Directors of August 1892 provided further detail of the rationale behind reconstruction and its intended outcomes. Though acknowledging that the firm had made a loss of £1823 in 1892, the report clung to the hope that the changes made had been far reaching enough to save the firm but that their effects had not yet been felt. Nonetheless, it was admitted that:

> The large reduction in the value of the ware manufactured and sold, without an apparent adequate decrease in the consumption of materials, fully accounts for the this adverse balance, notwithstanding the reduction in the expenses of the Company which have resulted from its reconstruction and other causes ... consequently the reductions which have already taken place have not sufficed to show a balance to the credit of the Profit and Loss account.[91]

Besides the savings arising from Arnoux's retirement, already referred to, the reductions were 'substantially' rent reduced by £1500 and debenture interest by £400. The report also contained a balance sheet laying out how the reduction of capital by £28,625 resulting from reconstruction had been utilized. This information is summarized in Table 7.4. Clearly the adverse balance was most serious, but the losses resulting from the depreciation of stocks of expensive ornamental wares cannot be ignored. The Directors also reported that they were enabled, 'By Mr. Campbell foregoing rent and interest due amounting altogether to £9924', to create a reserve fund of the same value and to further increase it by £375, the nominal value of 50 shares surrendered by Mr. Holdcroft. This fund was to be used to cover £765 spent in the reconstruction of the company and on Holdcroft's retirement. A further £1908 from the fund was set aside to 'bring the Walbrook stock of ware to Stoke prices for stock by a reduction of twenty per cent'.[92]

90 M.Mss. 245.
91 Ibid.
92 Ibid.

Table 7.4
Balance sheet, 1892

Item	Amount (£)
Extinction of adverse balance	23,817
Extinction of New Buildings Account	1768
Reduction in prices of:	
Ornamental goods	2563
Walbrook fixtures	100
Retirement of Mr. Holdcroft	375
Total	28,623

Source: M.Mss. 245, *Report of the Directors*, 1892.

Though losses in 1893 were approximately £1000 as against £5000 in 1892 the years immediately after the reconstruction did not feel the hoped for 'benefit of these and other reductions more fully'. By 1894 losses had started to climb once more, and The Report of the Directors to the Annual Meeting of Shareholders of that year made it all to clear that, whilst the value of ware manufactured and the value of ware sold had both continued to decrease, wages and salaries as a percentage of the value of the ware made, bad debts, stocks of goods and materials at Stoke, Walbrook and Liverpool, and the rent and debenture interest due had all continued to increase.[93] As a result, on 25 June 1894, the directors were 'compelled' to pass a resolution noting that 'it is impossible to find money to pay the interest due to Debenture Holders on February 11 last or to meet the companies liabilities' but that Mr. Campbell had 'expressed his willingness to enter as debenture holder and carry on the business'. At a special general meeting one month later a deed was completed giving full effect to this resolution, but as the 'arrangement for carrying this into effect' was not 'completed by the end of the year 11 August 1894 ... Mr. Campbell immediately after this meeting ... advanced the sum of £3100 to the Company for the payment of wages and other urgent liabilities, pending the completion of negotiations with the bank'.[94]

It was then, in the mid 1890s, only the 'irrational' degree of commitment displayed by John Fitzherbert Campbell, together with the willingness of the bank to extend overdraft facilities for a prolonged period of time, that enabled the firm to survive. This pattern of events not only offers evidence of 'how strong culture can be even in the face of a vociferous market' but is also typical

[93] M.Mss. 247, *Report of the Directors to the Annual Meeting of Shareholders*, 26 October 1894.

[94] Ibid.

of behaviour which, according to Lipartito, cannot be explained by 'some functional model'.[95] Moreover, it is probable that survival through the 'social drama' of reconstruction in 1892 and near collapse in 1894 served only to strengthen the existing culture.[96]

Indeed, this period in the firm's history served to intensify the involvement in and control over the firm of the Minton and Campbell families. Continuous losses were made during the last years of the century, rising to £16,000 in 1900, in which year John Fitzherbert Campbell gave notice to the firm and Company Secretary, Herbert Minton-Robinson that he 'by virtue of his appointment as Receiver, intends to take possession of the undertaking, property and assets of Mintons Ltd. on the 12 June 1900'.[97] Profitability returned in 1902, but thereafter a series of transfers continued to concentrate shares in the hands of John Fitzherbert Campbell and, increasingly, his son John Campbell. For many years thereafter the firm's directors continued to be drawn almost exclusively from the family. By 1931 the company was again facing adverse trading conditions and making a loss, but between 1902 and 1930 profits were made in every year except 1915, with the result that in April 1913 it had been possible to revoke John Fitzherbert Campbell's appointment as receiver, the company being 'now able to pay all interest in respect of "A" and "B" debentures, and to carry on business without [his] intervention as receiver'.[98]

Given the lack of fundamental strategic change, the recovery after the turn of the century must be ascribed largely to an exogenous revival in the firm's traditional markets. Whether the management in the late nineteenth century may be considered to have exercised good judgment, displayed fine instincts or simply to have been lucky must remain a moot point. However, with regard to the issue of survival at least, the role of a culture rooted in personal capitalism is undeniable. However, caution is required, for at Mintons a series of documents reveal the extent to which the 'social glue' of family and culture could become strained and contested.[99]

The first of these documents is a letter written by solicitor S. Herbert Cooper to Company Secretary Herbert Minton Robinson early in 1888 in response to a request that John Fitzherbert Campbell make a reduction in rent and debenture interest due to him from the company, reductions which, as we have seen, were

---

95 Lipartito, 'Culture and the Practice of Business History', p. 2. See Church's claim that the story of Kenricks is evidence of 'just how determined a family firm can be in resisting extreme pressures for change'. Church, *Kenricks*, p. 323.

96 A. Pettigrew, 'On Studying Organizational Cultures', *Administrative Science Quarterly*, Vol. 24 (1979), p. 570–1.

97 M.Mss. 575, *Note Signed by John Fitzherbert Campbell*, 8 June 1900.

98 M.Mss. 587–8, *Letters from Herbert S. Cooper and Co., Solicitors, to Mintons Ltd.*, 5/8 April 1913.

99 Lloyd-Jones *et al.*, 'Culture as Metaphor', p. 99.

granted in the early 1890s. Starkly highlighted is the reluctance of Campbell to grant the concessions being sought. Cooper began by noting that Campbell:

> observes that you anticipate that the profit and loss account now expected, and which he assumes is in the course of preparation, will show a loss on the trade of the last half year as great, at least, as that shown on the previous Balance Sheet. No doubt you have good ground for this expectation, and, assuming it to be realised, the question will arise as to how this great loss is to be accounted for in the past, and arrested in the future.
>
> Mr. Campbell feels that until – with the expected Balance Sheet before him, some definite answer is given to this question, it is premature to ask for the concessions applied for by your letter. At the same time, if the requirements of the Company make the payment of the rent and interest inexpedient – either as tending to cripple the business, or to delay the due and punctual payment of the Company's creditors, Mr. Campbell will for the present postpone the payments due to him. He feels however that no time should be lost in preparing the Balance Sheet, and in considering, in the light of it, the questions above suggested.[100]

It is known that by 1892 Campbell was owed nearly £10,000 in arrears on rent and debenture interest, thus the postponement suggested in 1888 must have become somewhat prolonged. Nonetheless, it is clear that, up until the last resort was reached, the stance adopted by Campbell was essentially that of a disinterested external investor.[101]

More striking yet are the tensions laid bare in an exchange of letters, dating from the very close of the century, between Cooper, Campbell and G. Mure Ritchie of Ritchie, Graham and Tindall of Glasgow. The first extant letter, though it was certainly preceded by others and probably also by a visit by Ritchie to the Minton factories in Stoke, sets out Ritchie's prognosis for the firm. To a very large degree this echoed that offered over many years by Deloitte, Dever, Griffith and Co. Ritchie, despite 'dribbling loss', found it 'difficult to believe that the business cannot be made to pay, whether by rigid economy here a little and there a little within the works'. However, more radically, he also suggested that the 'three businesses', i.e. tiles, earthenware and china, 'ought at once to be made perfectly independent of one another'.[102]

---

[100] M.Mss. 546, *Letter from S.H. Cooper to H.M. Robinson*, 27 February 1888.

[101] Rebuffed, the Company seem first to appealed to the memory of Campbell's father, Colin Minton Campbell, for Cooper was forced to write a further letter emphasizing that 'I pointed out in my last letter that the Executors of the late Mr. Campbell have nothing to do with the questions you raised, which lie entirely between the Company [and] Mr. John Fitzherbert Campbell'. M.Mss. 546, *Letter from S.H. Cooper to H.M. Robinson*, 28 April 1888.

[102] Ritchie explained that he meant that any internal transfer 'whether time or material, ought to be charged for as if given from outside sources, and I do not think the business as a whole will be likely to do much good until the present system is changed'.

Crucially, Ritchie, as the auditors had, felt, though this was a 'mere guess', that:

> the leakage is least likely to occur in the Tile Works, more likely in the Earthenware department, but most likely of all in the work for the high-class china, for which the firm is so famous ... [where] some of the materials are so costly, the operations are so manifold and these so delicate, that it is extremely difficult, even apart from the large proportion of unsuccessful trials, to arrive at anything like an exact cost.

In turn, Ritchie pressed the need for the works to be physically reorganized, eliminating 'unnecessary extra handling of materials'.

However, Ritchie also passed damning judgment on the incumbent management. Acknowledging that 'it looks a rather brutal way of putting it', Ritchie counselled that his recommendations 'proceed(s) on the assumption that the present management has tried and failed, and requires to be superseded'. Aware of his position as an outsider, both to the firm and to potting, Ritchie expected the existing regime to react jealously to his involvement, though he thought such a sentiment 'impossible in the case of a man like Mr. [Herbert Minton] Robinson'.[103] Further criticisms were voiced in a second letter from Ritchie, notably that he did feel that present chief designer 'fully discharges the functions [former Art Director] Arnoux did'. Moreover, Ritchie expressed his anxiety to meet Arnoux and John Campbell and to visit the factory again, bringing with him his 'scientific adviser'. Clearly, his relationship with the firm had been initiated by John Fitzherbert Campbell, whose confidence Ritchie found 'flattering'. Significantly, for our discussion of company culture, Ritchie wished for the time to remain a 'mere outsider', in order to avoid the 'risk of being somewhat too biased by the accumulated experience and traditions of the place and of therefore falling into some of the present errors'.[104]

The familial and commercial tensions hinted in these letters emerge with greater clarity in a draft letter from John Fitzherbert Campbell to his son and successor John. John and Arnoux, retired from the firm but clearly still in close contact with the Campbells, were to tour the works with Ritchie and to offer all the 'potting and scientific' information they could. Crucially, Campbell felt his son and Arnoux to be fitted to this task not only through their own experience and knowledge of both the firm and potting more generally, which was unparalleled in Arnoux's case, but because both opposed 'the continuation of a management that lowers the reputation of the firm'. Astonishingly, he further

[103] M.Mss 1185, *Letter from G. Mure Ritchie to S.H. Cooper*, 31 October 1899.

[104] M.Mss. 1186, *Letter from Ritchie to Cooper*, 14 December 1899. Ritchie added that with 'regards to the present management, I would shrink from elaborate conference from them because of this danger'.

asserted that mention of the Campbell name to the workers would assist them in their task as 'most of them prefer Campbells to Mintons'. There can be little doubt that morale must have been very low throughout the firm at what Campbell acknowledged was a 'tense' time.[105]

Unfortunately the archives do not reveal what, if anything, came of Ritchie's involvement or any suggestions he made. Nonetheless, these documents do force us to re-evaluate our assessment of the influence of personal capitalism and company culture at Mintons. First, it is necessary to reiterate that ultimately Campbell was not prepared to see the company fail, despite both his clear lack of respect for the incumbent management, composed of members of the Minton family and a few trusted employees, and the further personal loss of income he seemed likely to incur. However, perhaps unsurprisingly, familial connections did not necessarily make for easy relations. More importantly, the governance structure and style of the firm bound his hands as he watched the difficulties mount. The management, recruited through their affiliation with a cultural group (the family) could not easily be ousted, despite their apparent incompetence. In this case a governance structure that only imperfectly separated ownership and control certainly appeared to be a weakness.

Conclusion

How then are we to judge the story of Mintons in this period and what explanations can we offer for the way in which it unfolded? Strategically, the firm stuck to what it knew and was good at, making expensive high-class goods. Cultural factors have frequently been advanced in the past in order to explain similar patterns of strategic 'inertia'. But, in part due to evidential issues, the explanatory power of these arguments is often relatively weak. Interestingly, at Mintons evidence of the power of culture is most persuasive in relation to a positive outcome, that is to the survival of the firm. Here it seems useful to invoke the notion of culture as buttressing the rationales underpinning behaviour that was, in optimising terms, irrational. As Church notes, 'success ... might be measured differently from profit rates and take account of longevity'.[106]

---

[105] M.Mss. 1187–8, *Letters from John Fitzherbert Campbell to John Campbell*, 29 November 1899. It seems likely a second financial reconstruction was also under consideration, as Campbell hoped that it would not be necessary for the share capital to be 'wiped out'.

[106] Church, 'Ossified or Dynamic', p. 12. As Rowlinson and Procter argue, 'An interpretive approach to business history would require reflection on the subjective meanings of success and failure for both historical actors and historians'. Rowlinson and Procter, 'The Culture of Business History', p. 49.

More useful perhaps are the tight correlations to be traced between strategy and productive resources, including not only the physical and human resources of the firm but also its marketing structures and relatively weak embeddedness in local economic structures. Many strategic options were not open to the firm, or would have involved massive expense. Attention to issues of finance are important, for, more negatively, it is by no means clear that funds sufficient to overhaul the firm's plant and premises were available.

Any judgements made now but also take care to avoid making assumptions as to the clarity of signals from the market. The firm did continue throughout this period to dominate the sector in which it preferred to compete. Moreover, it is possible to claim that the auditors, though their reports contained many valid criticisms, fundamentally misunderstood the business. As Scranton has shown, shifting downmarket could also prove near fatal. At Gorham, élite Rhode Island silverware manufacturers, attempts to '"democratize the consumption of silverware ... failed emphatically' in the early 1920s.[107] Following the advice offered by the auditors may have destroyed the capabilities on which the long-run success of the firm was based.

On balance, this case-study demonstrates the interdependencies of strategy, resources, governance and culture. Though the firm was aware that it faced constraints arising from the growth of continental industries, changing patterns of demand, and shifts in the organization of markets it responded with neither product diversification, process innovation, or developments in marketing. Instead, placing its faith in the value of reputation, the firm embarked on a financial restructuring that drew deeply on the personal commitment of all involved. Though it did not lead to significant growth this approach did not, on the other hand, prevent a return to profitability and whilst the firm is no longer independent the renown attached to its name persists.[108] Thus, though it is possible to understand why Tweedale wished to 'sympathise' with Sheffield cutlers George Wostenholm and Sons, whose position and strategic responses showed many similarities to those of Mintons, 'as it tried to shed its company culture of quality', it is as important to stress that 'personal capitalism had both strengths and weaknesses'.[109] The example provided by Mintons demonstrates that both could be found in one firm and at the same time. This chapter has

---

107 Scranton, *Endless Novelty*, p. 319.

108 Indeed, in 1974 Gay and Smythe noted that, 'although Minton wares are held in the highest esteem, in 1960 the capital of the firm amounted to only £500,000 and profits were a mere £43,000. Presumably the directors of the firm had regarded growth as vulgar, something whi ch might tarnish the perfection of Minton bodies, decorations and glazes'. Gay and Smythe go on to note that although production did increase after the firm was acquired by Doultons on 1968, 'extreme care was taken to preserve Minton's reputation for [the] dedicated production of top quality wares'. Gay and Smythe, *The British Pottery Industry*, p. 88.

109 Tweedale, 'Strategies for Decline', p. 53; Lloyd-Jones and Lewis, 'Personal Capitalism and British Industrial Decline', p. 407.

sought to draw together the themes developed separately in earlier chapters by focusing on a single case-study. In the next two chapters the focus will shift again, to an examination of the district and industry as a system. Thus, the next chapter explores patterns of integration and inter-firm networks in the context of exchange relationships.

CHAPTER EIGHT

Patterns of integration in the pottery industry, c. 1860–1900

Introduction

Mintons were relatively poorly integrated into local networks. However, the majority of firms were more reliant on auxiliaries, particularly with regard to the supply of important inputs. Thus, this chapter will explore the patterns of integration and inter-firm relations displayed by the North Staffordshire pottery industry during the second half of the nineteenth century. The chapter is informed by Scranton's proposition that; 'where networks of partial process firms develop, external economies of scale may be captured while risks and costs ... are reduced through contracting relations, yielding a system of disintegrated production'.[1]

In order to explore this proposition in the context of the pottery industry a dual approach has been adopted, focusing on both individual firms and the wider business system. In the first part, industry wide trends in patterns of integration will be analyzed. These patterns will be shown to have been highly variegated and, across the different components of the manufacturing sector, marked by divergent trends both towards and away from greater integration. Proceeding from a recapitulation of the reconstruction of industry structure presented in Chapter 2, it will be demonstrated that whilst integration could offer potential internal economies of scale to the very largest producers the disintegrated structure delivered to the majority of firms an important external economy.

In the second part, industry wide trends will be further probed via a case study of the firm of Jesse Shirley and Sons, a leading supplier of bone and other key inputs to pottery production. First, the development of this firm will be positioned within the parameters suggested by industry wide trends and, second, those wider changes will be clearly related to changes in the day-to-day business activity of the firm. It will be argued that as adverse changes in the competitive environment impacted on pottery manufacturers many firms reacted by drawing yet more deeply on the district's disintegrated system of production rather than by introducing technological or organizational

1 Scranton, 'Diversity in Diversity', p. 35.

innovations. This reaction was reflected in the increasingly contingent behaviour displayed by Shirleys and its customers. Risk reduction and economies of flexibility were then perhaps even more important attributes of the disintegrated system than its ability to generate external economies. The example of Jesse Shirley and Sons will also serve to emphasize the role of the family firm in the development and functioning of inter-firm networks in the nineteenth century.

Industry wide trends

In Chapter 2, some indication of the structure of the pottery industry's auxiliary sector was given. Specifically, it was shown that both absolutely and relative to the manufacturing sector, the auxiliary sector expanded until the 1880s and thereafter contracted. It was hypothesized that this pattern resulted from, firstly, from the general growth of the industry and, secondly, from an increasing degree of integration amongst some manufacturing firms. Here we will examine aspects of those trends in greater depth in order to relate the growth and development of the auxiliary sector more closely to that of the manufacturing sector and to the strategies of manufacturing firms. The disintegrated system of production of the Potteries was rooted in the small-scale structure of pottery firms, the industry's low barriers to entry, often limited managerial resources, and small and informal sources of start-up capital. In particular, the relative size of many ancillary firms represented a clear disincentive to full backward integration for the majority of manufacturing firms firms. Jesse Shirley and Son's RV in the 1870s and 1880s made them larger than many pottery manufacturers. Moreover, not only were such firms often larger than many manufacturers but they also displayed a higher fixed capital intensity. In 1882 Wedgwoods, at that time employing 723 workers, had an RV of £1069, whilst in the same year Shirleys employed at most 30 workers, and often less, and had an RV of £375. That is, Wedgwoods had a worker to RV ratio of 1:1.5 and Shirleys one of, at least, 1:12.5.[2] Though Wedgwoods did not by the 1880s represent best practice, investment in advanced production techniques having lagged at the firm, it is nonetheless unlikely that even innovative firms such as J. and G. Meakin would have equalled the worker/RV ratio seen at Shirleys. The high fixed capital intensity of many ancillary firms relative to the majority of manufacturers must then inform any exploration of patterns of integration in the industry.

However, some large firms had by the third quarter of the nineteenth century integrated the functions performed by Shirleys and other ancillary firms, raising a number of questions. What patterns of growth did the ancillary

[2] Hanley Borough Rate Book, 1882.

trades display? Why did some manufacturers choose to integrate whilst others did not? Why did some of those firms pursuing greater integration then appear to use integration as a platform for diversification, primarily into material supply, in the 1880s? However, these firms remained the exception and, as has been indicated, patterns of integration were polarizing in this period. These patterns will be related in section two to changes in both the structure of the industry and in the strategies of individual firms.

Ancillary firms in the pottery industry supplied a derived demand that remained, for the most part, buoyant for the first three-quarters of the nineteenth century. The growth of the manufacture of bone china for example, which had emerged in North Staffordshire in the late eighteenth century in response to demand for a cheaper substitute for porcelains from the Far East, bone being added to ceramic bodies in order to produce a finer and more translucent ware, thus stimulated the material processing sector in which Shirleys operated. The origins of this technique are disputed but innovation and diffusion occurred rapidly in the first quarter of the nineteenth century, the number of firms in the Potteries manufacturing bone china rising from four to forty-four between 1807 and 1822.[3] Pottery manufacture already required the preparation of a variety of materials and many firms either possessed grinding pans, drying beds etc. or took materials to be ground at one of the multi-purpose mills, typically water-powered, with which the district was furnished.

Thus, the growth of the manufacture of bone china, and indeed of the industry in general, was such as to make specialization by firm viable in the supply and processing of this and other potters' materials. Of these specialist firms, Bourne and Hudson, the forerunners of Shirleys, was amongst the first, founded in 1820. However, the 'idea of a specialized firm doing the work seemed a relatively new one' to Belgian visitor Guillaume Lambert as late as 1863–4.[4] However, in the second half of the century firms such as Shirley were joined by others. Thus, many sub-sectors of the ancillary trades, such as material milling, grew and became more competitive. As Chapter 2 demonstrated, the number of ancillary firms grew and there was a tendency for them also to become larger, at least up until the 1880s. The first large independent ancillary firm, for example was Hanley based millers Goodwin and Sons, with an RV of £600 for their works on Fenton Rd, in 1882.[5]

[3] R. Pomfret, '"My Bones are Burned as an Hearth": The Origins of Jesse Shirley and Sons', *Northern Ceramic Society Journal*, Vol. 15 (1984), p. 149.

[4] Celoria, 'Ceramic Machinery of the Nineteenth Century', p. 15–16. Lloyd-Jones and Lewis apply Stigler's model of functional average costs to explore the emergence of specialization in the cotton industry, arguing that as an industry expands the 'magnitude of the functions subject to increasing returns may become sufficient to permit a firm to specialise in performing it' and that as expansion continues the sub-sector grows and becomes competitive. They cite the appearance of cotton machinery manufacturers in the period 1800–15. Lloyd Jones and Lewis, *Manchester and the Age of the Factory*, p. 171.

[5] Hanley Borough Rate Book, 1882.

Nonetheless, the average auxiliary firm remained small and a slight growth in average firm size was accompanied by falling concentration levels. In other words, the auxiliary trades were becoming more competitive and, at the same time, the 'system of disintegrated production' in the Potteries was being augmented rather than eroded as the industry's external competitive environment became more hostile.[6] How may these patterns be related to the strategies deployed by manufacturing and auxiliary firms? As Helper notes, such a pattern of development, also to be found in the American car industry in the 1980s, appears:

> to contradict the predictions of ... theorists that vertical integration should rise with increasing uncertainty.Their reasoning is that vertical integration allows decisions to be made sequentially; as the state of nature is revealed... In contrast, dealing with a financially independent supplier requires either a contract that provides in advance for every contingency or costly post-contract haggling. As uncertainty rises, so does the number of contingencies and therefore also the expense of contracting.[7]

In order to address this apparent contradiction Helper advances a 'new conceptual framework for supplier relations, one that is based on problem-solving mechanisms rather than on financial arrangements'.[8] The problem that pottery manufacturers faced in the last quarter of the century, in addition to falling prices, was not the threat of hold-up in the supply of inputs, the firms generating those inputs being 'thickly supplied and therefore easy to replace', nor rising marginal costs, but the increasing instability and unpredictability of their demand structure.[9]

As will be shown through an examination of the trading patterns at Shirleys, those firms which had not integrated the function of material milling, the vast majority of firms in the industry, displaced some of the burden of the rising number of contingencies they were experiencing onto partial process firms. Whilst it will become clear that both a firm such as Shirleys and its customers experienced rising costs as the transactions between them became both less frequent and less standardized, it is also probable that these were more than balanced, for the manufacturers at least, by an even greater rise in transaction

---

6 Hanley Borough Rate Books, 1862 and 1882; Stoke-upon-Trent Borough Rate Books, 1886 and 1898; Scranton, 'Diversity in Diversity', p. 35.

7 S. Helper, 'Strategy and Irreversibility in Supplier Relations: The Case of the US Automobile Industry', *Business History Review*, Vol. 65, No. 4 (1991), p. 782.

8 Ibid., p. 784. Helper also notes that de-integration may be the best available option under conditions of radical uncertainty.

9 R. Langlois and P. Robertson, 'Explaining Vertical Integration: Lessons from the American Automobile Industry', *Journal of Economic History*, Vol. 49, No. 2 (1989), p. 362.

costs between Shirleys and its sources of raw bones. De-integration permitted the industry to absorb and transmit the impact of contingency. Thus the economies of flexibility offered were probably as great an incentive towards the maintenance of disintegration as the levels of capitalization necessary to integration were a disincentive.

Moreover, the system offered further risk reduction, primarily by allowing firms to reduce the amount of working capital tied up in stocks of materials, as will be shown non-integrated pottery manufacturers operated what was essentially a hand-to-mouth policy in the sourcing of inputs.[10] The flexibility delivered to manufacturers flowed from the structure of the ancillary trades, that is from the large number of sellers, their ease of entry and lack of significant market share. Rising concentration in the supply of materials would have reduced the room for manoeuver enjoyed by pottery manufacturers. They would no longer have been able to exercise what Helper characterizes as the 'exit' or 'voice with cheating' modes of problem resolution by finding a new supplier or by using a number of suppliers concurrently.[11] The district did generate and rely on trust in mediating many financial relationships, but trust rarely outweighed self-interest. Moreover, the costs of switching were not high. The trade in standardized goods such as bone, flint and other minerals, coal, or crates, and the face-to-face relations promoted by the clustering of the industry made for low information costs and simple contracts.

However, before exploring this case study in greater detail it is important to note that whilst integration of an increasing range of functions was the exception it was not unknown and increased throughout this period. Furthermore, some integrated firms proved, through diversification, to be a major source of growth in the ancillary trades. It is not surprising that these integrated firms were also very large firms, and by 1882 all five Hanley firms falling into the giant-size category (Wedgwoods, Brown-Westhead, Moore & Co., J. and G. Meakin, Clementson and Sons, and E.J. Ridgway) had integrated backwards into material processing. Moreover, the mills these firms operated were very large in comparison to those of specialists such as Jesse Shirley and Sons. Meakin's mill had an RV of £551 and Clementson's £597. Amongst the specialists only Goodwin and Sons, with an RV of £600, matched in size the milling operations of the giant integrated firms. Integration was rare though amongst firms even in the large-size category. Powell, Bishop & Stonier and the Old Hall Pottery Co. were the exceptions, whilst earthenware manufacture J. Bevington, whose mill and manufactory, with respective RVs of £78 and £198, placed his firm in the medium-size category, was most unusual.[12]

10 Ibid., p. 370.

11 Helper, 'Strategy and Irrversibility'.

12 Hanley Borough Rate Book, 1882.

There was then a clear correlation between scale and integration in the pottery industry, a correlation accentuated with time. In 1862 such significant firms as Meakins, Clementsons, and Ridgways had all yet to integrate material processing. Why did they then proceed towards integration? The clear demarcation line between giant-size/integrated firms and large-size/non-integrated firms suggests that there was definite size threshold beyond which internalizing a function such as material processing yielded internal economies of scale greater than those generated externally by the disintegrated business system of the district. Not only were transaction costs between producer and specialist processor eliminated, at the expense of fixed capital investment, but because of the scale and greater regularity of trade being done information and transaction costs with sources of raw materials may well have been less than those experienced by a firm such as Shirleys. This effect would only have strengthened as supplies came to be dominated by an oligopolistic trade in bone ash imported from South America later in the century.

It is also significant that with the exception of Wedgwoods, a firm very akin to Mintons in age, culture, and resources, that the giant integrated Hanley firms of 1882 were relatively young, fast growing, and oriented more towards volume than quality. As the trade press noted in 1891; 'In such businesses as the Meakins and Johnson Bros., which have quadrupled themselves in the last ten years, it is certain that some less enterprising firms have had to surrender orders in their favour'.[13] In other words, these firms were pursuing and beginning to capture a greater market share, attempting to 'reap the full benefit of the greater facilities for which [they had] paid by effecting larger sales at lower prices than can be charged by those who have not [such] facilities'.[14] Integration, often flowing from an 'entrepreneurial decision to supersede an existing network of complementary activities', occurred in these firms as a result of systemic moves towards mass production that were as much organizational as technological.[15] Though the threat of hold-up was low, as has already been argued the 'assets involved' in many of the ancillary trades were 'generalized ones' in the district, integration offered not only internal economies of scale but also the greater co-ordination necessary to mass production.[16]

Nonetheless, it is apparent that integration also carried risks, not least of which was that the fixed capital costs associated with integration were independent of the volume and composition of the trade done by a firm. These risks were especially high in an industry, such as pottery, in which mass production was in itself innovatory. As Langlois and Robertson have observed

[13] *The Pottery Gazette*, August 1891, p. 733.

[14] *The Pottery Gazette*, March 1890, p. 223.

[15] Langlois and Robertson, 'Explaining Vertical Integration', p. 363. They also stress that 'central to the innovation of mass production is it's systemic character'. Ibid., p. 367.

[16] Ibid., p. 362.

there is 'when the nature of a product is still in flux a tendency ... for firms to wait for a resolution of consumer preferences before committing themselves to mass production' and the uncertainty of capital investment.[17] The integrating firms of the 1880s were then prime movers.

However, the pattern of diversification into material supply to other primary producers displayed by some of these integrated firms in the 1880s raises important questions. Was diversification a deliberate, expansionist strategy or a defensive reaction to changes in the market and the as yet uncertain nature of consumer preferences in ceramics?

This pattern of diversification is revealed by an exploration of the growth mechanisms within the ancillary trades. As was shown in Chapter 2, growth in the population of primary producers was almost solely generated by mobility, but amongst ancillary firms entry also had an important role to play. Table 8.1 demonstrates that entry firms represented just over half of the population of ancillary firms in Hanley in 1882.

Table 8.1
Biographical History of Auxiliary Firm Population: Hanley, 1882

	Size Category									
	Small		Medium		Large		Giant		Total	
Firm Type	No.	%	No.	%	No.	%	No.	%	No.	%
Survival:										
static	9	33	4	44	–	–	–	–	13	33
Mobile:										
up	–	–	4	44	1	33	–	–	5	13
down	–	–	–	–	–	–	–	–	–	–
All	9	33	8	89	1	33	–	–	18	46
Entry	18	67	1	11	2	66	–	–	21	54
Total	27	100	9	100	3	99	–	–	39	100

Source: Hanley Borough Rate Book, 1882.

Though, as might be expected, the majority of entry firms were small a significant feature of the population of ancillary firms in Hanley in 1882 was the appearance of mills owned and operated by some of the giant-sized, integrated manufacturing firms. Such firms have been recorded as participants

[17] Ibid., p. 362.

in the ancillary trades when they received separate listings in trade directories as potters' millers and manufacturers. Both the single medium entry firm in the ancillary population of 1882 (Brown-Westhead, Moore & Co.) and the two large entry firms (Clementson Bros. and J & G Meakin) fall into this category, as does one of the surviving medium sized firms (Powell, Bishop & Stonier). In 1862 only one firm, Livesey, Powell & Co., had combined integration with diversification.

The entry of these integrated manufacturing firms into the auxiliary sector will clearly have had an impact on existing smaller specialists. More interesting, though, are their motivations for entry. Had they recognized a business opportunity where their existing scale could potentially have quickly lead to market power or were they simply trying find a use for under-utilized physical resources, integration being difficult and costly to reverse. Helper argues that a 'buyer firm with power in its final-product market', the goal of these giant integrated concerns in the Potteries, 'can use that power to change the structure of its input markets'. However, it seems unlikely that these firms were attempting through diversification to induce greater concentration in the ancillary trades, which might in turn also have led to changes in the structure of the manufacturing sector by altering the balance of the disintegrated network.[18] As Wilson and others have argued, altering the atomistic structure of Britain's industries was beyond the scope of single firms acting alone. Moreover, though demand for potters' materials was being increased by the general expansion of the industry supply showed every sign of being met by a steady stream of small entrants. Indeed, declining concentration in the ancillary trades had not been halted by the entry of the far more heavily capitalized integrated firms. Furthermore, there was in the majority of these cases a clear lag between integration and diversification. Integration, as evidenced by the Rate Books, typically occurred in the early 1870s, and diversification, as evidenced by trade directories, in the early 1880s. Thus, it was the continuing lack of power these firms had in the final-product market that had forced them into an adaptive rather than intended strategy of diversification.

Thus, integrated firms, despite their attempts to move towards mass production, were, like all others in the Potteries, subject to increasingly unpredictable trade patterns in this period. Their decision to diversify rather than to divest reflected the implausibility of substituting at the margins with every shift in their cost or demand structures. Though Lazonick has argued that in the post-1945 cotton industry spinning, weaving, and, marketing firms readily combined and separated for the 'sake of short-term supply and demand advantages' and that this 'constituted precisely Coasian managerial decision-making', he goes on to argue that to 'reap the benefits of mass production, the

18 Helper, 'Strategy and Irreversibility', p. 790.

modern enterprise cannot shift its mode of operation with every change in relative factor prices' and that:

> the manager who integrates and disintegrates operations according to the ebb and flow of the market situation does so in lieu of the long-term planning of the organizationally interconnected and technically interrelated production and distribution processes that characterize the modern corporation.[19]

Integration followed by diversification amongst large pottery manufacturers in the 1880s was the result of the conjunction of a strategic decision to pursue mass production and a determination to maintain the resources necessary to that strategy in the face of difficult conditions rather than to enter rashly into any costly and possibly irreversible policy of divestment. As if to emphasize this point the giant integrated firms of the late nineteenth century, such as Meakins, remained industry leaders throughout much of the twentieth century. Nonetheless, vertical integration remained exceptional and as late as 1974 Gay and Smythe were able to assert that 'the preparation of materials ... are mainly undertaken by specialists on behalf of the manufacturers. Because the suppliers operate on a large scale ... the pottery manufacturers benefit from specialisation'.[20]

It was argued above that individual firms were unable to affect the structure of the manufacturing sectors through destabilizing the balance between manufacturing and auxiliary sectors. Nonetheless, by the turn of the century, as the auxiliary sector began to experience a distinct process of contraction, it was becoming clear that change in its structure could have unmistakeable consequences for manufacturers. Thus, in 1901, the trade press began to report that the idea of a trust was being floated by some manufacturers, in part because; 'potters ... are practically hopeless before the (unofficial) Coal Trust [and] the Millers' Trust'.[21] These complaints of the undue power being wielded by potters' millers were particularly vociferous in Longton, home to many small manufacturers. Thus, at the China Makers Dinner of the same year, combination was proposed as 'one of the best solutions to short bones, high coals and short prices'.[22] To a large degree, these changes flowed from an increasing reliance on South American sources of bone ash. As Bernard Moore noted before the *Tariff Commission*, 'Certain manufacturers use nothing but English bone, but it is more expensive'. The difficulty faced by millers and, in

---

19 Lazonick, 'The Cotton Industry, p. 40–1.

20 Gay and Smythe, *The British Pottery Industry*, p. 34.

21 *The Pottery Gazette*, January 1901, p. 65.

22 *The Pottery Gazette*, February 1901, p. 192. At the same dinner, E.V. Greatbach, chair of the North Staffordshire Chamber of Commerce, alluded to the interruption of bone supplies from South America.

turn potters, was that the importation of this material was highly ologopolistic in structure, 'as all the bone comes through three men in Liverpool'.[23] In defense Moore and others attempted to form a 'large milling combination for grinding the materials for manufacturers – perhaps the largest in the world'.[24]

Little is known of the nature and history of this 'combination', though its longevity and success must be in some doubt. Bernard Moore's daughter maintained that Moore had been 'part of a syndicate or group which attempted to monopolize supplies of bone' but that this 'speculation went disastrously wrong, and rather than declare himself bankrupt, Moore sold the family firm'. This was in 1905, at around the time Moore gave evidence to the *Tariff Commission*. Percy Shelley later claimed that 'the uncertainty of getting his materials, especially bone of a certain purity and quality, compelled [Moore] to build a small mill, which was a great worry and doubtless a great financial loss to him, and led to his becoming associated with the mill combine'.[25] In this matter, as in others, the Potteries failed to generate strong institutions that transcended the fragmented nature of the industry.

Jesse Shirley and Son, 1820–1890

In relating the growth and development of the firm of Jesse Shirley and Sons to the wider trends outlined above we can further illustrate the process of change in the patterns of integration displayed by the pottery industry in the latter half of the nineteenth century. The fortunes of the firm, founded in 1820, expanded decisively by a capital investment programme in the 1850s, and undergoing contraction in the 1880s, paralleled the development of the wider industry. The example provided by the firm first emphasizes an increase in specialization and then reinforces the impression of increasingly difficult trading conditions from the mid-1870s. In outlining the broad story of the firm we will also explore the role of the family and of personal capitalism in the development of inter-firm networks in the nineteenth-century. Subsequent sections will explore in more detail the activities of the firm, providing evidence of the way in which the disintegrated system functioned to absorb contingencies, reduce risks, and deliver economies of flexibility.

The firm was founded in 1820, though, as has been noted, a Belgian visitor to the Potteries in the 1860s thought specialization in this field relatively new. The firm was then a prime mover driven by the entrepreneurial activities of its founding partners, Bourne and Hudson.[26] Little is known of this partnership,

---

23 *Tariff Commission*, para. 114.

24 Ibid., para. 110.

25 Dawson, *Bernard Moore*, p. 14.

26 R. Pomfret, '"My Bones are Burned as an Hearth"', pp. 147–76.

though it seems likely that Hudson was a sleeping partner.[27] The family firm and personal capitalism have become key areas in debates over the organization and performance of British business. They have been seen as the seedbeds of both a conservative business culture and of an atomistic business structure.[28] However, the route to proprietary capitalism taken by Jesse Shirley emphasizes that there was in the nineteenth century no typical family firm. Family firms were to be found in every sector and were of every size and structure, from the giant cotton concern of Samuel Greg and Co. to the far smaller retail units of Nenadic's Edinburgh studies.[29]

Shirley's route to ownership of the firm was complex, being built on his previous employment under Bourne, marriage into the Bourne family, and finance from his own immediate family. The business went on to become a genuine inter-generational family firm, ownership passing to Jesse's sons. The firm remains an independent family business today.[30] Pomfret presents evidence that Jesse, born in 1822, was an employee of Bourne at the bone works from 1841 at the latest and that throughout the 1840s was the firm's most highly paid worker. How did Shirley move from the position of employee to that of employer? Pomfret makes reference to a 'family tradition' which holds that 'John Bourne married twice and, following his death, Jesse Shirley married his widow', for which there is supporting evidence. Jesse and his older brother Joseph each inherited one quarter of Bourne's estate and the appearance of J. Bourne-Shirley as a co-occupier of the Etruscan Bone Works in the Hanley Borough Rate Book of 1882 links the two family names in one person.

---

[27] Ibid., p. 169.

[28] Chandler, *Scale and Scope*; Elbaum and Lazonick, *The Decline of the British Economy*.

[29] M.B. Rose, 'The Role of the Family in Providing Capital and Managerial Talent in Samuel Greg and Company, 1784–1840', *Business History*, Vol. 19, No. 1 (1977), pp. 37–54; S. Nenadic, 'The Small Family Firm in Victorian Britain', *Business History*, Vol. 35, No. 4 (1993), pp. 86–113.

[30] By the 1880s the firm was controlled by Jesse's sons; Jesse (1848–1927), Henry Benjamin (1858–1910) and John Bourne-Shirley (1851–d. unkown). The fourth occupant of the works recorded in the rate book of 1882, another J. Shirley, was probably John, eldest son of Joseph, brother of Jesse snr. This John was recorded in the 1851 Census as a clerk, aged fifteen. The evidence thus supports Nenadic's claim that the 1880s represented a watershed in the fortunes of small firms, whereafter 'small-firm profits were better able to provide an income for more than one member of the family. There were, however, limits to this process. When E.N.W. Bennett entered Dunn, Bennett and Co. in 1910, aged sixteen, he was soon reminded by 'one of my older brothers, now married and commencing a family of his own ... that there were already three elder brothers at the factory and one in the London office and there was no future for me whatsoever'. Just as the family firm could be constrained by the size and attributes of the family, so the opportunities open to family members could be constrained by the growth of the firm. The nineteenth century family firm was indeed not a 'simple phenomenon'. *Census*, 1851 and 1861; Hanley Borough Rate Book, 1882; Nenadic, 'The Small Family Firm', pp. 91–3; E.N.W. Bennett, *Argentina Farewell*, (Privately Printed, 1977), p. 45; Nenadic, 'The Small Family Firm', p. 109.

Thus, the family might be shaped by business interests as much as the firm was by family priorities. As Nenadic notes, 'aspirant Victorian business men extensively exploited family realities and mythologies'.[31]

Marriage to Bourne's widow provided Shirley with an entry into business, but his own family played a vital role in supplying further financial and managerial resources and, perhaps most importantly, in integrating the firm into local business networks. Having gained control of a firm that had, at an early stage, assumed a central position in the district's emerging system of disintegrated production Shirley was also well placed to take advantage of rising demand in the industry's final-product market in the third quarter of the century. In particular, the Shirley family's financial reserves were central to the building of a new mill in 1857, shortly after Jesse gained control of the firm. As Scranton has observed, succession of moments of transition 'could often precipitate experiments in marketing, styling or technology'.[32] The new mill added significantly to the firm's capacity, suggesting that returns to the function of material processing were continuing to increase at that time. Thus, the potential for continued expansion in some specialisms also led to the heightened fixed capital intensity seen in ancillary firms such as Shirleys, moving integration further beyond the reach of the majority of manufacturers. This effect was further magnified by a concurrent decline in the concentration of the pottery industry.

The family's financial strength was derived from the retained profits of other business activities. These were mercantile in nature. Joseph Shirley was recorded in the census of 1851 as an 'Agent for Manufacturers' and unmarked ledgers stored with those of both Bourne and Hudson and Jesse Shirley and Sons, detailing a trade in china clay and stone carried out between Cornwall and the Potteries between 1844 and 1851, make it clear that he was a merchant.[33] Through this activity the family had built up reserves of capital, contacts, goodwill and trust in the district that supplemented those established by Jesse whilst Bourne's employee.[34] Many of Joseph's customers for clay and stone will also have been Jesse's customers for bone. Thus, the family and the firm were quickly integrated into the business networks of the district. As Cookson observed from a study of textile engineering firms in West Yorkshire, it was 'vital to be connected into a local network of technical and commercial

---

[31] Pomfret, '"My Bones are Burned"', p. 156–8; Nenadic, 'The Small Family Firm', p. 100.

[32] Scranton, *Figured Tapestry*, p. 166.

[33] Joseph's mercantile trade was largely conducted with Anthony Luke and Co., of Charleston, St. Austell, Cornwall.

[34] See Nenadic's claim that the family 'provided the entrepreneur with one of the best vehicles for reducing transaction costs through improved "intermediation" on the basis of family reputation'. 'The Small Family Firm', p. 89.

information' and that the family very often played a central role in the process of insertion.[35]

Evidence of a reduced but continuing trade in china clay and stone is also to be found in ledgers definitely belonging to the firm of Jesse Shirley and Sons, and the two brothers also jointly owned a number of residential properties. There is then a pattern of diversified business activity to be found within the Shirley family, a pattern emphasized as a positive aspect of the Greg family businesses in studies by Rose. Rose also notes that 'Many entrants to the cotton industry transferred capital amassed from profits earned as merchants, into large scale manufacturing concerns', and though the mercantile route was not typical of those entering the pottery industry as manufacturers it was appropriate to the trade carried out by Shirleys.[36]

During the first fifty years of its life then the firm of Jesse Shirley and Sons was able to establish itself and prosper as a key ancillary firm, one of a small cohort of larger independent specialists, as the industry which it served enjoyed continued expansion and growing demand. This growth and development has been related both to industry wide trends and to the centrality of families to localized inter-firm networks. However, in the late 1870s or early 1880s the firm underwent a process of contraction. In 1872 the firm owned and occupied three sites in Etruria with a combined RV of £375 (two mills and a smaller collection of offices, stabling etc.), but by 1882 the smaller Bells Mill (RV £169), though still owned by the executors of Jesse Shirley, stood unoccupied.[37] The firm survived but was clearly experiencing difficulties. However, as was shown in Chapter 3, pottery exports did not decline in volume in the last quarter of the century. Instead, pottery manufacturers were faced with a more erratic demand structure and falling prices. Shirley's problems must be traced primarily to that instability and its impact on the strategies of manufacturing firms, to change in the structure of the industry and to the growing competitiveness of the sub-sector in which they operated, in part a result of the diversification of large integrated manufacturers responding to the same pressures in their markets.

The business system supplying bone products to the pottery industry was built on a chain of relationships linking four components. These were: i. sources of raw bones, located primarily within the city and its immediate rural environs, ii. the processing firm, in this case Jesse Shirley and Sons., iii. pottery manufacturers, forming the largest and most valuable group of customers for the firms products, and, iv. customers for the by-products of processing, located mainly in the textile districts of Lancashire, Yorkshire, and the Midlands. These relationships displayed a series of marked differences

---

35 Cookson, 'Family Firms and Business Networks', p. 6.

36 M.B. Rose, 'Diversification of Investment by the Greg Family, 1800–1914', *Business History*, Vol. 21, No. 4 (1979), pp. 79–96; Rose, 'The Role of the Family', p. 39.

37 Hanley Borough Rate Books, 1872 and 1882.

from one another. For instance, the relationships between the processing firm and its two customer groups were carried out in quite different ways. All these relationships also changed over time.

The sources of the raw materials used by the firm, bone, coal and slack, will be examined first. From whom bone was bought, the pattern of transactions (i.e. frequency and volume of transactions), how purchases were handled and overall volume will all be examined. In all transactions carried out by the firm, whether with suppliers or customers, the frequency and consistency of transactions (whether or not orders are for simple, standard amounts, for example) is of particular interest, for, as Nicholas has emphasized, rising infrequency leads almost invariably led to rising transaction costs.[38]

In 1857 raw bones, those that needed to go through each stage of processing, were bought from six sources, all located in the city or its immediate rural environs. A much smaller quantity of bone in other forms, either ash or ready calcined, came from a further three sources, two of them located in Liverpool. The assumption must be that these were imported from South America, the dominant source of bone by the close of the century. The total expenditure on bone in 1857 was approximately £5234. By way of contrast total expenditure on the new mill stood at £1802 at the end of 1858, whilst the total wage bill for 1867 was £819. Clearly the firm's cost structure was very different to that of most pottery manufacturers, where wages predominated. However, high levels of expenditure on inputs probably ensured that the need for working capital was just as great. By 1867 suppliers of bone had risen by two to eleven and the total expenditure on bone had also increased to £6094. By 1884, expenditure on bone had declined to £5046, lower than that of nearly three decades earlier.[39]

However, most significantly, the smaller quantities of bone purchased by the firm in the 1880s came from a much wider network of smaller suppliers, twenty four in total, and whilst the majority of these were still to be found in the Potteries and its surroundings, others were to be found elsewhere, particularly to the south in the Black Country. The obvious consequence of these conflicting trends was that the amounts bought from individual suppliers tended to fall in both weight and value whilst transactions also became more infrequent. The bulk of bone processed no longer came from one or two dominant sources supplemented by a handful of suppliers used less often and for smaller amounts. By the 1880s sources of raw bone that can be characterized as petty had come to dominate. As will be shown, this more erratic sourcing of raw materials reflected the increasingly erratic orders being placed by the firm's customers. It was this increasing mass of petty transactions that pottery manufacturers, facing increasing uncertainty in their own markets, avoided through taking advantage of the disintegrated system. These changes

[38] Nicholas, 'Overseas Marketing Performance'.

[39] Ledgers, 1857, 1867 and 1884.

in the sourcing of raw bone can be illustrated more fully through studying one supplier, John Gray of Hagley, a Cheshire village to the northwest of the Potteries.

Gray supplied bone to Etruria in each of the three years examined in the second half of the nineteenth century, that is 1857, 1867 and 1884. In fact, Gray had also supplied bone to value of £2466, out of total bone purchases of £3264, in 1835. The relationship was then durable and, it may be assumed, characterized by a degree of loyalty. Continuity of involvement between Shirleys and other suppliers was not unknown. Thomas Culshaw of Newcastle-under-Lyme supplied bone for over a decade in the middle of the century, but the relationship with Gray was exceptional, reflecting the voume of trade between the two. Between July and December 1857 the value of bone purchased from Gray was barely less than fifty per cent of the total value of raw bone bought (£1229 out of £2617). Gray's deliveries were both regular and frequent, four or five a month at very nearly one weekly intervals. They did, however, range in both size and value, from one to ten tons and £12 to £76. The highest total value of raw bone supplied by any other local source in the same period was £64, though two lots of calcined bones with a total value of £370 were sourced locally and calcined bone and bone ash worth £565, again in two lots, was shipped from Liverpool[40].

By 1867 Gray was less important to Shirley. Over the whole of that year the value of his trade in bone with Jesse Shirley, at £1721, was little more than it been had in six months ten years earlier. The frequency and regularity of his deliveries had not altered significantly but their size and value had. This is not in itself indicative of Shirleys reacting to changing trading conditions with altered behaviour, but that conclusion is suggested by evidence from 1884. In that year Gray made only one delivery a month, with the exception of May in which there were two, and their size and value had also decreased. In total Gray supplied bone to the value of £368 and was now just one among a throng of petty suppliers, such as Ann Cain of Longton who between May and August supplied bone to the value of £9-17-2, or John Clewlow of Cheadle, whose many deliveries throughout the year attained a total value of only £62. Gray's decline, which might in itself have been caused by a number of unrelated factors, had not led to the emergence of a new, comparably dominant supply of raw bone; instead the dispersal of a multitude of lines of supply from an assortment of farmers and rag and bone men had been maximized.[41]

This changed relationship between the firm and sources of raw bone represented a flexible response by the firm to changes in the behaviour of primary manufacturers, heightened competition and uncertainty having led them to alter the way they purchased raw materials. However, though flexible,

[40] Ledger, 1857.

[41] Ledgers, 1867 and 1884.

the strategy also imposed penalties on the Shirleys and, as has been seen, the firm contracted in the early 1880s by mothballing one of its two mills. In particular, a multitude of irregular transactions led to opportunity costs in the form of management time devoted to both overseeing a now more complex, dispersed, and less reliable system and to the co-ordination of supply and demand in order to avert the threat of either plant under-utilization or inability to meet sudden orders. At the same time increased information and transaction costs were also incurred, as transactions become less routine and thus open to greater negotiation. Change in the pattern of transactions was also accompanied by changes in the way they were handled, particularly in terms of payment.

In 1857 Gray and other local suppliers of bone were paid in cash. However, the consistency of the trade done allowed payment to take the form of regular, rounded monetary sums bearing no relation to specific deliveries. In 1857 even the relatively large and distant deals with Liverpool were paid for with cash, though it is interesting that these were the only ones on which Shirleys paid commission, presumably to brokers. As the century progressed and trading patterns became more fragmented so to did methods of payment. By 1884 bone was being paid for with cash, cheques, bankers' drafts and payment in kind all employed, at times in combination and with no strong correlation between size or value of purchase and method used.

In comparison to bone the sourcing of coal and slack, necessary for the boiling, grinding and drying of bone was relatively simple and also displayed less change in the period under study. These differences may be attributed mainly to the large-scale structure of the mining industry in the region. Demand from the pottery and steel industries of the district had brought the local mining industry to maturity and all supplies of coal were local. In 1857 four sources were utilized, they were; Fox and Tinsley of Cobridge, Thomas Brindley also of Cobridge, Adderley and Dean of Norton and Charles Hale of Ford Green. Of these four Fox and Tinsley made both larger and more regular deliveries. However, Brindley also made very regular, though smaller, deliveries. Indeed, the two sources found close at hand in Cobridge, adjacent to Etruria, were essentially used in conjunction. By 1884 this picture, though altered in detail, remained similar in outline. The Butterley Colliery of Silverdale and The Hanley Colliery Company were being used in conjunction. Both collieries made deliveries in all twelve months of the year, though they tended to be paid rather differently. Butterley Colliery, with whom a marginally larger trade was done, were paid on only four occasions throughout the year (April, May, August, and November) whilst The Hanley Colliery was paid on a monthly basis, though with a delay of two months from delivery.[42]

---

[42] Given the frequent references to the use of credit within the district it is probable that collieries also allowed manufacturers to settle accounts quarterly. Indeed, the Cork, Edge and Malkin archive contains a letter from the Ivy House and Wheatley Brick and Marl Works apologizing for sending the firm an invoice, probably for clay, meant for another local firm.

Both collieries received cheques only and gave discount, typically in the order of five per cent. A much smaller trade was done with Henry Warrington of Hanley, who made deliveries in May, July, August, November and December. Warrington was paid with one bankers' draft and gave discount of 2.5%.[43] Clearly, much less flexibility was available to Shirleys in sourcing coal than was the case with raw bones.

Though few in number, the firm enjoyed an important relationship with customers located outside the Potteries, particularly in the middle decades of the century. In 1857 the firm did business with five such customers, two in Manchester and one a piece in Nottingham, Derby and Wolverhampton. The firms in Manchester both bought size and tallow, weak glues used in the cotton industry to give weight and strength to cheap cloth. The trade with one of these firms, J. & J.M. Worrall, was very substantial, greater in value than that with any individual pottery firm by a considerable margin. However, as with the supply of raw bone, the 1880s witnessed the collapse of all trade with firms and individuals located outside the district into a mass of smaller, more infrequent and much less valuable transactions. The Ledger for 1884 records sales not only of tallow, size and various bone products but also of rags, hay and manure. Again there is a concentration of customers located in textile districts, three in Manchester and one in Halifax, but none of these firms, including Vickers with whom business was being done in 1857, placed more than a handful of orders or spent more than £20 with Jesse Shirley and Sons throughout the course of the year.[44] These are indications that the changes to the supply of raw bones made by the firm bore a clear relationship to alterations in demand in the period under study. Again the costs incurred in supervising a greater volume of less valuable transactions may be inferred. It will now be shown that similar changes characterized trade with the firm's principal customers, ceramic firms located within the Potteries.

Examination of trade between the firm and pottery manufacturers will focus on the same features explored in the relationships between others components of the business system; by whom orders were placed, the size, value and frequency of those orders, how they were paid for and alterations in all of these factors over time. Furthermore, differences between business done inside and outside the Potteries will also be illustrated. These differences will be shown to have lain principally in the methods of payment most commonly used by pottery firms, which may, in turn, be related to circuits of credit prevalent within the district.

The letter, which concluded by 'apologizing for the innaccuracy and soliciting your further orders', was dated 1 August 1867 and the original invoice 1 April of that year. SD 1204/241, *Letter from the Ivy House and Wheatley Brick and Marl Works, Hanley*, 1 August 1867.

43 Ledgers, 1857, 1867 and 1884.

44 Ibid.

As might be expected pottery firms, as a group, were numerically more significant than any other group of customers throughout the second half of the century. Typically they also spent more than other types of customers, though none of them spent as much on bone products as Worralls spent on size and tallow in the 1850s. Of the fifteen customers recorded in the Ledger covering 1857 nine were pottery firms, fairly evenly distributed through the five towns. Three were to be found in the southern china townships of Longton and Fenton, three in the increasingly important centre of Hanley and its satellites and a further two to the north in Burslem and Tunstall, where earthenware in which bone was not an ingredient was the staple product. The final firm occupied a peripheral location in Brownhills. The Longton and Fenton firms did however spend more, placing more frequent and more valuable orders. For example Allerton and Co., the firm's most important pottery customer, took delivery of no less than seven lots of ground bone, each of twenty cwt., in July 1857 alone. Only in December 1857, a typically slack month in the pottery trade, were there less than five transactions between the two firms. The patterns displayed by J. Lockett, also of Longton, and Thomas Green of Fenton were very similar, though neither did quite as large a trade as Allerton and Co.[45] It is likely that for seven of the firm's nine local customers, Shirley was their only or principal source of ground bone. They operated what would today be defined as a preferred supplier sourcing strategy, rather than one of mulitple or parallel sourcing.

Certainly, these firms do not appear to have used 'competitive discipline ruthlessly against their partner'. Casson suggest that in a low-trust climate firms will '"shop around" its partners rivals, and use price comparisons to back up threats to switch trade away unless it gets a better deal'. There is no evidence that in 1857 Shirley's customers were making such switches in order to 'maintain the credibility of these threats'.[46] Conversely, the remaining pottery firm customers each placed only one order with Shirley in the six month period analyzed, suggesting that they too enjoyed stable relations with a preferred supplier and turned to another source, Shirley, only in exceptional circumstances. Firms seem to have sought and valued stability and loyalty in the local supply networks in which they participated. This finding clearly bears on the issue of trust in the context of the industrial district and, in turn, as we shall see, the delayed payments made by customers reflected Shirley's trust in them.

By 1884 the situation was in many ways very different. Pottery firms remained Shirley's most important customers and amongst these china manufacturers were still dominant. However, that firms from Longton and

[45] Ledger, 1857.

[46] M. Casson, *Enterprise and Competitiveness: A Systems View of International Business* (Oxford, Clarendon Press, 1990), p. 113.

Fenton were not now numerically predominant is indicative of the continued shifts within the district, the sectoral/spatial alignment of earthenware to the north, china to the south starting to become blurred. Finally, as in 1857, pottery firms were more likely to place multiple orders than other customers.[47]

However, the trade being done with these customers was quite different in complexion in a number of ways. In order to assess these changes we need to specify the nature of two sets of relationships. First, there are those between Shirley and long-term customers, with whom it might be expected that strong links involving notions of trust and reciprocity had been forged. Had these deteriorated? That Shirley still did business with firms with which it had traded in 1857 aids this inquiry. Second, focus will fall on firms whose relationships with Shirley were much newer; particularly those that can be identified as small new entrants to the industry. Were particular forms of inter-firm relationship associated with such firms, providing a link to industry-wide structural change?

The firm's customer base had certainly grown by 1884 but this growth had not compensated for the increasingly erratic demands made by the district's manufacturers. Orders were now patchy, often infrequent and generally smaller. In 1857 bone was ordered and supplied in near standard twenty cwt. lots, but in 1882 deliveries displayed a much greater range of sizes and values. Seemingly in response, many other products were also being supplied alongside bone and, perhaps most significantly, services as opposed to products had emerged as an important part of the firm's business. The firm was, therefore, diversifying its activities as the staple trade in ground bone became increasingly unpredictable and less valuable. There were still firms doing a large and relatively steady trade with Shirleys, but even these displayed a degree of contingent behaviour.

These changes in the day-to-day business activities of the firm may be related to two factors in the wider industry; that is to structural and strategic change. The latter point may best be seen in the change in the behaviour of established customers such as Allerton and Co., and T. and S. Green, of Longton and Fenton respectively. Shirleys had done business with both of these firms in 1857, when both had placed only orders for twenty cwt of ground bone at roughly weekly interval, the tempo of orders varying only slightly with the seasonal nature of the trade. However, in the altered trading conditions of the 1880s, were placing orders that were both smaller and less frequent than before. Robinson and Son, of Sutherland Road Longton, with whom Shirley had traded since at least 1867, provide another example. They appear to have done a very vigorous trade with their supplier, placing thirty separate orders in June 1884 alone for example, but when that trade is examined in detail it is seen to be composed of a mass of petty transactions. They too now bought bone in lots of lesser weight and value than previously

[47] Ledger, 1884.

and the majority of their orders were for the grinding of very small amounts of colour and glaze.

That long established customers behaved in this way is significant and suggests that irregular and infrequent ordering was now the norm rather than the exception. Indeed, most of the orders received by Shirleys were now from firms placing infrequent orders and most of the firms doing business with Shirleys placed infrequent orders. For example, of the twenty-four pottery firms transacting with Shirley in June 1884 fifty per cent placed two or less orders and typically carried on in the same way throughout the year. Their behaviour was then quite different to that of the firms placing infrequent orders at the mid-century.[48] Repeat trading was now less common, or certainly less reliable, strongly suggesting that switching was taking place, manufacturers exercising competitive discipline as they themselves experienced fluctuating demand and falling prices. Returning to the analysis of inter-firm relationships offered by Helper, those experienced by Shirley in this period may be characterized as 'voice with cheating'. Such relationships are not:

> explicitly nurtured [but are] maintained because of personal trust between individuals at the two firm or because of firms status as a traditional supplier. Over the decades that these relationships endure, fairly complex norms of reciprocity ... arose, as buyers and suppliers attempted to forge continuing relationships in an atmosphere characterized by both intense conflict and mutual dependency.[49]

The crucial attribute of the voice with cheating mode is that it does not, even in a tightly clustered industry such as pottery, preclude either reneging or buyers playing suppliers off against each other. The trust that Shirley had built up in the networks of the district could only do so much to override the imperatives of firms trying to reduce their cost and enhance their flexibility in an increasingly uncertain world.

In turn, the demands made of Shirley by manufacturers in the 1880s, if they were to have been met internally, would have required initial fixed capital investment, which, as we have seen, only the very largest manufacturers were either willing or able to make. Such investments would also have incurred the risk of the under-utilization when demand for the firm's finished product was slack. As has already been suggested a network of partial process firms did allow the pottery industry to benefit from external economies of scale and flexibility, the functioning and efficiency of which must be related to the physical clustering of the industry. Indeed, this pattern was perhaps only feasible given the tight spatial clustering of the district.

---

48 Ledgers, 1857, 1867 and 1884.

49 Helper, 'Strategy and Irreversibility', p. 802.

However, the rise of infrequent and petty ordering amongst the majority of Shirley's customers may be traced not only to change in the behaviour of established customers but also to structural change in the industry and, in particular, to a proliferation of small, new firms. Shirley's records display a clear correlation between infrequent ordering and small, new entrant firms such as Banks and Morley (RV £100) and E. Steel (RV £80), both of Hanley, or Shorter and Boulton of Stoke-upon-Trent (RV £83). Another manufacturer typical of this group was Thomas Bevington, china manufacturer of Burton Place, Hanley, whose firm (RV £204) had entered the industry between 1872 and 1882. Bevington placed just one order for twelve cwt. of best ground bone in June 1884. Small, new-entrant firm were also more likely than older customers to place orders for bone that were smaller, or to place orders only for grinding small amounts of glaze etc. Increasingy mobility within the firm population of the industry and quickening pace of entry and exit, both demonstrated in Chapter 2, had resulted in a decline in repeat trading and had, it may be surmised, emerged from and reinforced a growing climate of distrust.[50]

There were some exceptions to all these trends. For example the firm of Wm. Stubbs, earthenware manufacturers of Hanley, placed just one order with Shirleys in June 1884, buying twenty eight cwt. of ground bone, yet was a well established firm in the medium-size category. A further entirely new feature of the trade being done by Shirleys in the 1880s were the transactions between Shirleys and other ancillary firms such as the Hanley colour manufacturers Wengers (RV £45) or the large milling firm of E. & C. Challinors (RV £272). These transactions, again typically for small amounts of grinding rather than substantial quantities of materials, point to a rise in contingencies. It seems likely that with the greater irregularity of trade came increasing difficulties in co-ordination, leading in turn to occasional inability to meet demand in the short-term, hence the orders placed with a competing ancillary firm. 'Mushroom' firms impacted not only on the relationship of the industry to markets then but also on that with its ancillary trades.[51]

Furthermore the price the firm could charge for ground bone also seems to have fallen, from between ten and eleven shillings per cwt. in 1857 to around eight in 1884. In the context of the patterns of trade within the district and the non-occupancy of Bells Mill in 1882, the grinding of often petty quantities of materials for other firms, apparent in the ledger of 1884, must be seen not as a strategy of deliberate diversification but rather as a defense designed to minimize the under-utilization of plant, an adaptive rather than intended strategy.[52] The returns to specialization open to a firm such as Shirleys were

[50] Hanley Borough Rate Books, 1862, 1872 and 1882; Ledgers, 1857, 1867 and 1884.

[51] Ibid.

[52] Though rate books clearly show that Bell's Mill was unoccupied in 1882, minimal wages were still being paid with regard to this site in 1884, probably in relation to maintenance

becoming harder to capture. The evidence from this case study thus fleshes out the story set out in Chapter 2 of an auxiliary sector contracting from the 1880s onwards.

Some of the ways in which the disintegrated system of production in the Potteries delivered flexibility and risk reduction to manufacturing firms have been demonstrated in this examination of the day-to-day business activity of Shirley. However, that system, and the role played by firms such as Shirley, did not, of course, eliminate risk. Instead, risk was transferred or deferred and remained within the industry. In particular, methods of payment for transactions occurring within the district, as seen in the example of Jesse Shirley and Sons, went some way towards the informal reintegration of the industry along lines of credit and debt.

At Shirley, cash had been the principal or sole method of payment used in the 1850s, but by the 1880s bankers' drafts and bills of exchange dominated transactions within the district in a way not seen at the mid-century. Collapse in one link in the credit circuits of the later nineteenth-century could have wide ramifications; lean times, a preference for raising finance through retained profits, and the constant demand for working capital experienced by firms large and small, meant that there were many businesses which did not have the 'capital which it requires to meet an emergency'.[53] The result was that failures tended to run in series. In August 1896 it seemed as though 'The slackness of trade and low prices ... are beginning to bear fruit, and two failures have been announced in the present month'.[54] A more specific example may be drawn from March 1883:

> The present state of the trade is, to use a common phrase, 'in a regular jumble'. First of all John Plant and Co., China decorators, Stafford Street tumble over for a small amount-under £300. Then, like a row of bricks, follows the startling news that another has gone for £2000; and, as a sort of climax, comes Messrs. Wm. Kirkby and Co. with the respectable amount of £24,000.[55]

It is interesting that this chain began with a small partial process firm and 'climaxed' with a large manufacturer. The ancillary trades were clearly fully integrated into such chains. Thus, when Furnivals, a large grinder and supplier of flint and other potters' materials, failed in 1883 their liabilities of £33,883 included £23,015 owed to unsecured creditors, the majority of them local firms. The use of bankers' drafts and bills of exchange, so prominent in the

---

work. Just as was true of the large integrated manufacturers, under-utilization did not lead automatically to a costly and hard-to-reverse divestment.

[53] *The Pottery Gazette*, February 1893, p. 127.

[54] *The Pottery Gazette*, August 1896, p. 714.

[55] *The Pottery Gazette*, March 1883, p. 263.

many transactions carried out by Jesse Shirley with other local businesses, was central to the functioning of the disintegrated system. However, as Pomfret notes, 'In the advantage of the bill of exchange', that is its ability to circulate, 'also lay its danger ... the failure of one substantial trading concern could precipitate the failure of many others'.[56] Thus, methods of payment between firms within the Potteries, though they extended the flexibility inherent in the disintegrated system and eased liquidity problems, also carried dangers.

The evidence provided by Shirleys wage books, assuming a degree of correlation between the firm's demand for labour and its derived demand, suggests, however, that whilst both uncertainty and contingent strategies were on the increase the extent to which the industry experienced seasonal fluctuations lessened slightly in this period.[57] The impact of seasonality on the pottery industry was rooted in fluctuations in demand and in the practicalities of supply. Fashion had its seasons, as did the weather. The winter month were particularly hard, bringing both fewer orders and more difficult working conditions, the 'banks' of clay, very often stored outside by manufacturers, even freezing solid on occasion. These variations were held to be a 'greater factor in the cost of production than is generally acknowledged'.[58]

Wage patterns at Shirleys have been analyzed in order to determine the degree of fluctuation between the highest and lowest monthly wage bills. The wage pattern of 1844 was reconstructed first to provide a basis from which to explore changes in the second half of the century. In 1844, during what may be thought of as the formative stage of the disintegrated system in the Potteries, fluctuation was very marked. Much of the firm's workforce in that year worked for only a few weeks. As might be expected, January was the least wage intensive month, total wage bill £23-8-6, and June the most, at £48. In other words a degree of fluctuation of over one hundred per cent. January was also the least wage intensive month in 1867 and 1884, though, perhaps as a result of work on the new mill, it fell in July in 1857. The most wage intensive month was May in 1857 and 1884 and March in 1867. However, by 1857 the degree of fluctuation had dropped to around fifty per cent where it remained in 1867. An increase of a few percentage points in the degree of fluctuation in 1884

---

[56] *The Pottery Gazette*, September 1883, p. 160; Pomfret, '"My Bones are Burned"', p. 160.

[57] The principal change in employment patterns at the firm in the period under study was decline in seasonal or part-time working. The workforce grew very little in absolute terms but those workers employed for all or the greater part of the year did come to representa larger and larger proportion of the workforce.

[58] *The Pottery Gazette*, March 1897, p. 315. Similarly, it was reported in Febraury 1891 that the 'principal topic of manufacturers during the past month has undoubtedly been the weather. It has been cold. Clay was frozen, pumps were frozen, water ceased to run, clay became scarce and flint scarcer, and it seemed in some quarters as if orders were congealed too'. *The Pottery Gazettem*, February 1891, p. 151.

suggests that, though the trend was not particularly marked, greater uncertainty in that period was also compounded by rising seasonality.[59]

Conclusion

This chapter has demonstrated that the growth and development of a population of auxiliary firms in the Potteries led to the creation of a tightly clustered 'system of disintegrated production', yielding external economies of scale, economies of flexibility, and reduced risks. These attributes became more important in the last quarter of the nineteenth century as adverse changes in the market forced many pottery manufacturers into a search for strategies able to meet the increasing number of contingencies they faced. The development of this disintegrated system was congruent with concurrent changes in the structure of the pottery industry, particularly the proliferation of small-scale firms from the mid-1870s and a subsequent decline in concentration ratios. At the same time, however, a small group of much larger firms was emerging and some of these firms sought to exit from the disintegrated system by integrating an ever-greater range of functions. The returns to integration were, though, still uncertain and hard to capture, and in the context of a changing competitive environment and changes in the structure of the industry some of these firms were forced in to an adaptive strategy of diversification in the 1880s.

Many of these industry wide developments were reflected at the micro-level in the story of Jesse Shirley and Son, the growth and development of the firm mirroring that of the industry it served. Changes in the material sourcing strategies of manufacturers and in buyer/supplier relations in the industry were to be seen in the trade between the firm and its well established customers, who ordered and paid for bone, other materials, and services in increasingly erratic patterns. The impact of structural changes in the wider industry, on the other hand, was to be seen in the firm's newer customers, many of them small entrants displaying less loyalty and liable to use Shirley in a yet more irregular way. As a result the firm had itself to minimize its commitment to lines of supply and, eventually, contracted in the 1880s, leaving one of its three sites unoccupied. The firm did, however, survive and remains an independent family firm today.

However, this disintegrated structure may also have been one factor in creating in the Potteries a systemic bias towards small-scale enterprises unable to make the three pronged investment in manufacturing, marketing and management, which Chandler argues began to distinguish American and German business from the late nineteenth century. In the Potteries, just as in the American jewellery industry in the same period, there was 'spatial

---

[59] Wage Books, 1844, 1857, 1867 and 1884.

flexibility with a vengeance, but the question of who would capture its benefits would unsettle the trade for decades'.[60] Increasingly, the trade press and the largest firms in the industry, including many of those integrated firms examined here, argued that the further growth and development of the industry in the Potteries was being constrained by this same unresolved question. In the next chapter the attempts made by these firms to gain greater influence over the industry by building industry-wide organizations will be explored.

60 Scranton, 'Diversity in Diversity', p. 35.

CHAPTER NINE

"An indissoluble mutual destiny": Business associations in the Potteries

Introduction

This chapter will explore the proposition that industrial districts encourage and depend upon the development of extra-firm institutions, which act to temper competition and foster co-operation. Such institutions emerge from the general tendency of firms in industrial districts to form networks at the local level through a variety of economic and social institutions and arrangements. Some economic linkages in the Potteries were examined in the preceding chapter, and the second half of the nineteenth century saw a series of attempts to establish organizations able to represent the interests of the business community in North Staffordshire, and of the pottery industry in particular. As Scranton notes, associationism may 'signal a maturing industrial district'.[1] These bodies included the *North Staffordshire Exchange*, the *North Staffordshire Chamber of Commerce*, and the *Potteries Board of Arbitration*. Though voluntary, these organizations were intended by their promoters to have a regulatory and unifying effect on the highly fragmented and competitive pottery industry. Their intended functions were, at times, explicitly interventionist, but each in turn failed.

It will be argued that the failure of these institutions was related to the fundamental problem of developing unity in the face of the 'individual assumptions' prevailing in the business community of the district.[2] As a result these bodies failed to engender sufficient support or to develop a 'distinctive collective identity'.[3] The failure of these institutions demonstrates the difficulty of creating cohesion in a highly competitive industrial district, and is a reminder that the concept of the industrial district is as yet vague on the conditions under which a balance between competition and co-operation will

---

[1] P. Scranton, 'Webs of Productive Association in American Industrialization: Patterns of Institution-formation and their Limits, Philadelphia, 1880–1930', *Journal of Industrial History*, Vol. 1, No. 1 (1998), p. 12.

[2] *The Sentinel*, 12 February 1859, p. 6.

[3] Staber, 'Embeddedness', p. 157.

be struck.[4] Furthermore, as the industry came under increased pressure in the 1880s and 1890s the earlier institutional failures became a symbol of the industry's problems, focusing attention on the issue of its highly competitive structure.

In order to explore these issues, the first section of the chapter will deploy the conceptual framework of Alfred Marshall, who viewed institutional forms as key agents in the historical evolution of industrial districts. Marshall's model has undergone considerable refinement. Piore, Sabel and Zeitlin, in particular, have reinvigorated the concept, emphasizing the role of qualitative factors in encouraging innovation and flexibility in industrial districts.[5] More recent developments have sought to explore the mechanisms whereby the 'social embeddedness' characteristic of clustered industries constrains and facilitates economic actors, in particular by promoting trust and tacit understandings.[6] Institutional building, so the literature suggests, may be one of the most important means through which such qualities are nurtured and exploited.

In the second section a brief chronology of institutional developments in the Potteries will be provided, and related to the typology of associations proposed by Scranton.[7] The pattern revealed will be related to broad shifts in the structure of the industry, in the competitive environment in which it operated, and in the strategies deployed by firms. The third section will then examine the factors responsible for the failure of institutional developments in the Potteries. The central role of a group of leading businessmen in the establishment of these institutions will be explored, and their aims and objectives outlined. Four factors contributed to the failure of this hierarchy to provide a focal point for collaboration.[8] First; the atomistic structure of the industry, and in particular the divide between a few large firms and the mass of small enterprises; second, cultural divisions, closely related to those of structure and rooted in issues of religion, politics, place of birth, the age of firms, and in the prevalence of personal capitalism within firms; third, sectoral divisions, particularly between

---

[4] Staber claims that the mix of competition and cooperation characteristic of industrial districts is 'not a commodity to be possessed or engineered but a condition that reflects cultural consistency, normative backing and conformity to agreed-upon-rules'. 'Embeddedness', p. 169.

[5] See; Piore and Sabel, *The Second Industrial Divide*; Sabel and Zeitlin, 'Historical Alternatives'.

[6] Staber, 'Embeddedness' perhaps provides the best introduction to this literature.

[7] Scranton, 'Webs of Productive Association'.

[8] Many researchers see embeddedness as a quality amenable to active promotion. Sydow, for example, argues that inter-firm networks may be co-ordinated 'with the help of trade associations or other collective organisations. J. Sydow, 'Flexible Specialization in Regional Networks', in Staber *et al.*, *Business Networks*, p. 24. Similarly, Staber argues that 'associations' broad scope places them in a strategic position as overlapping foci'. Staber, 'Embeddedness', p. 164.

earthenware and china manufacturers; and, finally, civic rivalry between the six townships of the district.[9]

The picture that emerges is a complex one. The factors shaping associational activity, in terms of both of the impulse towards it and its rejection, were highly inter-related, but above all else it was structural divisions which were the prime factor in the failure of the pottery industry to identify and act upon a set of common business interests. A final section will provide basic conclusions as to how this investigation of institutional developments in the Potteries can inform our understanding of the historical evolution of industrial districts. In particular, it will be argued that there is a need to further refine the concept in order to gain a deeper understanding of the diversity of industrial districts.

Institutional Forms in the Concept of the Industrial District

Alfred Marshall, who attempted to define the characteristics and attributes of industrial districts, first gave the concept coherent form. Most relevant here is Marshall's focus on the ways in which co-ordination occurs between firms within industrial districts.

Marshall was undoubtedly interested in what may be termed conscious co-ordination, or the 'various forms of co-operation in which there is some constructive purpose'.[10] Marshall argues that the principal benefit achieved through association is that derived from 'parcelling out of demand for various sorts of the same class of products [so] that each business can specialize its plant on a narrow range of work, and yet keep it running with but little interruption'.[11] In other words, association can act to guarantee realization of the external economies of scale characteristic of industrial districts by encouraging firms to concentrate on core competencies. It must be noted though that he goes on to claim that this 'specialization is however thoroughly effected without conscious effort in the Lancashire cotton industry'.[12] Thus, his preference is clearly for what may be termed market co-ordination, and he notes that:

> The broadest, and in some respects most efficient forms of constructive co-operation are seen in a great industrial district where numerous

---

[9] Staber notes that Saxenian 'argues that the political environment is an important causal factor in network development'. Staber, 'Networks and Regional Development', p. 18. For civic rivalry in the Potteries, see, Stobart and Thomas, 'Cultural Capital'.

[10] Marshall, *Industry and Trade.*, p. 599.

[11] Ibid., p. 601.

[12] Ibid., p. 601. For an exploration of how this was achieved and, in particular, of the contribution of merchants, see, Broadberry and Marrison, 'External Economies of Scale'.

> specialized branches of industry have been welded almost automatically into an organic whole.[13]

Here he is referring to the kinds of network explored in the last chapter. Moreover, Marshall noted the many negative effects often associated with conscious co-ordination, such as 'desire to get the better of others in buying or selling' which characterizes many examples of association and 'develops a strong and even anti-social temper in a few of them'.[14]

Piore, Sabel, and Zeitlin have developed Marshall's ideas along both empirical and theoretical lines. For example, the analyses of both recognize that industrial districts, consisting of clusters of many small and medium-size firms, depend upon co-ordination, and that co-ordination is typically sought through a balance of conscious and automatic action. The later scholars, however, place greater emphasis than Marshall on the social dimensions of industrial districts, and assign to conscious co-ordination a more central and positive role. For Marshall, the most important attributes of an industrial district were external economies of scale and progressive specialization by firm, whereas Piore, Sabel, and Zeitlin place their main emphasis on the emergence of flexible specialization. They define the industrial district in terms of three characteristics; first, a 'highly differentiated' relationship with the market, in which products are 'constantly altered', second, the use of multi-purpose technologies and, third, 'regional institutions that balanced co-operation and competition among firms so as to encourage permanent innovation'.

Institutional arrangements are not subordinate to markets and technology; the three characteristics are 'mutually dependent'.[15] They identify three basic institutional forms, the municipal system, the paternalist or welfare capitalist firm, and the federated family firm. In order for an industrial district to exploit its adaptive and innovative potential these institutions are required 'to create an environment in which ... firms are discouraged from reducing wages and cutting prices rather than creating new products and production processes'. [16]

Piore, Sabel, and Zeitlin claim that through such institutional arrangements industrial districts are able to develop a 'distinctive combination of industrial fragmentation and commercial co-ordination'. However, they also contend that this co-ordination is rarely achieved, in Marshall's terms, purely automatically, but that it requires 'policing'.[17] The effectiveness of this policing is, in their analysis, a function of the district as a whole and, in particular, of a powerful identity of common interests inculcated from birth. Thus, 'each new

---

13 Marshall, *Industry and Trade*, p. 599.

14 Ibid., p. 599.

15 Sabel and Zeitlin, 'Historical Alternatives', p. 144.

16 Ibid., p. 144.

17 Ibid., p. 144–7 and p. 149.

generation' through 'automatic and collective induction ... learned the rules of competition and whom they could trust to abide by them'. This identification of common interests penetrated deep into the life of the district, attached moral sanctions to certain behaviour, and 'created a community across and within generations that protected the economy as a whole against the consequences of short-term calculations of advantage'.[18] Their analysis of this community of interests bears some resemblance to Marshall's concept of 'industrial atmosphere', but is more complex and instrumental. Indeed, Staber argues that Piore and Sabel's 'analysis of territorially bounded networking goes beyond standard agglomeration and transaction cost reasoning by emphasizing the *qualitative* social and institutional factors which facilitate quantitative external economies of co-location'.[19]

Thus, where Marshall was interested in the free interplay of market forces and in the ability of 'industrial atmosphere' to give firms competitive advantage in international markets, through guaranteeing supplies of skilled workers for example, Piore, Sabel and Zeitlin focus on the role of the district in moderating internal competition. In fact, they pay little attention to the firm, their focus is firmly on what Scranton has called the 'broad vitality of the industrial district'.[20] At this level, businessmen attempted to found institutions that were 'fashioned to ... establish rules of business conduct, thus regulating competition through governance practice [and] to engage shared dilemmas collectively'.[21]

Marshall in fact derived one of his few examples of 'pure constructive cooperation' from the pottery industry, quoting at length from the literature of the *British Pottery Manufacturers Association*. Marshall concludes that in this case 'Cooperative action ... does not seem to involve centralized control' or any 'drift to use it as a means of maintaining prices at higher levels than would otherwise prevail'. There is, however, reason to suppose that Marshall overestimated both the cohesion and the impartiality of this body. Thus, at the *Truck Acts Committee* of 1907, the industry was represented not by the *British Pottery Manufacturers Association* but by the *Joint Committee of the Pottery*

[18] Ibid., p. 154. One way in which institutions could police competition was by 'overseeing complex wage stabilization systems designed to eliminate wage cutting and ruinous price wars'. Similarly, Scranton notes that in 'older industrial districts' institutions were 'fashioned to ... establish rules of business conduct, thus regulating competition through governance practice'. Scranton, 'Webs of Productive Association', p. 9. However, as will be shown, it is doubtful that the *Potteries Board of Arbitration* ever achieved this aim.

[19] Staber, 'Business Networks and Regional Development', p. 8.

[20] Scranton, *Figured Tapestry*, p. 165.

[21] Scranton, 'Webs of Productive Association', p. 9. Noting the difficulties associated with such projects, Scranton goes on to note how the concept of '"fragmented governance" brings into play issues critical to the functioning of industrial districts: the means through which relational rules and routines for business competition are established and maintained'. Ibid., p. 19.

Manufacturers of Great Britain. This frequent reforming and renaming of organizations was also typical of the industry in the nineteenth century. Moreover, it is clear from the evidence of William Burton, Chairman of the *Joint Committee* and an ex Wedgwood chemist, that his organization did not represent the whole industry, for 'outside our association there are a certain number of pottery manufacturers over whom we have no control and for whom I cannot speak, against whom all these things are alleged'.[22] Burton was attempting to draw a distinction between 'rough' and 'respectable' firms, much as some in the *Exchange* and *Chamber of Commerce* had done three decades earlier. He also acknowledges his association's inability to sanction non-members. What patterns of institutional-building may be traced then in the nineteenth century?

Associations in the Potteries, 1850–1882

This chapter examines three key institutions active in the years 1851–1882; these were; the *Potteries* and then *North Staffordshire Chamber of Commerce*, the *North Staffordshire Exchange*, and the *Potteries Board of Arbitration*. Though having distinct functions these institutions were closely related, but the *Chamber of Commerce* could trace its origins to the late eighteenth century.[23]

Informal association between the regions pottery manufacturers began in the 1760s in connection with the building of turnpikes, was put on a more formal though still temporary basis in the early 1780s, and culminated in late 1784 in the formation of a 'Committee of Commerce for the Manufactory of Pottery'.[24] However, as Bowden noted, 'The history of these early organisations of great industrialists is in many cases extremely obscure, and it is difficult ... to distinguish between informal or temporary groupings for concerted action in specific cases, and formally constituted bodies for exerting continuous pressure on economic policies'.[25] This judgement remained true of the Potteries in the first half of the nineteenth century. A *Chamber of Commerce* was again formed in 1831, to regulate prices, but was largely inactive until 1836 when it responded to the formation of the *National Union of Operative Potters*.[26] Though the manufacturers had 'failed to organise successfully to fix selling

22 *Truck Acts*, Vol. 3, p. 271.

23 As with so much in the earlier history of the North Staffordshire pottery industry, Joisah Wedgwood was at the centre of institutional activity in the late eighteenth century and was Chairman of the Potteries *Committee of Commerce*. This latter organization was predated perhaps only by those in Birmingham, Manchester and Edinburgh, all three of which it was in communication with. Thomas, *Rise of the Staffordshire Potteries*, p. 142–3.

24 Ibid., p. 142–3.

25 Ibid., p. 142.

26 This seems to have been a common motive for association. See, Scranton, 'Webs of Productive Association', p. 21.

prices' they were 'determined to fix piece prices'.[27] This pattern was replicated in manufacturers' organizations throughout the rest of the century, combination was always more effective in response to pressure from trades unions than from the market or other firms within the industry.

With the unions defeated in the Great Strike and Lockout of 1836 the *Chamber* again became dormant until it was 'resuscitated' in 1851 and 'for many years continued in full vigour'.[28] Much of the strength of the *Chamber* in the third quarter of the century has been attributed to the leadership of its first Chairman, M.D. Hollins. During this period the *Chamber*, meeting fortnightly, established a 'Commercial Tribunal' for the 'settlement of mercantile disputes', committees to regulate the size of wares and the terms and conditions of employment of apprentices, and lobbied the Treasury for reduction in the indenture stamp.[29] The *Chamber* also reacted decisively and successfully to a strike among cratemakers in 1853, closing fifty factories, but in 1860 failed to defend its Foreign Price List in the face of violations by smaller manufacturers. In 1866 a lockout, though prosecuted 'with the perfect unanimity of the employers', was unsuccessful in defending annual hiring.[30] The *Chamber* was then, in Scranton's typology, a classic 'area sectoral' organization rooted in a 'monoculture' industrial district, an environment that was to prove conducive to co-operation amongst, for example, the furniture firms of Grand Rapids.[31]

The *Chamber* was clearly becoming weaker during the late 1860s and collapsed at some point in the early 1870s, it being noted in 1874 that it had been active 'until lately'.[32] The *Chamber* was reconstituted in 1874. The immediate spur to attempts to strengthen the association was the growth of trade unionism in the industry, the body being 'instituted as a counterpoise to those combinations'.[33] However, these moves also had a wider purpose, which was to:

> form into one general association the different commercial institutions which have hitherto existed in North Staffordshire, ... and to ally them together under the name of a Chamber of Commerce for the whole district ... Our object is to amalgamate and embrace all classes of Manufacturers.[34]

The *Potteries Chamber of Commerce* thus became the *North Staffordshire Chamber of Commerce*, enlarged to include the iron, steel, and coal industries

---

27 Burchill and Ross, *History of the Potters' Union*, p. 65.
28 *Keates and Fords' Directory*, 1882.
29 Burchill and Ross, *A History of the Potters' Union*, p. 119.
30 *Staffordshire Advertiser,* 17 November 1866.
31 Scranton, 'Webs of Productive Association', p. 12–4 and p. 25.
32 *Staffordshire Advertiser*, Paper Cuttings, Vol. 4, HBRL, p. 142.
33 Ibid., p. 142.
34 Ibid., p. 142.

of the district alongside pottery. In other words, the 'area sectoral' institution was to be transformed into one that was 'area cross-sectoral'.[35] Nonetheless, membership, which had begun to fall before 1874, continued to decline and by March 1882 stood at just sixty-four. By January 1883 the trade press was reporting rumours of the 'move that is being made to resuscitate the "Chamber of Commerce" at Hanley'.[36]

A second key institutional development, again 'area sectoral' or 'cross-sectoral', was the *North Staffordshire Exchange*, which existed for a few months in 1859 and then again from 1875 to 1882. The first meeting of subscribers to the proposed Exchange was held on January 17th 1859. Present were twenty-six of the eighty or ninety firms and individuals who had already subscribed. Rules and Regulations were agreed upon, a fourteen strong Committee of Management established, and Mr. Wm. Bates unanimously elected first Chairman. The inaugural session of the *Exchange* was held on February 8th and it was felt that 'eighty names of subscribers seems ... a very hopeful sign'. The meeting of April 5th was 'one of the largest and most influential ... yet'. However, by May of the same year attendance had begun to fall, the *Exchange* had 'drooped', and on October 4th 'terminated its short existence'. The few members present resolved that:

> seeing with regret that the attendance on the 'Change had not improved since the meeting in July, [we] are of the opinion that it would be useless to continue the Exchange any longer, and ... resolve to close the same at once, but with a hope that ere long the advantages of an Exchange will be more generously appreciated and an Exchange for North Staffordshire permanently established.[37]

It was concluded that the 'time had not yet arrived when the district generally could appreciate' the advantages of an exchange, but there was no thorough analysis of why the *Exchange* had failed in 1859.[38] In time, the general growth

---

35 Scranton, 'Webs of Productive Association', p. 15.

36 *The Pottery Gazette*, January 1883, p. 60.

37 *The Sentinel*, 22 January 1859, p. 5; Ibid., 12 February 1859, p. 6; Ibid., 9 April 1859, p. 4 and Ibid., 21 May 1859, p. 4. In the same report it was noted that 'the attendance on the 'Change last Monday was but a slight improvement on the two or three previous meetings. Business has scarcely recovered from the derangement of the election ... Prior to the election the members, and especially many of the manufacturers, seemed to have become convinced of the importance of a more regular attendance, and to act upon such a conviction ... But then came the election and the usual ... excitement attending it; from that time to the present the Exchange has drooped, and many of the virtuous members before alluded to seem now to have forgotten their good resolutions'. Thus, actual attendance was of more importance than nominal membership. *The Sentinel*, 6 October, p. 8.

38 Thus, committee member F. Wragge admitted that 'he had nothing in the shape of an explanation to offer ... but has still not changed his opinion as to the importance and value of an Exchange to the district'. Ibid., p. 8. Similarly, Scranton claims that Philadelphia's Full-

of the industry was seen as perhaps a sufficient condition for success, it being hoped that a second *Exchange* would emerge from the reformed and enlarged *North Staffordshire Chamber of Commerce* of 1874.

The two institutions were intended to complement one another. It was hoped that 'if the Chamber of Commerce were successful an Exchange would grow out of it'.[39] It was decided that 'ample time should be given for consideration of the subject' and the *Exchange* was not re-opened until early 1875. The new *Exchange* was considerably larger than its predecessor and at its opening could boast 160 subscribers, 'representing all the great interests and principal establishments of the district ... including most of the leading ironmasters, colliery proprietors, china and earthenware manufacturers, professional men and tradesmen'.[40] The greater size of the second Exchange was reflected in its greater longevity and by January 1877 it was felt that the organization could 'now be looked upon as one of the permanent institutions' of the Potteries. It was recognized nonetheless that without such a central, inclusive institution the district was 'materially weakened', thus there was issued an appeal:

> to the manufacturers, the ironmasters, the coal owners and managers, the agents and all who have the welfare of North Staffordshire at heart, to attend the Exchange every Wednesday, to do as much business as they can there, and to encourage their friends to imitate their example, for by doing so they guarantee its success.[41]

However, by early 1878 membership, though still standing at 131, had begun to fall, and in January 1881 the *Exchange* was suspended for a period of two years following a collapse in attendance. The suspension was subsequently confirmed as permanent.

The *Potteries Board of Arbitration*, the third key institutional form developed in the Potteries faced quite different problems. The *Board* was founded in 1868 and owed much to the advocacy of union leader William Owen, who drew inspiration from a similar body founded in the Nottingham hosiery trade by A.J. Mundella in 1860. Aware perhaps that in Nottingham leading manufacturers had 'benefitted from improved industrial relations and uniformity of rates', arbitration was taken up with enthusiasm by leading firms in the Potteries, the seventy to eighty manufacturers who joined, claimed by

---

Fashioned Hosiery Manufacturers' Association 'developed no overarching analysis that might have provided a foundation for a wider ... appreciation of collective needs'. Scranton, 'Webs of Productive Association', p. 22.

39 *Staffordshire Advertiser*, Paper Cuttings, Vol. 4, HBRL, p. 142. Unity was again a specific aim; an 'enlarged and comprehensive' body was viewed as 'the means for pulling the district more together'. Ibid., p. 142.

40 Ibid., p. 142. Though in theory 'cross-sectoral', all of these activities were essentially focused on pottery manufacture.

41 *Staffordshire Advertiser*, 27 January 1877.

trade unionist Arthur Hollins to employ eighty per cent of the district's workforce, were essentially the same grouping who formed the core of the *Chamber of Commerce* and the *Exchange*. M.D. Hollins, Chairman of the *Chamber of Commerce* for over twenty years from 1851, was the Board's first President.[42]

The involvement of an important union figure in the formation of the Board would seem to indicate the establishment of friendly and co-operative relations between capital and labour in the Potteries, a factor recognized in recent research as important to realizing flexibility in disintegrated business networks.[43] Indeed, Church claims that the board in Nottingham was instrumental in allowing large manufacturers to 'build up stock without fear of being undercut by unfair employers'. According to Mundella the whole tenor of the hosiery trade was altered. The question was no longer 'who shall screw down wages the most [but] who shall buy the best material and produce the best article'.[44] Thus, the large manufacturers active in the *Potteries Board* largely viewed it, as they did also the *Chamber of Commerce* and the *Exchange*, as a means for creating greater stability in various aspects of the trade, not only in terms of wage levels but in the whole process of negotiation and in the relationship between wages, prices and margins.

However, the *Potteries Board*, which was intended to function when disputes arose over the interpretation of existing annual agreements, always made at Martinmas, largely failed to develop more conciliatory arrangements between employers and workers. Instead, the unions quickly 'fell into the trap of using arbitration as a substitute for annual negotiations', a situation which proved advantageous to the manufacturers.[45] In Nottingham too the unions eventually became 'completely reliant on the success and continuation of the Board, having rejected the policy of negotiation from strength'.[46]

Initially, the manufacturers refrained from using the *Board* to push through wage reductions, fearing that if they did they would be unable to resist

---

[42] R. Church, 'Technological Change and the Hosiery Board of Conciliation and Arbitration, 1860–1884', *Yorkshire Bulletin*, Vol. 15 (1963), p.57; Burchill and Ross, *History of the Potters' Union*, p. 125.

[43] M. Gertler and T. Rutherford, 'Regional-Industrial Networks and the Role of Labour', in Staber *et al.*, *Regional Business Networks.*

[44] Church, 'Technological Change', p. 57. This is an excellent restatement of the belief, prevalent in the industrial district literature, that associations may aid in setting the terms of competition in an industry

[45] Burchill and Ross, *History of the Potters' Union*, p. 123. See also J.H. Porter, 'Wage Bargaining under Conciliation Agreements, 1860–1914', *Economic History Review*, Vol. 23, No. 3 (1970), pp. 460–475. Porter argues that 'the formation of Boards appears to have taken place when unions had sufficient strength to convince employers that conciliation and arbitration were necessary, but insufficient power to make an openly militant policy more attractive for themselves. This point was usually reached on the upswing of the trade cycle when membership was increasing'. Ibid., p.461.

[46] Church, 'Technological Change', p. 57; Porter, 'Wage Bargaining', p. 460.

demands for price reductions from buyers. However, manufacturers began to face an increasingly hostile environment from the mid-1870s, and in both 1876 and 1879 a reduction of ten per cent was demanded and, under the Chairmanship of Lord Hatherton, awarded in 1879. As in many arbitration processes from this period Hatherton's decision was guided largely by falling selling prices and 'a vague opinion on the "general state of the trade"'.[47] Separate branch submissions for the restoration of 'Hatherton's pennies' were made by the unions in 1880 but were refused by the umpire, Thomas Brassey M.P. Defeat led the unions to discuss both federation and withdrawal from a *Board* that had disappointed their expectations. This latter move played into the manufacturers' hands, who, in 1881, refused to reconvene a body that they now claimed had been destroyed by the men. During the ensuing strike the manufacturers held firm, in part through he co-operation of those still working, who refused to engage new hands without a written note of dismissal from their previous employer, forcing operatives back to work after six weeks.

Thus, in November 1882, at the first annual hiring after the strike, the manufacturers were able simply to refuse to negotiate, confirming the pattern of employer strength in the arbitration process. However, attention to the national picture demonstrates that unions tended to be disadvantaged in all industries where arbitration was tried. The example of the *Potteries Board* clearly fits in with Porter's finding that:

> the majority of wage arbitrations took place during the Great Depression ... when only 9 out of the 61 wage awards gave advances whilst 35 gave reductions ... the greatest concentration took place between 1974 and 1879, when the fall in average selling prices was particularly rapid [and] only two advances were made in comparison with 28 reductions.[48]

As elsewhere umpires in the Potteries tended to be 'lawyers, politicians, or employers ... it is unlikely that they would have been invited to arbitrate if they had not shared the conventional view of political economy'.[49] The result was that when, for example, unionist George Bloor asked to see manufacturers' books during the arbitration of 1880, arguing that the 'manufacturers knew what the men were earning but the men knew nothing of the income of their masters', his appeal was rejected as 'opposed to every principle of political

---

47 Porter, Wage Bargaining', p. 464. In 1879, the employers' principal arguments for a reduction were; the depressed state of the trade, increased foreign competition and reduced prices. Lord Hatherton was clearly impressed with these claims, for in explaining the award he made he commented that 'the trade is depressed to such an extent as to require some reduction in the cost of production ... nor was it possible to increase the selling price while the trade was in its current state. I deeply regret therefore that my award must be against the workmen'. Burchill and Ross, *History of the Potters' Union*, p. 126–32.

48 Porter, 'Wage Bargaining', p. 463–5.

49 Ibid., p. 462.

economy'.[50] Thus, the success of pottery manufacturers in using arbitration to force through wage reductions says little about their unity. Willingness to use the mechanism in this way can instead be seen as tacit acknowledgment of the intensely competitive nature of the industry. Moreover, it was a tactic likely only to exacerbate competition.

The *Board* was not officially terminated, with the agreement of both sides, until 1892, but was only very intermittently active for the last ten years of its existence. The example of the *Board of Arbitration* also serves here as a contrast to the other institutions, for it was the only one in which unrepresentativeness did not prove a bar to achieving the manufacturer's aims. The inability of the *Board,* as limited in its membership as the *Exchange* or *Chamber*, to apply sanctions to or otherwise coerce non-members did not matter, because the firms which did not participate were very unlikely to pay wages higher than those set at arbitration.[51]

Crucially, these institutional developments took place against a background of significant shifts in the structure of the industry and of equally significant changes in the competitive environment. It was shown in the previous chapter, these forces had led in turn to change in the strategies pursued by many firms. Changes to structure, environment, and strategy together form the context in which these attempts to build organizations, identify common interests, and act in unison occurred. As Scranton expresses it, 'configurations of opportunity and hazard press individual firms towards webs of association'.[52] The growth in the size of the industry, through both the growth of surviving firms and the appearance of many new entrants, appeared to have enlarged the potential constituency of these institutions. Indeed, Sabel and Zeitlin explicitly associate 'municipal' institutional forms with 'dispersed' production.

However, despite the considerable growth shown by a handful of well established and already large firms, such was the volume of small new entrants that, as was shown in Chapter 2, both average firm size and levels of concentration declined throughout this period. These trends had become particularly marked by the early 1880s, when institutional collapse occurred. Many small new firms were owned and run by operatives turned businessmen, the industry's structure was associated with a high proportion of first-generation entrepreneurs, using ageing plant and financially insecure. These factors were to prove critical to the fortunes of key institutions.

Moreover, as the structure of the industry was becoming increasingly competitive, so the external environment was also becoming more hostile. Foreign competitors emerged for the first time, tariff barriers were raised in

---

[50] *The Pottery Gazette*, March 1881, p. 233.

[51] Interestingly, as we have seen in earlier chapters, two very large firms, Mintons and Copelands, also abstained from the crucial arbitration of 1879, believing that market segmentation protected them from the forces to which other firms were exposed.

[52] Scranton, 'Webs of Productive Association', p. 12.

important markets, and prices experienced sustained downward pressure. The industry appeared to many to be facing 'crisis' in the 1880s and 1890s. Within these long-run changes it is possible also to discern relationships between short-term cycles and the institutions in question, in terms of both their formation and failure. Thus, for example, at the time of the first *Exchange* in 1859 the *Sentinel*, a local paper, noted that the trade was characterized by a 'torpid state of affairs' and a 'timid convalescence which, in the midst of abundance, still recalls the commercial panic'.[53] In 1874, the year in which the *Potteries Chamber of Commerce* sought to bolster its membership by opening its doors to the non-potting trades, there was by a sharp fall in the value of British ceramic exports, whilst the years 1879–82, leading up to and culminating in the collapse of both the *Exchange* and *Chamber,* were also marked by a clear downward trend in ceramic prices.

However, the relationship between trade depression and institutional developments was complex. For some firms in the Potteries depression acted as a spur to association as a defensive measure, but, as will be seen, deep seated problems of co-ordination within the industry and low levels of trust drove others to reject the same path. Similar trends can be seen in other industries and regions. Scranton found that in Philadelphia 'each crisis led some manufacturers to confront collectively the contingency confronting their operations', but, 'whether due to "possessive individualism" or sheer cussedness', these attempts failed to gather a 'sufficient ... critical mass'.[54] Farnie too ties the fortunes *Manchester Royal Exchange*, as expressed in fluctuating levels of membership, to trade cycles.[55] However, Farnie was observing these effects in a much larger, well-established body, not one trying to secure its position. We may thus expect the impact of trade cycles to have been more severe in the case of the *North Staffordshire Exchange*. However, the contemporary press in Manchester believed that 'It may even be said that the worse the business is, or, in other words, the more difficult it is to obtain business, the more necessary it is to become a member of the Exchange', highlighting again the tension between defensive, collective reactions to depression on the one hand and calculative, individualistic reactions on the other.[56]

Thus, institutions did not fail simply because of the impact of either short or long-term trade cycles, though recent studies by Sydow and Gertler and Rutherford have questioned the '"flexibility of flexible specialisation",

---

53 *The Sentinel*, 1 January 1859, p. 8.

54 Scranton, *Figured Tapestry*, p. 130.

55 However, Farnie found that whilst membership 'increased during times of boom', only a 'severe and prolonged crisis' would result in falling membership'. D.A. Farnie, 'An Index of Commnercial Activity: The Membership of the Manchester Royal Exchange, 1809–1948', *Business History*, Vol. 21, No. 1 (1979), p. 102.

56 Farnie, 'An Index of Commercial Activity', p. 104.

especially in recessionary times' and found 'mutual distrust among hard-pressed enterprises'.[57] Instead, it is necessary to consider together these cycles and the shifts taking place in the structure of the industry. As was shown in the preceding chapter change in the competitive environment was accompanied by changes in the strategies used by firms in the Potteries. In particular, firms turned increasingly to reactive, contingent strategies; in other words they placed greater demands on the ability of the district to effect 'automatic' co-ordination. At the same time these strategies were accompanied by a decrease in the stability of relationships between firms trading with one another within the district. Congruent with this was the rising tide of complaint about the behaviour of some firms, particularly small firms, seen in the trade press. Some also associated 'unfair' or 'illegitimate' business practices with the china manufacturers of the southern townships, Longton and Fenton, further exacerbating tension by giving it an explicitly civic and sectoral dimension.

The pottery industry was then increasingly populated by ever more firms, often using outdated and limited resources, financially weak, exploited by buyers and agents, and less attuned to the 'moral economy' of industry and district posited by Sabel and Zeitlin. Simultaneously, Hanley appeared to be becoming ever more powerful in both industrial and civic terms. The structural, cultural, sectoral, and civic balances of the district were all developing in ways likely to inhibit association. These changes will now be explored in more detail and related to the structure, functions, aims, and failure of the institutions in question.

The socio-economic context of associational failure

The key institutions studied may be said to have had two broad aims; to regulate the industry and to unify it. In terms of regulation they sought to stabilize the prices and supply of inputs, particularly raw materials, and to stabilize selling prices and wages. Unity was to both grow out of and reinforce this increased stability. It was also hoped to project the district as a whole in both national and international terms. *The Sentinel* was careful to stress that this greater unity and stability would not result in a loss of competitiveness. Indeed, individual advantage was seen as a product of association. The *Exchange* would promote 'the truth that the more enterprising and united a district is the more prosperous its individual members must be'. It was in effect acknowledged that the 'district model favors cooperation only insofar as collaboration has competitive consequences'.[58] This establishes the scope of the

---

[57] P. Scranton, 'Review of Staber et al. *Regional Business Networks*', *Business History,* Vol. 39, No. 3 (1997), p. 181.

[58] *The Sentinel*, 12 February 1859, p. 6; Staber, 'Embeddedness', p. 151.

governance intentions of associational activists. What mechanisms would aid or hinder their realization?

Scranton claims that the 'decentralized ... governance' structures of industrial districts lead of 'necessity ... to a focus on trust'. In turn, in the industrial districts of the past, 'frequent face-to-face dealings, shared ethnic/religous backgrounds, and common business political values all contributed to the construction of reciprocity and high-trust relations'.[59] An examination of the key institutions operating in the Potteries highlights the role-played by a small group of leading businessmen. Small-scale business may have dominated the district numerically, but large local pottery manufacturers, despite arguing to the contrary, were highly influential in promoting various sections of the industry through these trade institutions.

A good example of such men was Col. Michael Daintry Hollins, Chairman of the *Potteries Chamber of Commerce* from its revival in 1851, first President of the *Potteries Board of Arbitration* from 1868, and a member of the Committee of Management of the *Exchange* of 1859. An examination of the career and profile of Hollins and others active in promoting greater organization will illustrate the range of structural, cultural, sectoral and civic divides that inhibited these institutions from becoming established in the district. Effective 'social embeddedness' cannot be read off in a simple way from the mere fact of intense spatial clustering. A survey of pronouncements from and about the Exchange and other institutions will then demonstrate the extent to which sectional interests were reflected in the aims and functions of these bodies.

Born in Manchester, in 1815, and trained as a doctor, Hollins had many connections with the Potteries and the pottery industry. Related by marriage to the Minton family he joined this important and influential firm in 1839, as head of the commercial department. He was made a partner in 1845, the firm trading at that time under the name of Minton, Hollins and Co., and took control of the tile department. When Herbert Minton died in 1859 he assumed joint partnership of the firm with Colin Minton-Campbell. In 1868 the partnership was dissolved, the tile department, under Hollins' control, became an entirely independent company and moved to a new factory at Cliffe Vale, Stoke-upon-Trent. This firm, with an RV of £1432 in 1879, fell into the giant-size category. Hollins' non-commercial interests and activities spanned a panoply of civic positions and voluntary organizations. He was a Justice of the Peace, Improvement Commissioner, and Chief Bailiff for Stoke-upon-Trent, and represented the town on Staffordshire County Council from 1888–90. He was a Colonel in the Local Volunteers, contributed financially to many local churches, and always lived close to the Potteries, dying in 1898 at Whitmore

---

59 Scranton, 'Webs of Productive Association', p. 19–20.

Hall, situated in a village just a few miles to the west of Newcastle-under-Lyme.[60]

Other businessmen active in promoting association displayed similar profiles. Colin Minton-Campbell, Hollins' partner at Mintons between 1859–68, was a leading proponent of the second *Exchange* of the 1870s and early 1880s. Campbell too came from outside the Potteries, joining the firm of his uncle Herbert in 1842. By the 1870s he controlled both Mintons and the Campbell Tile Co. and had rentier interests in local rail and water supply companies. His activities outside business were, if anything more numerous than those of Hollins. Elected M.P for Stoke-upon-Trent in 1874 he was also Mayor of that town from 1880–3, Deputy Lieutenant of the County in 1868 and High Sheriff in 1869. He contributed generously to local churches, to other charities and public works, gave land for a library, served as an officer in three local military bodies and also continued to live in North Staffordshire until his death. Robert Heath, coal and iron master, founding subscriber to the first *Exchange* and first President of the second *Exchange,* was likewise an M.P. for Stoke-upon-Trent, and Deputy Lieutenant and then High Sheriff of Staffordshire.[61]

Though Berghoff has stressed the specificity of nineteenth century British business elites, arguing that 'In reality, provincial business communities offer a colourful picture of highly diverse local elites' existing under 'very different social and economic conditions', the example of Hollins, Campbell, Heath and others supports his further conclusion that 'quite universal features' can be discerned. These included:

> a high willingness to support political parties, to stand for local election contests, to accept seats on town councils, to join the magistracy and the staggeringly time and money-consuming involvement in charitable movements of all sorts ... Rich businessmen were often local worthies, just as local worthies often were rather wealthy.[62]

However, more important that their fit with the national picture is the degree of alignment between the profiles of the business elite in the Potteries and local norms. Here, a number of wide gulfs can be found, including in religious and political allegiances. A series of comparisons drawn from the work of Berghoff and Möller will emphasize the breadth of these divisions in the Potteries.[63]

---

[60] Stuart, *People of the Potteries*, p. 123–4.

[61] Ibid., p. 55–6, p. 119.

[62] H. Berghoff, 'Regional Variations in Provincial Business Biography: The Case of Birmingham, Bristol and Manchester, 1870–1914', *Business History*, Vol. 39, No. 4 (1995), p. 64, p. 68.

[63] H. Berghoff and R. Möller, 'Tired Pioneers and Dynamic Newcomers? A Comparative Essay on English and German Entrepreneurial History, 1870–1914', *Economic History Review*, Vol. 47, No. 2 (1994), pp. 262–87.

Religion has long been posited as an important element in business networks. Caunce has recently suggested that the prevalence of Non-conformism contributed to the cohesion and dynamism of the woollen industry in the West Ridings, and Staber has argued that religious beliefs are 'possible meaning systems supporting business cooperation', sustaining 'community values which span social classes and thus play an integrative role in dynamic districts'.[64] In both Manchester and Birmingham in the late nineteenth century, the 'Non-conformist community ... represented the highest echelons of [the] political and social elite', but in the Potteries Hollins, Campbell, and Heath were all members of the Church of England.[65] Their Anglicanism was shared by others playing key roles in the *Chamber of Commerce* and *Exchange*. These included; pottery manufacturers Thomas Peake and William Webberley of the Committee of Management of the *Exchange* of 1859, W. Adams and E.C. Challinor of the Committee of the reformed *Chamber of Commerce* of 1874, and H.T. Davenport, solicitors F. Bishop and W. Keary, and mining engineer C.J. Homer of the Committee of the *Exchange* in 1875.

However, where Non-conformism predominated not only in the highest echelons of local elites in Manchester and Birmingham but also across the samples analyzed by Berghoff (fifty-five per cent in Birmingham and fifty-two per cent in Manchester) Anglicanism was even weaker in the Potteries.[66] In a sample of 116 businessmen active in the pottery industry in the second half of the nineteenth century, seventy-two per cent of those whose religious affiliations could be traced were Non-conformists.[67] Moreover, given the strength of Non-conformism in the working population of the district, and the degree of mobility between the workbench and the 'managers sanctum', it is probable that Non-conformism was even more typical of the owners of small-firms, certainly under-represented in the sample, than this suggests.[68] It was the unwillingness of just such small firms and entrepreneurs to enter into association which, it is argued, condemned the institutional developments examined here to failure

Hollins, Campbell, Heath, and the other Anglicans were also typically Conservative in politics. This again conflicted markedly with the composition of the wider business community of the Potteries, where, amongst the same sample of 116, just twenty-five per cent of those whose political affiliations could be determined were Conservatives. Political and religious affiliations

[64] S. Caunce, 'Complexity, Community Structure and Competitive Advantage within the Yorkshire Woolen Industry, c. 1700–1850'. *Business History*, Vol. 39, No. 4 (1997), pp. 27–43; Staber, 'Embeddedness', p. 165.

[65] Berghoff, 'Regional Variations', p. 78; Stuart, *People of the Potteries*, p. 123–4, p. 55–6 and p. 119

[66] Berghoff, 'Regional Variations', p. 78.

[67] Drawn from Stuart, *People of the Potteries*.

[68] *The Pottery Gazette*, December 1880, p. 1058.

were central in the nineteenth century to building the informal local networks around which formal bodies were likely to be constructed.[69] Even where no controversy was involved, political differences were important at a personal level, if only because they reduced opportunities for social interaction. Thus, 'because business networking occurs not among organizations but ("boundary spanning") individuals who link organizations, it is important to pay attention to the micro-level social and political aspects of networks'.[70]

Many of the leading proponents of closer association were differentiated from the wider business community of the district in two further important ways; that is by the age of their firms and by their place of birth. Comparison with the work of Berghoff would again seem to suggest that these were particularly powerful issues in the Potteries. Not only Hollins, Campbell, Davenport and Adams but also other important associational activists, such as William Woodall, Godfrey Wedgwood, James Maddock, and the Ridgways, represented multi-generational firms, many of them founded in the late eighteenth or early nineteenth centuries. Though Berghoff and Möller claim to have found very few examples of 'Smilesian operative-to-employer' careers, the proportion of first generation entrepreneurs in their sample, fifty per cent, is not insignificant. However, in the sample of 116 Potteries businessmen only thirty-five per cent came from families with existing interests in the pottery industry. The small-scale structure of the industry was clearly reflected in a higher proportion of first generation entrepreneurs.[71]

Furthermore, the central figures of Hollins and Campbell, though they had local connections, were both born outside the district. Whereas Berghoff and Möller found that sixty-one per cent of 1328 businessmen active in Birmingham, Manchester and Bristol between 1870 and 1914 were born outside those towns, eighty per cent of the sample of Potteries businessmen were born in the district and its immediate environs. The centrality of the local population to the business community of the district was repeated in all other sections of the community, particularly amongst working potters, as is demonstrated in the work of Dupree, Hall, and Whipp.[72] Local roots played a

---

[69] Though Berghoff argues that 'generally, a move took place towards a fusion of local elites on the basis of wealth and social standing, regardless or religious traditions and convictions', a process that, it will shown, occurred in the Potteries in this period. Berghoff, 'Regional Variations', p. 79.

[70] Staber, 'Networks and Regional Development', p. 10.

[71] Berghoff and Möller, 'Tired Pioneers', p. 266–7.

[72] Dupree, *Family Structure*; Whipp, *Patterns of Labour*; R. Hall, 'Women in the Labour Force: A Case Study of the Potteries in the Nineteenth Century', Occasional Paper No. 27 (1986), Department of Geography and Earth Science, Queen Mary College, University of London. Scranton also emphasizes the importance of entrepreneurial origins, noting, for example, that two large Philadelphia manufacturers, Search and Dolan, 'came to textile manufacturing not from the shop floor ... Neither had the intense and perhaps confining identification with factory life that possessed so many of their industrial colleagues'. A

vital role in the formation of the cultures of both the business and working communities of the district, and were a further attribute not shared by some of the leading promoters of association.

Many of those active in institutional developments in the Potteries in second half of the nineteenth century were then sharply differentiated in socio-economic and cultural terms from the mass of the business community. Moreover, a number of references allow us to infer that these issues did result directly in individuals not joining the *Exchange* and other institutions. For example, in April 1859 *The Sentinel* reported that 'we have heard individuals say they would have nothing to do with the Exchange because certain persons were its main projectors'. The paper counselled that 'to predict failure in such a case as this, and by absence, shaking the head, shrugging the shoulders, and whispering innuendoes against it – or by allowing mere personal antipathies to interfere would be unworthy of the enterprising men of this district'.[73] Instead, it was argued, the *Exchange* would be 'just what our enterprising men – not merely what its projectors, but they and their successors – shall choose to make of it'.[74] At the reconstitution of the *Chamber* and *Exchange* in 1874 M.F. Blakiston acknowledged that, 'Knowing North Staffordshire so well, I know the importance of having as chairman one whose position was completely impartial. We all have our little jealousies, and must get over them as well as we can'.[75]

The differentiation of the promoters of association from many in the industry was reflected in the institutions they attempted to build, which were unrepresentative in sectoral and civic terms. This is demonstrated by an analysis of the composition of the *Chamber of Commerce* in 1866. In that year the *Potteries Chamber of Commerce* had seventy-seven subscribing members. *Keates and Ford's Directory* of the same year records a total of 215 pottery firms, a figure that probably did not include all the smallest firms. Thus, the *Chamber* represented, at most, a little over one third of all manufacturers.[76] However, if the membership figures are disaggregated by location then under-representation can be seen to have been particularly chronic in certain parts of the district. These figures are presented in Table 9.1. As the data demonstrates, firms from the three northern townships of Tunstall, Burslem, and Hanley accounted for seventy-five per cent of the *Chamber's* membership. Similarly, in 1882, twenty-five members, or seventy-four per cent, of the thirty-four strong Council of the *Chamber of Commerce* were drawn from Hanley and

---

generalization perhaps, but also true of Hollins and Campbell. Scranton, *Figured Tapestry*, p. 168.

73 *The Sentinel*, 9 April 1859, p. 4.

74 Ibid., p. 4.

75 *Staffordshire Advertiser*, Vol. 4, HBRL, p. 142.

76 *Keates and Ford's Directory of the Staffordshire Potteries and Newcastle*, (Keates and Ford, Hanley, 1865–6).

Burslem alone. Fenton contributed just one council member and Longton none. At that time firms from Longton and Fenton represented thirty-nine per cent of the industry and those from Hanley and Burslem forty-eight per cent. It is hardly surprising that 'Longton manufacturers ... held aloof from this institution under the impression that it was a clique of "large" makers on the "other side" simply to push their particular brands'. Nor, as a corollary, that during the strike of 1881 it was reported that 'Longton stands aloof during the struggle'.[77] In turn, nearly sixty per cent of the Committee of Management of the *Exchange* in 1875 was composed of individuals and firms from Stoke-upon-Trent, Hanley, and Burslem. Longton and Fenton together contributed, at most, twenty-six per cent of the membership of the Committee.[78]

Table 9.1
Membership of the Potteries Chamber of Commerce by location, 1866

Location	No. of firms	% total pop	No. in Chamber	% of no. in Town	% of Chamber
Longton	68	32	10	15	14
Fenton	14	7	4	29	5
S-o-T	9	4	5	56	6
Hanley	52	24	29	56	38
Burslem	49	23	16	32	21
Tunstall	23	11	13	57	17
Total	215	100	77	–	100

Source: Keates and Ford's Directory, 1865–6.

However, the cultural, civic, and sectoral divisions outlined above did not apply to all those active in these institutional developments. Important positions in all the institutions in question were filled by members of prominent non-conformist manufacturing families. These included John Maddock, Edwin Powell, and John Ridgway. These non-conformists were also typically Liberal in politics. In turn, some participants were china manufacturers from Longton. However, where men such as Ridgway were differentiated from Hollins, Campbell, and others by their religious and political affiliations they were

[77] *Keates and Ford's Directory*, 1882; *The Pottery Gazette*, January 1883, p. 60; *The Pottery Gazette*, December 1880, p. 1058.

[78] *Staffordshire Advertiser*, Paper Cuttings, Vol. 4, HBRL, p. 142. Given the spatial distribution of firms in the district, civic under-representation also translated into sectoral under-representation, in particular of china manufacturers.

united by the size of their firms, all falling into the large or giant size-categories. This may suggest that size of firm was the prime determinant of businessmen's attitudes to formal association. Given their characterization of the *Chamber* as a self-interested clique of large makers this was clearly the impression held by smaller firms in Longton, an impression confirmed by the tenor of statements made by both those active in the *Exchange* and other institutions, and by the local press.

As already noted, these statements suggest that the *Exchange*, *Chamber of Commerce*, and *Board of Arbitration* were intended to fulfil three broad functions; to unify, regulate, and promote the industry as a whole. Thus, the *Sentinel* hoped that Hanley would soon boast 'capacious and majestic' Exchange Buildings, 'adapted to the development of our incalculable mineral wealth, to increase the fame and therefore extend the sale of our unrivalled pottery'.[79] The Exchange Buildings, never built, would not only be 'consecrated to the spirit of enterprise' but would also:

> prove a true mart of commerce ... a temple of concord, equally sacred to the spirit of brotherhood, which shall animate those who have a common origin, common wants and an indissoluble mutual destiny; and a centre of intelligence from which shall go forth influences which shall quicken and reward legitimate emulation, but which shall cause hurtful ignorance to disappear, and before which willful prejudice and unholy jealousy shall expire.[80]

This appeal to common interests, expressed most powerfully as an 'indissoluble mutual destiny', was reinforced when, in August 1859, it was urged that 'each individual must feel "I am the Exchange, unless I attend there will be no Exchange"'.[81] As Staber notes 'pressures to conform to institutional expectations may be felt as persuasion, as when association leaders appeal to their members' sense of solidarity'. However, he also argues that in the absence of coercive mechanisms, 'regulative institutions' are generally only 'effective if they are *endorsed* by subordinates because they accept rules as fair and reasonable'.[82] Large manufacturers in the Potteries lacked both coercive power over and the endorsement of much of the industry.

The *Sentinel* was particularly fervent in its support for the first *Exchange*, proclaiming also that 'The prosperity of this Exchange will qualify individual assumptions, defeat and ring the knell of local ... monopolies, and supersede local sectional ascendancies by the elevation of the whole'.[83] The motivations

---

79 *The Sentinel*, February 1859, p. 6.
80 Ibid., p. 6.
81 *The Sentinel*, 6 August 1859, p. 4.
82 Staber, 'Embeddedness', p. 159–60.
83 *The Sentinel*, 12 February 1859, p. 6.

of the proponents of association can be traced then, at least in part, to an identification of the divided and highly competitive structure of the industry and district with negative effects on individual firms.

These same themes characterized the relaunch of the *Chamber of Commerce* and *Exchange* in 1874–5. The bodies were intended to operate in tandem, 'An Exchange is wanted to bring together the ... various trades and interests of the district, while the Chamber of Commerce would bring the district into more intimate communication with the outside world'. Above all it was hoped that, in contrast to the experience of twenty years previously, 'it will prove that the different classes of manufacturers are not competing interests but that ... the interests of each [are] connected with the interests of every other'.[84] Burslem earthenware manufacturer Anthony Shaw not only hoped that through 'the exchange of commodities or money transactions ... much might be done to facilitate their business transactions', but also that there 'would be ... an exchange of ideas, and gentlemen would be able to meet and compare notes as to what was for the interest of the community at large'. M.F. Blakiston, Clerk of the Peace, enlarged on this theme, looking 'forward to the movement as a very important one', hoping that 'if there had been, as some said, local and petty jealousy in the past, it would be speedily supplanted by generous rivalry'.[85]

Similarly, the report of the Council of the *Chamber of Commerce* claimed in March 1882 that the Chamber:

> is not a local institution, representing any one town; it is not a class institution, representing any one set of interests; it is not a potters' institution, though, unfortunately, the work has been chiefly left to potters to do. Lastly it is not a political institution, but the representative of all the commercial and manufacturing and mining interests of this important centre of industry.[86]

However, as has been shown, the *Chamber* and *Exchange* clearly had come to represent the interests not of all but of a particular 'class' of manufacturers, located in particular towns within the district. The bias of these institutions was occasionally made explicit. Thus, when the *Sentinel* looked to the first *Exchange* to 'supersede local sectional ascendancies' it asserted that this end would be achieved only 'if ... the majority of the leading manufacturers ... will come into the project. They will, and then the smaller ones must. It is merely a question of time'. In August 1859 it was noted that still missing from the *Exchange* were 'many of what Mr. Grose ... facetiously called "the dogs", but we suppose that we need not trouble about them, for if only the "hares" are

[84] *Staffordshire Advertiser*, Paper Cuttings, Vol. 4, HBRL, p. 142.
[85] Ibid., p. 142.
[86] *Keates and Ford's Directory*, 1882.

there the dogs will most certainly follow'.[87] The 'dogs' referred to small firms and the 'hares' to larger and more 'respectable' business houses, but the expression of such sentiments can only have served to further alienate the former from the latter.

It was then primarily the atomistic structure of the industry, and in particular tension between large and small firms, which inhibited the *Chamber* and *Exchange* from realizing their unifying and regulatory aims. Tension between large and small manufacturers, which increased throughout the last three decades of the century as trade depression continued, centred on the perceived negative impact on the industry as a whole of the presence of many small firms. Large firms argued that small firms were the principal cause of low prices, threatened the reputation of the district as a whole, and tended to worsen labour relations for all. In essence, large firms were advancing the belief that 'Competition ... is the soul of trade. However, there are limits to all things, and even competition in trade has reached a point at which it will be wise to halt'. They pointed to a spirit of 'unhealthy competition ... so ingrained ... that manufacturers have, in cases which are known, accepted orders at an absolute loss'.[88] The *Exchange* and *Chamber of Commerce* were defeated by the very thing that they were intended to ameliorate; the atomistic, competitive structure of the industry. They could generate no sense of common interests. As a result, the industry persisted with 'individualistic, wasteful and extravagant methods of production, while by a better system twenty five per cent might be saved and the diminishing and lost markets be reconquered'.[89]

Similar structural weaknesses have been identified by Scranton in Philadelphia, where the failure to 'convince the tenloom men for whom every yard carried its tiny contribution to an accumulation of capital that would build *their* firms as Dornan, Bromley, and the others had built theirs' regularly defeated collaborative schemes. The 'small operators sought individual gain, not a restrictive collaboration with bigger firms that surely would the latter but cut deeply into his narrower base'.[90] As will be shown, it was again the search for 'individual gain' that defeated the price agreements attempted in the Potteries in the two decades after the institutional failures of 1881–2. However, as Scranton suggests, institutional failure turned on practical as well as structural and cultural factors. The function of the institutions, especially the

---

[87] *The Sentinel*, 12 February 1859, p. 6.

[88] *The Pottery Gazette*, December 1891, p. 1126; *The Pottery Gazette*, October 1899. Contemporaries recognized that the small-scale structure of the industry was becoming more pronounced. Hence, it was noted that, 'many small firms have started into existence ... The proprietors in these cases have no more hands than they can look after themselves, and being content with little more than workmen's wages, they have undersold the older and larger firms'. *The Pottery Gazette*, March 1888, p. 227.

[89] *The Pottery Gazette*, February 1896, p. 134.

[90] Scranton, *Figured Tapestry*, p. 73.

Exchange, conflicted with the strategies deployed by many firms, whilst also adding further pressure to their scant resources.

This conflict arose because the *Exchange* was intended to regularize, in a quite simple way, the flows of commodities and transactions taking place in the district. Mr. Bates, Chairman of the first *Exchange*, hoped that 'members would, as the firm he represented intended, set apart Monday for purchasing all raw materials and to fix to meet the sellers "on 'Change"'. This they would do because 'it is ten to one but sellers of potters materials – local and distant – will make first to the Exchange; to the spot on which they shall meet with the greatest number of buyers within the shortest space of time, and with the least trouble'.[91] The *Sentinel* added that members 'will purchase "on 'Change" whatever can be purchased by sample, or description – whether clays, colours, chemicals, grain, straw or other articles, and they will pay there too'.[92] However, as was demonstrated in the last chapter, few firms in the Potteries ordered or paid for raw materials in such a rigid weekly pattern. To do so would very often have conflicted with the pattern of orders that they received, would have entailed either holding excessive stocks of materials or, on occasion, being unable to meet sudden demands, and would have required regular flows of ready cash. These problems have also been shown to have become more acute during the period in question as the industry's demand structure became more unpredictable and buyers asked for ever longer terms of credit. The *Exchange* conflicted with the 'automatic' co-ordination of the disintegrated system of the Potteries industrial district.

Moreover, the 'hand-to-mouth' strategies developed to meet these demands were particularly prevalent amongst small firms, increasing in number throughout this period. Given these strategies, small firms viewed 'automatic' co-ordination as means to achieving flexibility, not in order to innovate but simply to survive. The decrease in average firm size and industrial concentration in the last quarter of the nineteenth century thus worked against association, re-emphasizing the central role played by structural factors in the failure of the Potteries to generate formal bodies to supplement the institutional networks proposed by models of the industrial district.

In contrast, the strategies of the largest firms in the industry were evolving in ways that required greater stability. Some, as was shown in Chapters 5 and 7, were developing agency networks in marketing with the aim of gaining more accurate information about, and perhaps greater control over, demand. Some were also integrating backwards into the sourcing and processing of more and more raw materials. A few had even switched from being buyers to being large-scale suppliers of important inputs. It has already been shown that earthenware manufacturer Anthony Shaw, active in both the North and South

---

[91] *The Sentinel*, 22 January 1859, p. 4.

[92] Ibid., p. 4; *The Sentinel*, 12 February, p. 6.

American markets, viewed the *Exchange* as a means of facilitating transactions, and it is likely, given the trends outlined above, that conducting all transactions on the *Exchange* would have reduced both information and transaction costs for some large firms. With economies of scale not decisive in the pottery industry the *Exchange* represented a way of giving greater structure to inter-firm networks without internalizing more functions. But the firms able to lever membership of the *Exchange* in this way were probably few in number. The 'critical, multiple dilemmas' undoubtedly facing the Potteries varied from firm to firm and sector to sector.[93]

If the *Exchange* and *Chamber of Commerce* could not find the common ground on which to build an inclusive notion of the 'trade' then they were also unlikely to succeed in their third aim of raising the national profile of the industry and the district. A desire to emulate other manufacturing districts perceived to have higher national profiles did motivate the business elite of the Potteries. The most famous and prestigious provincial exchange was the *Manchester Royal Exchange*, and the 'great benefit which Manchester ... had derived from the establishment of [an] Exchange' was referred to directly at the first meeting of the *Exchange* of 1859.[94]

However, if the business elite of the Potteries were looking to the new *Exchange* to promote a greater identity of interests then Manchester was an ill-chosen model. Farnie has described the Royal Exchange as 'the centre of the most important aspect of Manchester's life', centralizing 'the supply of information ... as the indispensable basis for all transactions', but goes on to define it as a 'slaughterhouse' and 'an area of competition rather than of collaboration'.[95] Furthermore, the Manchester Exchange kept alive the type of Smilesian ideology that, by offering encouragement to under-resourced small capitalists, leading manufacturers in the Potteries increasingly identified as responsible for the ruinously competitive structure of the industry. Farnie notes that the Exchange 'undoubtedly remained a seedplot of individualism [and] a belief in the beneficial function of vertical mobility ... was especially cherished by members of the Manchester Exchange'. Neither was the leadership of the two institutions comparable for in Manchester the 'Chairmen of the proprietors were typical "Manchester man" and were rarely recruited from the largest firms in the industry'.[96]

A sense that the prominent local men involved in institutional developments in the Potteries felt frustrated on the national stage surfaced again at the *Exchange* of 1875. Anthony Shaw admitted that 'they were rather late in the

---

[93] Scranton, 'Webs of Productive Association', p. 25.

[94] *The Sentinel*, 22 January 1859, p. 5.

[95] Farnie, 'Index of Commercial Activity', p. 97; Farnie, *English Cotton*, p. 192.

[96] Farnie, 'Index of Commercial Activity', p. 99–100; Farnie, *English Cotton*, p. 294.

field in establishing an Exchange', whilst Sir Charles Adderley, speaking as a outside observer, may have touched a raw nerve when observed that:

> He had always looked upon the Potteries as a most singular resemblance in modern times to the groups of Grecian republics which were always divided although they had common interests. It was not so much the multiplication as the division that he objected to. He objected to the way in which that important borough of Stoke-on-Trent, numbering a great deal more than 100,000 inhabitants, and having one of the most important industries, divides its counsel seven times over, and so reduces its influence, not only on the Legislature, but on the world with which its great trade was connected.[97]

This identification of division as a constraint on development was echoed and extended in the *Sentinel*, which saw the small-scale structure of the industry reflected in a smallness of outlook or spirit:

> Our district has attained great dimensions, become wealthy ... It is high time that prejudices peculiar to small towns shall yield to ideas and habits more city like, more thoroughly national and cosmopolitan ... Nothing will better serve [than the Exchange] to modify or extinguish local jealousies and animosities-the result mainly of narrowness of soul.[98]

As has been shown neither the *Exchange* or the *Chamber of Commerce* proved strong enough to serve this function, and in the last two decades of the nineteenth century institutional developments in the Potteries were largely restricted to unsuccessful attempts to reach informal price agreements.

Prices and the terms of competition

Calls for co-ordinated rises in selling prices had frequently been made in the trade press, but had rarely resulted in the active promotion of schemes until the 1890s. As competitive pressures mounted some firms turned again to a collaborative approach. However, those same pressures once more exposed the ineffective nature of local institutions, and competition again prevailed over co-operation. The first attempt to raise prices after the institutional failures of 1881–2, announced as a 'New Combination of Manufacturers: How to Save the Potting Trade', took place in 1888. The un-named members of the combination condemned 'Selfish isolation' and deplored the impact of intense competition

---

97 *Staffordshire Advertiser*, Paper Cuttings, Vol. 4, HBRL, p. 142.

98 *The Sentinel*, 9 April 1859, p. 4.

within the industry. Small firms were condemned for dragging prices and reputations downward through producing lower standard products:

> We do not quarrel with cheapness, if the cheapness if brought about without impoverishing the producers, but cheapness which tends to make the capital in a trade unremunerative and unsafe, and which reduces the labour towards the point of starvation ought to be subject to wholesome checks.[99]

Implicit in this statement were two assumptions also held by some of those active in the *Exchange* and the *Chamber of Commerce;* namely that the behaviour of sections of the industry had a negative impact on all others, and that some forms of competition could be proscribed unfair or illegitimate. It was recognized that the influence of the small firm sector was growing and that large firms, though growing individually, were being disadvantaged by structural shifts. Critically, and as an indication of the terms of competition understood as just by this group, it was hoped that 'before long things will revert to a position somewhat similar to that they used to occupy, and that the larger manufacturers will be those who alone control the general spirit of the markets'.[100]

The proposed combination received no further mention and for the remainder of the century no other alliance managed to replace division with unity. There was often such pessimism about these schemes that their failure was almost guaranteed. Each vulnerable manufacturer felt that his own selfless action in pushing for higher prices, no matter how welcome they would have been, served only to leave his business open to the predatory actions of others. Thus, he too would refrain from alliance and join those hunting for any order that could be secured. An earthenware manufacturer expressed this dilemma in 1891:

> the primary cause of failure in all past combinations of manufacturers has been in the fact of a few grasping manufacturers holding aloof and there by getting orders whilst those in combination have been positively without.[101]

Spatial clustering had not led manufacturers to trust one another in the Potteries; firms had to operate in a 'context of "*localized opportunism,*" blunting or constraining efforts at sustaining trade solidarity'.[102] The next attempt at combination took place in 1898, when *The Pottery Gazette* reported

---

99 *The Pottery Gazette*, February 1859, p. 152.

100 *The Pottery Gazette*, May 1884, p. 536.

101 *The Pottery Gazette*, August 1891, p. 724.

102 Scranton, 'Webs of Productive Association', p. 12 (emphasis in the original).

that 'several large manufacturers have been engaged in the last few days in organising a meeting of manufacturers to consider the question' of prices, it being 'no secret that ... selling prices of pottery, particularly earthenware, have for a long time been disastrously low'. The report urged 'upon manufacturers the wisdom of acting well together in a concrete body ... The time is opportune for a careful and full consideration of the whole question, and we hope to see active co-operation'.[103] As in the 1850s and 1870s the drive again originated amongst large firms. By August 1898 the meeting had been held and was 'absolutely agreed'. A temporary committee was appointed to consider the whole issue and report to a further meeting 'to be held shortly', but, despite the trappings of committees and meetings, the scheme was still being referred to as the 'proposed alliance in the earthenware trade' in January of the following year.[104]

The response of 'A Manufacturer', highlighted the difficulties that such schemes faced. The correspondent began by affirming that:

> I would gladly support any scheme for securing an advance in the price of china and earthenware if anyone will submit one likely to secure that end. I do not associate myself with the present scheme, because I am quite sure that it can never have that end.[105]

The author's scepticism stemmed from a critique of the way in which the majority of firms in the industry set their selling prices. Depressed prices were the result, in this view, not of a competitive business structure or an increasingly competitive environment but of widespread ignorance of cost accounting and political economy. Thus:

> Manufacturers, instead of going closely into the question of the cost of production, have, in scores of cases, regulated their own selling prices by the prices charged by their competitors. This is the insanity of which I complain-the insanity which has been the cause of all the evil. There is only one sound business way, only one honest way of determining the selling price of an article you make. You must base it on the cost of production, and regulate it by the laws of supply and demand.[106]

This was a clear indication that some firms would simply refuse to join any pricing agreement. Manufacturers, it was argued, had no interests in common;

---

[103] *The Pottery Gazette*, July 1898, p. 827. The *Gazette* added, almost by way of a threat, that, 'firms of large capital, and some of them long-standing, have been seriously contemplating realising their capital, and voluntarily leaving the trade in which they are not making any money. Ibid., p. 827.

[104] *The Pottery Gazette*, January 1899, p. 67.

[105] *The Pottery Gazette*, February 1899, p. 81.

[106] Ibid., p. 81.

neither the clustering of the industry or any sense of collective identity should have any bearing on prices determined properly by the cost of inputs and demand and supply mechanisms. The argument, displaying no 'solidarity sentiments', is an implicit rejection of the claim that the particular 'process of socialization' which takes place in an industrial district protects its 'economy as a whole against the consequences of short-term calculations of advantage'.[107]

The doubts of the above correspondent were well founded for the alliance soon failed. In May 1899 it was noted that:

> Ostensibly intended to strengthen the position of manufacturing potters, and to assure them of that union which is strength, it [the Potters Alliance] has, for one result, helped to demonstrate the extreme weakness and insecurity, to use no stronger terms, of much of the great industry by which we are supported in North Staffordshire.[108]

This observation appeared in an article entitled 'The Evils of Potting with Insufficient Capital'. Clearly the failure of the Potteries to develop collaborative organizations was again being traced to the atomistic, small-scale structure of the industry.

Given more favourable conditions, particularly in terms of demand, sections of the industry did find a degree of unity. In June 1899 'Customers were astounded to receive ... intimation after intimation, that in consequence of the increased cost of materials etc., prices will be increased'.[109] By the close of the year manufacturers in Longton, largely those that had not joined the *Exchange* and the *Chamber of Commerce*, were described as 'unanimous over further price rises'.[110] The rises held up into the following spring and were pushed on. These developments received the support of the trade press, so often critical of small firms, the 'china manufacturers' being 'without doubt, justified in the further price rises of which they have given notice'. However, cohesion was not the cause of an advance in selling prices. Instead, unity emerged after the fact, and, moreover, could not be sustained as demand slackened once more. As the century closed and a new one dawned the business men of the Potteries, though they 'shared social, economic and cultural bonds, talked out their difficulties with one another ... ultimately were left to struggle with them alone, preserving an autonomy they cherished and clung to'.[111]

---

[107] Sabel and Zeitlin, 'Historical Alternatives', p. 154.

[108] *The Pottery Gazette*, May 1899, p. 551.

[109] *The Pottery Gazette*, July 1899, p. 671.

[110] *The Pottery Gazette*, November 1899, p. 1277.

[111] Scranton, *Figured Tapestry*, p. 131.

Conclusion

This chapter has clearly demonstrated that active co-operation was extremely difficult to achieve in the Potteries in the late nineteenth century. It is not true, in the Potteries at least, that a 'singular sectoral commitment reinforced a sense of collective mission'.[112] The fragmented structure of the industry was reflected in the fragmented and weak organizations examined here, the structural divisions of the industry mirrored in and compounded by the civic divisions of the district. As in Philadelphia, 'industrial structure set limits on the organization of manufacturers interests'.[113]

Analysis of the failure of the pottery industry to identify common interests, to act in unison, or to balance competition with co-operation has been rooted here in a perspective which sees industrial structure as the basic foundation of network relations. This chapter has been closely informed by the reconstruction of the growth and development of the Potteries' industrial structure carried out in Chapter 2. Some of the implications of business structure for the *Exchange* and other institutions turned on very practical issues. Drawing on the reconstruction of economic linkages carried out in Chapter 8, it has been argued that different sized firms, often deploying different resource mixes, had developed different strategies and different network relations. These differences made doing business on the *Exchange* more or less viable for different firms, and membership of the *Chamber of Commerce* more or less attractive. Neither body proved capable of reconciling and including these basic differences through either power or persuasion.

However, close attention to the 'social underpinnings' of the organizations examined here, and to those of the wider district with which they largely conflicted, has demonstrated, in Casson and Rose's words, 'the importance of social and political networks to inter-institutional relations'.[114] Analysis of social and cultural structures certainly extends the structural analysis of institutional failure in the Potteries. Nonetheless concentration on issues such as religious and political affiliations remains a relatively crude way of accessing the meaning and importance that actors, either individually or as groups, attached to their position in the structure and networks of the Potteries industrial district. Similarly, institutional failure cannot be ascribed simply to a culture of individualism and independence amongst the personal capitalists of the Potteries, though this undoubtedly played its part. It is clear that personal capitalism characterized the style of governance of all firms in the industry, but it is equally clear that the owners of these firms were highly differentiated in terms of their interests, values and priorities. Scranton has persuasively argued

---

[112] Scranton, 'Webs of Productive Association', p. 25.

[113] Scranton, *Figured Tapestry*, p. 60.

[114] M. Casson and M.B. Rose, 'Institutions and the Evolution of Modern Business: Introduction', *Business History*, Vol. 39, No. 4 (1997), p. 6.

that further studies will undoubtedly reveal 'differing constructions of an "entrepreneurial culture"' at an inter-district level.[115] But these differing constructions clearly also existed at the intra-district level, rending what we may term the political economy of the district. Under a range of internal and external pressures the Potteries endured in this period a crisis in the frameworks that ordered its development.

[115] Scranton, 'Webs of Productive Association', p. 27.

CHAPTER TEN

Conclusion

Business structure

A concern for recovering the details of business structure has formed the cornerstone of this study. The 'ideal-typical' industrial district of the literature, with its 'many' largely small and medium-sized firms, is a vague abstraction. As Staber observes, district researchers have tended to define districts 'a priori ... as agglomerations of numerous small firms' and have not modelled district development as an 'explicitly dynamic phenomenon'.[1] Thus, it is necessary to specify as closely as possible of how many firms an industrial district is comprised, the relative weight of identifiable size groupings and the mechanism whereby that structure emerged and continued to evolve. This task is vital to our ability to contextualize the exploration of issues central to the industrial district concept, and, indeed, to business history.

The Potteries industrial district was populated by many firms, and the majority of these firms were, relative to both local and national standards, small or medium-sized. But the picture is also subtler than this suggests. In particular, the business structure was far from static. The total number of firms fluctuated markedly in the period under study, and the actual roster of firms even more so. Moreover, some firms were very large relative to both those typical of other industries and those of pottery industries in other countries. Growth mechanisms, at the level of the firm and the industry, are also important. In particular, change in the size structure of the industry was fuelled almost entirely by the growth of individual firms following a 'Marshallian' path to maturity. For technological reasons, the majority of firms, large and small, integrated the most important functions.

However, integration did not necessarily predict an oligopolistic structure. Instead, local factor conditions and institutional infrastructures encouraged and supported a highly competitive environment. These conditions also led to an intensification of that competitive structure in the middle decades of our period of study and sustained personal capitalism as the characteristic form of ownership and governance for firms. The relevant factor conditions were, in simple terms, 'thick' supplies of physical and human resources. These resources had distinctive

---

[1] U. Staber, 'An Ecological Perspective on Entrepreneurship in Industrial Districts', *Entrepreneurship and Regional Development*, Vol. 9 (1997), p. 46.

qualities that were important to the strategies of firms, but in relation to structure their ready availability was their most salient characteristic. The institutional framework encompassed sources of start-up and working capital, much of it in the form of credit. Proximity, strengthened by shared and tacit knowledge bases, reinforced these infrastructures, reducing transaction costs and disseminating information. Factor conditions and local institutions had three principal effects on the structure of the industry; they made it easy to enter, ensured a ready supply of potential entrants and aided the survival and growth of a proportion of those entrants.

Auxiliary firms also played an important role, providing a range of inputs and important services, but rarely specialized in central production functions. Moreover, in most areas, the auxiliary sector progressively shrank relative to manufacturing sector. Only towards the close of our period of study did a significant new area of specialization open up with the emergence of dedicated lithographic firms. Discussion of the functions undertaken by firms prompts consideration of issues of strategy.

Structure and strategy

Here, we initially adopt a very broad definition of strategy as a basic orientation towards the market. In particular, closely related to the structure of an industry is the balance of economies of scale and scope available to it and the extent to which those economies are realized either internally or externally. Strategically, firms in the Potteries pursued differentiation, but, in aggregate, the cluster was also responsible for a prodigious output. Economies of both scale and scope were vital to the Potteries. That such economies were not mutually exclusive for either firms or industries is not acknowledged often enough in the literature on industrial districts, which privileges notions of flexible specialization.

How were these various economies realized? As Broadberry and Marrison have demonstrated, a highly developed mercantile system was central to the ability of the Lancashire cotton industry to reap both economies of scale and scope.[2] The same was true of the Potteries, particularly with regard to economies of scale. Though they may not always have acted in the best interests of individual manufacturers, merchants, aggregating and then 'parcelling out' demand, did provide the industry, despite its small-scale structure, with access to world markets.[3] The Potteries did not generate a dedicated mercantile system comparable to that found in Manchester, but still benefited from the sophistication and maturity of the British mercantile sector. Also like Lancashire,

---

2 Broadberry and Marrison, 'External Economies of Scale'.

3 Marshall, *Industry and Trade*, p. 601.

the Potteries' strengths lay with high-quality goods at the top-end of the market, where mercantile specialization was most beneficial.

The historic localization of the industry meant that entrepreneurs and, perhaps more importantly, skilled workers, were embedded in a distinctive social 'milieu' with strong 'spontaneous and emergent qualities'.[4] The district played an important role in generating vital human resources and was thus important to the competitive advantages enjoyed by individual firms in numerous ways. However, as has already been indicated, production displayed a high degree of integration within firms. At the same time, the largest firms in the industry did not necessarily compete on volume and price. Indeed, it must be stressed that relatively very large and long-lived firms most reliably captured economies of scope. That is, these economies were to a considerable degree internal, providing the most powerful explanation of the growth of individual firms in the Potteries in this period. Flexibility was necessarily located as much within as between firms. This suggests the salience of perspectives on the firms that stress the importance of resources, capabilities and related transaction costs. In particular, the returns to some capabilities, including those central to a strategy of differentiation, proved hard to capture for those firms most reliant on the resources of the district. This finding raises questions about the ability of the Potteries industrial district to generate high-trust networks, a central focus of the industrial district literature.

Networks and entrepreneurs

Clustering and network formation are closely associated throughout the literature on regional development. In particular, there is a strong assumption that clustering greatly facilitates network formation and that networks represent the optimum co-ordination mechanism, especially for firms and industries pursuing strategies of flexible specialization. Thus, Staber highlights how networking has been proposed 'as a *necessary* strategy for obtaining critical resources and for connecting to sources of information'.[5] In this context, the relative absence of networks in a district is treated as an imperfection leading to inefficient co-ordination. However, this approach does not take account of the way in which task of co-ordination varies from district to district according to a range of factors, not least of which is structure.

Instead, this study may suggest the need for a broader perspective on the issue of co-ordination and the range of mechanisms available. As Marshall would surely have agreed, co-ordination mechanisms exist on a continuum that stretches from, at one extreme, market solutions to, at the other, hierarchical solutions.

---

4 Staber, 'Embeddedness', p. 174.

5 Staber, 'Networks and Regional Development', p. 1.

Crucially, it needs to be recognized that firms and industries will shift position on this continuum in response to changing conditions. Thus, in the Potteries in the last quarter of a century there was a tendency, in concert with the increasing use of contingent or hand-to-mouth strategies, to reduce reliance on network-like solutions to problems of co-ordination as the external environment became more hostile. Aggressive pursuit of advantage, or simply survival in some cases, prevailed. Intra-district trust declined and levels of opportunism probably grew.[6] But manufacturing firms dealing with Jesse Shirley and Sons, for example, were able to lever economies of flexibility that probably would not have been available had they persisted with the stable, reciprocal relationships that had been typical at the mid-century. There may have been long-term negative effects associated with this broad response, on investment for example, but it is far from clear these were anymore deleterious than those flowing from heightened co-operation would have been. Co-operation can very easily shade into collusion. As Casson has noted;

> Networking *per se* does not necessarily advance economic development, and may even retard it. The type of network is crucial so far as economic impact is concerned. Even the 'right sort of network' may have no impact if the members ... do not utilise it properly. It is suggested that successful networks are usually composed of entrepreneurial individuals.[7]

It is not suggested that networks played no role in the Potteries in this period, certainly they were important to firm foundings for example. However, the claim that they carried the burden of inter-firm co-ordination problems cannot, on the evidence, be sustained.

An acknowledgement that market-like structures and behaviour conditioned and characterized strategy in the Potteries industrial district prompts consideration of the issue of entrepreneurship. Again, this is a factor highlighted by the emphasis placed here on business structure. In particular, it is important to reinstate the founding of a firm as a central entrepreneurial act. It was the pattern of such founding decisions that ultimately determined the structure of the industry. In the Potteries, as in almost every other sector and place in nineteenth century, that decision was typically embodied in a private firm, whether held by the family or a partnership. The firm did matter and we cannot, for the Potteries at least, accept Sabel and Zeitlin's contention that 'Firms were not enduring units of production but rather temporary combinations of machines and skills directed

---

[6] See; A. Popp, 'Trust in an Industrial District: The Potteries, c.1850–1900', *Journal of Industrial History*, Vol. 3, no. 1 (2000), pp. 29–53.

[7] Casson, 'Analysing Regional Business Networks', p. 2. Casson goes on to note that 'horizontal networks', the type most conspicuous by their absence in the Potteries, 'may inhibit co-ordination by promoting conflict over the distribution of profit'. Ibid., p. 9.

to the achievement of particular tasks'.[8] Impermanence represented failure, and for no one more than the proprietor.[9] Recombinations of resources and capital did happen all the time, but more often than not they were not an outgrowth of strategy but a reaction to contingency or calamity.

An emphasis on entrepreneurship is a reminder that specific problems of co-ordination were set within a wider context of industry or district governance. What frameworks prevailed at this level? Here we widen the discussion to highlight the importance of what might be termed the business culture of the district or, alternatively, the political economy of district development.[10] In the introduction to this study, it was proposed that such cultural or ideological frameworks be conceived of as a dialogue. This conceptualization creates space for an acknowledgement of the potential for dissent and conflict. In this regard, evidence from the Potteries thus forms a useful corrective to the picture of the 'ideal-typical' industrial district in which unitary and consensual systems of norms and value are held to govern the behaviour of actors in the local context.

The political economy of district development in the Potteries took as its principal subject and existed in a dynamic, almost dialectical relationship with issues of industry structure. Whether we label it business culture or political economy, governance systems at level of the district were both a determinant and an outcome of structural change. What was the central dynamic of this relationship?

Structure and culture in place and time

The structure of the industry, that is the number of firms of which it was comprised and their size, structure and governance, conditioned understandings of what firms in the Potteries did and how they did it. They legitimized particular organizational forms. But these understandings were not static. They changed as innovations either proposed new organizational forms or questioned the validity of those that already existed. Thus, it was that it came to be observed that:

> looking backward and forward, it can scarcely be doubted that the next decade will see the practical extinction of the small factory – at least as regards crockery. Competition, ever growing keener will cut profits down

---

8 Sabel and Zeitlin, 'Historical Alternatives', p. 149.

9 Witness the protracted humiliation of the failure of Titus Price's firm in Arnold Bennett's *Anna of the Five Towns* (London: Penguin, 1969).

10 As John Quail argues, 'Business history has not noticeably concerned itself with questions of ideology. The discipline generally studies business from the standpoint of what was done and how it was done ... [but] the assumptions made by businessmen and managers of the past on the way a business could or should be run have not really been considered'. J. Quail, 'The Proprietorial Theory of the Firm and its Consequences', *Journal of Industrial History*, Vol. 3, No. 1 (2000), p. 1.

> to the last farthing ... This, of course means capital, means large turnovers and large factories. Whether the smaller businesses are eaten up by the large, or the trust system introduced, remains to be seen, but ... the small manufactory is doomed.[11]

That the prophecy did not come to pass for very many years is, for the moment, less important than the fact that it was made. The process of adjustment predicted was not simply technological or organizational, but also ideological and cultural. That is, adjustment compelled reflection on beliefs about the economic system and about the role of individuals within that system. More specifically, adjustment questioned the role of independent, proprietary manufacture.

As Marshall and Hobson recognized, the forces that seemed to impel adjustment were complex and flowed from several sources, including technology and the market. Their impacts were not always obvious. For example, relatively stable technologies could, in the long run, have as destabilizing an impact on business structure as those that were more innovatory. Though technological change certainly accelerated from the 1870s onwards it was never revolutionary and was always incremental. At the same time, encouraged by clustering, second-hand plant circulated freely and cheaply. This had three effects; it facilitated entry, reduced demand for new machinery and led to sub-optimal efficiency in many firms. The concept of 'redundancy', an outcome of the 'thickness' of industrial districts, is posited as an important source of flexibility in clusters. Redundancy as a positive attribute of clustered industries is largely conceptualized in terms of institutional infrastructures and arrangements, giving an industry as a whole the ability to learn from the mistakes and failures of individual firms and entrepreneurs and to adapt. Scranton, however, extends the concept of beneficial redundancy to factors conditions, arguing that the 'broad vitality' of the Philadelphia textile complex to a process whereby:

> failed firms leave behind substantially devalued plant and equipment for others to activate, mill space is readily occupied and old machines may be so cheaply bought as to be profitably operable or sufficiently adaptable to be modified for new purposes that eluded their former owners. So long as this sequence is viable a species of non-kin succession recurs; collapses may open the way for new starts as much as successes offer example for them to emulate.[12]

However, acknowledgement that plant had to be substantially devalued in order to be profitably worked is an indication of the marginal nature of the firms thus encouraged into existence. The cycle of collapse and entry identified by Scranton certainly occurred in the Potteries and the firms it created, often financially

---

11 *The Pottery Gazette*, November 1900, p. 1248.

12 Scranton, *Figured Tapestry*, p. 165.

insecure, tended on the basis of their cheap but inefficient resources, to compete on price and to behave opportunistically, driving down prices industry wide and undermining the differentiation sought by those investing in design capabilities. Thus they also threatened the reputation of the district by cutting costs and making products of poorer quality. Staber claims that 'redundant network structure ... makes the system "error friendly"', but the Potteries appear to have been too error friendly.[13] Inefficiency was punished in individual cases but was not in the process eliminated from the system as a whole.

Moreover, the cycle of failure and entry created not only firms too weak to resist pressure to reduce prices but also systemic excess capacity and over-production. Farnie observed a similar effect in Lancashire earlier in the century:

> The ranks of the employers were swelled during each successive phase of expansion by a new influx of recruits with limited means and were then decimated during the subsequent depression, so creating a market in second-hand machinery, facilitating entry by new aspirants and exposing the trade to repeated bouts of over-production and underselling.[14]

At the same time, there was a rise in intra-district opportunistic behaviour. Firms gave hidden discounts for cash, copied competitors designs at the request of buyers, cut profit margins to the bone in order to secure orders from other local firms and refused to co-operate on a wide range of issues, such as proposed marketing initiatives.

As has been argued throughout this study, change in the external environment, including the rise of foreign competition and cyclical and secular changes in markets, figured significantly in the forces driving adjustment and exposing underlying rigidities. As Marshall observed:

> even a little obstinacy or inertia may ruin an old home of an industry whose conditions are changing; and ... the opening out of new sources of supply or new markets for sale may quickly overbear the strength which old districts have inherited from past conditions.[15]

The example of Mintons demonstrated how such rigidity could be combined with considerable resilience in a single firm. But approaches that focus only on either the impact of external forces or on the individual firm do not tell the whole story. Intense competition and low levels of trust and co-operation were as much properties of the system as a whole as they were products of the attitudes and behaviour of individual actors. Moreover, in so far as falling levels of trust may be related to ease of entry then that growing distrust occurred because of rather

---

13 Staber, 'Networks and Regional Development', p. 19.

14 Farnie, *English Cotton*, p. 210.

15 Marshall, *Industry and Trade*, 287.

than despite spatial clustering. The North Staffordshire pottery industry palpably failed or refused to recognize that it shared an 'indissoluble mutual destiny'.[16]

Increasingly, both internal and external pressures brought to the fore and made contentious issues of industry structure, giving rise to a language that contrasted the legitimate and illegitimate in relation to organizational forms and behaviour. The scope of the entrepreneurship that we identified above as the wellspring of the growth and development of the industry's structure became a highly contested issue. The Potteries industrial district did facilitate entrepreneurship, but to a degree that provoked a crisis in local frameworks of understanding that had previously legitimized or even celebrated independent manufacture. From an embeddedness perspective on regional networks, entrepreneurship is socially constructed in such a way as to balance the twin imperatives of ambition and co-operation and the twin claims of self and collective-interests. Why was that balance so how to achieve in the Potteries in the late nineteenth century?

Again structural factors are important to this question at two levels, one immediate, the other operating at a more fundamental level. First, new entrants, though likely to be deeply imbued with potting skills and lore, needed to be integrated into the business community. This was not easy and required time that few them were afforded. As Staber notes, 'if entry and exit are uncontrolled, [network] boundaries are fluid and impossible to maintain'.[17] Thus, many firms, especially not only small firms, looked to their own interests, acted in opportunist ways and did not recognize a unified notion of the 'trade' simply because of the day-to-day pressures placed on them by an intensely competitive environment and their own insecurity. However, any lack of cohesion was driven by cultural as well as economic imperatives.

In the Potteries these cultural imperatives derived much of their force from a powerful combination of history and what Scott and Storper have called 'the politics of place'.[18] The dynamic relationship between structure and culture was played out in the context of both space and history. Notions of continuity, inheritance and custodianship were, and still are, very powerful in the Potteries. Just as it was argued that there were legitimate and illegitimate forms of participation in the industry and fair and 'unwholesome' forms of competition, as attacks focused on the damage inflicted by 'the unjustifiable intrusion of thoughtless men who aspire to be in business on their own account', so it was also argued that there 'true potters' and pretenders.[19] If entrepreneurship was to be redefined in the local context as a role for which all men were not equally entitled or equally entitled then an alternative, 'legitimate' model of

---

[16] *The Sentinel*, 12 February 1859, p. 6.

[17] Staber, 'Networks and Regional Development', p. 14.

[18] A. Scott and M. Storper, 'Regional Development Reconsidered', in H. Ernste and V. Meier (eds.), *Regional Development and Contemporary Industrial Response* (London: Bellhaven Press, 1992)

[19] *The Pottery Gazette*, December 1898, p. 1393.

entrepreneurship had to be constructed. The alternative model that did emerge, inchoate though it was, drew heavily on the past to construct the figure of the 'true potter', a figure that was, by extension, representative not only of the trade but also of the district. It was hoped, in part through this act of redefining the role and scope of entrepreneurship within the district, that 'before long things will revert to a position somewhat similar to that they used to occupy, and that the larger manufacturers will be those who control the general spirits of the market'.[20] However, a constant flow of new entrants continued to block the potential institutional response of greater horizontal integration.

Structural tensions were tightly intertwined with those in the district's business community and, being compounded by geography, may be usefully modelled using the understanding of place proposed by Doreen Massey. Massey argues that both individuals and groups, drawing on 'deeply essentialist and internalist ways of thinking about ... place and its character', construct their sense of place with reference to the twin co-ordinates of space and time. Through this process people both claim a place for themselves and claim that they are representative of that place. However, what such views fail to recognize is that places and the identities attached to them are always multiple and nascent, continually being formed and reformed. Thus, places are 'hybrid' and the location of a 'multiplicity of readings'. Moreover, as was true of the Potteries in the late nineteenth century, the 'claims and counter-claims about the present character of a place depend in almost all cases on particular rival interpretations of its past'. In turn, 'conflicting interpretations of the past, serving to legitimise a particular understanding of the present, are put to use in a battle over what is to come ... competing histories of the present [are] wielded as arguments over what should be the future'.[21] Such arguments were the essence of debates over structure, strategy and entrepreneurship in the Potteries in the late nineteenth century.

Deploying Massey's understanding of place, it is possible to identify some of the rival claims within the business community of the Potteries and to map some of the conflicts on which attempts to balance competition and co-operation and self and collective-interests foundered in this period. Was the Potteries a place of art or of 'rude manufacture', of craft or mechanization, or, most importantly perhaps, of established interests or fresh opportunities? All of these questions were vigorously debated by contemporaries and came to be polarized around the structural and strategic tensions between large and small firms. These divisions, themselves related to spatial clustering, increasingly placed limits on the extent of 'cultural consistency, normative backing and conformity to agreed-upon-rules' held to be characteristic of the 'ideal-typical' industrial district. Potters may have compete[d] vigorously' but they did not 'define their self-interest collectively

20 *The Pottery Gazette*, May 1884, p. 536.

21 Massey, 'Places and their Pasts', p. 183.

within the social context of the district'.[22] Issues of place and representativeness may be thought of as part of the '*content* of social relations' in the Potteries, reconstruction of which, Staber argues, aids in the exploration of business behaviour. If, as Lipartito argues, the concept of business culture can articulate the behaviour of firms at a deep, non-functional level, then sufficiently nuanced approaches to social embeddedness may help to articulate the district a similar non-functional level.

Trajectories

However, finally, mapping divisions within the district also returns us to the notion of divergent developmental paths introduced at the outset of this study. There it was suggested that the industry faced a range of choices; between batch and mass production, between skilled-labour and mechanization, between personal and corporate capitalism. These were, in turn, correlated with the cultural choices outlined above. Such choices were made many times over, by individual entrepreneurs, managers and firms and were expressed through the birth of new firms and the evolution of those already extant.

In doing so actors exercised their reflectiveness and asserted the importance of individual agency, but at the same time that vital agency was circumscribed, the co-ordination of the district loosely coupled and its frameworks of governance contested. Thus, as the industry and district advanced towards survival throughout the twentieth century and on into the twenty first, change was incremental, the dynamics of clustering complex and sometimes chaotic.

---

[22] Staber, 'Embeddedness', p. 169 and p. 151–2.

Bibliography

Primary Sources

Business Records

Boulton and Co.; T. Willet and Co. and Wengers and Co., miscellaneous catalogues, Horace Barks Reference Library, Hanley

John Challinor and Co., Co. No. 16372, PRO

Cork, Edge and Malkin archive, SD. 1204, Horace Barks Reference Library, Hanley

Dunn, Bennett and Co. archive (Privately held)

Hand Collection, PA/Hand/–, Horace Barks Reference Library, Hanley

James MacIntyre and Co. Co. No. 38217, Companies House

Minton Archive, Royal Doulton Ltd., London Road, Stoke-on-Trent, Staffs.

Jesse Shirley and Son archive, Jesse Shirley and Son, Etruria, Staffs.

Journals and Newspapers

The Illustrated London News; Staffordshire Potteries Special Supplement, 30 August 1884

Staffordshire Advertiser, Horace Barks Reference Library, Hanley

Staffordshire Sentinel, Horace Barks Reference Library

Staffordshire Mercury, Horace Barks Reference Library, Hanley

Paper Cuttings Volume 4, Horace Barks References Library, Hanley

The Pottery and Glass Trades Gazette, Horace Barks Reference Library, Hanley

Local Records

Census Returns:

Etruria, 1841, 1851, 1861 and 1871; Burslem, 1841, 1851, 1861 and 1871

Rate Books:

Burslem, 1914; Fenton, 1914; Hanley, 1862, 1872, 1882 and 1914; Longton, 1847 and 1913; Stoke-on-Trent, 1914; Tunstall, 1913

Trade Directories

Keates and Ford's Directory of the Staffordshire Potteries and Newcastle (Hanley: Keates and Ford, 1865–6)
Keates and Ford's Directory of the Staffordshire Potteries and Newcastle (Hanley: Keates and Ford, 1882)
Keates and Ford's Directory of the Staffordshire Potteries and Newcastle (Hanley: Keates and Ford, 1889)
Keates' Gazetteer of the Staffordshire Potteries and Newcastle (Hanley: Keates and Ford, 1892)
Kelly's Directory of the Staffordshire Potteries, Newcastle and District (Hanley: Staffordshire Sentinel, 1907)
Post Office Directory of Staffordshire (London: Kelly and Co., 1872)
Slater's Commercial Directory (Manchester: Isaac Slater, 1853)
Slater's Commercial Directory (Manchester: Isaac Slater, 1862)

Interviews

J.C.M. Shirley, Jesse Shirley and Son., Etruria, Staffs, 1990
J.W. Ravenscroft, John Tams Ltd., Longton, Staffs, 1990
P. Bennett, Dunn, Bennett and Co., Newcastle-under-Lyme, Staffs., 1996

Official (UK)

P.P. *Report of the Royal Commission on the Working of the Factory and Workshop Act, 1875*
P.P. *First Report of the Royal Commission on the Depression in Trade and Industry, 1886.*
Annual Statement of the Trade of the United Kingdom with Foreign Countries and British Possessions, 1875–1914
Report on the Pottery Industry in France (1899), Cd. 9526, Vol. XII
Technical Instruction in Germany: Report on Special Technical Schools for the Ceramic Industries, Dr. F. Rose, Miscellaneous Series of Trade Reports, No. 615 (1904), Cd. 1767, Vol. XCVI
Memorandum on German Ceramic Industries and German Trade in Ceramic Products, Miscellaneous Series of Trade Reports, No. 653 (1906), Cd. 2683–17
Report on the Employment of Compounds of Lead in the Manufacture of Pottery, their Influence upon the Health of the Workpeople with Suggestions as to Means which might be Adopted to Counteract their Evil Effects, T.E. Thorpe and T. Oliver, Cd. 9207
Census of Production in the United Kingdom, 1907: Final Report
Final Report of the Truck Acts Committee (1908)

Official (Foreign)

W. Burgess, 'Staffordshire vs. American Pottery', *Reports of the Consuls of the United States*, Vol. 37, No.s 132–135 (Washington: Government Printing Office, 1892)

Secondary Sources

D.H. Aldcroft, 'The Entrepreneur and the British Economy, 1870–1914', *Economic History Review*, Vol. 17 (1964), pp. 113–34.

P. Bartrip, '"Petticoat Pestering": The Women's Trade Union League and Lead Poisoning in the Staffordshire Potteries, 1890–1914', *Historical Studies in Industrial Relations*, Vol. 2, No. 2 (1996), pp. 3–26.

S.H. Beaver, 'The Potteries: A Study in the Evolution of a Cultural Landscape', *Presidential Addesses Delivered to the Institute of British Geographers*,

M. Bellandi, 'The Industrial District in Marshall', in E. Goodman, J. Bamford and P. Saynor (eds), *Small Firms and Industrial Districts in Italy* (London: Routledge, 1989).

A. Bennett, *The Old Wives' Tale* (London: Dent, 1954).

A. Bennett, *Anna of the Five Towns* (London: Penguin, 1969).

E.N.W. Bennett, *Argentina Farewell* (Privately published pamphlet).

E.N.W. Bennett, *The Origins of the Bennetts of Grove House, Cobridge* (Privately published pamphlet, 1976).

M. Berg, 'Inventors of the World of Goods', in K. Bruland and P. O'Brien, *From Family Firms to Corporate Capitalism: Essays in Business and Industrial History in Honour of Peter Mathias* (Oxford: Clarendon Press, 1998).

H. Berghoff, 'Regional Variations in Provincial Business Biography: The Case of Birmingham, Bristol and Manchester, 1870–1914', *Business History*, Vol. 37, No. 1 (1995), pp. 64–85.

H. Berghoff and R. Möller, 'Tired Pioneers and Dynamic Newcomers? A Comparative Essay on English and German Entrepreneurial History, 1870–1914', *Economic History Review*, Vol. 47, No. 2 (1994), pp. 262–87.

N. Bishnell, *Pottery Cost Accounts*, (Hanley: British Pottery Manufacturers' Federation, 1921).

R.L. Blaszczyk, 'The Aesthetic Moment: China Decorators, Consumer Demand and Technological Change in the American Pottery Industry, 1865–1900', *Winterthur Portfolio*, Vol. 29 (1994), pp. 121–53.

R.L. Blaszczyk, '"Reign of the Robots": The Homer Laughlin China Company and Flexible Mass Production', *Technology and Culture*, Vol. 36, No. 4 (1995), p. 863–911.

R.L. Blaszczyk, *Imagining Consumers: Design and Innovation from Wedgwood to Corning* (Baltimore, Md.: John Hopkins University Press, 2000).

P. Booth, 'Herbert Minton: Nineteenth Century Pottery Manufacturer', *Staffordshire Studies*, (1991), pp. 65–85.

J.H.Y. Briggs, '"The Radical Saints of Shelton": The Ridgway Family, Methodist Pottery Manufacturers', in D. Jeremy (ed), *Business and Religion in Britain* (Aldershot, Gower, 1988).

S. Broadberry and A. Marrison, 'External Economies of Scale in the Lancashire Cotton Industry, 1900–1930', Unpublished paper, (2000).

C. Buckley, *Potters and Paintresses: Women Designers in the Pottery Industry, 1870–1955* (London: Women's Press, 1990).

F. Burchill and R. Ross, *A History of the Potters' Union* (Hanley: Ceramic and Allied Trades Union, 1977).

M. Casson, *Enterprise and Competitiveness: A Systems View of International Business* (Oxford: Clarendon Press, 1990).

M. Casson, 'Entrepreneurship and Business Culture' in J. Brown and M.B. Rose (eds), *Entrepreneurship, Networks and Modern Business* (Manchester: Manchester University Press, 1993).

M. Casson, 'Analysing Regional Business Networks: An Economic Perspective', Discussion paper, Department of Economics, University of Reading, (1999).

S.A. Caunce, 'Complexity, Community Structure and Competitive Advantage within the Yorkshire Woolen Industry, c. 1700–1850', *Business History*, Vol. 39, No. 4 (1997), pp. 27–43.

F. Celoria, 'Ceramic Machinery of the Nineteenth Century in the Potteries and in Other Parts of Britain', *Staffordshire Archaeology*, Vol. 2 (1973), pp. 10–48.

F. Celoria, 'Reports of the US Consuls on the Staffordshire Potteries, 1883–1892', *Journal of Ceramic History*, Vol. 7 (1974), pp. 43–54.

A.J. Chandler, *Scale and Scope: The Dynamics of Industrial Capitalism* (Cambridge, Mass.: Harvard University Press, 1990).

S.D. Chapman, 'Quantity versus. Quality in the British Industrial Revolution: The Case of Printed Textiles', *Northern History* Vol. 21 (1985), pp. 175–92.

S.J. Chapman, *The Lancashire Cotton Industry: A Study in Economic Development* (Clifton, N.J.: Augustus M. Kelley, 1973).

R. Church, 'Technological Change and the Hosiery Board of Conciliation and Arbitratio, 1860–1884', *Yorkshire Bulletin*, Vol. 15 (1963), pp. 52–60.

R. Church, 'The Effect of the American Export Invasion on the British Boot and Shoe Industry, 1885–1914', *Journal of Economic History*, Vol. 28, No. 223–54.

R. Church, *Kenricks in Hardware: A Family Business, 1791–1966* (Newton Abbott: David and Charles, 1969).

R. Church, *The Great Victorian Boom, 1850–1873* (Basingstoke: Macmillan, 1979).

R. Church, 'New Perspectives on the History of Products, Firms, Marketing and Consumers in Britain and the United States since the Mid-nineteenth Century', *Economic History Review*, Vol. 52, No. 3 (1999), pp. 405–35.

R. Church, 'Ossified or Dynamic? Structure, Markets and the Competitive Process in the British Business System of the Nineteenth Century', *Business History*, Vol. 42, No. 1 (2000), pp. 1–20

K. Clay, 'Trade, Institutions and Credit', *Explorations in Economic History*Vol. 34, No. 4 (1997), pp. 495–521.

D.C. Coleman, 'Failings and Achievements: Some British Businesses, 1910–1980', *Business History*, Vol. 29, No. 4 (1987), pp. 1–17.

D.C. Coleman and C. Macleod, 'Attitudes to New Techniques: British Businessmen, 1800–1950', *Economic History Review*, Vol. 34, No. 4 (1986), pp. 588–611.

E. Collard, *Nineteenth Century Pottery and Porcelain in Canada* (Montreal: McGill University Press, 1967).

G. Cookson, 'Family Firms and Business Networks: Textile Engineering in Yorkshire, 1780–1830', *Business History*, Vol. 39, No. 1 (1997), pp. 1–20.

P.L. Cotterell, '"Lo, ... Nineveh and Tyre": British Trading Anxieties and Official Reactions, 1870–1929', in D.H. Aldcroft and A. Slaven, *Enterprise and Management: Essays in Honour of P.L. Payne* (Aldershot: Scolar, 1995).

F. Crouzet, *The Victorian Economy* (London: Methuen, 1982).

A. Dawson, *Bernard Moore: Master Potter, 1850–1935* (London: Richard Dennis, 1982).

M. Dupree, *Family Structure in the Staffordshire Potteries, 1840–1880* (Oxford: Clarendon Press, 1995).

M. Eason, 'Business, Training and Education: Sheffield, c. 1880–1940' (Unpublished Ph.D., Sheffield Hallam University, 1997).

A. Eatwell and A. Werner, 'A London Staffordshire Warehouse', *Journal of the Northern Ceramic Society*, Vol. 8 (1991), pp. 91–124.

B. Elbaum, 'The Steel Industry before World War One', in B. Elbaum and W. Lazonick (eds), *The Decline of the British Economy* (Oxford: Oxford University Press, 1987).

B. Elbaum and W. Lazonick (eds), *The Decline of the British Economy* (Oxford: Oxford University Press, 1987).

N. Ewins, '"Supplying the Present Wants of Our Yankee Cousins ...": Staffordshire Ceramics and the American Market, 1775–1880', *Journal of Ceramic History*, Vol. 15 (1997), pp. i–154.

D.A. Farnie, *The English Cotton Industry and the World Market, 1815–1896* (Oxford: Oxford University Press, 1979).

D.A. Farnie, 'An Index of Commercial Activity: The Membership of the Manchester Royal Exchange, 1809–1948', *Business History*, Vol. 21, No. 1 (1979), pp. 97–106.

W.H. Fraser, *The Coming of the Mass Market, 1850–1914* (Basingstoke: Macmillan, 1981).

M. French, 'Structure, Personality and Business Strategy in the US Tyre Industry: The Siberling Rubber Company, 1922–1964', *Business History Review*, Vol. 67, No. 1 (1996), pp. 246–78.

P.J. Frost, L.F. Moore, M.R. Louis, C.C. Lundberg and J. Martin (eds), *Organizational Culture* (London: Sage, 1985).

W. Garside and H. Gospel, 'Emplyers and Managers: Their Organizational Structures and Changing Industrial Strategies', in C. Wrigley (ed), *A History of British Industrial Relations, 1875–1914* (Brighton: Harvester, 1982).

P.W. Gay and R.L. Smythe, *The British Pottery Industry* (London: Butterworth, 1974).

M. Gertler and T. Rutherford, 'Regional-industrial Networks and the Role of Labour', U. Staber, N. Schaefer and B. Sharma, *Regional Business Networks: Prospects for Prosperity* (Berlin: de Gruyter, 1996).

G.A. Godden, *Jewitt's Ceramic Art of Great Britain, 1800–1900* (London: Barrie and Jenkins, 1972).

E. Goodman, J. Bamford and P. Saynor (eds), *Small Firms and Industrial Districts in Italy* (London: Routledge, 1989).

T.R. Gourvish, 'British Business and the Transition to a Corporate Economy: Entrepreneurship and Management Structures', *Business History*

P. Halfpenny, 'Joseph Clementson: A Potter "Remarkable for Energy of Character"', *Northern Ceramic Society Journal*, Vol. 5 (1984), pp. 177–205.

R. Hall, 'Women in the Labour Force: A Case Study of the Potteries in the Nineteenth Century', Occasional Paper No. 27 (1986), Department of Geography and Earth Sciences, Queen Mary College, University of London.

M.T. Hannan and G.R. Carroll, *Dynamics of Organizational Populations: Density, Legitimation and Competition* (Oxford: Oxford University Press, 1992).

B. Harrison, 'Industrial Districts: Old Wine in New Bottles?', *Regional Studies*, Vol. 26, No. 5 (1992), pp. 469–83.

S. Helper, 'Strategy and Irreversibility in Supplier Relations: The Case of the US Automobile Industry', *Business History Review*, Vol. 65, No. 4 (1991).

J.A. Hobson, *The Evolution of Modern Capitalism: A Study of Machine Production* (London: Walter Scott, 1906).

J. Jones, *Two Hundred Years of Design and Production at Mintons* (Shropshire: Swan Hill Press, 1995).

P. Joyce, *Work, Society and Politics: The Culture of the Factory in Later Victorian England* (London: Methuen, 1982).

J.R. Kinghorn and J.V. Nye, 'The Scale of Production in Western Economic Development: A Comparison of Official Statistics in the US, Britain, France and Germany, 1903–13', *Journal of Economic History*, Vol. 56, No. 1 (1996), pp. 90–112.

M.W. Kirby, 'Institutional Rigidities and Economic Decline: Reflections on the British Experience', *Economic History Review*, Vol. 45, No. 4 (1992), pp. 637–60.

T. Kono, 'Changing a Company's Strategy and Culture', *Long range Planning*, Vol. 27, No. 5 (1994), pp. 85–97.

P. Krugman, *Geography and Trade* (Camridge, Mass.: M.I.T. Press, 1993).

A. Lamb, 'The Press and Labour Response to Pottery-making Machinery in the North Staffordshire Pottery Industry', *Journal of Ceramic History*, Vol. 9 (1977), pp. 1–7.

A. Lamb, 'Mechanization and the Application of Steam Power in the North Staffordshire Pottery Industry', *North Staffordshire Journal of Field Studies*, Vol. 17 (1977), pp. 59–64.

N. Lamoreaux, *The Great Merger Movement in American Business, 1898–1904* (Cambridge: Cambridge University Press, 1985).

R. Langlois, 'Creating External Capabilities: Innovation and Vertical Disintegration in the Microcomputer Industry', *Business and Economic History*Vol. 19, No. 2 (1990), pp. 93–102.

R. Langlois and P. Robertson, 'Explaining Vertical Integration: Lessons from the American Automobile Industry', *Journal of Economic History*, Vol. 49, No. 2 (1989), pp. 361–75.

W. Lazonick, 'Review of C. Sabel and J. Zeitlin (eds), *Worlds of Possibilities*', *Business History Review*, Vol. 73, No. 2 (1999), pp. 309–13.

M.J. Lewis, 'The Growth and Development of Sheffield's Business Structure, 1880–1930' (Unpublished Ph.D., Sheffield City Polytechnic, 1989).

K. Lipartito, 'Culture and the Practice of Business History', *Business and Economic History*, Vol. 32, No. 2 (1995).

H. Livesay, 'Entrepreneurial Dominance in the Businesses Large and Small, Past and Present', *Business History Review*, Vol. 63, No. 1 (1989), pp. 1–21.

J. Llobrera, D. Meyer and G. Nammacher, 'Trajectories of Industrial Districts: Impact of Strategic Intervention on Medical Industrial Districts', *Economic Geography*, Vol. 76, No. 1 (2000), pp. 68–98.

T.A. Lloyd, *The History of Methodism in the Potteries* (Privately Published, 1988).

R. Lloyd-Jones and A.A. Le Roux, 'The Size of Firms in the Cotton Industry: Manchester, 1815–1841', *Economic History Review*, Vol. 33, No. 1 (1980), pp. 72–82.

R. Lloyd-Jones and A.A. Le Roux, 'Marshall and the Birth and Death of Firms: The Growth and Size Distribution of Firms in the Early Nineteenth Century Cotton Industry', *Business History*, Vol. 24, No. 1 (1982), pp. 141–55.

R. Lloyd-Jones and M.J. Lewis, *Manchester and the Age of the Factory: The Business Structure of Cottonopolis in the Industrial Revolution* (London, Croom Helm, 1988).

R. Lloyd-Jones and M.J. Lewis, 'Personal Capitalism and British Industrial Decline: The Personally Managed Firm and Business Strategy in Sheffield, 1880–1920', *Business History Review*, Vol. 68, No. 3 (1994), pp. 364–411.

R. Lloyd-Jones and M.J. Lewis, *British Industrial Capitalism since the Industrial Revolution* (London: UCL Press, 1998).

R. Lloyd-Jones, M.J. Lewis and M. Eason, 'Culture as Metaphor: Company Culture and Business Strategy at Raleigh Industries, c. 1945–60', *Business History*, Vol. 41, No. 3 (1999), pp. 93–133.

R. Lloyd-Jones and M.J. Lewis, 'Regional Business Networks in Historical Perspective: The British Bicycle Industry, 1870–1914', in T. Slaven (ed.), *Business History, Theory and Practice: Proceedings of the Conference on Business History and Theory* (Glasgow: Centre for Business History in Scotland, 2000).

R. Lloyd-Jones and M.J. Lewis, *Raleigh and the British Bicycle Industry: An Economic and Business History, 1870–1960* (Aldershot: Ashgate Publishing, 2000).

T.A. Lockett, *Davenport Pottery and Porcelain, 1794–1887* (Newton Abbott, David and Charles, 1972).

T.A. Lockett and G.A. Godden, *Davenport: China, Earthenware and Glass* (London: Barries and Jenkins, 1989).

A. Marrison, 'Businessmen, Industries and Tariff Reform in Great Britain, 1897–1914', *Business History*, Vol. 25, No. 2 (1983), pp. 148–78.

A. Marshall, *Industry and Trade: A Study of Industrial Technique and Business Organization; and of Their Influences on the Conditions of Various Classes and Nations* (Basingstoke: Macmillan, 1919).

A. Marshall, *Principles of Economics* (Basingstoke: Macmillan, 1952).

J. Martin, S.B. Sitkin and M. Boehm, 'Founders and the Elusiveness of a Cultural Legacy', in P.J. Frost, L.F. Moore, M.R. Louis, C.C. Lundberg and J. Martin (eds), *Organizational Culture* (London: Sage, 1985).

W. Mass and W. Lazonick, 'The British Cotton Industry and International Competitive Advantage: The State of the Debate', *Business History*, Vol. 32, No. 4 (1990), pp. 9–65.

D. Massey, 'Places and their Pasts', *History Workshop Journal*, Vol. 39 (1995), pp. 182–92.

D. McCloskey, *Economic Maturity and Entrepreneurial Decline: British Iron and Steel, 1870–1913* (Cambridge, Mass.: Harvard University Press, 1973).

N. McKendrick, 'Josiah Wedgwood: An Eighteenth Century Entrepreneur in Salesmanship and Marketing Techniques', *The Economic History Review*, Vol. 12, No. 3 (1960), pp. 408–33.

N. McKendrick, 'Josiah Wedgwood and Cost Accounting in the Industrial Revolution', *Economic History Review*, Vol. 23, No. 1 (1970), pp. 45–67.

J. Melling, 'Review of C. Sabel and J. Zeitlin (eds), *Worlds of Possibilities*', *Business History*, Vol. 40, No. 3 (1998), pp. 174–5.

A.H. Morgan, 'Regional Consciousness in the North Staffordshire Potteries', *Geography*, Vol. 27 (1942), pp. 95–102.

S. Moss, *An Economic Theory of Business Strategy* (Oxford: Martin Robinson, 1981).

A. Moyes, 'Victorian Industrial Structure and Inter-industry Relations in the Potteries: A Framework and Exploratory Analysis', *North Staffordshire Journal of Field Studies*, Vol. 19 (1979), pp. 39–59.

S. Nenadic, 'The Small Family Firm in Victorian Britain', *Business History*, Vol. 35, No. 4 (1993), pp. 86–113.

L. Newton, 'Regional Bank-Industry Relations During the Mid-Nineteenth Century: Links Between Banks and Manufacturing in Sheffield, c. 1850 to c. 1885', *Business History*, Vol. 38, No. 3 (1996), pp. 64–83.

S. Nicholas, 'Agency Contracts, Institutional Modes and the Transition to Foreign Direct Investment by British Manufacturing Multinationals Before 1939', *Journal of Economic History*, Vol. 43, No. 3 (1983), pp. 675–86.

S. Nicholas, 'The Overseas Marketing Performance of British Industry, 1870–1914', *Economic History Review*, Vol. 37, No. 4 (1984), pp. 489–506.

G. Dei Ottati, 'Trust, Interlinking Transactions and Credit in the Industrial District, *Cambridge Journal of Economics*, Vol. 18 (1994), pp. 529–46.

P.L. Payne, 'The Emergence of the Large-scale Company in Great Britain, 1870–1914', *Economic History Review*, Vol. 20, No. 1 (1967), pp. 519–42.

P.L. Payne, 'Family Business in Britain: An Historical and Analytical Survey', in A. Okochi and S. Yasuoka (eds), *Family Business in the Era of Industrial Growth* (Tokyo: Tokyo University Press, 1984).

A. Pettigrew, 'On Studying Organizational Cultures', *Administrative Science Quarterly*, Vol. 24 (December 1979), pp. 570–581.

M. Piore and C. Sabel, *The Second Industrial Divide: Possibilities for Prosperity* (New York: Basic Books, 1984).

S. Pollard, *Britain's Prime and Britain's Decline: The British Economy, 1870–1914* (London, Edward Arnold, 1989).

R. Pomfret, '"My Bones are Burned as an Hearth": The Origins of Jesse Shirley and Sons', *Northern Ceramic Society Journal*, Vol. 15 (1984), pp. 147–75

A. Popp, 'Trust in an Industrial District: The Potteries, c. 1850–1900', *Journal of Industrial History*, Vol. 3, No. 1 (2000), pp. 29–53.

A. Popp, 'Specialty Production, Personal Capitalism and Auditors' Reports: Minton Ltd., c. 1870–1900', *Accounting, Business and Financial History*, Vol. 10, No. 3 (2000), pp. 347–69.

J.H. Porter, 'Wage Bargaining Under Conciliation Agreements, 1860–1914', *Economic History Review*, Vol. 23, No. 3 (1970), pp. 460–75.

M.E. Porter, *Competitive Strategy: Techniques for Analysing Industries and Competitors* (New York: Free Press, 1980).

D. Pye, *The Nature and Art of Workmanship* (Cambridge: Cambridge University Press, 1968).

J. Quail, 'The Proprietorial Theory of the Firm', *Journal of Industrial History*, Vol. 3, No. 1 (2000), pp. 1–28.

Report of the Tariff Commission, Volume 5: The Potteries (London: King and Son, 1907)

F. Rhead and G. Rhead, *Staffordshire Pots and Potteries* (London: Hutchinson, 1906).

M.B. Rose, 'The Role of the Family in Providing Capital and Managerial Talent in Samuel Greg and Company, 1784–1840', *Business History*, Vol. 19, No. 1 (1977), pp. 37–54.

M.B. Rose, 'Diversification of Investment by the Greg Family, 1800–14', *Business History*, Vol. 21, No. 4 (1979), pp. 79–96.

N. Rosenberg, *Exploring the Black Box: Technology, Economics and History* (Cambridge, Cambridge University Press, 1994).

M. Rowlinson and S. Procter, 'The Culture of Business History and the History of Business Culture', in T. Slaven (ed.), *Business History, Theory and Practice: Proceedings of the Conference on Business History and Theory* (Glasgow: Centre for Business History in Scotland, 2000), pp. 45–57.

M. Russo, 'Technical Change and the Industrial District: The Role of Inter-firm Relations in the Growth and Transformation of Ceramic Tile Production in Italy', in E. Goodman, J. Bamford and P. Saynor, *Small Firms and Industrial Districts in Italy* (London: Routledge, 1989).

C.F. Sabel and J. Zeitlin, 'Historical Alternatives to Mass Production: Politics, Markets and Technology in Nineteenth Century Industrialization', *Past and Present*, No. 108 (1985), pp. 133–76.

C.F. Sabel and J. Zeitlin, 'Stories, Strategies, Structures: Rethinking Historical Alternatives to Mass Production', in C.F. Sabel and J. Zeitlin (eds), *Worlds of Possibilities: Flexibility and Mass Production in Western Industrialization* (Cambridge: Cambridge University Press, 1997).

J. Sarsby, *Missuses and Mouldrunners: An Oral History of Women Pottery Workers at Work and at Home* (Milton Keynes: Open University Press, 1988).

S.B. Saul, *The Myth of the Great Depression, 1873–1896* (Basingstoke: Macmillan, 1982).

E.H. Schein, *Organizational Culture and Leadership* (San Francisco: Josey-Bass, 1992).

A. Scott and M. Storper, 'Regional Development Reconsidered', in H. Ernste and V. Meier (eds), *Regional Development and Contemporary Industrial Response* (London: Bellhaven Press, 1992).

P. Scranton, *Proprietary Capitalism: The Textile Manufacture at Philadelphia, 1800–1885* (Cambridge, Cambridge University Press, 1983).

P. Scranton, *Figured Tapestry: Production, Markets and Power in Philadelphia Textiles, 1885–1941* (Cambridge, Cambridge University Press, 1989).

P. Scranton, 'Diversity in Diversity: Flexible Production and American Industrialization, 1880–1930', *Business History Review*, Vol. 65, No. 1 (1991), pp. 27–90.

P. Scranton, 'Build a Firm, Start Another: The Bromley and Family Firm Entrepreneurship in the Philadelphia Region', *Business History*, Vol. 35, No. 4 (1993), pp.115–51.

P. Scranton, *Endless Novelty: Specialty Production and American Industrialization, 1865–1925* (Princeton, N.J.: Princeton University Press, 1997).

P. Scranton, 'Webs of Productive Association in American Industrialization: Patterns of Institution-formation and their Limits, Philadelphia, 1880–1930', *Journal of Industrial History*, Vol. 1, No. 1 (1998), pp. 1–34.

A. Shadwell, *Industrial Efficiency: A Comparative Study of Industrial Life in England, Germany and America* (London: Longmans, Green & Co., 1906).

U. Staber, 'Networks and Regional Development: Perspectives and Unresovled Dilemmas', in U. Staber, N. Schaeffer and B. Sharma (eds), *Regional Business Networks: Prospects for Prosperity* (Berlin: de Gruyter, 1996).

U. Staber, 'Social Embeddedness of Industrial District Networks', in U. Staber, N. Schaeffer and B. Sharma (eds), *Regional Business Networks: Prospects for Prosperity* (Berlin: de Gruyter, 1996).

U. Staber, 'An Ecological Perspective on Entrepreneurship in Industrial Districts', *Entrepreneurship and Regional Development*, Vol. 9 (1997), pp. 45–64.

M.J. Stern, *The Pottery Industry of Trenton: A Skilled Trade in Transition, 11850–1929* (New Brunswick, N.J., Rutgers University Press, 1994).

J. Stobart, 'Patterns of Urban Retailing: Suburbanisation, Centralisation , and Hierarchies in the Potteries Conurbation, 1872–1932', *Journal of Local and Regional Studies* Vol. 18, No. 1 (1998), pp. 11–26

J. Stobart and C. Thomas, 'Cultural Capital and Competition in the Five Towns', (Unpublished paper, Coventry University and Staffordshire University).

H.J. Stratton, 'Technological Development of the American Pottery Industry', *Journal of Political Economy* (October, 1932), p. 661–76.

D. Stuart, *People of the Potteries: A Dictionary of Local Biography, Vol. 1* (Keele, Staffs.: Department of Adult Education, University of Keele, 1985).

J. Sydow, 'Flexible Specialization in Regional Networks', in U. Staber, N. Schaefer and B. Sharma (eds), *Regional Business Networks: Prospects for Prosperity* (Berlin: de Gruyter, 1996).

S. Taylor, 'Tradition and Change: The Sheffield Cutlery Trades, 1870–1914', (Unpublished Ph.D., University of Sheffield, 1988).

F. Thistlethwaite, 'The Atlantic Migration of the Pottery Industry', *Economic History Review*, Vol. 11, No. 2 (1958), pp. 264–78.

J. Thomas, *The Rise of the Staffordshire Potteries* (Bath, Adams and Dart, 1971).

G. Timmins, 'Concentration and Integration in the Sheffield Crucible Steel Industry', *Business History*, Vol. 24, No. 1 (1982), pp. 61–78.

C. Triglia, 'Small-firm Development and Political Subcultures', in E. Goodman, J. Bamford and P. Saynor, *Small Firms and Industrial Districts in Italy* (London: Routledge, 1989).

J. Turnbull, 'Staffordshire Potters and Scottish Merchants', *Journal of the Northern Ceramic Society*, Vol. 9 (1992), pp. 115–22.

G. Tweedale, 'Strategies for Decline: George Wostenholm and Son and the Sheffield Cutlery Industry', *Transactions of the Hunter Archaeological Society*, Vol. 17 (1993), pp. 43–56.

G. Tweedale, *Steel City: Entrepreneurship, Strategy and Technology in Sheffield, 1743–1993* (Oxford: Clarendon Press, 1995).

W.H. Warburton, *A History of Trade Union Organization in the North Staffordshire Potteries* (London: Allen and Unwin, 1931).

L. Weatherill, *The Pottery Trade and North Staffordshire, 1660–1760* (Manchester: Manchester University Press, 1971).

L. Weatherill, 'Capital and Credit in the Pottery Industry Before 1770', *Business History*, Vol. 24, No. 4 (1982), p. 238–258.

L. Weatherill, 'The Business of the Middleman in the English Pottery Trade Before 1780', *Business History*, Vol. 28, No. 3 (1986), pp. 51–76.

R.H. Whipp, '"The Art of Good Management": Managerial Control of Work in the British Pottery Industry, 1900–1925', *International Review of Social History*, Vol. 29, No. 3 (1984), pp. 359–85.

R.H. Whipp, 'The Stamp of Futulity: The Staffordshire Potters, 1880–1905', in R. Harrison and J. Zeitlin (eds), *Divisions of Labour: Skilled Workers and Technological Change in the Nineteenth Century* (Brighton: Harvester, 1985).

R.H. Whipp, 'Women and the Social Organization of Work in the Staffordshire Pottery Industry, 1900–1930', *Midland History*, Vol. 12 (1987), pp. 103–21.

R.H. Whipp, *Patterns of Labour: Work and Social Change in the Pottery Industry* (London: Routledge, 1990).

B.R. Williams, 'The Pottery Industry', in D. Burn, *The Structure of British Industry: A Symposium, Vol 2* (Cambridge, Cambridge University Press, 1958).

J.F. Wilson, *British Business History, 1720–1994* (Manchester: Manchester University Press, 1995).

J.F. Wilson, 'Industrial History: Towards a Definition', *Journal of Industrial History*, Vol. 1, no. 1 (1998), pp. 1–8.

W. Woodall, 'Potters in Rhineland', *English Illustrated Magazine,* (1890)

J. Zeitlin, 'Why Are There No Industrial Districts in the UK?', in A. Bagnasco and C. Sabel (eds), *Small and Medium Enterprises* (London: Pinter, 1995).

Index of business firms and other actors

Author and subject index